W9-BBX-452

Universal Design in Higher Education

From Principles to Practice

SECOND EDITION

Edited by

Sheryl E. Burgstahler

HARVARD EDUCATION PRESS

Cambridge, Massachusetts

Second Printing, 2015

Copyright © 2015 by the President and Fellows of Harvard College

All rights reserved. No part of this publication may be reproduced or transmitted in any form or by any means, electronic or mechanical, including photocopy, recording, or any information storage and retrieval systems, without permission in writing from the publisher.

Library of Congress Control Number 2015936476

Paperback ISBN 978-1-61250-816-0
Library Edition 978-1-61250-817-7

Published by Harvard Education Press,
an imprint of the Harvard Education Publishing Group

Harvard Education Press
8 Story Street
Cambridge, MA 02138

Cover Design: Saizon Design
Cover Photo: © Hero Images/Corbis

The typefaces used in this book are ITC Stone Serif for text and ITC Stone Sans for display.

*This book is dedicated to people
who look beyond their own disabilities and other differences
to promote a more inclusive world for everyone.*

Contents

Foreword

Colleges and universities in the United States strive to educate their students to become responsible global citizens and future leaders within a challenging learning environment informed by cutting-edge scholarship. Everyone on our campuses should have an opportunity to participate in all that we offer, whether from the perspective of a learner, a teacher, a researcher, or a staff member, or from the perspective of our many visitors who take advantage of our on-site and online offerings. What we make available must be accessible to and usable by everyone, and our values—such as integrity, diversity, excellence, collaboration, and innovation—should reflect this view.

Over the years, the list of characteristics considered to represent "diversity" at our institutions has expanded significantly to include race, ethnicity, nationality, gender, sexual orientation, religion, age, socioeconomic status, and ability. Everyone benefits from what individuals from traditionally underrepresented groups bring to our learning communities; their participation increases our ability to address pressing societal issues and prepare our students for global citizenship and leadership. We simply cannot afford to waste the talents, creativity, or brilliance of anyone.

Sheryl Burgstahler, founder and director of the DO-IT (Disabilities, Opportunities, Internetworking, and Technology) and Access Technology Centers at the University of Washington, has been tireless in finding allies in the United States and abroad to promote the adoption of inclusive practices that serve all students at all types of postsecondary institutions. In this book, some of these allies—students with disabilities, scholars, and practitioners—share examples of such practices and the principles of universal design that inform them. Instead of designing courses, technology, services, and resources for the "typical" person and then reactively making modifications for those who find those offerings unwelcoming, inaccessible, or unusable, universal design *proactively* addresses the needs and preferences of people with a broad range of abilities and other characteristics during the purchase, design, and deployment processes.

The authors of this book make a compelling case for adopting universal design in *all* postsecondary offerings in order to support a diverse educational community and an inclusive approach to academic excellence. There is something here for everyone.

Michael K. Young
President, Texas A&M University
Professor of Public Policy
Bush School of Government and Public Service

Preface

My husband Dave, son Travis, and I have a beach house on Hood Canal in Washington State, a natural waterway that extends for about fifty miles and separates the Kitsap Peninsula from the Olympic Peninsula. Several years ago, we expanded our deck at the beach house to include an attractive ramp that wraps around one side of the house, connecting the level of the deck with that of the sidewalk below. It was interesting to hear the reactions of our neighbors and others who visited the house during the renovation. Almost everyone commented on the ramp and, in most cases, asked which of our elderly friends or relatives was going to use it. They seemed surprised that we did not have anyone in particular in mind. In fact, most beneficiaries have been children with pull toys and people moving items from the garage to the deck. This approach is an example of universal design (UD)—proactively designing a space to meet the needs of potential visitors with a wide range of physical capabilities. The design feature itself sends the message to anyone who requires its use, "We expected that you would come to our home. You are welcome here."

With me at 5'1" and Dave at 6'5", I've noticed that it is easy for each of us to identify design features that impact us personally, but less so the other way around. In our home, I didn't notice that the ceiling over the steps to the basement is low until my husband hit his head on it. People who are newly embracing a UD approach are challenged to change their perspective to one where they look to address the needs of individuals with a wide range of characteristics whenever they create something—an academic course, a website, a service, and so on. If we all did so, wouldn't our world be more accessible, comfortable, and inclusive?

Although UD strives to make opportunities accessible to everyone, it can be argued that individuals with disabilities benefit the most from the flexible, adaptable design features it promotes. This is a worthy outcome since people with disabilities are generally not as successful as others in academic studies, careers, and other life activities. Their success is impacted by many stakeholders, as illustrated in Figure P.1—people with disabilities themselves; parents and family members; peers; K–12 teachers, counselors, and support staff; postsecondary administrators, faculty, and staff; legislators and policy makers; government service providers; and community leaders and group members. The Disabilities, Opportunities, Internetworking, and Technology (DO-IT) Center at the University of Washington (UW), with funding from federal, state, and private sources, has addressed issues in most of these areas with projects, publications, and web resources (see http://www.washington.edu/doit/).

FIGURE P.1   Stakeholders Who Impact the Success of People with Disabilities in Higher
Education

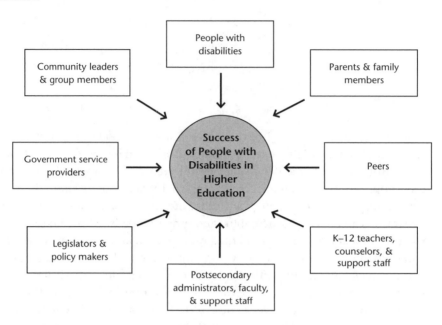

Because individuals with disabilities play a role in their own success, there is a need for interventions that help them prepare for college and careers. As part of the AccessSTEM project, DO-IT created a critical junctures model (see Figure P.2) to identify key steps that lead to the success of people with disabilities in science, technology, engineering, and mathematics (STEM) fields. Based on a literature review and more than twenty years of practice in the field, the model also highlights inputs or interventions (e.g., mentoring, peer support, technology access) that can support them on their journey.

Besides developing personal skills to achieve their goals, individuals with disabilities benefit from societal changes that level the playing field. The content of this book lies in that domain. It promotes the proactive practice of universal design in higher education (UDHE). By "higher education" I mean educational opportunities provided through colleges and universities. Consistent with the social model of disability that looks first to products and environments instead of to the individual to identify access barriers, UD encourages anyone designing a course, service, technology, building, or other application to consider the great diversity of characteristics that users possess, such as those with respect to ability, language, race, ethnicity, culture, gender, sexual orientation, and age. Results from such proactive thinking during the design process can reduce the need for disability-related accommodations once the product or environment is created. You'll see how UD doesn't replace other design considerations, but, in concert with those considerations, makes a design better—UD makes a course better, UD makes a building better, UD makes technology better.

FIGURE P.2   AccessSTEM: Progress of Teens with Disabilities Toward Careers: Project Inputs Leading Students to Critical Junctures

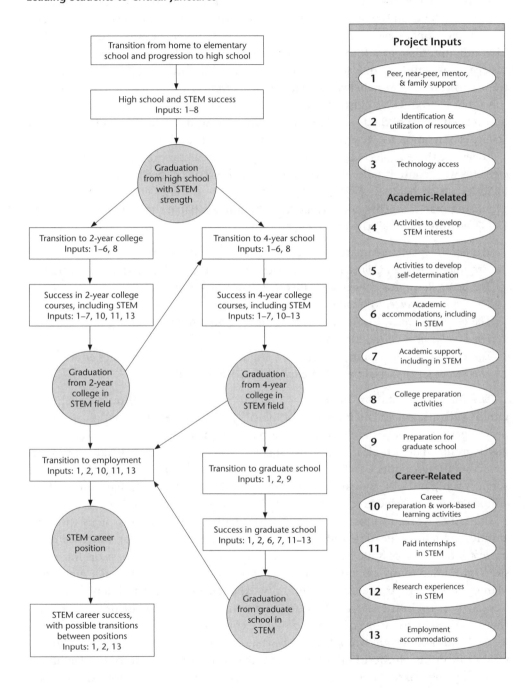

Copyright © 2011, 2008, 2006, Sheryl Burgstahler, University of Washington. Permission is granted to copy these materials for educational, noncommercial purposes provided the source is acknowledged.

The inspiration and much of the content for this book emerged from three DO-IT projects funded by the Office of Postsecondary Education of the U.S. Department of Education. DO-IT staff worked with more than forty collaborating institutions in creating professional development materials and programs to help postsecondary faculty and administrators fully include students with disabilities in their courses and services. The online Center for Universal Design in Education (CUDE) emerged from these efforts to disseminate research, guidelines, promising practices, and resources for the application of UD to instruction, services, physical spaces, and technology. Content related to STEM fields was enhanced through multiple grants from the National Science Foundation for AccessSTEM, AccessComputing, and other initiatives.

Together, these projects led to the development of a comprehensive collection of websites with content tailored to the needs and interests of specific stakeholders that includes a searchable knowledge base of questions and answers, case studies, and promising practices. This AccessCollege collection, available through a link from the DO-IT website, includes the following "rooms":

The Faculty Room, for instructors and academic administrators;
The Student Services Conference Room, for student service administrators and staff;
The Board Room, for college and university administrators;
The Student Lounge, for students with disabilities;
The Veterans Center, for student veterans and related services;
The Employment Office, for employers;
The STEM Lab, for science, technology, engineering, and mathematics educators;
The Center for Universal Design in Education, for all educators.

The forty-seven authors of this book ensure that voices of multiple stakeholder groups with respect to the implementation of UDHE are heard. Although no single person perfectly represents a stakeholder group, sharing a sample of perspectives from many groups makes it clear that every stakeholder—faculty, administrators, student services staff, researchers, technology companies, online learning designers, technical support staff, and others—can play a role in creating a more inclusive campus. Specific stakeholder perspectives presented in the chapters are listed in Table P.1.

DO-IT has worked to increase the successful participation of individuals with disabilities in higher education and employment since 1992. Before that, I focused more narrowly on the accessible design of information technology. My passion for inclusion—grounded in my personal, academic, and professional experiences—runs deep. Many of my thoughts coalesced around my experiences with a child named Rodney (see Chapter 16) in the late 1970s. Much of my time with Rodney focused on finding ways to adjust an existing computer so that he could use it with his mouth wand. As I worked with Rodney, my view came to be that most of the obstacles he faced did not reside within his physical limitations, but rather within the design of the facility or technology he was trying to use. It was clear that the designers did not expect someone like Rodney to use the product or environment they created. But why not? There have always been children like Rodney in the world. Sometimes society chooses not to see them. Sometimes well-meaning people try to protect them from a harsh world

TABLE P.1   Stakeholder Perspectives Within Chapters of This Book

Stakeholder	Chapters With Stakeholder View
Undergraduate and graduate students with disabilities	6, 12
Faculty and teaching assistants	4, 5, 9, 18, 20, 21, 22
Student service providers	7, 12
Technology specialists	16, 17
Researchers	3, 8
Assessment experts	10
Architects	14
Partnerships of multiple stakeholders	23, 24

and, as an unintended result, further isolate them. Sometimes others consider them incapable of reaching education and career goals typical of their peers.

I joined forces with others who asked simple questions like, "Why can't people who are blind use this computer?" We rejected the simple answer, "Because they are blind." We asked, "But why can't the computer adjust to a person's blindness?" Over time, our work in both the DO-IT and Access Technology Centers at UW has increasingly addressed the UD of mainstream technologies along with the development and support of specialized, assistive technologies for individuals with disabilities.

Although progress has been made, many obstacles exist today that could have been avoided through the proactive application of UD practices. People like Rodney and his allies need to keep pushing for a world that is more inclusive. UD provides one avenue for moving this agenda forward.

The first edition of this book was published in 2008. So why is there a need for a new edition? What is different in the field of UDHE since 2008? Three trends are described here:

- Much more practice in UDHE is reported in the literature, although I have been disappointed in the small amount of attention in the area of UD of student services and in the inclusion of UD topics within course curricula.
- Research is beginning to emerge to document the efficacy of the application of UD to instruction, although more research is needed in this area and to address the impact of the application of UD to informal science learning.
- Civil rights complaints regarding the inaccessible design of technology used at postsecondary institutions in the U.S. have resulted in campuses developing proactive policies and procedures to ensure that the technology they procure, develop, and use is accessible to individuals with disabilities. There has been increasing interest in the proactive approach of UD as part of the remedy for these violations.

The growth in terminology used for concepts related to UD continues to contribute to the alphabet soup of acronyms both within and outside of the U.S. Much work outside of the U.S. in the domain of UD has taken place under different names, such as *design for all* and *inclusive design*. Although references are made to these bodies of work, given length restrictions for this book, we could not cover them to the degree I would prefer. Acknowledging this limitation, I and other chapter authors have made an attempt to make the basic content relevant within any culture.

So how can we engage more individuals in the worthy effort to promote UDHE? The DO-IT website hosts an online book that complements the printed book you are reading. The online *Universal Design in Higher Education: Promising Practices* (http://www.washington.edu/doit/universal-design-higher-education-promising-practices) is continually growing with reports of practices that can be replicated by others. You and your colleagues are encouraged to submit an article for publication; author guidelines are provided in that book's preface. You are also encouraged to add promising practices to the DO-IT Knowledge Base. Also supported by the UDHE initiative is an online community of practice (CoP) of individuals interested in learning more about and sharing UDHE practices. Join this UDHE CoP by sending a request to doit@uw.edu.

I have always considered UD to be an old idea with a new name, an ideal more than a fully achievable result, a process more than a set of prescriptive practices, and a journey more than a destination. I hope you enjoy sharing the journey with me and the other authors of this book.

Special thanks are extended to those who engaged in DO-IT's UDHE initiative, and the authors and peer reviewers who contributed to both editions of the book. I would also like to thank the many DO-IT Center staff members who helped this project come together, in particular: Rebecca Cory, Linda Tofle, and Rebekah Peterson for the first edition, and KC Lynch, Kayla Brown, and Elizabeth Lee for the second.

This book is based on work supported by the U.S. Department of Education Office of Postsecondary Education (grant numbers P333A990042, P333A020044, and P333A050064) and the National Science Foundation (grant numbers CNS-0837508, CNS-1042260, and HRD-0833504). Any opinions, findings, and conclusions or recommendations are those of the authors and do not necessarily reflect the policy or views of the federal government. The Principles of Universal Design were conceived and developed by the Center for Universal Design at North Carolina State University. Use or application of the Principles in any form is separate and distinct from the Principles and does not constitute or imply acceptance or endorsement by the Center for Universal Design of the use or application.

PART 1

Introduction

In Part 1, Sheryl Burgstahler provides a summary of the history, principles, and applications of universal design (UD). She highlights approaches to implementing UD in higher education and gives an overview of the contents of this book with a guide for finding answers to specific questions.

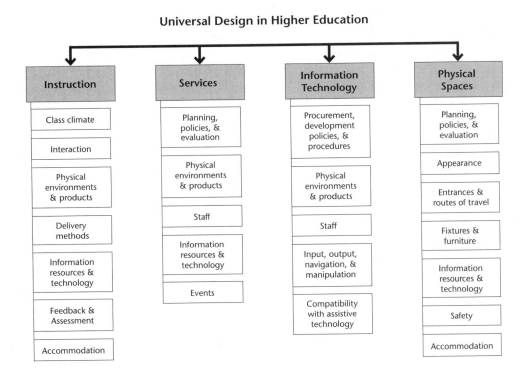

Universal Design in Higher Education

Instruction	Services	Information Technology	Physical Spaces
Class climate	Planning, policies, & evaluation	Procurement, development policies, & procedures	Planning, policies, & evaluation
Interaction	Physical environments & products	Physical environments & products	Appearance
Physical environments & products	Staff	Staff	Entrances & routes of travel
Delivery methods	Information resources & technology	Input, output, navigation, & manipulation	Fixtures & furniture
Information resources & technology	Events	Compatibility with assistive technology	Information resources & technology
Feedback & Assessment			Safety
Accommodation			Accommodation

Source: S. Burgstahler (2014). *Applications of Universal Design in Education.* Seattle: University of Washington.
http://www.washington.edu/doit/applications-universal-design-education

1

Universal Design in Higher Education

Sheryl E. Burgstahler

Universal design (UD) has a rich history in applications to commercial products and archi-tecture. The UD approach holds promise for making educational products and environments more inclusive of all students, faculty, staff, and visitors. This chapter includes historical highlights, design approaches, the definition and principles of UD, the process of UD, and applications of UD in higher education (UDHE). The chapter ends with an outline of the content of this book and a guide for locating answers to specific questions addressed therein.

What if there were a paradigm for higher education that simultaneously addressed issues of diversity, equality, accessibility, social integration, and community? What if this approach went beyond the design of more inclusive instruction to provide guidance for making physical spaces, student services, and technology more welcom-ing to, accessible to, and usable by everyone on campus? The application of UD in higher education can do all of this and more. While you can never finish implement-ing UDHE, it is easy to get started taking incremental steps toward the ideal. Apply-ing UDHE is a journey and, like any exciting journey, requires goal setting, research, planning, diligence, engagement, observation, adjustments, and being open to a dif-ferent way of thinking. This chapter gives an overview of the world of UDHE, and the remaining chapters provide road maps for the journey itself.

The design of any product or environment, including those used in education, involves myriad factors, among them purpose, aesthetics, safety, industry standards, usability, and cost. Traditional design often focuses on the average user. In contrast, UD promotes an expanded goal to make products and environments welcoming and useful to groups that are diverse with respect to many dimensions, including gender, race, ethnicity, age, socioeconomic status, ability, veteran status, disability, and learn-ing style. Originally applied in the fields of architecture, consumer product design, and information technology, UD has more recently emerged as a paradigm to address diversity and equity in the design of a broad range of educational applications, including educational software, on-site and online instruction, and student services. Used in this context, a *paradigm* is "a theory or a group of ideas about how something should be done, made, or thought about" (*Merriam-Webster's Collegiate Dictionary*, n.d.a). The dominant paradigm refers to the collection of values or system of thought in a society that is widely held at a given time. For the group that has adopted the paradigm, it provides an almost unconscious, internalized framework that affects the way they think that things should work and often goes without question. Paradigm shifts—when the collection of values or system of thought changes from what was once dominant to something new—are rare.

Together, the authors of the chapters in this book make the case that postsecondary institutions should adopt a paradigm shift with respect to how they address the needs of a diverse student body that includes students with a wide variety of abilities. This chapter provides foundational information that supports their case.

DIVERSITY IN HIGHER EDUCATION

Once the exclusive domain of the young, able-bodied, Caucasian male, the postsecondary student body of today is more than half female and includes significant populations of racial and ethnic minorities, international students, those with low socioeconomic status, veterans, individuals whose age is older than that of the typical college student, and other groups; and the student population is expected to increase in diversity in the coming years (The Lawlor Group, n.d.). In particular, the enrollment of students with disabilities, once rare, has grown to an estimated 11% of the student body in the United States (National Center for Education Statistics, 2013). Many of the disabilities students report are "invisible," including those that affect abilities to learn, pay attention, and interact socially. Veterans of recent wars are adding to the growing pool of college students with multiple disabilities. As represented in Figure 1.1, myriad aspects of diversity will continue to be reflected in postsecondary student bodies worldwide and, as illustrated in Figure 1.2, some individuals have multiple minority status.

Legislation, research, practice, and debate in the areas of civil rights, social justice, and multicultural education shed light on postsecondary diversity issues with respect to socioeconomic, racial, ethnic, and gender status (e.g., Hackman & Rauscher, 2004; Nieto, 1996; Pliner & Johnson, 2004). This body of knowledge can be used to inform campus efforts related to another characteristic that contributes to diversity on any campus: variations in student abilities. For example, although the ruling of the U.S. Supreme Court in the 1954 *Brown v. Board of Education of Topeka* case applied to racial segregation when it established that separate education is not equal education, this principle has informed approaches to disability issues, resulting in a push toward inclusion in all educational opportunities rather than separate schools and programs for students with disabilities.

The discussion below elucidates a few of the challenges faced by students with various physical, sensory, learning, attention, and communication characteristics and shares examples of ways an institution can proactively ameliorate potential barriers to its offerings.

FIGURE 1.1   Student Characteristics

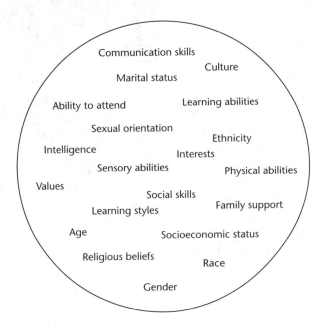

- *Physical differences*. Some facilities are not designed for students who are large; providing a few larger chairs in a classroom can make these students more comfortable. Spaces that are not wheelchair-accessible cannot be used by some students and instructors; designing level surfaces and ramps and flexible spaces that offer multiple seating options for all potential participants addresses this problem. Some individuals use assistive technology that emulates the functions of a standard keyboard but not a mouse. Campuses can avoid erecting barriers by developing and using websites and software applications that can be operated with the keyboard alone.
- *Visual differences*. Web content that requires the ability to distinguish one color from another presents a barrier to access for people who are color-blind; webmasters can avoid this by making mindful color and design choices. A standard computer screen is inaccessible to individuals who are blind. Campuses can avoid this barrier by providing computer systems that are able to convert screen text to braille or speech. However, since this technology can only read text, individuals who are blind can only make sense of the content within graphic images if webmasters provide alternative text descriptions. Individuals who have limited vision and use software to enlarge screen images can view only a small portion of content at one time. Campus units that deploy cluttered web pages and inconsistent page layouts make navigation difficult. Printed materials, videos, televised presentations, and/or other materials with visual content also erect access barriers unless alternatives (e.g., large print formats, tactile materials, audio versions, or electronic text) are provided.

- *Hearing differences.* Unless the audio content of videos and other multimedia is captioned or transcribed, it creates a barrier to the content for students who are deaf. Although some communication methods, such as e-mail, are fully accessible to individuals with hearing impairments, they may be unable to fully participate in on-site, telephone, or videoconference discussions unless sound amplification, sign language interpreters, real-time captions, or other access alternatives are provided.

FIGURE 1.2   A young African American woman who has a disability uses computing resources and tools to prepare for college.

- *Learning differences.* Course content delivered in a single mode, such as by lecture, creates a barrier to access for students with a wide variety of learning styles, strengths, and preferences; using a variety of teaching methods can make the content accessible to more students (e.g., Claxton & Ralston, 1978; Dunn & Griggs, 2000; Gardner, 1983; Rose, Meyer, & Hitchcock, 2005). Websites that change formats from one page to the next, crowd too much content on the screen, or move to new content using timers rather than user control erect barriers to students with specific learning disabilities that affect the ability to read, write, or process information; these students benefit when webmasters avoid these site characteristics. When time provided to complete a test is inadequate, students with learning disabilities that affect processing speed are placed at a disadvantage; creating assessments without unnecessary time constraints allows all students to demonstrate their knowledge. Some students with learning disabilities that affect their ability to interpret written text are at a disadvantage when printed textbooks are the only option; offering accessibly designed electronic books benefits all students who wish to read using computer-based speech output.
- *Attention differences.* Students exhibit a wide range in their ability to pay attention to content as it is presented. Some students may find it difficult to pay attention to a lecture, lab, or other activity. Instructors can avoid erecting barriers by providing a printed outline or other organizational tool.
- *Communication differences.* Communication differences can relate to hearing ability, brain injuries, autism spectrum disorders, native language, culture, age, or other factors. E-mail and other modes of communication that do not require the ability to hear or speak are fully accessible to individuals with speech and hearing impairments and may also be desirable for students in courses where the spoken language is not their native language. However, fast-paced, on-site, or online discussions, teleconferences, or audio conferences may limit the participation of these individuals.

Discussions like this support the view of disability as simply a diversity issue. Some have even argued for terminology that is a better reflection of this view. For example, a term that is increasingly used to refer to students who have neurological conditions, such as those on the autism spectrum, is *neurodiversity* (e.g., Griffin & Pollak, 2009); using similar language, a person without a neurological condition that would be labeled a disability might be called *neuro-typical*. Focusing on difference rather than deficit supports the social model of disability and other integrated approaches within the field of disability studies that consider variations—such as those with respect to gender, size, socioeconomic status, race, ethnicity, and ability—a normal part of the human experience. Thus, disability is viewed simply as one aspect of a spectrum of human variations. One view is that "impairment is an individual limitation, while a disability is a socially imposed restriction. Not being able to walk is an impairment but lack of mobility is a disability (a socially created situation)" (Seale, 2014, p. 23). Not being able to see is an impairment, but not having access to documents in an accessible format creates a disability for this person. When a wheelchair user is allowed to participate in a marathon, her impairment did not result in a disability because the organizers created an inclusive event. Using this perspective, a *disability* is the extent to which a person is limited in performing an activity or accessing a resource; if the activity or resource is designed to be accessible, a disability is not created. Although this distinction between impairment and disability may be appealing to many, it is not always reflected in legislation and the provision of services.

A significant gap exists in the achievement of postsecondary degrees for students with disabilities compared with their peers without disabilities (Belch, 2004; National Council on Disability, 2003; Wagner, Newman, Cameto, & Levine, 2005). However, success stories demonstrate that opportunities do exist for students with disabilities who successfully overcome barriers imposed by inaccessible facilities, curricula, websites, electronic files, online and on-site instruction, student services, and other aspects of college and university environments (Disabilities, Opportunities, Internetworking, and Technology [DO-IT], 1993–2014; Stern & Woods, 2001). In general, factors that affect retention of a diverse student body occur at both individual (e.g., socioeconomic status, study skills) and institutional (e.g., policies, procedures) levels (Berge & Huang, 2004; Braxton, Sullivan, & Johnson, 1997; Tinto, 1993). Specifically, with respect to disabilities, educators have recommended interventions to reduce the gap in postsecondary success between students with and without disabilities so that:

- Students with disabilities can develop self-determination skills so they can effectively advocate for reasonable accommodations and otherwise be better prepared to succeed in the college environment (Getzel & Thoma, 2008).
- Postsecondary institutions can make their physical environments, technology, services, and courses more welcoming and accessible to students with disabilities (Burgstahler & Cory, 2008).

The authors of this book address the second issue. While some institutions and individuals may feel a moral obligation to make their offerings welcoming and accessible to students with disabilities, in many countries there is a legal requirement to do so (Fernie & Henning, 2006). Such legislation requires that universities and other entities avoid discrimination and provide reasonable adjustments for people with disabilities. Internationally, the United Nations has developed the Convention on the Rights of Persons with Disabilities to "promote, protect, and ensure the full and equal enjoyment of all human rights and fundamental freedoms by all persons with disabilities, and to promote respect for their inherent dignity" (2006, Article 1). The accommodation approach and proactive approaches to providing access to individuals with disabilities are presented in the next two sections of this chapter.

THE ACCOMMODATION APPROACH TO ACCESS

Higher education policies and practices with respect to students with disabilities have evolved over time. In early years, institutions of higher education excluded many people with disabilities by adopting discriminatory enrollment policies and designing inaccessible courses, facilities, and services (Welsh, 2002). Demands for the admission of otherwise qualified students with disabilities and for services to support them came from multiple groups, including injured veterans returning from World War II who were eligible for college funding through the GI Bill, students with disabilities who were mainstreamed in precollege education and prepared for college studies, parents who wanted more academic and career options for their children, and those inspired by the civil rights movements for women and minorities to extend similar rights to people with disabilities. In the U.S., these efforts eventually led to civil rights mandates for people with disabilities (Welsh & Palames, 2002) that include Section 504 of the Rehabilitation Act of 1973, the Americans with Disabilities Act of 1990 (ADA), and the latter's 2008 Amendment Act (ADAAA). The ADA considers a person with a disability to be any individual who has

- a physical or mental impairment that substantially limits one or more major life activities of such individual;
- a record of such an impairment; or
- being regarded as having such an impairment (ADAAA, Section 12102).

Examples of major life activities include, but are not limited to, caring for oneself, performing manual tasks, seeing, hearing, eating, sleeping, walking, standing, lifting, bending, speaking, breathing, learning, reading, concentrating, thinking, communicating, and working, and also include the operation of major bodily functions, such as immune system, cell growth, digestive, bowel, bladder, neurological, brain, respiratory, circulatory, endocrine, and reproductive functions. Disabilities covered by legislation include, but are not limited to, those that are related to hearing, learning, mental health, speech, mobility, and sight. According to the ADA, no otherwise qualified individual with a disability shall, solely by reason of that disability, be excluded from, denied the benefits of, or subjected to discrimination under programs of a covered entity, including an institution of higher education. In the ADA, *qualified*, with respect to postsecondary education, means an individual with a disability who—with or without reasonable modifications to rules, policies, or practices; the removal of architectural, communication, or transportation barriers; or the provision of auxiliary aids and services—meets the essential eligibility requirements for the receipt of services or the participation in programs or activities provided by a public entity (ADA, Section 12101). Soon after the ADA was passed in the U.S., governments around the world enacted similar laws protecting the rights and guaranteed access of citizens with disabilities—beginning with Australia, New Zealand, Japan, the United Kingdom, and Germany.

Using an accommodation process for addressing the inaccessible design of program offerings is deeply rooted in the culture of most postsecondary institutions. An *accommodation* occurs when an adjustment or modification is made to a product or environment so that it is accessible to an individual with a disability. A focus on accommodations is grounded in a medical model or "deficit model" of disability, in which a professional identifies an individual's functional limitations or "deficits" and prescribes a cure, rehabilitation, or adjustments that allow this person to fit into an established environment or use an existing product (Jones, 1996; Loewen & Pollard, 2010; Moriarty, 2007; Swain & Lawrence, 1994). In higher education, the student typically provides documentation of a disability to a specified office at the institution before requesting accommodations. The institutional representative determines what accommodations are "reasonable" and shares this information with appropriate faculty and staff members. Examples of accommodations include materials in alternate formats (e.g., braille, accessible PDF files), extra time on exams, sign language interpreters, and movement of classes to wheelchair-accessible locations. Thus, the institution recognizes the inaccessibility of a course, service, physical space, or a technology to a specific student, views the individual's "deficit" (the disability) as the "problem," and offers an accommodation as a "solution" to that person's problem.

The accommodation approach only comes into play when a specific individual tells the institution that he is unable to fully benefit from an offering. Thus, securing accommodations requires extra effort for students with disabilities beyond that required of other students and may result in students receiving materials later than other students because of the time it takes to convert them to alternate formats. In and of itself, this approach does not improve the overall design of the course or other offerings for individuals seeking access in the future.

Providing accommodations does not benefit all students with disabilities on campus. This is because many students with disabilities potentially eligible for accommodations—an estimated 60% of the population of students with disabilities who receive special education services in high school (Wagner, Newman, Cameto, Garza, & Levine, 2005)—choose not to seek accommodations in higher education. This may be because they expect that they do not need an accommodation, have insufficient knowledge of the services offered, want to avoid potential negative social reactions to their disability, or perceive that the services will not be useful to them (Marshak, Van Wieren, Ferrell, Swiss, & Dugan, 2010).

The accommodation model does not always provide an equitable experience for students with disabilities and can lead to an unnecessary dependence on a student service office. For example, Professor A routinely provides course readings in a format that is inaccessible to students who use screen reader software to read aloud text in the documents because they are blind or because they have learning disabilities that impact their reading ability. Students in Professor A's class who need accessible documents (e.g., documents that include text and formatting that can be accessed with a screen reader) may rely heavily on the disability services office to convert these materials into an accessible format, sometimes resulting in them receiving course content at a later time than other students. In contrast, Professor B routinely provides course materials in an accessible format. Students in his class who are blind or have learning disabilities do not need to rely on the disability services office at all for document conversion. Such proactive approaches to access are described in the next section.

In summary, negative aspects that occur when an accommodation-only approach is applied include:

- The process for securing accommodations marginalizes students with disabilities by requiring a segregated process for gaining access.
- An accommodation does not always result in content and experiences equivalent to those of other students.
- Accommodations can create an unnecessary dependency on a student service office.
- The value associated with an accommodation does not extend to students with disabilities who choose not to self-disclose nor to other students in a class who might benefit from it.
- An accommodation for one student does not in and of itself make a course or other offering more accessible to students in the future.

PROACTIVE APPROACHES TO ACCESS

To a great extent, campus responses to students, staff, faculty, and visitors with disabilities focus on compliance with civil rights laws designed to create a more inclusive world and open doors to education, employment, and community involvement for individuals with disabilities. When U.S. President George H. W. Bush signed the ADA, he stated the following:

> With today's signing of the landmark Americans with Disabilities Act, every man, woman, and child with a disability can now pass through once-closed doors into a bright new era of equality, independence, and freedom. (The U.S. Equal Employment Opportunity Commission, 2002)

Throughout the world, various fields of practice have promoted the proactive design of products and environments that reduce negative outcomes of the accommodations-only approach by eliminating deficits in the products or environments that make them inaccessible to some individuals. This approach aligns with the social model of disability and other integrated approaches within the field of disability studies. Proponents of proactive design suggest that all of these variations should be considered at every step in the design process in order to create products and environments—including courses, technology, facilities, and student services—that are welcoming to, usable by, and accessible to a broad audience (DePoy & Gibson, 2008a, b; Gabel & Peters, 2010).

Using a variety of terminology—*usable design, accessible design, inclusive design, design for all, barrier-free design, user-centered design, sustainable design, universal access,* and *universal design*—efforts have been made to design products and environments that avoid the creation of barriers to specific people, with individual countries embracing this terminology and evolving in unique ways (Ostroff, 2011). What they have in common is a paradigm shift in design approaches from a focus on the average or "typical" user to consideration of a broad range of human characteristics (Myers, Lindberg, & Nied, 2013). They all promote the proactive design of products and environments to reach a broad audience.

Whereas accommodation is a reactive approach to provide access to an individual, proactive approaches strive to ensure access to a potential audience with a wide range of characteristics. Three proactive design approaches are described in the paragraphs that follow. The third, universal design (UD), perhaps the most comprehensive of all proactive approaches, is the topic of the remaining sections of this chapter and its application to higher education is the topic of this book.

Barrier-Free and Accessible Design

The term *barrier-free design* originated in the mid-twentieth century to describe efforts to remove physical barriers to people with disabilities in the built environment (Ostroff, 2011). The term *accessible design* has also been used to address similar issues (Iwarsson & Stahl, 2003). After World War II, veterans who sustained injuries in the war, other people with disabilities, and their advocates led a barrier-free movement that drove changes in public policies, laws, and design standards. Further inspired by the civil rights movements of women and racial minorities, disability rights leaders made a positive impact on the accessibility of not only the built environment, but also education, public places, transportation, and information technology (U.S. Department of Justice, 2005). For example, the U.S. Architectural Barriers Act of 1968 requires that all buildings designed, constructed, altered, or leased with federal funds meet minimum accessibility requirements to remove physical barriers to individuals with disabilities. Section 504 of the Rehabilitation Act of 1973 prohibits discrimination on the basis of disability in covered public programs and services. Accessible design of the built environment came to the forefront of public awareness in the U.S. with the passage of the ADA in 1990. As a result of legislation, the U.S. Architectural and Transportation Barriers Compliance Board (U.S. Access Board) created standards for the construction and renovation of facilities. People often equate accessible design to compliance with federal standards; some even label accessible environments as "ADA-compliant" (Iwarsson & Stahl, 2003).

Some standards and guidelines for the accessible design of specific products have been developed. For example, guidelines have been developed for the accessible design of homes (e.g., Gulatee, 2007). Regarding technology, the international World Wide Web Consortium developed web content accessibility guidelines (n.d.) and the U.S. Access Board developed standards for the accessibility of information technology used by the federal government in response to Section 508 of the Rehabilitation Act.

Although the focus of barrier-free and accessible design is typically on disability, making a product or environment accessible to individuals who have disabilities often benefits others, as illustrated by the following examples:

- A noisy environment in airports prohibits access to audio output of running television programs for many people, which is very similar to barriers faced by people with hearing impairments; including captions on videos ensures access to a diverse audience.
- Some people for whom English is a second language experience reading difficulties similar to those of people with some types of learning disabilities; software that provides vocabulary support (e.g., built-in access to word definitions) benefits a diverse audience.
- Workers who need to operate a computer when their hands are performing other tasks face access challenges similar to those who use a hands-free input method because of physical limitations; speech control benefits a diverse audience.

Usable Design

Usability has been defined as "the extent to which a product can be used by specified users to achieve specified goals with effectiveness, efficiency, and satisfaction in a specified context of use" (International Organization for Standardization, 1998). Usability engineers are concerned with subjective views on how well a design enables performance and contributes to well-being (Iwarsson & Stahl, 2003). Usability takes into account how easily users can learn how to operate a product, achieve their goals, and remember how to perform tasks when they return to the product at a later time. Some usability professionals today consider accessibility "a necessary precondition for usability" (Iwarsson & Stahl, 2003, p. 62). However, in practice, many do not routinely include people with disabilities in usability tests (Bergman & Johnson, 1995; Burgstahler, Jirikowic, Kolko, & Eliot, 2004). Such an oversight results in products that are not usable by a diverse audience.

It should be noted that designs that are technically accessible to people with disabilities may not be very usable. For example, a very complicated table presented on a website could be marked up in such a way that a person who is blind could access the content with a screen reader, but, because of the table's complexity, may be too confusing for this individual to use.

Universal Design

The UD of products and environments has a history that predates the use of the term *universal design*. Marc Harrison (1928–1996), a professor of industrial engineering at the Rhode Island School of Design, was a pioneer in what later became known as UD. Harrison sustained a traumatic brain injury as a child. His experiences through years of rehabilitation gave him insight and inspiration for his work. He challenged a design philosophy that focused on individuals of average size and ability by promoting the idea that products and environments should be designed for people of all abilities. For example, his design of a food processor—with large and easily pressed buttons, large grasp handles, and bold, high-contrast labels—demonstrated that making a product more usable by consumers with visual and mobility impairments made it more usable by everyone (Hagley Museum and Library, n.d.).

Ronald Mace, a wheelchair user as well as an internationally recognized architect, product designer, and educator, coined the term *universal design* in the 1970s. Like Harrison, Mace challenged the conventional practice of designing products for the average user and promoted a design approach that led to a more accessible and usable world for everyone. At the Center for Universal Design (CUD) at North Carolina State University, he defined UD as "the design of products and environments to be usable by all people, to the greatest extent possible, without the need for adaptation or specialized design" (CUD, 2008, p. 1). UD promoters argue that disadvantages associated with disabilities are primarily imposed by the inaccessible design of products and environments (Jones, 1996; Swain & Lawrence, 1994). UD features in a product or environment are integrated into the design so that they do not stand out and so that they foster social integration. An example of UD is a sidewalk that has curb cuts to make it usable by people who are walking, using wheelchairs, pushing baby strollers, and rolling delivery carts. Although some researchers and practitioners have used UD in the context of providing access for individuals with disabilities or, even more narrowly, to individuals with certain types of disabilities, the definition of UD is much broader than that, clearly stating its consideration of and benefit to *all people* in the design process.

Other terms are used to describe design approaches identical to or similar to UD. The Design for All Europe organization defines *design for all* as "design for human diversity, social inclusion, and equality" (Kercher, 2008). *Inclusive design* is defined by the British Standards Institute (2005) as the "design of mainstream products and/or services that are accessible to, and usable by, as many people as reasonably possible . . . without the need for special adaptation or specialised design" (Engineering Design Centre, 2013). In Canada, the Inclusive Design Institute (n.d.) defines *inclusive design* as a design approach that considers "the full range of human diversity with respect to ability, language, culture, gender, age, and other forms of human difference." *Universal access* terminology has been mainly used in reference to computer-based applications (Stephanidis, 2009). With the aim to prevent the exclusion of any group, including people with disabilities, from gaining full benefits from information technologies, universal access approaches to design embrace human-centered approaches to human-computer interactions. Emphasis is on knowing potential product users, where "users" is defined broadly.

Some researchers and practitioners have tailored the general definition of UD to specific applications. For example, Universal Smart Home Design has been described as "the process of designing products and housing environments that can be used to the greatest extent possible for people of all ages, abilities, and physical disabilities" (Schwab, 2004). UD has also been defined in legislation. For example, with a focus on information technology, UD is defined in the U.S. Assistive Technology Act of 1998 as:

> a concept or philosophy for designing and delivering products and services that are usable by people with the widest possible range of functional capabilities, which include products and services that are directly usable (without requiring assistive

technologies) and products and services that are made usable with assistive technologies. (Assistive Technology Act, 1998)

The common thread in all these applications is that a diverse group of potential users can fully benefit from a product or environment in an inclusive setting (National Council on Disability, 2004). With UD, the user is not expected to adjust to the limitations of an inflexible product or environment; rather, the application is expected to adjust to the needs and preferences of the vast majority of its potential users. As illustrated in Figure 1.3, UD integrates both accessible and usable design features and seeks to make it possible for everyone to participate in an inclusive setting without being singled out.

The *universal* in UD represents an ideal with respect to the audience for a specific product or environment. However, no application will be fully usable by every human being; in many cases this is not even desirable. For example, designing an electric saw that can be easily operated by everyone, including a five-year-old child, is neither necessary nor desirable. UD does, however, require inclusive practices that address access and use issues related to diverse characteristics of members within the broadly defined population for whom the application is intended. For example, when instructors apply UD to a postsecondary course, they consider the great diversity of their potential students (e.g., anyone who meets the entrance requirements of the institution as well as a particular course). Considerations include level of ability to move, see, hear, read, learn, and process information; stature; age; race; ethnicity; culture; socioeconomic status; learning style and preference; dexterity; native language; intelligence; and gender. Considering that most characteristics (e.g., the ability to see) can be measured on a continuum, the traditional view of a person "having a disability" or "not having a disability" is overly simplistic. Everyone has different abilities that are likely to change over the course of a lifetime. The design of a product or environment with which an individual wishes to interact and the specific task at hand determine whether a user needs a specific ability. An uncaptioned video requires the ability to hear well enough to understand the content; a captioned video does not.

The *design* in UD reinforces the characteristic that UD is a proactive process rather than a reactive one. Universally designed products and environments have built-in features that anticipate the needs and preferences of a diverse group of users. For example, the director of a registration office is applying UD when she anticipates that a student who is blind may at some time need to register for a class and directs her technical staff to take steps to ensure that the online registration system is accessible to someone who is blind and using screen reader technology.

It should be noted that designs that are technically *accessible* and *usable* may not provide good examples of UD because they are not *inclusive*. A main entrance to a building that has stairs and a separate ramp for wheelchair users is technically accessible and usable. However, this approach is not as inclusive as a sloping ramp to a main entrance without stairs, which allows everyone to approach and enter the building together.

Even universally designed products can be poorly designed in other ways. Adding captions to a poorly designed video presentation only makes the poorly designed

FIGURE 1.3   Characteristics of Universal Design

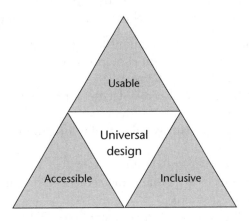

video accessible to a broader audience. To be most effective, UD is *paired* with best practices in the field in which it is applied.

PRINCIPLES AND GUIDELINES FOR UNIVERSAL DESIGN

In the mid-90s at the CUD, with funding from the U.S. Department of Education, a group of product developers, architects, environmental designers, and engineers established the following set of seven principles of UD and related guidelines to consider in the design of any product or environment (CUD, 1997).

1. *Equitable use.* The design is useful and marketable to people with diverse abilities. Guidelines for this principle are as follows:
   - Provide the same means of use for all users: identical whenever possible; equivalent when not.
   - Avoid segregating or stigmatizing any users.
   - Provisions for privacy, security, and safety should be equally available to all users.
   - Make the design appealing to all users.

2. *Flexibility in use.* The design accommodates a wide range of individual preferences and abilities. Guidelines for this principle are as follows:
   - Provide choice in methods of use.
   - Accommodate right- or left-handed access and use.
   - Facilitate the user's accuracy and precision.
   - Provide adaptability to the user's pace.

3. *Simple and intuitive use.* Use of the design is easy to understand, regardless of the user's experience, knowledge, language skills, or current concentration level. Guidelines for this principle are as follows:
   - Eliminate unnecessary complexity.
   - Be consistent with user expectations and intuition.

- Accommodate a wide range of literacy and language skills.
- Arrange information to be consistent with its importance.
- Provide effective prompting and feedback during and after task completion.

4. *Perceptible information.* The design communicates necessary information effectively to the user, regardless of ambient conditions or the user's sensory abilities. Guidelines for this principle are as follows:
   - Use different modes (pictorial, verbal, tactile) for redundant presentation of essential information.
   - Provide adequate contrast between essential information and its surroundings.
   - Maximize "legibility" of essential information.
   - Differentiate elements in ways that can be described (i.e., make it easy to give instructions or directions).
   - Provide compatibility with a variety of techniques or devices used by people with sensory limitations.

5. *Tolerance for error.* The design minimizes hazards and the adverse consequences of accidental or unintended actions. Guidelines for this principle are as follows:
   - Arrange elements to minimize hazards and errors: most used elements, most accessible; hazardous elements eliminated, isolated, or shielded.
   - Provide warnings of hazards and errors.
   - Provide fail-safe features.
   - Discourage unconscious action in tasks that require vigilance.

6. *Low physical effort.* The design can be used efficiently, comfortably, and with a minimum of fatigue. Guidelines for this principle are as follows:
   - Allow user to maintain a neutral body position.
   - Use reasonable operating forces.
   - Minimize repetitive actions.
   - Minimize sustained physical effort.

7. *Size and space for approach and use.* Appropriate size and space is provided for approach, reach, manipulation, and use regardless of the user's body size, posture, or mobility. Guidelines for this principle are as follows:
   - Provide a clear line of sight to important elements for any seated or standing user.
   - Make reach to all components comfortable for any seated or standing user.
   - Accommodate variations in hand and grip size.
   - Provide adequate space for the use of assistive devices or personal assistance. (Story, Mueller, & Mace, 1998, pp. 34–35)

The authors expected that these general principles and guidelines could apply to any design discipline and be used to evaluate existing designs, guide the design process, and educate designers and consumers about the characteristics of more accessible, usable, and inclusive products and environments (Story, Mueller, & Mace, 1998, p. 32). From this foundation, the authors also expected that practitioners would develop design standards and compliance tests for specific fields. For example, a practitioner could apply principle 5, "Tolerance for error," to an online course—even though offering courses online was a rare practice when the principle was written—by providing helpful feedback that includes redirecting students who make specific selection errors as they engage with the course materials.

Some researchers and practitioners have used CUD's seven principles of UD as a foundation on which to develop application frameworks with guidelines, performance indicators, and/or checklists of promising practices to help practitioners implement UD in specific situations. Vanderheiden and Vanderheiden (1992) developed specific guidelines for information technology. Hogan (2003) developed an Inclusive Employment Checklist and an Inclusive Marketing Checklist for companies to use when applying UD to issues regarding employees and products, respectively. Ensign (1993) developed a UD checklist for playgrounds. As presented in the next chapter of this book, several researchers and practitioners have developed frameworks for the application of UD to teaching that include the universal design for learning (UDL) (Meyer, Rose, & Gordon, 2014). Similarly, DO-IT, which hosts the Center for Universal Design in Education (CUDE) at the University of Washington, developed checklists of UD practices for instruction (Burgstahler, 2015a), but also many other college and university settings, such as computer labs (Burgstahler, 2012a), student services (Burgstahler, 2015b), and specific student service units (DO-IT, n.d.a; n.d.b) as described in other chapters of this book.

THE PROCESS OF UNIVERSAL DESIGN

The term *design* can be used as a verb or as a noun. As a noun, *design* represents the characteristic of a product or environment; as a verb, it refers to the *process* of creating a product or environment. Thus, UD is a process as well as a goal. As stated by Story, Mueller, and Mace (1998, p. 2):

> It is possible to design a product or an environment to suit a broad range of users, including children, older adults, people with disabilities, people of atypical size or shape, people who are ill or injured, and people inconvenienced by circumstance. [Yet] it is unlikely that any product or environment could ever be used by everyone under all conditions. Because of this, it may be more appropriate to consider universal design a process, rather than an achievement.

Vanderheiden and his colleagues at the University of Wisconsin's Trace Center have used the following definition of UD as a process for designing consumer products:

> Universal design is the process of creating products (devices, environments, systems, and processes) which are usable by people with the widest possible range of abilities, operating within the widest possible range of situations (environments, conditions, and circumstances), as is commercially practical. Universal design has two major components:
>
> 1. Designing products so that they are flexible enough that they can be directly used (without requiring any assistive technologies or modifications) by people

with the widest range of abilities and circumstances as is commercially practical, given current materials, technologies, and knowledge; and

2. Designing products so that they are compatible with the assistive technologies that might be used by those who cannot efficiently access and use the products directly. (Vanderheiden & Tobias, n.d., p. 1)

For example, in applying the process of UD to consumer electronics—including those used at a postsecondary institution—the Electronic Industries Alliance suggested that companies (1) know the user; (2) make the product adjustable; (3) provide alternatives and redundancies; (4) make functions conspicuous; (5) provide adequate feedback; (6) make the design forgiving; (7) strive first for accessibility, then for compatibility (with assistive technology); and (8) evaluate the product (Electronic Industries Alliance, 1996).

UD as a process requires a macro view of an application (e.g., choosing teaching strategies), as well as a micro view of subparts of the application (e.g., facilitating small-group discussions). It also requires that *universe* be defined as broadly as possible. In this context, the universe is a "set that contains all elements relevant to a particular discussion or problem" (*Merriam-Webster's Collegiate Dictionary*, n.d.b). For example, in a course, the universe would include the wide diversity in characteristics of students eligible to take the course, as well as curriculum, facilities, and technology used in the course. A list of steps for applying UDHE was informed by a review of the literature and the experiences of a leadership team led by the DO-IT Center (2012) for more than a decade with funding from the U.S. Department of Education. They are described below (Burgstahler, 2015c, pp. 1–2) and summarized in Figure 1.4.

1. *Identify the application.* Specify the product or environment to which you wish to apply universal design.
2. *Define the universe.* Describe the overall population (e.g., users of service), and then describe the diverse characteristics of potential members of the population for which the application is designed (e.g., students, faculty, and staff with diverse characteristics with respect to gender; age; size; ethnicity and race; native language; learning style; and abilities to see, hear, manipulate objects, read, and communicate).
3. *Involve consumers.* Consider and involve people with diverse characteristics (as identified in Step 2) in all phases of the development, implementation, and evaluation of the application. Also gain perspectives through diversity programs and student services, such as the campus disability services office.
4. *Adopt guidelines or standards.* Create or select existing universal design guidelines or standards. Integrate them with other best practices within the field of the specific application.
5. *Apply guidelines or standards.* Apply universal design in concert with best practices within the field, as identified in Step 4, to the overall design of the application, all subcomponents of the application, and all ongoing operations (e.g., procurement processes, staff training) to maximize the benefit of the application to individuals with the wide variety of characteristics identified in Step 2.

FIGURE 1.4 Universal Design as a Process

6. *Plan for accommodations.* Develop processes to address accommodation requests (e.g., purchase of assistive technology, arrangement for sign language interpreters) from individuals for whom the design of the application does not automatically provide access. Make these processes known through appropriate signage, publications, and websites.

7. *Train and support.* Tailor and deliver ongoing training and support to stakeholders (e.g., instructors, computer support staff, procurement officers, volunteers). Share institutional goals with respect to diversity and inclusion and practices for ensuring welcoming, accessible, and inclusive experiences for everyone.

8. *Evaluate.* Include universal design measures in periodic evaluations of the application; evaluate the application with a diverse group of users; and make modifications based on feedback. Provide ways to collect input from users (e.g., through online and printed instruments and communications with staff).

APPLICATIONS OF UNIVERSAL DESIGN IN HIGHER EDUCATION

The UD definition and UD principles can be applied to many educational products (e.g., websites, curricula, scientific equipment) and environments (e.g., classrooms, computer labs, buildings, libraries, online courses) (DO-IT, n.d.b). To emphasize its application to educational settings, "educational" could be added to CUD's UD definition, so that the definition of universal design in education (UDE) is "the design of *educational* products and environments to be usable by all people, to the greatest extent possible, without the need for adaptation or specialized design."

Practicing UDHE instead of providing accommodations alone holds promise for making institutions more inclusive, both for students who disclose disabilities and request accommodations and for those with disabilities who do not disclose, UDHE benefits *all* students, including those with various learning styles and technological expertise, those whose native language is not English, those who are older than the average student, and those who are members of racial and ethnic minority groups. So, how can you recognize a universally designed product or environment? It is helpful to remember that UD

- is applied proactively,
- makes a product or environment welcoming to all potential users,
- is usable by and accessible to people with a broad range of characteristics, and
- is offered in an inclusive setting.

Strategies for applying UDHE are unique to a specific application. For example, Table 1.1 lists the seven principles of UD, each matched with examples of its application to products and environments in higher education (Burgstahler, 2012b). Organizing UD strategies around specific areas of focus within the institution—instruction, services, information technology, and physical spaces—can make them more useful to individuals with specific roles at the institution. Figure 1.5 provides examples of UDHE practices in these four areas.

UD is a promising approach for integrating what we know about gender, race, ethnicity, age, disability, and other diversity issues into implementation frameworks that can be routinely applied to all aspects of higher education. In summary, UDHE

- has a *goal* of making all aspects of campus offerings usable by faculty, staff, students, and visitors;
- *values* access, equity, and inclusion, and considers differences in ability, as with other diversity characteristics, to be part of the normal human experience and "disability" to be largely a social construct;
- is a *proactive process* for creating flexible educational products and environments that are welcoming to, accessible to, and usable by everyone; and
- provides a *foundation* for the development of strategies for the design of all on-site and online products and environments found in higher education.

On many campuses today, embracing UDHE requires a paradigm shift from

- a medical or deficit model to a social model of disability;
- viewing disability as a deficit to viewing disability as a diversity characteristic;
- viewing inaccessibility as a problem caused by a person's impairment to viewing inaccessibility as a problem caused by the inaccessible design of products and environments;
- a design focus on the average or typical person to a design focus on individuals with a wide range of characteristics; and
- a reactive accommodations-only approach to providing access to students with disabilities to a proactive UD approach that minimizes the need for, but is well prepared to offer, reasonable accommodations when needed.

Applying UDHE does not reduce quality, but it may reorient the roles of faculty, student service administrators, and disability service units. In an accommodation

TABLE 1.1   Examples of Universal Design Principles Applied to Higher Education Practices

UD Principle	Example of UDHE Practice
1. *Equitable use.* The design is useful and marketable to people with diverse abilities.	*Career services.* Job postings in formats accessible to people with a broad range of abilities, disabilities, ages, and racial/ethnic backgrounds.
2. *Flexibility in use.* The design accommodates a wide range of individual preferences and abilities.	*Campus museum.* A design that allows a visitor to choose to read or listen to the description of the contents of display cases.
3. *Simple and intuitive.* Use of the design is easy to understand, regardless of the user's experience, knowledge, language skills, or current concentration level.	*Assessment.* Testing in a predictable, straightforward manner.
4. *Perceptible information.* The design communicates necessary information effectively to the user, regardless of ambient conditions or the user's sensory abilities.	*Dormitory.* An emergency alarm system with visual, aural, and kinesthetic characteristics.
5. *Tolerance for error.* The design minimizes hazards and the adverse consequences of accidental or unintended actions.	*Instructional software.* A program that provides guidance when the student makes an inappropriate selection.
6. *Low physical effort.* The design can be used efficiently, comfortably, and with a minimum of fatigue.	*Curriculum.* Software with on-screen control buttons that are large enough for students with limited fine motor skills to select easily.
7. *Size and space for approach and use.* Appropriate size and space is provided for approach, reach, manipulation, and use, regardless of the user's body size, posture, or mobility (The Center for Universal Design, 1997).	*Science lab.* An adjustable table and flexible work area that is usable by students who are right- or left-handed and have a wide range of physical characteristics and abilities (Burgstahler, 2015d).

model, the student is typically responsible for presenting documentation to disability service staff who then determine reasonable accommodations and, as appropriate, tell faculty and staff to implement them. In the UDHE model, there is more shared responsibility as faculty and staff take on greater roles in creating welcoming, accessible, and inclusive environments, and engage with disability service personnel, who provide a consulting role regarding these efforts in addition to their traditional role of specifying accommodations for individuals. Effective results require active engagement of the student as well. Table 1.2 articulates the potential roles of students with disabilities, disability services staff, faculty, and student service administrators when UDHE is embraced.

Changing attitudes about diversity and disability are embodied in how the postsecondary community discusses access problems. For example, a professor might say, "My course videos are not accessible to Dylan because *he* is deaf." A professor who embraces the UD approach might say, "Dylan cannot access the content presented in my course videos because they are not captioned." A fully UD-enlightened professor could say, "Dylan can access the content in my course videos because I provide captions that benefit students who are deaf or hard of hearing, whose native language is

FIGURE 1.5   Examples of Universal Design in Higher Education

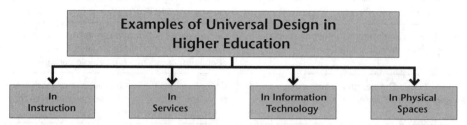

In Instruction	In Services	In Information Technology	In Physical Spaces
• A statement on a syllabus that invites students to meet with the instructor to discuss learning needs.	• Part of a service counter that is at a height accessible from a seated position.	• Captioned videos.	• Clear directional signs that have large, high-contrast print.
• Multiple delivery methods that motivate and engage all learners.	• Staff that are aware of resources and procedures for providing disability-related accommodations.	• Alternative text for graphic images on web pages so that individuals who are blind and using text-to-speech technology can access the content.	• Restrooms, classrooms, and other facilities that are physically accessible to individuals who use wheelchairs or have other mobility challenges.
• Flexible curriculum that is accessible to all learners.	• Pictures in publications and on websites that include people with diverse characteristics with respect to race, age, gender, and disability.	• Procurement policies and procedures that promote the purchase of accessible products.	• Furniture and fixtures in classrooms that are adjustable in height and allow arrangements for different learning activities and student groupings.
• Examples that appeal to students with a variety of characteristics with respect to race, ethnicity, gender, age, and interest.	• A statement in publications that states how to request special assistance, such as a disability-related accommodation.	• Standards for the universal design of websites.	• Emergency instructions that are clear and visible and address the needs of individuals with sensory and mobility impairments.
• Regular, accessible, and effective interactions between students and the instructor.	• A student service website that adheres to accessibility standards of the U.S. federal government (see http://www.section508.gov/).	• Comfortable access to computers for both left- and right-handed students.	• Nonslip walking surfaces.
• Allowing students to turn in parts of a large project for feedback before the final project is due.	• Printed materials that are easy to reach from a variety of heights and without furniture blocking access.	• Software and websites that are compatible with assistive technology.	
• Class outlines and notes that are on an accessible website.	• Printed publications that are available in alternate formats (e.g., electronic, large print, braille).	• Computers that are on adjustable-height tables.	
• Assessing student learning using multiple methods.			
• Faculty awareness of process and resources for disability-related accommodations.			

not mine, who wish to search through the content for specific topics, who want to know the spelling of technical words that I use, and/or who want to reformat the content into their own study materials." UD-enlightened educators recognize accessibility barriers that reside in a product or environment and take proactive steps to avoid them. Rather than viewing disability as an individual's problem to be dealt with by disability service offices, they see inclusion as a responsibility of everyone engaged in the community.

CUDE (DO-IT, n.d.a) maintains an online resource that includes introductory materials, links to resources, a news feed, a list of published articles related to UDHE (DO-IT, n.d.c), and a knowledge base of questions and answers, case studies, and promising practices. Practitioners can use these materials to stay abreast of the latest developments in the field.

TABLE 1.2 **Stakeholder Roles on a Universally Designed Campus**

Stakeholder	Role
Student with disability	Apply self-determination skills, including self-advocacy, to address access issues.
Disability services staff	Consult on universal design. Authorize and arrange reasonable accommodations.
Faculty or student service administrator	Apply universal design. Provide reasonable accommodations.

CONCLUSION

In an era of rapidly changing demographics, it may be impossible (and may not be particularly useful) to describe the "typical" student; it may be more useful to describe diversity within the student body. An institution that does not adequately address diversity issues limits the ability of specific groups to thrive and limits the institution's ability to achieve its academic goals. UD is consistent with the social model of disability, addresses a range of diversity issues, and has the potential to improve campus offerings while it reduces the need for individual accommodations. UDHE challenges postsecondary institutions to make all of their products and environments welcoming to, accessible to, and usable by everyone. Some researchers and practitioners, including authors of chapters in this book, consider the practice of infusing UD into all aspects of higher education a next step toward destigmatizing disability and ensuring equity, while making all members of the campus community feel welcome. The inclusive educational programs that result benefit from the unique perspectives of all participants.

THE AUTHORS AND CONTENT OF THIS BOOK

The content of this book documents applications of UDHE by individuals, institutions, and associations. Although there are differences in UD terminology used by the authors, "the goal is profound: we can and should make our human-made world as accessible and usable as possible for as diverse a user population as possible" (Story, 2011, p. 43). The book emerged from decades of experiences of educators, administrators, and researchers who share this common goal. Chapter authors share a passion for creating educational environments that value all learners and recognize the promise of UD practices for doing that. The authors present a variety of perspectives, experiences, and outcomes with respect to the application of UDHE to:

- instruction,
- physical spaces,
- technology, and
- student services.

To limit the size of this volume, efforts regarding UDHE in the U.S. as well as specific benefits of UD to students with disabilities are emphasized; although authors

TABLE 1.3 Questions Answered in This Book

If This Is Your Question	Find Your Answer in Chapter(s):
What are the history and applications of UDHE?	1, 2, 11, 13, 15, 16
How can I apply UD to instruction?	2, 3, 4, 5, 6, 7, 8, 9, 21, 22
How does UD relate to teaching and learning theories, philosophies, and models?	2
What evidence base supports UD of instruction?	3
How can I apply UD to assessments?	2, 10
How can I apply UD to an e-learning course?	2, 15, 18
How can I incorporate UD concepts in a course?	20
How do students with disabilities perceive the value of UD for their learning?	6
How can I provide faculty development on UD?	2, 8, 21, 22, 23, 24
How can I apply UD to a student service unit?	11, 12
How is a universally designed physical space different than one that is simply "ADA-compliant"?	13, 14
How can I design web content to be accessible to and usable by everyone?	15, 16, 17, 18
How can I promote a campuswide adoption of UD?	19, 23, 24

also acknowledge the value of UD to other student populations, as well as to faculty, staff, and visitors worldwide. Many of the authors have disabilities, but it is unknown exactly how many because a UD process was employed in developing the book; thus, accommodations were not needed for any author. UD strategies are also employed in presenting the content of this book. It is available in an accessible electronic format for people who are blind. The chapters are organized into four parts that guide its readers:

Part 1: Introduction
Part 2: Universal Design of Instruction in Higher Education
Part 3: Universal Design of Student Services and Physical Spaces in Higher Education
Part 4: Universal Design of Technology in Higher Education
Part 5: Promotion and Institutionalization of Universal Design

Each part begins with a summary of the section's focus and a recurring diagram of UDHE examples that highlights the section topic. Each chapter begins with an abstract summarizing its content. There are overview chapters for each of the four major UDHE application areas covered in the book. These chapters are easy to identify by their inclusion of the subtitle "From Principles to Practice." Each overview chapter ends with a description of the subsequent chapters that relate to the topic. Chapters are ordered so that the content builds on previous chapters, but they are self-contained and thus can be read out of the order presented. Supplementing a traditional table of contents and index, Table 1.3 (above) helps readers locate answers to specific questions.

REFERENCES

Americans with Disabilities Act of 1990. 42 U.S.C.A. § 12101 *et seq.*

Americans with Disabilities Act Amendments Act of 2008. 42 U.S.C.A. § 12102 note (2011)

Architectural Barriers Act of 1968. 42 U.S.C. § 4151 *et seq.*

Assistive Technology Act of 1998 Pub.L. No. 105-394 Stat 2432.

Belch, H. A. (2004). Retention and students with disabilities. *Journal of College Student Retention: Research, Theory, & Practice, 6*(1), 3–22.

Berge, Z. L., & Huang, Y. (2004). A model for sustainable student retention: A holistic perspective on the student dropout problem with special attention to e-learning. *DEOSNEWS, 13*(5). Retrieved from http://www.ed.psu.edu/acsde/deos/deosnews/deosnews13_5.pdf

Bergman, E., & Johnson, E. (1995). Towards accessible human-computer interaction. In J. Nielsen (Ed.), *Advances in human-computer interaction* (Vol. 5). Norwood, NJ: Ablex.

Braxton, J. M., Sullivan, A. V., & Johnson, R. M. (1997). Appraising Tinto's theory of college student departure. In J. C. Smart (Ed.), *Higher education: Handbook of theory and research* (Vol. XII, pp. 107–164). New York: Agathon.

Brown v. Board of Education, 347 U.S. 483 (1954).

Burgstahler, S. (2012a). *Equal access: Universal design of computer labs.* Seattle: University of Washington. Retrieved from http://www.washington.edu/doit/equal-access-universal-design-computer-labs

Burgstahler, S. (2012b). *Universal design in education: Principles and applications.* Seattle: University of Washington. Retrieved from http://www.washington.edu/doit/universal-design-education-principles-and-applications

Burgstahler, S. (2015a). *Equal access: Universal design of instruction.* Seattle: University of Washington. Retrieved from http://www.washington.edu/doit/equal-access-universal-design-instruction

Burgstahler, S. (2015b). *Equal access: Universal design of student services.* Seattle: University of Washington. Retrieved from http://www.washington.edu/doit/equal-access-universal-design-student-services

Burgstahler, S. (2015c). *Universal design: Process, principles, and applications.* Seattle: University of Washington. Retrieved from http://www.washington.edu/doit/universal-design-process-principles-and-applications

Burgstahler, S. (2015d). *Universal design in education: Principles and applications.* Seattle: University of Washington. Retrieved from http://www.washington.edu/doit/universal-design-education-principles-and-applications

Burgstahler, S., & Cory, R. (2008). *Universal design in higher education: From principles to practice.* Cambridge, MA: Harvard Education Press.

Burgstahler, S., Jirikowic, T., Kolko, B., & Eliot, M. (2004). Software accessibility, usability testing and individuals with disabilities. *Information Technology and Disabilities, 10*(2). Retrieved from http://itd.athenpro.org/volume10/number2/burghsta.html

Center for Universal Design (CUD). (1997). *The principles of universal design, version 2.0.* Raleigh: North Caroline State University. Retrieved from http://www.ncsu.edu/ncsu/design/cud/about_ud/udprinciplestext.htm

CUD. (2008). *About UD.* Raleigh: North Carolina State University. Retrieved from http://www.ncsu.edu/ncsu/design/cud/about_ud/about_ud.htm

Claxton, C. S., & Ralston, Y. (1978). *Learning styles: Their impact on teaching and administration.* Washington, DC: American Association for Higher Education.

DePoy, E., & Gibson, S. (2008a). Disability studies: Origins, current conflict, and resolution. *Review of Disability Studies, 4*(4), 33–40.

DePoy, E., & Gibson, S. (2008b). Healing the disjuncture: Social work disability practice. In K. M. Sowers & C. N. Dulmus (Series Eds.), & B. W. White (Vol. Ed.), *Comprehensive handbook of social work and social welfare: Volume 1, The profession of social work* (pp. 267–282). Hoboken, NJ: Wiley.

Disabilities, Opportunities, Internetworking, and Technology (DO-IT). (n.d.a). *The Center for Universal Design in Education (CUDE).* Seattle: University of Washington. Retrieved from http://www.washington.edu/doit/programs/center-universal-design-education

DO-IT (n.d.b). *Resources for student services staff.* Seattle: University of Washington. Retrieved from http://www.washington.edu/doit/programs/accesscollege/student-services-conference-room/resources/resources-student-services-staff

DO-IT. (n.d.c). Published articles and books about universal design in higher education (UDHE). Seattle: University of Washington. Retrieved from http://www.uw.edu/doit/programs/center-universal-design-education/resources/published-books-and-articles-about-universal

DO-IT. (1993–2014). *DO-IT snapshots.* Seattle: University of Washington. Retrieved from http://www.washington.edu/doit/programs/do-it-scholars/snapshots

DO-IT. (2012). *AccessCollege: Systemic change for postsecondary institutions.* Seattle: University of Washington. Retrieved from http://www.washington.edu/doit/accesscollege-systemic-change-postsecondary-institutions

Dunn, R., & Griggs, S. A. (2000). *Practical approaches to using learning styles in higher education.* Westport, CT: Greenwood.

Electronic Industries Alliance. (1996). *Resource guide for accessible design of consumer electronics: Linking product design to the needs of people with functional limitations.* Arlington, VA: Author.

Engineering Design Centre. (2013). *Definitions of inclusive design.* Cambridge: University of Cambridge.

Ensign, A. (Ed.). (1993). *Universal playground design.* Lansing, MI: PAM Assistance Centre.

Fernie, T., & Henning, M. (2006). From a disabling world to a new vision. In M. Adams & S. Brown (Eds.) *Towards inclusive learning in higher education: Developing curricula for disabled students* (pp. 23–31). Ablingdon, Oxford, UK: Routledge.

Gabel, S., & Peters, S. (2010). Presage of a paradigm shift: Beyond the social model of disability toward resistance theories of disability. *Disability & Society, 19*(6), 585–600.

Gardner, H. (1983). *Frames of mind.* New York: Basic Books.

Getzel, E. E., & Thoma, C. A. (2008). Experiences of college students with disabilities and the importance of self-determination in higher education. *Career Development and Transition for Exceptional Individuals, 31*(2), 77–84.

Griffin, E., & Pollak, D. (2009). Student experiences of neurodiversity in higher education: Insights from the BRAINHE project. *Dyslexia, 15*(1), 23–41.

Gulatee, R. (2007). Creating accessible homes: A checklist for accessibility. *Exceptional Parent Magazine, 37*(7), 28.

Hackman, H., & Rauscher, L. (2004). A pathway to access for all: Exploring the connections between universal instructional design and social justice education. *Equity & Excellence in Education, 37,* 114–123.

Hagley Museum and Library. (n.d.). *The Marc Harrison collection.* Wilmington, DE: Author. Retrieved from http://www.hagley.org/

Hogan, G. (2003). *The inclusive corporation.* Athens, OH: Swallow Press/Ohio University Press.

Inclusive Design Institute. (n.d.). *What is inclusive design?* Toronto, Ontario: Author.

International Organization for Standardization. (1998). *Guidance on usability.* (ISO 9241-11).

Iwarsson, S., & Stahl, A. (2003). Accessibility, usability and universal design—positioning and definition of concepts describing person-environment relationships. *Disability and Rehabilitation, 25*(2), 57–66.

Jones, S. R. (1996). Toward inclusive theory: Disability as social construction. *NASPA Journal, 33,* 347–354.

Kercher, J. (2008). *Names and mission statements: The evolving message of design for all.* EIDD Design for All Europe. Retrieved from http://www.designforalleurope.org/Design-for-All/Articles/Names-and-Mission-Statements-the-evolving-message-of-Design-for-All/

The Lawlor Group (n.d.). *Trends for 2013: Demographic trends in higher education.* Eden Prairie, MN: Author. Retrieved from http://www.thelawlorgroup.com/trends-2013-2.

Loewen, G., & Pollard, W. (2010). The social justice perspective. *Journal of Postsecondary Education and Disability, 23*(1), 5–18.

Marshak, L., Van Wieren, T., Ferrell, D. R., Swiss, L., & Dugan, C. (2010). Exploring barriers to college student use of disability services and accommodations. *Journal of Postsecondary Education and Disabilities, 22*(3), 151–165.

Merriam-Webster's Collegiate Dictionary (11th ed.). (n.d.a). Paradigm. In *Merriam-Webster's Collegiate Dictionary*. Chicago: Encyclopedia Britannica Company. Retrieved from http://www.merriam-webster.com/dictionary/paradigm

Merriam-Webster's Collegiate Dictionary (11th ed.). (n.d.b). Universe. In *Merriam-Webster's Collegiate Dictionary*. Chicago: Encyclopedia Britannica Company. Retrieved from http://www.merriam-webster.com/dictionary/universe

Meyer, A., Rose, D. H., & Gordon, D. (2014). *Universal design for learning: Theory and practice*. Wakefield, MA: CAST Professional Publishing. Retrieved from http://udltheorypractice.cast.org (free registration required)

Moriarty, M. A. (2007). Inclusive pedagogy: Teaching methodologies to reach diverse learners in science instruction. *Equity and Excellence in Education, 40*(3), 252–265.

Myers, K. A., Lindberg, J. J., & Nied, D. M. (2013). *Allies for Inclusion: Disability and Equity in Higher Education*. Hoboken, NJ: Wiley Periodicals, Inc.

National Center for Education Statistics. (2013). *Digest of education statistics*. (NCES 2014-015). Washington, D. C.: U.S. Department of Education. Retrieved from http://nces.ed.gov/fastfacts/display.asp?id=60

National Council on Disability. (2003). *People with disabilities and postsecondary education—position paper*. Retrieved from http://www.ncd.gov/publications/2003/Sept152003

National Council on Disability. (2004). *Design for inclusion: Creating a new marketplace*. Washington, DC: Author. Retrieved from http://www.ncd.gov/publications/2004/10282004

Nieto, S. (1996). *Affirming diversity: The sociopolitical context of multicultural education* (2nd ed.). White Plains, NY: Longman.

Ostroff, E. (2011). Universal design: An evolving paradigm. In W. Preiser & K. H. Smith (Eds.), *Universal design handbook* (2nd ed.), (pp. 1.1–1.11). Chicago: McGraw-Hill Professional.

Pliner, S., & Johnson, J. (2004). Historical, theoretical, and foundational principles of universal instructional design in higher education. *Equity & Excellence in Education, 37*, 105–113.

Rose, D. H., Meyer, A., & Hitchcock, C. (Eds.). (2005). *The universally designed classroom: Accessible curriculum and digital technologies*. Cambridge, MA: Harvard Education Publishing Group.

Schwab, C. (2004). A stroll through the universally designed smart home for the 21st century. *The Exceptional Parent, 34*(7), 24–28.

Seale, J. K. (2014). *E-learning and disability in higher education. Accessibility research and practice*. London: Routledge, Taylor & Francis.

Section 504 of the Rehabilitation Act of 1973, as amended. 29 U.S.C. § 794.

Section 508 of the Rehabilitation Act of 1973, as amended. 29 U.S.C. § 794(d).

Stephanidis, C. (2009). Universal access and design for all in the evolving information society. In C. Stephanidis (Ed.). *The universal access handbook* (pp. 1-1–1-11). Boca Raton, FL: CRC Taylor & Francis Group.

Stern, V., & Woods, M. (2001). *Roadmaps and rampways*. Washington, DC: American Association for the Advancement of Science.

Story, M. F. (2011). Universal design: An evolving paradigm. In W. Preiser & K. H. Smith (Eds.), *Universal design handbook* (2nd ed.), (pp. 4.3–4.12). Chicago: McGraw-Hill Professional.

Story, M. F., Mueller, J. L., & Mace, R. L. (1998). The principles of universal design and their application. In M. F. Story, M. L. Mueller, & R. L. Mace. *The universal design file: Designing for people of all ages and abilities*, pp. 32–36. Raleigh, NC: Center for Universal Design. Retrieved from http://www.ncsu.edu/ncsu/design/cud/pubs_p/docs/udffile/chap_3.pdf

Swain, J., & Lawrence, P. (1994). Learning about disability: Changing attitudes or challenging understanding? In S. French (Ed.), *On equal terms: Working with disabled people* (pp. 87–102). Oxford, UK: Butterworth Heinemann.

Tinto, V. (1993). *Leaving college: Rethinking the causes and cures of student attrition*. (2nd ed.). Chicago: University of Chicago Press.

United Nations. (2006). *Report of the Ad Hoc Committee on a Comprehensive and Integral International Convention on the Protection and Promotion of the Rights and Dignity of Persons with Disabilities*. Retrieved from http://www.un.org/disabilities/convention/conventionfull.shtml

United States Department of Justice. (2005). *A guide to disability rights laws.* Washington, DC: U.S. Department of Justice, Civil Rights Division. Retrieved from http://www.ada.gov/cguide.pdf

The U.S. Equal Employment Opportunity Commission. (2002). *Remarks of President George Bush at the signing of the Americans with Disabilities Act.* Retrieved from http://www.eeoc.gov/eeoc/history/35th/videos/ada_signing_text.html

Vanderheiden, G., & Tobias, J. (n.d.). *Universal design of consumer products: Current industry practice and perceptions.* Madison: University of Wisconsin Trace Research and Development Center. Retrieved from http://trace.wisc.edu/docs/ud_consumer_products_hfes2000/index.htm

Vanderheiden, G. C., & Vanderheiden, K. R. (1992). *Guidelines for the design of consumer products to increase their accessibility to people with disabilities or who are aging* (Working Draft 1.7). Madison: University of Wisconsin Trace Research and Development Center. Retrieved from http://trace.wisc.edu/docs/consumer_product_guidelines/toc.htm

Wagner, M., Newman, L., Cameto, R., Garza, N., & Levine, P. (2005). *After high school: A first look at the postschool experiences of youth with disabilities. A report from the National Longitudinal Transition Study2 (NLTS2).* Menlo Park, CA: SRI International.

Wagner, M., Newman, L., Cameto, R., & Levine, P. (2005). *Changes over time in the early postschool outcomes of youth with disabilities: A report of findings from the National Longitudinal Transition Study (NLTS) and the National Longitudinal Transition Study-2 (NLTS2).* Menlo Park, CA: SRI International.

Welsh, P. & Palames, C. (2002). A brief history of disability rights legislation in the United States. *Universal Design Education Online.* Retrieved from http://www.udeducation.org/resources/61.html

World Wide Web Consortium. (n.d.). *Web Content Accessibility Guidelines (WCAG) Overview.* Cambridge, MA: Author. Retrieved from http://www.w3.org/WAI/intro/wcag

This chapter is based on work supported by the U.S. Department of Education Office of Postsecondary Education (grant numbers P333A990042, P333A020044, and P333A050064) and the National Science Foundation (Cooperative Agreement number HRD-0227995, grant numbers CNS-1042260 and HRD-0833504). Any opinions, findings, and conclusions or recommendations are those of the author and do not necessarily reflect the policy or views of the federal government, and you should not assume its endorsement.

PART 2

Universal Design of Instruction in Higher Education

Part 2 begins with a chapter by Sheryl Burgstahler that provides an overview of the history, principles, and applications of universal design (UD) to instruction. The authors of the following chapters share perspectives, research, and strategies for applying UD to teaching methods, curriculum, and assessment.

Universal Design in Higher Education

Instruction	Services	Information Technology	Physical Spaces
Class climate	Planning, policies, & evaluation	Procurement, development policies, & procedures	Planning, policies, & evaluation
Interaction	Physical environments & products	Physical environments & products	Appearance
Physical environments & products	Staff	Staff	Entrances & routes of travel
Delivery methods	Information resources & technology	Input, output, navigation, & manipulation	Fixtures & furniture
Information resources & technology	Events	Compatibility with assistive technology	Information resources & technology
Feedback & Assessment			Safety
Accommodation			Accommodation

Source: S. Burgstahler (2015). *Applications of universal design in education.* Seattle: University of Washington. Retrieved from http://www.washington.edu/doit/applications-universal-design-education

2

Universal Design of Instruction
From Principles to Practice

Sheryl E. Burgstahler

Good teachers have employed inclusive practices since the beginning of time. Over the past two decades, increasing numbers of articles about the application of universal design (UD) for making instruction more inclusive in higher education have appeared in the literature. The author of this chapter provides an overview of frameworks for applying UD to teaching methods, materials, and assessments in on-site and online learning environments. Educators may find these insights useful as the characteristics of the students in their courses become increasingly diverse.

What might be the first response of a professor when a student who is blind enrolls in her art history class? Would she look forward to the unique perspective this student brings to her field and classroom? Would she be eager to learn how a person with a visual impairment might experience art? Would the tone and content of her communication make the student feel welcomed? An important first step in creating a welcoming and inclusive classroom environment for all students is to truly value diversity in its many forms, including, in this case, to see differences in visual abilities as simply a normal part of the human experience, rather than an extraordinary burden to be dealt with.

For many instructors and institutions, the primary approach for addressing the inaccessible design of instruction is through the provision of accommodations to individual students with disabilities. In contrast, as summarized in Chapter 1 of this book, faculty who embrace the universal design paradigm proactively design courses to address a student body that is increasingly diverse with respect to race, ethnicity, native language, culture, age, learning style, background knowledge, ability, gender, veteran status, and other characteristics. This chapter provides an overview of history, terminology, frameworks, and practices for the application of UD to teaching and learning in on-site and online environments in higher education.

OVERVIEW

Good teachers have long used teaching methods that reach a student body with a wide range of characteristics. Taking steps to make instruction appropriate for a diverse audience has been recognized as a best practice for fostering the academic and social growth of all students (Gurin, Dey, Hurtado, & Gurin, 2002). In an exploratory study, postsecondary faculty reported that flexible instructional practices and the ability to monitor and quickly adjust teaching methods benefit students with a range of disabilities. They also reported as beneficial the general practices of cooperative learning, contextual learning, computer-assisted instruction, constructive learning, scaffolding, online instruction and assessment, the provision of organizing tools for students, multimodal instruction, peer editing, criterion-based learning, extended time for exams and projects, and testing in the same manner as teaching (Silver, Bourke, & Strehorn, 1998).

At the Center for Universal Design (CUD), a group of architects, product designers, engineers, and environmental design researchers established seven principles of UD to provide guidance in designing all products and environments to be usable by all people, to the greatest extent possible (CUD, 1997, 2008). Researchers and practitioners have applied these principles to specific educational products and environments, including information technology (e.g., websites, educational software, video presentations), physical spaces (e.g., classrooms, labs), and services (e.g., advising, registration). UD, as defined by CUD, can be applied to any product or environment in higher education, as discussed in Chapter 1 and the remaining chapters of this book. For example, the UD principle "Simple and intuitive use" is applied when instructors present material in a clear, straightforward manner, taking care to consider the wide range of potential language skills and background knowledge of their students. "Flexibility in use" requires that students have choices regarding how they interact with the content. UD practices maximize these options. To further demonstrate the applicability of the CUD principles to postsecondary teaching, each of the seven principles of UD is listed in Table 2.1, along with one example of its application to instruction. In all such applications of UD, instructors anticipate the presence of students with diverse abilities, disabilities, and other characteristics, and make design decisions that benefit all of these individuals, rather than focusing only on the average or "typical" student. Universally designed curricula and instructional practices are welcoming to, accessible to, and usable by all potential students.

Applying UD reduces, but does not eliminate, the need for accommodations for students with disabilities. For example, providing a sign language interpreter in every class, just in case someone might need one, is unreasonable; this service is best provided as an accommodation for a specific student who is deaf and enrolled in a specific course. However, captioning videos in an online course means that no accommodations or product redevelopment will be necessary if a student who is deaf enrolls in the class. And, as a bonus, captions benefit students who want to search through the video for specific topics, who need to see the spelling of vocabulary with which they are not familiar, whose first language is not the one in which the video content is presented, and who have audio processing difficulties. Thus, planning ahead

TABLE 2.1 Applications of the Seven Principles of Universal Design to Instruction

UD Principle	Example of How UD Might Be Applied to Instruction
1. *Equitable use.* The design is useful and marketable to people with diverse abilities.	A professor's website is designed so that it is accessible to everyone, including students who are blind and use text-to-speech software.
2. *Flexibility in use.* The design accommodates a wide range of individual preferences and abilities.	A museum, visited as a field trip for a course, allows each student to choose to read or listen to a description of the contents of display cases.
3. *Simple and intuitive.* Use of the design is easy to understand regardless of the user's experience, knowledge, language skills, or current concentration level.	Control buttons on science equipment are labeled with text and symbols that are simple and intuitive to understand.
4. *Perceptible information.* The design communicates necessary information effectively to the user regardless of ambient conditions or the user's sensory abilities.	A video presentation projected in a course includes captions.
5. *Tolerance for error.* The design minimizes hazards and the adverse consequences of accidental or unintended actions.	Educational software provides guidance and/or background information when the student makes an inappropriate response.
6. *Low physical effort.* The design can be used efficiently and comfortably and with a minimum of fatigue.	Doors to a lecture hall open automatically for people with a wide variety of physical characteristics.
7. *Size and space for approach and use.* Appropriate size and space is provided for approach, reach, manipulation, and use regardless of the user's body size, posture, or mobility (The Center for Universal Design, 1997).	A flexible science lab work area has adequate workspace for students who are left- and right-handed and for those who need to work from a standing or seated position (Burgstahler, 2015c, p. 2).

through UD may save time in the long run and benefit many students in a class in addition to a student who is deaf.

At a meeting in 1997, a group of researchers and developers recommended steps for implementing UD in the development of educational curricula:

> Publishers should prepare, and teachers should select, instructional materials that are supportive and inclusive of students who have wide disparities in their abilities to see, hear, speak, read, etc. . . . To achieve that end, we recommend that all developers of instructional materials adopt the concept of universal design and implement it in their products. Further, we recommend that teacher-training programs prepare teachers for teaching in environments where the goals, methods, and materials are universally designed. (Orkwis & McLane, 1998, p. 13)

Meeting participants hoped that publishers would collaborate with educators to make the application of UD standard for all curricula. They recommended the following first steps for curriculum developers (Orkwis & McLane, 1998, pp. 14–15):

1. Provide all text in digital format.
2. Provide captions for all audio.

3. Provide educationally relevant descriptions for images and graphical layouts.
4. Provide captions and educationally relevant descriptions for video.
5. Provide cognitive supports for content and activities:
   - summarize big ideas,
   - provide scaffolding for learning and generalization,
   - build fluency through practice, and
   - provide assessments for background knowledge.
6. Include explicit strategies to make clear the goals and methods of instruction.

Progress toward more accessible curricula has been enhanced by the U.S. Department of Education's endorsement of a common National Instructional Materials Accessibility Standard (NIMAS) (Rose, Meyer, & Hitchcock, 2005). NIMAS provides a foundation for the development of a variety of formats of printed materials. However, since NIMAS is not widely implemented, educators continue to struggle with acquiring textbooks and other materials in alternate formats for students with disabilities. Although pedagogical, legal, and ethical arguments can be made for developing accessible educational materials, few available curriculum products at any educational level fully embrace accessible design. The following sections describe different terminology and frameworks for applying UD to teaching and learning products and environments.

TERMINOLOGY AND FRAMEWORKS

Some organizations have created frameworks for addressing issues related to the application of UD. *Framework* in the context of this chapter refers to "a set of ideas or facts that provide support for something" (*Merriam-Webster's Collegiate Dictionary*, n.d.). Figure 2.1 lists some of the myriad dimensions that a UD framework for teaching and learning might address—values, goal, definition, scope of application, principles, guidelines, exemplary practices, process, evaluation, and support. Ideally, relevant stakeholders (e.g., students with disabilities, disability support services, instructors, e-learning designers, IT specialists) are considered and engaged in the development of each dimension of a framework.

Terminology for applying UD to various aspects of teaching and learning includes *universally designed teaching, universal instructional design, universal design for learning, universal design for instruction*, and *universal design of instruction*. Related frameworks share the vision of equitable educational offerings and the goal of applying UD to ensure that all students have meaningful access to course materials, activities, and assessments in an integrated setting (Bar, Galluzzo, & Sinfit, 1999; Campbell, 2004; Mino, 2004). Although the frameworks are similar in the instructional practices they recommend, there are differences in the definitions, principles, and guidelines they embrace, as well as the scope of instructional practices they address. In all frameworks, UD practices allow students with diverse abilities and other characteristics to learn and demonstrate knowledge through multiple channels—including reading, listening, viewing, manipulating, experimenting, discussing, and responding to questions—each of which is available in formats accessible to all students.

FIGURE 2.1 Potential Dimensions of a Framework for Applying UD to Teaching and Learning

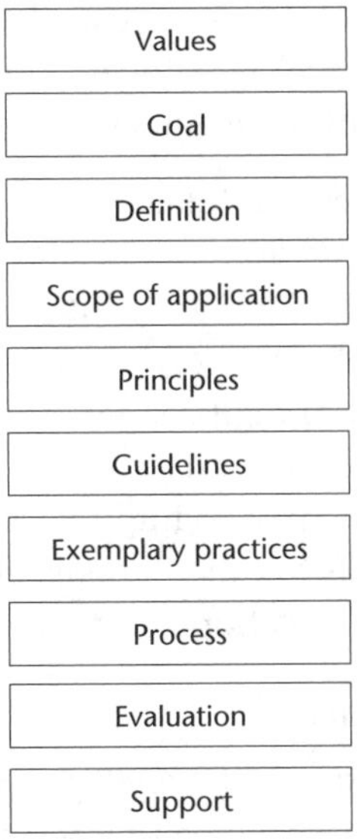

Values
Goal
Definition
Scope of application
Principles
Guidelines
Exemplary practices
Process
Evaluation
Support

Universally Designed Teaching (UDT)

Frank Bowe was a deaf professor and leader in disability rights advocacy and legislation. In his 1978 book, *Handicapping America: Barriers to Disabled People*, he argued that society handicaps people with disabilities by designing inaccessible facilities, equipment, and programs, and he advocated for a wide application of accessible design practices to correct this situation. He pointed out that disability is primarily an interaction between a person and an environment. Thus, the impact of a disability may be significant in some situations, but irrelevant in others. For example, being a wheelchair user is not relevant if a lecture hall is wheelchair-accessible. As an early promoter of the application of UD in higher education, Bowe recognized that UD addresses the most pressing needs of individuals with disabilities, and encouraged educators to think more broadly to consider the needs of students from minority ethnic/racial cultures, with different learning styles, and for whom traditional approaches to instruction are inconvenient. Bowe charged "educators and schools to take steps to reach out to nontraditional students. This means that educators need to plan for inclusion of such students" (Bowe, 2000, p. 107). Further, he affirmed that "[t]he principles of universal design place responsibility for making curricula, materials, and environments accessible to and usable by all students upon the teacher and the school" (Bowe, 2000, p. 4).

Bowe summarized that universally designed curricula and materials present information in multiple ways, offer multiple ways for students to interact with and respond to content, provide multiple ways for students to find meaning in the material, and make effective use of technology. Bowe emphasized that when UD practices are applied, only a small minority of students will need disability-related accommodations. In his book *Universal Design in Education* (2000), Bowe operationalized CUD's seven principles of UD and corresponding guidelines by applying them to educational settings that include physical spaces, teaching, and technology. In his "Tip Sheet for Universally Designed Teaching" (Bowe, 2000, pp. 5–6), Bowe organized UD practices under the following eight basic guidelines:

1. Become aware of your own culture's teachings and how those affect you as an educator.
2. Provide students with options for demonstrating knowledge and skills.
3. Offer instruction, and accept student work, at a distance.
4. Alert students to availability of digitized texts (e-books).
5. Offer students information in redundant media.
6. Provide the support students need to improve accuracy and speed.
7. Translate important materials to other languages as needed by your students.
8. Choose physically accessible locations for your classes.

Universal Instructional Design (UID)

The term *universal instructional design* (UID) refers to a theoretical model for the application of UD in higher education developed by researchers and practitioners at the University of Minnesota (Higbee & Goff, 2008; Lightfoot & Gibson, 2005; Silver, Bourke, & Strehorn, 1998). UID is

> a means for providing equity in access to higher education for all students by encouraging faculty to rethink their teaching practices to create curricula and courses that include all learners. Although initially many postsecondary educators perceived that the focus of UID was access for students with disabilities, the intent of this theoretical model is to consider all possible students who might be taking a course and then design the course accordingly. (Higbee, 2008, p. 61)

Components of UID build from the work of Chickering and Gamson (1987) on best practices for undergraduate instruction and include:

- creating welcoming classrooms;
- determining the essential components of a course;
- communicating clear expectations;
- providing constructive feedback;
- exploring the use of natural supports for learning, including technology, to enhance opportunities for all learners;
- designing teaching methods that consider diverse learning styles, abilities, ways of knowing, and previous experience and background knowledge;
- creating multiple ways for students to demonstrate their knowledge; and
- promoting interaction among and between faculty and students. (Higbee, 2008, p. 62)

Chapter 5 of this book describes specific examples of the application of these eight components to postsecondary instruction.

Universal Design for Learning (UDL)

Researchers at the Center for Applied Special Technology (CAST) concluded that the "idea of UD transfers readily from the built environment to the learning environment, but the *principles* and *techniques* do not" (Rose, Harbour, Johnston, Daley, & Abarbanell, 2006, p. 1). Applying the results of brain and learning research and the capabilities of information technology, CAST defined UDL as "a research-based set of principles that together form a practical framework for using technology to maximize learning opportunities for every student" (Rose & Meyer, 2002, p. 5). UDL has been applied more generally to curriculum that does not use technology as well. UDL supports the goal of UD as well as that of differentiated instruction to effectively teach students with different backgrounds, levels of readiness, primary languages, preferences, interests, and abilities in the same class. UDL provides "rich supports for learning, and reduces barriers to the curriculum, while maintaining high achievement standards for all" (CAST, n.d.b, p. 1). A key premise of UDL is that a curriculum should include alternatives to make it accessible and applicable to students with different backgrounds, learning styles, abilities, and disabilities and to minimize the need for assistive technology.

Three principles guide the application of UDL (Rose, Meyer, & Hitchcock, 2005):

- multiple means of representation;
- multiple means of action and expression; and
- multiple means of engagement.

UDL guidelines, organized under each principle, promote the development of curriculum that includes options for (1) perception; (2) language, expressions, and symbolism; (3) comprehension; (4) physical action; (5) expressive skills and fluency; (6) executive functions; (7) recruiting interest; (8) sustaining effort and persistence; and (9) self-regulation. The UDL research team developed a total of thirty-two specific checkpoints for the nine guidelines. For example, checkpoint 2.5 argues that it is important to "illustrate through multiple media":

> In formal schooling, there is a marked tendency to present the majority of information in language, specifically in printed text. Many students for whom language is not a particular strength thus face persistent barriers not experienced by others. The experimental studies on the option of illustrating key concepts nonlinguistically listed here span a range of media. There is extensive research to support the representation of information through a variety of formats: video, diagram, image, music, animation, and more. The scholarly reviews and opinion pieces provide more classroom-based perspectives on the importance of using a range of media to convey content to students. (CAST, 2011)

In a UDL curriculum:

- *Goals* provide an appropriate challenge for all students.
- *Materials* have a flexible format, supporting transformation between media and multiple representations of content to support all students' learning.

- *Methods* are flexible and diverse enough to provide appropriate learning experiences, challenges, and support for all students.
- *Assessment* is sufficiently flexible to provide accurate, ongoing information that helps teachers adjust instruction and maximize learning. (Hitchcock, Meyer, Rose, & Jackson, 2002, p. 8)

Many examples of UDL in precollege curricula have been shared in the literature. More recently, some researchers and practitioners have articulated the relevance of UDL to postsecondary instruction (Rose et al., 2006). Postsecondary examples of "multiple means of representation" include giving directions in multiple ways (e.g., orally as well as via handout, whiteboard, website), sharing outlines to help students follow a lecture presentation (Stein, 2013), and utilizing multiple mediums to present content (e.g., video presentations, lectures, small-group discussions) (Izzo, Murray, & Novak, 2008). Examples of "multiple means of engagement" include asking students to repeat directions given by an instructor, facilitating discussions where students add their thinking to that of others, and providing both cooperative learning and independent learning opportunities (Stein, 2013), as well as making learning motivating and relevant to all students (Izzo, Murray, & Novak, 2008; Poore-Pariseau, 2013). Examples of "multiple means of action and expression" are using whiteboards to record responses and using checklists to keep track of steps toward the completion of a task (Stein, 2013), as well as using multiple types of assessments such as those presented in written format, in multimedia, and in individual and group presentations (Izzo, Murray, & Novak, 2008). CAST efforts have led to the publication of many books and online resources, including UDL on Campus (CAST, n.d.a). Chapter 4 in this book provides a concrete example of the application of UDL to a postsecondary course.

Universal Design for Instruction (UD*forI*)

Researchers within the Center on Postsecondary Education and Disability (CPED) at the University of Connecticut—after a review of the literature on UD, effective instruction in postsecondary education, and effective practices for teaching students with learning disabilities—concluded that the UDL principles were not comprehensive enough to cover applications of UD to postsecondary instruction. Therefore, they chose to build their framework on CUD's principles for UD. Not convinced that these seven principles adequately covered all instructional applications in higher education, they added two more principles to CUD's list of seven:

- *A community of learners.* The instructional environment promotes interaction and communication among students and between students and faculty.
- *Instructional climate.* Instruction is designed to be welcoming and inclusive. High expectations are espoused for all students. (McGuire, Scott, & Shaw, 2003, p. 13)

Chapter 22 in this book is devoted to this framework, which is called Universal Design for Instruction (UD*forI*; the *for* is included in the acronym in the remainder of this chapter to distinguish it from the UDI—universal design of instruction—framework discussed in the next section). Included in Chapter 22 is a table with the nine principles of UD*for*I, each matched with a definition of the principle and examples of its practice in postsecondary education.

Universal Design of Instruction (UDI)

Since 1992, the Disabilities, Opportunities, Internetworking, and Technology (DO-IT) Center at the University of Washington—funded by the U.S. Department of Education, the National Science Foundation, the State of Washington, and other sources—has engaged in a Universal Design in Higher Education (UDHE) initiative to promote the application of UD to all aspects of postsecondary education. DO-IT has strong roots in the UD of technology, particularly within higher education. Over the course of a decade, DO-IT engaged with more than forty postsecondary institutions nationwide in its development and application of a framework for the UD of a wide variety of products and environments integral to postsecondary institutions—technology, physical spaces, student services, and instruction. These efforts led to the publication of the first edition of this book and to the formation of the Center for Universal Design in Education (CUDE) (DO-IT, n.d.a).

Soon after DO-IT's UDHE leadership team began to offer professional development to postsecondary faculty and administrators nationwide, they concluded that the basic definition and principles of UD developed by the CUD can be directly applied to create inclusive instructional products and environments (see examples in Table 2.1), but the terminology used by CUD is somewhat foreign to educators (Burgstahler, 2007a, b). They also concluded that all three UDL principles are supported by UD principles but use jargon more familiar to educators. However, the scope of UDL principles is narrower than that of UD principles and does not include all potential applications of UD in the postsecondary arena that may impact learning, such as physical aspects of computer and science labs (see Figures 2.2 and 2.3, respectively). With respect to the two new principles developed within the UD*for*I framework—a community of learners and instructional climate—the DO-IT team did not find these additions necessary as principles, but rather considered them to be aspects of instruction to which the original UD and UDL principles can be applied in an effort to ensure related practices are inclusive. Consequently, leaders in the UDHE initiative chose to adopt the CUD definition, principles, and guidelines of UD, but embrace UDL principles, as the foundation for its framework for the universal design of instruction (UDI). However, they encourage faculty to avoid preoccupation with jargon by applying the definition of UD and ensuring that their UD practices are

- developed proactively,
- designed to make instruction welcoming to all potential students,
- accessible to and usable by students with a broad range of abilities and other characteristics, and
- offered to all students in an inclusive setting.

As DO-IT's projects unfolded, postsecondary faculty requested examples for the application of UDI to specific instructional products (e.g., textbooks, videos, websites) and environments (e.g., classrooms, computer labs, online learning). In response to these requests, DO-IT's UDHE initiative leadership operationalized UDI into a checklist of promising practices that demonstrate how UD can be applied to (1) the overall design of instruction, (2) specific aspects of learning environments, and (3) the determination of accommodations when universally designed instruction does not fully address the needs of a specific student with a disability (e.g., there is a need for a sign language interpreter).

The initial and later versions of the UDI checklist were based on reviews of literature that identified promising practices that embody the UD paradigm to make instruction more inclusive of individuals with diverse characteristics (e.g., Bowe, 2000; Burgstahler, 2008; Burgstahler & Doe, 2006; DO-IT, n.d.b; Higbee, 2008; Moriarty, 2007; Rose et al., 2006; Rose & Meyer, 2002; Scott, McGuire, & Shaw, 2003; Silver et al., 1998) as well as experiences of the UDHE leadership team. Team members taught UDI practices to faculty on more than forty campuses. In an iterative process, the UDI checklist evolved with input from new literature in the field and formative feedback from participating faculty and administrators. Many UD practices recommended by the UDHE leadership team were inspired by best practices and accommodations for students with specific disabilities and then generalized in such a way as to benefit all students in a course (e.g., Burgstahler & Gleicher, in press; Souma & Casey, 2008). Rather than organizing the practices under UD principles and guidelines, the team clustered them under specific aspects of instruction. The initial eight subcategories were class climate, physical environment and products, delivery methods, information resources and technology, interaction, feedback, assessment, and accommodations; in later iterations, feedback and assessment were combined into one category because they are so interrelated (Burgstahler, 2015a, 2012). Always a working document, the most current list of UDI guidelines and practices is maintained in the regularly updated online publication *Equal Access: Universal Design of Instruction* (Burgstahler, 2015a) on the CUDE website (DO-IT, n.d.a). Educators are encouraged to suggest improvements and to tailor the checklist to specific courses. They are also encouraged to send references for additional articles on UDHE to include in CUDE's list of published articles, books, and chapters on UDHE (DO-IT, n.d.c).

Although DO-IT's UDI checklist is used to guide educators in ensuring that all instructional products and environments (e.g., the design of a syllabus, physical layout of classroom or lab) are welcoming to, accessible to, and usable by a great majority of students (which minimizes the need for individual accommodations), planning for accommodations is addressed in CUDE's UDI framework as one of the guidelines:

> *Plan for accommodations for students whose needs are not met by the instructional design.* Know how to arrange for accommodations. Know campus protocols for getting materials in alternate formats, rescheduling classroom locations, and arranging for other accommodations for students with disabilities. Make sure that assistive technology can be made available in a computer or science lab in a timely manner. Ensure the course experience is equivalent for students with accommodations. (Burgstahler, 2015a, p. 5)

Each example included in DO-IT's UDI checklist is explicitly tied to specific UD and UDL principles. These examples encourage faculty to avoid unnecessary jargon and clearly explain concepts and terms; present new terminology on a whiteboard or projected image at the start of the class; provide outlines, summaries, study guides, and other cognitive supports in both printed and electronic formats; provide both oral and printed instructions; post a syllabus online early enough to allow students to read course materials before the first class session; minimize time constraints and distractions; announce assignments well in advance of due dates; and otherwise create an inclusive class that maximizes the potential learning of all students. A single document cannot capture all potential applications of UDI. However, DO-IT's evolving checklist provides a place to start. Table 2.2 includes a partial list of UDI practices organized around specific aspects of instruction and including references to UD and UDL principles that each practice applies.

DO-IT's UDHE collaborative work in the development of the UDI framework led to the operationalization of UD principles to many other aspects of the postsecondary environment that can affect academic achievement. UDHE initiative leaders contributed to the development of checklists that oper-

FIGURE 2.2   A student with one arm engages in a computer lab with peers.

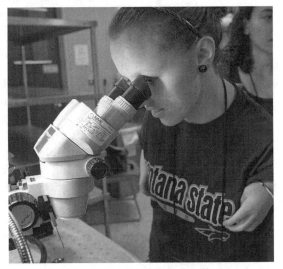

FIGURE 2.3   A student with a disability peers through the lens of a microscope in a science lab.

ationalize UD principles to academic departments, computer labs, student service units, online learning, and other aspects of a postsecondary learning environment that are discussed in other chapters of this book (DO-IT, n.d.a).

The Relationship of UD to Teaching and Learning Philosophies, Theories, and Models

Some frameworks have integrated into their principles and guidelines other best practices for instruction such as the guidelines for undergraduate instruction proposed by

Chickering and Gamson (1987). One concern about this approach is that these guidelines, like many evidence-based instructional practices, were based on research that did not routinely include or report on students with a wide variety of characteristics, including disabilities. Another is that the Chickering and Gamson list has not been informed by research since 1987. In contrast, rather than choosing specific teaching practices to integrate into the framework, DO-IT's UDI framework promotes the integration of UD along with an instructor's choice of best practices. Examples of UDI practices applied to Chickering and Gamson's guidelines are noted in Table 2.3. The application of UDI makes these practices fully inclusive of a student population with diverse characteristics.

Separation of UD practices from other best practices in a field is consistent with other applications of UD. The UD of a building does not ensure that all building codes and best practices in architectural design are incorporated into the design. Instead, UD offers a lens through which to view all design decisions to ensure that a building is welcoming, accessible, and inclusive. Similarly, UDI does not replace, but rather complements, other evidence-based teaching practices. Without good teaching practices, applying UD will simply make a poorly conceived course, and its related materials, more accessible. Thus, it can be argued by those who value inclusion that all universally designed instruction is not necessarily good instruction, but all good instruction is universally designed.

Applying UDI does not require that educators abandon their adopted teaching and learning philosophies, theories, and models, such as cooperative learning, constructive learning, and differentiated instruction (Hall, Strangman, & Meyer, 2003; Santangelo & Tomlinson, 2009); self-paced and computer-assisted instruction (Svinicki, 1999); learner-centered instruction (Barr & Tagg, 1995; Mino, 2004); and sociocultural approaches to teaching and learning (O'Loughlin, 1992). Instead, instructors who embrace UD can rethink the mix of strategies they use and ensure that the overall mix, as well as the implementation of each strategy, is welcoming to, accessible to, and usable by students with a wide variety of characteristics. Some philosophies, such as differentiated instruction, are more compatible with UD because of the flexibility they promote, but embracing UD may encourage practitioners to be more proactive and intentional about ensuring inclusiveness (Mason & Orkwis, 2005). Examples of how UD might be applied to teaching practices associated with different teaching and learning philosophies are presented in Table 2.4.

Pairing UD with evidence-based teaching practices is a powerful combination. Similarly, once a specific instructional practice is selected by an instructor—such as a small-group discussion, a "flipped" classroom, a lecture, or a group project—UD can be employed to ensure that the practice is implemented in such a way that it is appropriate for and accessible to all students. So rest assured that UD can be applied to whatever new teaching trend emerges after the publication of this book! Because of its promotion of multiple teaching methods, instructors may find that embracing a UD approach may actually lead them to incorporating more teaching approaches. For example, cooperative learning combined with UD applications may lead a faculty member to explore ways to apply a constructivist approach.

TABLE 2.2   UDI Guidelines, Examples, and Pairing with UD and UDL Principles

UDI Guideline	Example of UDI Practice
Class climate. Adopt practices that reflect high values with respect to diversity, equity, and inclusiveness.	*Avoid stereotyping.* Offer instruction and support based on student performance and requests, not simply on assumptions that members of certain groups (e.g., students with certain types of disabilities or from a specific racial/ethnic groups) will automatically do well or poorly or require certain types of assistance. [UD 1]
Interaction. Encourage regular and effective interactions between students and the instructor, employ multiple communication methods, and ensure that communication methods are accessible to all participants.	*Promote effective communication.* Employ interactive teaching techniques. Face the class, speak clearly, use a microphone if your voice does not project adequately for all students, and make eye contact with students. Consider requiring a meeting with each student. Supplement in-person contact with online communication. Use straightforward language, avoid unnecessary jargon and complexity, and use student names in electronic and in-person communications. [UD 1, 2, 4, 5; UDL 3]
Physical environments/products. Ensure that facilities, activities, materials, and equipment are physically accessible to and usable by all students, and that all potential student characteristics are addressed in safety considerations	*Arrange instructional spaces to maximize inclusion and comfort.* Arrange seating to encourage participation, giving each student a clear line of sight to the instructor and visual aids and allowing room for wheelchairs, personal assistants, sign language interpreters, captionists, and assistive technology. Minimize distractions for students with a range of attention abilities (e.g., put small groups in quiet work areas). Work within constraints to make the environment as inclusive as possible. Encourage administrators to apply UD principles in facility design and renovation. [UD 2, 6, 7]
Delivery methods. Use multiple instructional methods that are accessible to all learners.	*Provide cognitive supports.* Summarize major points, give background/contextual information, deliver effective prompting, and provide scaffolding tools (e.g., outlines, class notes, summaries, study guides, and copies of projected materials with room for notes). Deliver these materials in printed form and in a text-based electronic format. Provide opportunities for gaining further background information, vocabulary, and practice. [UD 2, 3, 4, 5; UDL 1, 3]
Information resources/technology. Ensure that course materials, notes, and other information resources are engaging, flexible, and accessible for all students.	*Select materials early.* Choose printed materials and prepare a syllabus early to allow students the option of beginning to read materials and work on assignments before the course begins. Allow adequate time to arrange for electronic and other alternate formats to be obtained. [UD 5; UDL 2, 3]
Feedback and assessment. Provide specific feedback on a regular basis using multiple, accessible methods and tools, and adjust instruction accordingly.	*Provide regular feedback and corrective opportunities.* Allow students to turn in parts of large projects for feedback before the final project is due. Give students resubmission options to correct errors in assignments and exams. Arrange for peer feedback when appropriate. [UD 5; UDL 2, 3]
Accommodation. Plan for accommodations for students whose needs are not met by the instructional design.	*Know how to arrange for accommodations.* Know campus protocols for getting materials in alternate formats, rescheduling classroom locations, and arranging for other accommodations for students with disabilities. Ensure that the course experience is equivalent for students with accommodations and those without. [UD 1, 2, 4, 6] (Burgstahler, 2007b, pp. 2–5).

TABLE 2.3   UDI Applied to Chickering and Gamson's Principles of Good Practice

Principle of Good Practice in Undergraduate Education	Example of How UD Might Be Applied to the Principle
Encourages contact between students and faculty.	Include a statement on class syllabus inviting students to meet with instructor to discuss disability-related and other learning needs.
Develops reciprocity and cooperation among students.	Assign group work for which learners must support each other and that places a high value on different skills and roles. Encourage multiple ways for students to interact with each other (e.g., in-class discussion, group work, Internet-based communication).
Encourages active learning.	Provide multiple ways for students to participate, ensuring that all students, including those with disabilities, can actively participate in class activities.
Gives prompt feedback.	Regularly assess student progress using multiple, accessible methods and tools and adjust instruction accordingly.
Emphasizes time on task.	Ensure that all students have adequate time to complete tasks, including students with disabilities.
Communicates high expectations.	Keep expectations high, including those for students with disabilities, and provide accommodations to level the playing field rather than give unfair advantage.
Respects diverse talents and ways of learning (Chickering & Gamson, 1997).	Adopt practices that reflect high values with respect to diversity, equity, *and* inclusiveness.

Similarly, specific academic supports for postsecondary students can incorporate UD to make them more inclusive. For example, instructors can apply UD to freshman learning communities (Hotchkiss, Moore, & Pitts, 2006; Minkler, 2002; Soldner, Lee, & Duby, 1999)—environments in which freshmen engage in courses and extracurricular activities as a cohort—by ensuring that all aspects of these communities are welcoming, accessible to, and inclusive of a broad audience. As one step toward universally designed learning communities, coordinators can ensure that participating instructors employ UD in their courses. They can also make sure that publications and websites for their communities are welcoming and accessible to a broad audience by including accessible formats, content that explains how to obtain accommodations and other assistance, and pictures of participants with diverse characteristics. In addition, UD can be applied to teaching and learning centers, libraries, computer and science labs, and other places that support student learning (DO-IT, n.d.a).

The Process of UD

DO-IT's UDI framework includes a process for applying universal design to all aspects of instruction. Key steps for an instructor are to clearly identify the objectives of a course, choose a variety of teaching and assessment strategies, select course materials, and then apply UD to each strategy and curriculum material. Adapting the general

TABLE 2.4   UDI Applied to Practices Associated with Teaching and Learning Philosophies

Strategy Employed by a Specific Teaching/Learning Philosophy	Example of How UD Might Be Applied to the Strategy
The *differentiated instruction* strategy of initial and ongoing assessment of student readiness and growth (Hall, Strangman, & Meyer, 2003; Tomlinson, 2001).	Use multiple and accessible assessments (e.g., oral presentations, demonstrations, portfolios, and projects) that take into account the diverse characteristics of potential students.
Computer-assisted self-paced instruction based on *behaviorist theory* (Svinicki, 1999).	Ensure that content is culturally relevant to a broad audience, that captions or transcriptions are provided for auditory output, and that text descriptions are provided for the content of graphic images.
The *constructivist* approach for the instructor to serve as a resource to help students access and utilize information resources and share information with peers (Fosnot, 1996; Hodson & Hodson, 1998; Osborne, 1996).	Make sure resources and communication options are accessible to all learners, including those for whom English is a second language; those with low-level reading skills; and those who have physical, learning, or sensory disabilities.
The *learning-centered instruction* focus on the student as learner and the instructor as the facilitator of learning (Barr & Tagg, 1995; Harrison, 2006; Kame'enui, Carnine, Dixon, Simmons, & Coyne, 2002).	Ensure that learning is defined in such a way that it does not discriminate against any students and is assessed in multiple ways.
The *sociocultural approach* to teaching and learning based on the notions that learning is situated in contexts, each student has a unique cultural perspective, and communication in the learning process is very important (O'Loughlin, 1992).	Ensure that the views of *all* students are heard, considered, and valued in the classroom.

process for applying UD to any product or environment, as presented in Chapter 1, the instructor can take the following steps, which are also summarized in Figure 2.4 (Burgstahler, 2015a):

1. *Identify the course.* Describe the course, its learning objectives, and its overall content.
2. *Define the universe.* Describe the overall population of students eligible to enroll in the course and then consider their potential diverse characteristics (e.g., with respect to gender; age; ethnicity and race; native language; learning style; and abilities to see, hear, manipulate objects, read, and communicate).
3. *Involve students.* Consider perspectives of students with diverse characteristics, as identified in Step 2, in the development of the course. If they are not available directly from students, gain student perspectives through diversity programs and the campus disability services office.
4. *Adopt instructional strategies.* Adopt overall learning and teaching philosophies and methods (e.g., differentiated instruction, constructivism, computer-assisted instruction, the "flipped" classroom) and integrate them with UD practices to ensure the full inclusion of all students.

5. *Apply instructional strategies.* Apply UD strategies in concert with good instructional practices (both identified in Step 4) to the overall choice of course teaching methods, curricula, and assessments. Then apply UD to all lectures, classroom discussions, group work, handouts, web-based content, labs, fieldwork, assessment instruments, and other academic activities and materials to maximize the learning of students with the wide variety of characteristics identified in Step 2.

6. *Plan for accommodations.* Learn campus procedures for addressing accommodation requests (e.g., arranging for sign language interpreters) from specific students for whom the course design does not automatically provide full access. Include this information in the syllabus.

7. *Evaluate.* Monitor the effectiveness of instruction through observation and feedback from students with the diverse set of characteristics identified in Step 2, assess learning, and modify the course as appropriate.

From the perspective of an instructor, the *universe* referred to in the UDI framework includes anyone who is qualified to enroll in a specific course. Any UDI practice employed is designed to make all the curricula, teaching methods, technology, and assessments used in the course welcoming to, accessible to, and usable by all potential students. For example, if an instructor decides to adopt a "flipped" classroom approach—by having students view online video presentations before class and then engage in interactive activities during class sessions—and use this UDI process, she will be reminded to make sure that the videos are captioned and the classroom activities are designed to engage all students, including those with disabilities and those whose primary language is not the one in which the course is taught.

Detailed work takes place at each basic step of the process. For example, if a professor decides that lecture followed by large-group discussion is the best way to deliver a specific lesson (Step 4), he can incorporate UD into this instructional approach by choosing to:

- Welcome all students by name, interacting with them as they enter the classroom.
- Arrange seating to encourage participation, give each student a clear line of sight to the instructor and visual aids, and allow room for wheelchairs, personal assistants, and assistive technology.
- Make expectations clear.
- Give students scaffolding tools (e.g., provide outlines, class notes, summaries, graphic organizers, copies of projected materials with room for taking notes) and provide alternative formats (e.g., large print, braille) upon request.
- Face the class; speak clearly; use a microphone, if appropriate; and make eye contact with all students.
- Use large, bold fonts on uncluttered overhead presentation slides and speak aloud all content presented with visual aids.
- Present content in a logical, straightforward manner and in an order that reflects levels of importance. Avoid unnecessary jargon and complexity; define new terms and acronyms. Summarize major points. Give background or contextual information.

FIGURE 2.4   A Process for the Application of UDI

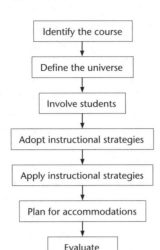

- Provide multiple examples of specific concepts to make them relevant to individuals with diverse characteristics with respect to age, ability, gender, ethnicity, race, socioeconomic status, interests, and so on.
- In discussions, encourage the sharing of multiple perspectives. Demonstrate and demand mutual respect. Seek out a student's point of view and respond patiently.
- Avoid segregating or stigmatizing any student by drawing undue attention to a difference (e.g., a disability).
- Repeat questions asked by students to ensure that all students have heard them.
- Put class notes and assignments on a website in a text-based format.
- Provide multiple types of assessment.

Comparison of Frameworks

Although many researchers and practitioners agree that applying UD to instructional practices can make meaningful learning available to a diverse student body, multiple frameworks for its implementation in higher education have emerged. Characteristics of the five frameworks discussed in this chapter are summarized below.

- *Universally designed teaching (UDT).* Applying CUD's definition of UD and seven principles of UD, Bowe explained how UD can be applied to a wide variety of products and environments at all levels of education and created eight guidelines and corresponding examples of practices specific to the design of teaching materials and environments.
- *Universal Design for Instruction (UDforI).* McGuire, Scott, and Shaw at the University of Connecticut added two UD principles to CUD's list of seven to make the total set more relevant to postsecondary instruction, incorporating teaching strategies that benefit students with learning disabilities specifically and undergraduate stu-

dents in general. They created definitions for each of the nine UD*forI* principles and examples for their application to postsecondary instruction.

- *Universal instructional design (UID).* The eight guidelines developed by Higbee and colleagues at the University of Minnesota were based on CUD's work in UD as well as best practices for teaching undergraduate students. From this framework they created examples for applications to postsecondary instruction.
- *Universal design for learning (UDL).* Rose and his colleagues at CAST created a definition of UDL, three principles, nine guidelines, and thirty-two checkpoints originally focused on the development and delivery of flexible technology-based curriculum at the K–12 level, and built on these efforts to apply UDL to promote postsecondary learning.
- *Universal design of instruction (UDI).* Burgstahler and collaborators in DO-IT's UDHE initiative at the University of Washington embraced the CUD definition of UD along with both of the UD and UDL sets of principles and guidelines to operationalize UD into a checklist of UDI practices organized under specific aspects of instruction. The UDI framework also includes a process for the application of UDI; a model for how UDI can be applied to established teaching philosophies, theories, and methods; and complementary guidelines for the application of UD to online learning programs, academic departments, computer and science labs, tutoring centers, and other postsecondary offerings that impact student learning.

Perhaps this discussion of five frameworks reminds you of the famous quote by computer scientist Andrew S. Tanenbaum (1988, p. 254): "The nice thing about standards is that you have so many to choose from." Although there are multiple frameworks for the application of UD to teaching and learning from which to choose, they are very similar in terms of the teaching practices they promote. During the process of applying UD, instructors can choose practices suggested within these frameworks as well as develop their own practices by applying the definition of UD and ensuring that the new strategy

- is applied proactively,
- makes instruction welcoming to all potential students,
- is accessible to and usable by students with a broad range of characteristics, and
- is offered to all students in an integrated setting.

Some of the most powerful UD strategies are in response to specific challenges faced by faculty in their courses. Robbin Zeff shared the following examples of straightforward, practical outcomes from faculty training in the Ivy Access Initiative, which was funded by the U.S. Department of Education:

> [A] computer science professor who had received criticism from his students for not providing enough contextual background for his lectures started opening his lectures with an overview of key concepts and their importance. A psychology professor added flexibility in the execution of his final exam by offering students the option of a take-home or in-class exam. And a math/statistics faculty member started distributing copies of overheads to the entire class so that students could use them for

reference and review. He also began to deliver his lectures with a greater focus on his audience. The changes he made included making eye contact with students, pausing when appropriate, and being more specific in his descriptions. (Zeff, 2007, p. 37)

But which teaching qualities provide the greatest benefit to students with disabilities? In an informal, online discussion conducted by the author of this chapter, high school and college students with a wide variety of disabilities were asked, "What are the qualities of a good teacher?" Their responses can be summarized as follows. A good teacher

- is well prepared,
- is a good role model,
- makes expectations clear,
- is approachable,
- gets to know students,
- respects students and maintains privacy,
- does not make assumptions about a student's capabilities,
- encourages students,
- is patient,
- challenges students,
- helps students apply knowledge,
- is open to new ideas,
- is enthusiastic,
- facilitates the exchange of ideas between students and between teacher and students, and
- adjusts to the unique needs of students.

No one in the discussion specifically mentioned disability, but many of the qualities suggested reflect the inclusive nature of UD. Simply stated, good teaching for students with disabilities is good teaching for all students. This should be welcome news to professors afraid that they need to adopt entirely new teaching approaches in order to fully engage students with diverse characteristics in their courses.

Specific UD Considerations for Online Learning

Information technology is well suited to delivering the multiple instructional options characteristic of UD. In 1995 the author of this chapter co-taught the first online course offered through the University of Washington. The course presented an overview of assistive technology for people with disabilities. She and her co-instructor, Professor Norm Coombs at the Rochester Institute of Technology, who happens to be blind, set out to make the content and interactions fully accessible to anyone with a disability who might enroll in the course. A series of DO-IT videos, which were captioned and audio described and presented in VHS format, were mailed to the students. Electronic mail and a text-based listserv distribution list were used for communication. There was no World Wide Web, but a gopher server developed at the University of Minnesota was used to organize text-based course materials. Other online resources were accessed through Telnet and file transfer protocols. When the instructors were asked if students with disabilities were enrolled in course offerings, they were proud to say they did not know. There was no need to disclose a disability when all of the materials and communications were in accessible formats. Dr. Coombs disclosed his blindness, but only because of its relevance to the course content.

Fast forward to today. Over the past few decades there have been dramatic increases in the variety of technologies used in online learning, in the number of online courses offered, and in the number of students taking these courses, including students who have disabilities (Allen & Seaman, 2009; Kim-Rupnow, Dowrick, & Burke, 2001; Kinash, Crichton, & Kim-Rupnow, 2004; Phillips, Terras, Swinney, & Schneweis, 2013). Although these trends make accessibility issues more complex as well as more important to address, in applying UD to online learning, practitioners must still address both pedagogical and technical issues. Access barriers can occur with the technology used, such as with functions of the campus learning management system (LMS), as well as the methods and products selected and developed by instructors, such as videos and PDF files. Ultimately, a universally designed course should support a student's preferred access methods (e.g., speech input, alternative keyboard, the keyboard alone) and output preferences (text, audio, video, graphical), and be customizable.

It is encouraging to note that the popular Quality Matters Rubric of eight benchmarks for high quality online courses includes accessibility and usability as the eighth benchmark that should be applied to all of the other benchmarks—course overview and introduction, learning objectives (competencies), assessment and measurement, instructional materials, course activities and learning interaction and engagement, course technology, and learner support (Quality Matters, n.d.). The national standards for quality online courses published by the International Association for K–12 Online Learning (2011) also include accessible design recommendations for both technology and learning activities.

However, many online learning (alternatively called distance learning, e-learning, cyber learning, distance education, or online education) courses unintentionally erect barriers to individuals with disabilities (Burgstahler, 2002, 2006, 2007a; Coombs, 2010; Fichten et al., 2009; Keeler & Horney, 2007; Kim-Rupnow, Dowrick, & Burke, 2001; National Council on Disability, 2004; Schmetzke, 2001). Students with disabilities report inaccessible features such as disorganized web content, uncaptioned videos, and PDF files and other course materials that cannot be read by screen readers (Gladhart, 2010). In one study, almost half of the respondents with disabilities who engaged in online courses reported that they "perceived their disability to have a negative impact on their ability to succeed in online courses" and close to 70% of these students had not disclosed their disabilities to their online instructors (Roberts, Crittenden, & Crittenden, 2011). Another study found that female students with learning disabilities taking online courses perceived the learning environments to be less supportive and less satisfactory than females without learning disabilities; female students reported that the academic services were not sufficiently considerate of their needs and they were less content with the courses overall (Heiman, 2008).

To create an accessible environment, practitioners can apply UD to the o design of the online course (e.g., choosing which CMS features to employ) as as specific course products (e.g., providing text alternatives to describe the content in graphic images) and communication methods (e.g., ensuring that discussions are accessible to students with all types of disabilities). UD can also be built into an assignment. For example, if an instructor chooses working in small groups as a teaching strategy for a specific assignment, instead of individual groups being told they need to use a specific communication tool (e.g., phone conferencing, bulletin board, online chat, e-mail), groups could be required to select a communication method through which everyone can actively participate in group "meetings." For example, in an online course taught by the author of this chapter, small groups were assigned to complete a project and answer specific questions to report their work. The first thing they were told to do was decide which mode of communication they would employ so that all students could attend group "meetings" and fully engage in the collaboration. One group reported back that they used e-mail, at least in part, because one of the participants was deaf and could not easily engage using the synchronous communication modes offered. Actually, the majority of groups used asynchronous communication options, usually because this mode of communication, when compared to phone conferences and real-time chat sessions, worked best when group members lived in different time zones and/or had different daily schedules. Asynchronous communication also works well for individuals with slow input speeds. Even though one member disclosed her deafness, members of groups were not required to disclose disabilities or any other characteristics that contributed to their communication preference; they just needed to reach consensus on the communication tool they would use. In this course, if not for her voluntary disclosure, not even the instructor would have known she was deaf because the class was universally designed. For example, captions were provided on all video presentations.

Online instructors and institutions tend to employ an accommodations-only model rather than one that is proactive in dealing with accessibility and usability (Barnard-Brak & Sulak, 2010; Kim-Rupnow, Dowrick, & Burke, 2001; Kinash, Crichton, & Rupnow, 2004). However, many strategies for making online learning accessible to students with disabilities are reported in the literature (e.g., Burgstahler, 2012; Coombs, 2010; Fichten et al., 2009; Keeler & Horney, 2007; Pearson & Koppi, 2006; Rangin, 2011; Savidis & Stephanidis, 2005; Seale, 2014). For example, DO-IT (n.d.a, p. 1) has suggested these first steps for designing an accessible online course:

- Include a statement on the syllabus about how to request a disability-related accommodation and how to report a design feature of the course that is not accessible.
- Make learning objectives, expectations, assignments and due dates, grading rubrics, assessment questions, and other course elements clear.
- Use consistent and predictable screen layouts and single columns when possible.
- Structure lesson pages and documents using the heading feature of the product you are using (e.g., Word, PDF).

- Make sure the text of links describes the resource linked to rather than using wording like "click here."
- Make sure that color is not the only way to convey important information, and make background screens plain and with high contrast to text.
- Share definitions of terms that might be unknown to some students.
- Provide alternative text to describe important content presented in images.
- Caption videos or, when it's not possible to do so, provide transcriptions.
- Design HTML, Word, PowerPoint, and PDF documents in accessible formats.

There are also published guidelines for how UD can be applied to distance learning programs as a whole. Efforts by DO-IT's UDHE initiative collaborators on sixteen campuses (DO-IT, 2012) led to the list of characteristics of a universally designed online learning program documented in Table 2.5. It includes subcategories representing key stakeholder groups—students and potential students, distance learning designers, distance learning instructors, and program evaluators. Challenges reported in work related to the development of these guidelines include getting multiple stakeholders to work together, gaining faculty and staff buy-in, and overcoming technical problems such as presenting videos, coding math characters, and dealing with inaccessible PDF files and other online materials. However, it was concluded that these challenges were worth overcoming because "employing universal design principles as Internet-based distance learning courses are created can bring us closer to making learning accessible to anyone, anywhere, at any time" (Burgstahler, Corrigan, & McCarter, 2005).

Most publications about online learning do not address access issues for people with disabilities or UD. Even a study that used a database of nearly five hundred thousand courses taken by over forty thousand technical and community college students, which revealed the performance gap between online and face-to-face courses and how the size of that gap differs across student subgroups defined by gender, age, race, and grade point average, missed the opportunity to explore similar research questions with respect to students with disabilities (Xu & Jaggars, 2014). Not surprisingly, many online courses are not accessible to all students with disabilities. In one study, 80% of online learning faculty surveyed had not considered the needs of students with disabilities in their courses and less than 12% had "partially" considered the needs of students with disabilities in developing their courses (Bissonnette, 2006). In another study, a low percentage of faculty reported being aware of strategies to ensure the accessibility of their online courses (Gladhart, 2010). Often, online faculty do not feel confident that they have the knowledge, technology, and support to accommodate students with disabilities in their courses (Roberts, Park, Brown, & Cook, 2011). The results of three studies (Burgstahler, 2007a) suggest the need for accessibility training for distance learning personnel that includes content related to access challenges for people with disabilities, legislative requirements, UD guidelines, design techniques, and resources. Training for instructors, technology leaders and support staff, and other stakeholder groups should be tailored to these groups and include on-site and online options. Besides specialized training, it is important to integrate UD into more general professional development offerings such as how to use the campus LMS.

TABLE 2.5   Characteristics of Distance Learning Programs That Are Accessible to All Students

For Students and Potential Students

1. The distance learning home page is accessible to individuals with disabilities (e.g., it adheres to Section 508, World Wide Web Consortium, or institutional accessible-design guidelines/standards).

2. A statement about the distance learning program's commitment to accessible design for all potential students, including those with disabilities, is included prominently in appropriate publications and websites, along with contact information for reporting inaccessible design features.

3. A statement about how distance learning students with disabilities can request accommodations is included in appropriate publications and web pages.

4. A statement about how people can obtain alternate formats of printed materials is included in publications.

5. The online and other course materials of distance learning courses are accessible to individuals with disabilities.

For Distance Learning Designers

6. Publications and web pages for distance learning course designers include:
   a. a statement of the program's commitment to accessibility;
   b. guidelines/standards regarding accessibility;
   c. resources.

7. Accessibility issues are covered in regular course designer training.

For Distance Learning Instructors

8. Publications and web pages for distance learning instructors include:
   a. a statement of the distance learning program's commitment to accessibility;
   b. guidelines/standards regarding accessibility;
   c. resources.

9. Accessibility issues are covered in training sessions for instructors.

For Program Evaluators

10. A system is in place to monitor the accessibility of courses and, based on this evaluation, the program takes actions to improve the accessibility of specific courses and to update information and training given to potential students, actual students, course designers, and instructors (Burgstahler, 2006, p. 86).

RESEARCH AND PRACTICE

Research and practice with respect to social justice, civil rights, and multicultural education explore diversity issues including gender, race, ethnicity, socioeconomic status, and age (e.g., Hackman & Rauscher, 2004; Knowles, 1980; Pliner & Johnson, 2004). Research and practice also shed light on the great variety of learning styles, preferences, and strengths present in a typical course (Claxton & Ralston, 1978; Dunn & Griggs, 2000; Kolb, 1981; Wooldridge, 1995) and the challenges that some instructional approaches present to individuals with these characteristics. A *learning style* has been described as a combined reaction to environmental, emotional, and physiological issues, and sociological factors (Dunn & Griggs, 2000). Learning preferences include those that are visual, tactile, auditory, and kinesthetic (Wooldridge, 1995). It has been found that a person's *dominant learning style* as a converger, diverger, assimilator, or accommodator affects how she experiences learning (Claxton & Ralston, 1978; Svinicki & Dixon, 1987). The theory of multiple intelligences—spatial, linguistic, logical-mathematical, bodily-kinesthetic, interpersonal, intrapersonal, musical, and naturalistic (Gardner, 1983)—describes the variety of ways that people perceive the world and sheds light on aspects of diversity found in educational settings. Although the linguistic and logical-mathematical intelligences are most frequently addressed in traditional curricula, educators who apply UD consider a more balanced offering of materials and approaches that address all types of learning differences. They use multiple modes of delivery; provide multiple ways for students to interact with each other, the instructor, and the course content; and offer multiple ways for students to demonstrate their learning. Ideally, learners can choose among learning alternatives those that best meet their needs.

The largest collection of published research studies that provide some support for the identification of promising UD instructional practices was compiled in a multiple-stage process by researchers at CAST (CAST, 2012). They distilled descriptions of three learning networks and developed three corresponding UDL principles—multiple means of representation, action and expression, and engagement—from studies in neuroscience, neuropsychology, and cognitive neuroscience. Through an iterative meta-analysis of published research, UDL researchers organized evidence-based teaching practices around the three principles. Nearly one thousand articles were selected as an evidence base for three UDL guidelines tied to each principle. Unfortunately, the collection of studies as a whole provides little insight into the efficacy of UDHE because the vast majority of the studies are at the precollege level, focus on the development of reading and writing skills, evaluate the implementation of one specific strategy in a specific content area at a specific academic level, and do not test the application of combinations of UDL strategies with students who have a wide variety of disabilities and other characteristics. Although this research base provides evidence of effective practices in specific settings, some feel that a "claim that UDL has been scientifically validated through research cannot be substantiated at this time" and without "an adequate base of primary research, an analysis of research evidence that establishes UDL as a scientifically validated intervention is not possible (Edyburn, 2010, p. 34).

A very small but growing body of research supports the efficacy of UD as a collection of instructional strategies that bolster the success of individuals in a diverse, postsecondary student population (DO-IT, n.d.c). Reports of research that compare the student outcomes of the same course taught with and without the application of UD are beginning to appear in the literature. For example, Beckman (2009) offered two versions of a graduate course in information management, teaching one session with lecturing as the primary instructional method (i.e., a control group) and the other "treatment" section with lectures and small-group discussions. Students in the treatment group reported that "the instructor was open to a variety of points of view" more often than did students in the control group; they also performed better on essay exam questions than did students in the control group. Both groups performed at the same level on multiple-choice and fill-in-the-blank exam questions. In another example that was part of the evaluation of one of DO-IT's projects in its UDHE initiative, collaborators delivered faculty training using content in the UDI checklist. Outcomes and impact were assessed using multiple measures. Post-training surveys of faculty suggest increased knowledge and skills after their participation in professional development, and an intention to incorporate specific UD strategies into their teaching practices. A quasi-experimental research study produced evidence of increased grade point averages of students with disabilities in courses taught by trained faculty members when compared to students with disabilities in courses they taught before training; whereas students with disabilities in a comparison group of untrained faculty did not show an increase in grade point averages over the same time period (Burgstahler & Moore, submitted for publication; DO-IT, 2009). A weakness of most studies, like these two examples, is that they are conducted in courses that do not include enough students with a wide range of disabilities and other characteristics to analyze an intervention's success with specific subgroups. In other studies faculty reported positive outcomes from UD training to improve their teaching (e.g., Langley-Turnbaugh, Blair, & Whitney, 2013).

Several published articles have reported the positive reactions of students to a wide range of UD strategies (e.g., Durre, Richardson, Smith, Shulman, & Steele, 2008) and to the application of multiple modes of instruction in specific classes (e.g., Kortering, McClannon, & Braziel, 2005). In a survey of another study, students rated highly the UD features in course websites (Carter, Leslie, & Kwan, 2011). In the UK, Jane Seale, a leader in promoting accessible e-learning in higher education, points out the value of participatory design and other methodologies that "liberate" disabled students' voices and offer opportunities for critical self-reflection (Seale, 2014). Participatory design incorporates early and continual engagement of users as collaborative partners with researchers, tests in real-life contexts, and development and evaluation within iterative cycles until an acceptable solution is reached (e.g., Bjerknes & Bratteteig, 1995). For example, Seale employed a participatory design approach to explore the complex interactions between students and technologies in e-learning (Seale, 2014).

The next chapter of this book provides a review of nineteen published articles in peer-reviewed journals that report the outcomes of UD interventions at the postsecondary level. Results of the literature review reveal an increase in the rate of articles published in this area since 2000, with only three studies using experimental or quasi-experimental designs. Overall, the studies support UD practices for students and training for faculty and reflect the value of UD for all students, not just those with disabilities.

Although some researchers report faculty members' lack of interest in applying UD to their teaching (e.g., Lomardi, Murray, & Gerdes, 2011), there is evidence that UD is being embraced by some campuses and presented to faculty nationwide as a means to make their courses more accessible (e.g., Burgstahler, 2007b; Burgstahler & Doe, 2006; Getzel, Briel, & McManus, 2003; Gordon, Gravel, & Schifter, 2009; Gradel & Edson, 2009–2010; Harrison, 2006; Kame'enui et al., 2002; Ouellett, 2004; Shaw & Scott, 2003; Smith & Buchannan, 2012). Much of this training has included UD as a strategy to help faculty serve students with disabilities more effectively in their courses (Getzel, Briel, & McManus, 2003; Office of Postsecondary Education, n.d.). Some researchers have tested the efficacy of such training. For example, one study developed pre- and post-surveys for students to complete in courses where instructors are trained in UD practices; positive results of the training were suggested when surveys regarding trained instructors were compared with surveys regarding those who did not receive training (Schelly, Davies, & Spooner, 2011).

Anecdotal evidence and reported practices also support the application of UD to instruction that occurs outside of a traditional academic course, including informal science learning (Crawford & Burgstahler, 2013; Reich, Price, Rubin, & Steiner, 2010) and conference presentations (e.g., Burgstahler, 2015b). For example, the author of this chapter regularly employs UD when she delivers presentations:

> All presentation videos are captioned, website resources are universally designed, handouts are provided in alternate formats, presentation visuals use large bold fonts and are uncluttered, a microphone is used by the presenter, and, before the audience arrives, chairs are moved so that any wheelchair users who might attend have multiple options for positioning themselves in the room. Efforts are also made to speak slowly and clearly, describe orally all content that is presented visually, avoid unnecessary jargon, define terms that might be unfamiliar to some attendees, make eye contact with and engage many members of the audience, and repeat questions asked by attendees before answering them. These proactive steps on the presenter's part minimize the need for special accommodations; typically, the only disability-related accommodation requested in these presentations is a sign language interpreter or real-time captioner by an individual who is deaf; such arrangements would be requested ahead of time by the participant from the event sponsor. Particularly positive feedback given by attendees includes appreciation for the flexibility of the seating arrangement by individuals who use wheelchairs, for video captions by attendees who are deaf and by those whose first language is not English, for orally describing visual content by individuals who are blind, and for providing materials in multiple formats by many. (Burgstahler, 2011, p. 19:7)

Clearly, further research is needed to test the efficacy of UD instructional practices when applied to postsecondary instruction with students who have a wide range of characteristics. Multiple methods should be considered. Although more traditional experimental methodologies are valuable for studying teaching practices, techniques from fields of design research—such as usability testing, user- or learner-centered design, contextual design, action research, and cooperative inquiry (Nesset & Large, 2004)—can bring a product-design mind-set to the research base for UDHE and allow for the engagement of students in the design process. For example, a design-based research approach—which is commonly used in computer products that go through multiple versions until all the bugs are worked out—could be applied to testing UD qualities of an online course through iterative cycles of design. Research steps would include implementation of the current design, evaluation with students with a variety of characteristics, informed redesign of the course, implementation of new

design, and so on (Cobb, Confrey, diSessa, Lehrer, & Schauble, 2003; C(
& Bielaczyc, 2004). Such an approach carries experimentation into re.
refines the design so that it continues to work better in practice, and has the po...
to explore the experiences of students with a wide variety of characteristics, including
disabilities. After all, it is not enough to see how well the class performs as a whole
when a UD practice is employed; we need to know how effective it is for individuals
with diverse characteristics. Without a strong research base, practitioners will continue to identify "promising" practices rather than "research-based" practices with
respect to the application of UD in instructional settings.

Social and related models of disability as well as UD have been addressed in recent
legislation and by organizations worldwide. For example, the IMS Global Learning
Consortium (2004), whose goal is to advance open architecture technology that can
improve educational participation and attainment worldwide, proposed the following definition of disability and accessibility as applied in an educational setting:

> In this document, the term disability has been re-defined as a mismatch between the
> needs of the learner and the education offered. It is therefore not a personal trait but
> an artifact of the relationship between the learner and the learning environment or
> education delivery. Accessibility, given this re-definition, is the ability of the learn-
> ing environment to adjust to the needs of all learners. Accessibility is determined
> by the flexibility of the education environment (with respect to presentation, con-
> trol methods, access modality, and learner supports) and the availability of adequate
> alternative-but-equivalent content and activities. (IMS Global Learning Consortium,
> 2004, Section 2)

This recommendation embodies the UD approach as it promotes the proactive
design of flexible products to meet the needs of all learners.

The Higher Education Opportunity Act (HEOA) of 2008 in the U.S. promotes the
application of UD and other strategies to make postsecondary education more accessible to students with disabilities (Gordon, Gravel, & Schifter, 2009). HEOA established the statutory definition for UDL to be a guiding educational practice that

- provides flexibility in the ways information is presented, in the ways students
  respond or demonstrate knowledge and skills, and in the ways students are
  engaged; and
- reduces barriers in instruction; provides appropriate accommodations, supports,
  and challenges; and maintains high achievement expectations for all students,
  including students with disabilities and students who are limited English profi-
  cient. (The Higher Education Opportunity Act, 2008)

CONCLUSION

The application of UD to instruction holds promise for addressing the needs of a student body that is increasingly diverse with respect to race, ethnicity, native language,
culture, age, learning style, background knowledge, ability, gender, veteran status,

and other characteristics. Several different frameworks and related terminology have emerged for applying UD to teaching and learning; together they provide options for principles, guidelines, teaching strategies, and application processes. All frameworks reflect a goal of inclusive instruction and support practices that encourage instructors to consider the needs of students with a broad range of characteristics as they develop flexible strategies that make instruction inclusive and engaging for all students. Since each course is unique, a particular implementation of UD must rely on the expertise of the instructor to select and apply appropriate UD practices at both macro and micro levels.

The authors of the remaining chapters in Part 2 of this book further explore the application of UD to teaching and learning. In Chapter 3, Kelly Roberts, Maya Satlykgylyjova, and Hye-Jin Park provide a summary of published empirically based studies. In Chapter 4, Jenna Gravel, Laura Edwards, Christopher Buttimer, and David Rose reflect on how they have universally designed a course at Harvard University. Similarly, in Chapter 5, Jeanne Higbee shares how she has applied UD to a college course at the University of Minnesota. In Chapter 6, past and present students with disabilities—Imke Durre, Michael Richardson, Carson Smith, Jessie Amelia Shulman, and Sarah Steele—share their perspectives on UDI. Al Souma and Deb Casey discuss the benefits of UD for students with psychological disabilities in Chapter 7. In Chapter 8, Craig Spooner, Patricia Davies, and Catherine Schelly discuss how they measured the effectiveness of a UD intervention. In Chapter 9, Karen Myers shares her experience with incorporating UD in administration courses. Finally, in Chapter 10, Leanne Ketterlin-Geller, Christopher Johnston, and Martha Thurlow explain how UD principles can be applied to assessments in higher education, building guidelines from applications of UD to large-scale testing instruments in precollege education.

REFERENCES

Allen, I. E., & Seaman, J. (2009). *Learning on demand: Online education in the United States.* Retrieved from http://www.sloanconsortium.org/publications/survey/pdf/learningondemand.pdf

Bar, L., Galluzzo, J., & Sinfit, S. D. (1999). *The accessible school: Universal design for educational settings.* Berkeley, CA: MIG Communications.

Barnard-Brak, L., & Sulak, T. (2010). Online versus face-to-face accommodations among college students with disabilities. *The American Journal of Distance Education, 24,* 81–91.

Barr, R. B., & Tagg, J. (1995). From teaching to learning—a new paradigm for undergraduate education. *Change, 27*(6), 12–25.

Beckman, P. (2009). Universal design for learning: A field experiment comparing specific classroom actions. In *Proceedings of the Americas Conference on Information Systems (ACIS '09).* Retrieved from http://aisel.aisnet.org/amcis2009/10

Bissonnette, L. (2006). *Meeting the evolving education needs of faculty in providing access for university students with disabilities.* Retrieved from http://spectrum.library.concordia.ca/8741/

Bjerknes, G., & Bratteteig, T. (1995). User participation and democracy: A discussion of Scandinavian research on system development. *Scandinavian Journal of Information Systems, 7*(1), 73–97.

Bowe, F. G. (1978). *Handicapping America: Barriers to disabled people.* New York: Harper & Row.

Bowe, F. G. (2000). *Universal design in education: Teaching nontraditional students.* Westport, CT: Bergin and Garvey.

Burgstahler, S. (2002). Distance learning: Universal design, universal access. *AACE Journal, 10*(1), 32–61. Retrieved from http://www.editlib.org/index.cfm?fuseaction=Reader.ViewAbstract&paper_id=17776

Burgstahler, S. (2006). The development of accessibility indicators for distance learning programs. *Association for Learning Technology Journal, 14*(1), 79–102.

Burgstahler, S. (2007a). Accessibility training for distance learning personnel. *Access Technologists Higher Education Network (ATHEN) E-Journal, 2*. Retrieved from http://athenpro.org/node/56

Burgstahler, S. (2007b). Lessons learned in The Faculty Room. *Journal on Excellence in College Teaching, 18*(3).

Burgstahler, S. (2008). Universal design of instruction: From principles to practice. In S. Burgstahler, & R. Cory. (Eds.), *Universal Design in Higher Education; From Principles to Practice* (pp. 23–43). Cambridge, MA: Harvard Education Press.

Burgstahler, S. (2011). Universal design: Implications for computing education. *ACM Transactions on Computing Education, 11*(3), 19-1–19-17.

Burgstahler, S. (2012). *Real connections: Making distance learning accessible to everyone*. Seattle: University of Washington. Retrieved from http://www.washington.edu/doit/real-connections-making-distance-learning-accessible-everyone

Burgstahler, S. (2015a). *Equal access: Universal design of instruction*. Seattle: University of Washington. Retrieved from http://www.washington.edu/doit/equal-access-universal-design-instruction

Burgstahler, S. (2015b). *Equal access: Universal design of your presentation*. Seattle: University of Washington. Retrieved from http://www.washington.edu/doit/equal-access-universal-design-your-presentation

Burgstahler, S. (2015c). *Universal design of instruction (UDI): Definitions, principles, guidelines, and examples*. Seattle: University of Washington. Retrieved from http://www.washington.edu/doit/universal-design-instruction-udi-definition-principles-guidelines-and-examples

Burgstahler, S., Corrigan, B., & McCarter, J. (2005). Steps toward making distance learning accessible to students and instructors with disabilities. *Journal of Information Technology and Disabilities, 11*(1). Retrieved from http://www.rit.edu/~easi/itd/itdv11n1/brgstler.htm

Burgstahler, S., & Doe, T. (2006). Improving postsecondary outcomes for students with disabilities: Designing professional development for faculty. *Journal of Postsecondary Education and Disability, 18*(2), 135–147.

Burgstahler, S., & Gleicher, R. (in press). Applying universal design to address the needs of postsecondary students on the Autism Spectrum. *Journal of Postsecondary Education and Disability*.

Burgstahler, S., & Moore, E. (submitted for publication). Impact of faculty training in UDI on the grades of their students with disabilities.

Campbell, D. (2004). Assistive technology and universal instructional design: A postsecondary perspective. *Equity and Excellence in Education, 37*(2), 167–173.

Carter, I., Leslie, D., & Kwan, D. (2011). Applying universal instructional design to course websites by using course evaluations. *Collected Essays on Learning and Teaching, 5*, 119–125.

Center for Applied Special Technology (CAST). (n.d.a). UDL on campus. Wakefield, MA: Author. Retrieved from http://udloncampus.cast.org/home#.VD2OsSiri8U

CAST. (n.d.b). What is universal design for learning? Retrieved from http://www.cast.org/research/udl/

CAST. (2011). UDL guidelines - Version 2.0: Checkpoint 2.5: Illustrate through multiple media. Retrieved from http://www.udlcenter.org/research/researchevidence/checkpoint2_5

CAST. (2012). UDL guidelines - Version 2.0: Research evidence. Retrieved from http://www.udlcenter.org/research/researchevidence/

The Center for Universal Design (CUD). (1997). The principles of universal design, version 2.0. Raleigh: North Caroline State University. Retrieved from http://www.ncsu.edu/ncsu/design/cud/about_ud/udprinciplestext.htm

CUD. (2008). About UD. Raleigh: North Carolina State University. Retrieved from http://www.ncsu.edu/ncsu/design/cud/about_ud/about_ud.htm

Chickering, A. W., & Gamson, Z. F. (1987). *Seven principles for good practice in undergraduate education.* Washington, DC: American Association for Higher Education. (ERIC Document Reproduction Service No. ED282491).

Claxton, C. S., & Ralston, Y. (1978). *Learning styles: Their impact on teaching and administration.* Washington, DC: American Association for Higher Education.

Cobb, P., Confrey, J., diSessa, A., Lehrer, R., & Schauble, L. (2003). Design experiments in educational research. *Educational Researcher, 32*(1), 9–13.

Collins, A., Joseph, D., & Bielaczyc, K. (2004). Design research: Theoretical and methodological issues. *Journal of the Learning Sciences, 13*(1), 15–42.

Coombs, N. (2010). *Making online teaching accessible: Inclusive course design for students with disabilities.* San Francisco: Jossey-Bass.

Crawford, C., & Burgstahler, S. (2013). Promoting the design of accessible informal science learning. In S. Burgstahler (Ed.), *Universal design in higher education: Promising practices.* Seattle: DO-IT, University of Washington. Retrieved from http://www.washington.edu/doit/promoting-design-accessible-informal-science-learning

DO-IT (Disabilities, Opportunities, Internetworking, and Technology). (n.d.a). *The Center for Universal Design in Education.* Seattle: University of Washington. Retrieved from http://www.washington.edu/doit/programs/center-universal-design-education/overview

DO-IT. (n.d.b). *How can I get started in making my distance learning course accessible to all students?* Seattle: University of Washington. Retrieved from http://www.washington.edu/doit/how-can-i-get-started-making-my-distance-learning-course-accessible-all-students?112

DO-IT. (n.d.c). *Published articles and books about universal design in higher education (UDHE).* Seattle: University of Washington. Retrieved from http://www.washington.edu/doit/programs/center-universal-design-education/resources/published-books-and-articles-about-universal

DO-IT. (2009). *Final report of the AccessCollege project to the Office of Postsecondary Education, U.S. Department of Education.* University of Washington, Seattle.

DO-IT. (2012). *AccessCollege: Systemic change for postsecondary institutions.* Seattle: University of Washington. Retrieved from http://www.washington.edu/doit/accesscollege-systemic-change-postsecondary-institutions

Dunn, R., & Griggs, S. A. (2000). *Practical approaches to using learning styles in higher education.* Westport, CT: Greenwood.

Durre, I., Richardson, M., Smith, C., Shulman, J. A., & Steele, S. (2008). Universal design of instruction: Reflections of students. In S. Burgstahler & R. Cory (Eds.), *Universal Design in Higher Education: From Principles to Practice* (pp. 83–96). Cambridge, MA: Harvard Education Press.

Edyburn, D. L. (2010). Would you recognize universal design for learning if you saw it? Ten propositions for new directions for the second decade of UDL. *Learning Disability Quarterly, 33*(1), 33–41

Fichten, C. S., Ferraro, V., Asuncion, J. V., Chwojka, C., Barile, M., Nguyen, M. N., Klomp, R., & Wolforth, J. (2009). Disabilities and e-learning problems and solutions: An exploratory study. *Educational Technology and Society, 12*(4), 241–256.

Fosnot, C. T. (1996). *Constructivism: Theory, perspectives, and practice.* New York: Teachers College Press.

Gardner, H. (1983). *Frames of mind: The theory of multiple intelligences.* New York: Basic Books.

Getzel, E. E., Briel, L. W., & McManus, S. (2003). Strategies for implementing professional development activities on college campuses: Findings from the OPE-funded project sites (1999–2002). *Journal of Postsecondary Education and Disability, 17*(1), 59–78.

Gladhart, M. A. (2010). Determining faculty needs for delivering accessible electronically delivered instruction in higher education. *Journal of Postsecondary Education and Disability, 22*(3), 185–196.

Gordon, D. T., Gravel, J. W., & Schifter, L. A. (Eds.). (2009). *A policy reader in Universal Design for Learning.* Cambridge, MA: Harvard Education Press.

Gradel, K., & Edson, A. (2009–2010). Putting universal design for learning on the higher ed agenda. *Journal of Educational Technology, 38*(2), 111–121.

Gurin, P., Dey, E. L., Hurtado, S., & Gurin, G. (2002). Diversity and higher education: Theory and impact on educational outcomes. *Harvard Educational Review, 72*(3), 330–366.

Hackman, H., & Rauscher, L. (2004). A pathway to access for all: Exploring the connections between universal instructional design and social justice education. *Equity and Excellence in Education, 37*(2), 114–123.

Hall, T., Strangman, N., & Meyer, A. (2003). *Differentiated instruction and implications for UDL implementation*. Wakefield, MA: National Center for Accessing the General Curriculum.

Harrison, E. G. (2006). Working with faculty toward universally designed instruction: The process of dynamic course design. *Journal of Postsecondary Education and Disability, 19*(2), 152–162.

Heiman, T. (2008). Females with learning disabilities taking on-line courses: Perceptions of the learning environments, coping and well-being. *Journal of Postsecondary Education and Disability, 21*(1), 4–14.

Higbee, J. L. (2008). The faculty perspective: Implementation of universal design in a first-year classroom. In S. Burgstahler & R. Cory (Eds.), *Universal Design in Higher Education: From Principles to Practice* (pp. 61–72). Cambridge, MA: Harvard Education Press.

Higbee, J. L., & Goff, E. (2008). *Pedagogy and student services for institutional transformation: Implementing universal design in higher education*. Minneapolis: Regents of the University of Minnesota, Center for Research on Developmental Education and Urban Literacy.

Higher Education Opportunity Act (HEOA) of 2008. *20 U.S.C. § 1003(24)*

Hitchcock, C., Meyer, A., Rose, D., & Jackson, R. (2002). Providing new access to the general curriculum: Universal design for learning. *Teaching Exceptional Children, 35*(2), 8–17.

Hodson, D., & Hodson. J. (1998). From constructivism to social constructivism. A Vygotskian perspective on teaching and learning science. *School Science Review, 79*(289), 33–41.

Hotchkiss, J., Moore, R. E., & Pitts, M. M. (2006). Freshman learning communities, college performance, and retention. *Education Economics, 14*(2), 197–210.

IMS Global Learning Consortium. (2004). *IMS AccessForAll meta-data overview*. Retrieved from http://www.imsglobal.org/accessibility/accmdv1p0/imsaccmd_oviewv1p0.html#1632526

International Association for K–12 Online Learning. (2011). *Version two national standards for quality online courses*. Vienna, VA: Author.

Izzo, M., Murray, A., & Novak, J. (2008). The faculty perspective on universal design for learning. *Journal of Postsecondary Education and Disability, 21*(2), 60–72. Retrieved from http://eric.ed.gov/?id=EJ822094

Kame'enui, E. J., Carnine, D. W., Dixon, R. C., Simmons, D. C., & Coyne, M. D. (2002). *Effective teaching strategies that accommodate diverse learners (2nd ed.)*. Upper Saddle River, NJ: Pearson Prentice Hall.

Keeler, C. G., & Horney, M. (2007). Online course designs: Are special needs being met? *The American Journal of Distance Education, 21*(2), 61–75.

Kim-Rupnow, W. S., Dowrick, P. W., & Burke, L. S. (2001). Implications for improving access and outcomes for individuals with disabilities in postsecondary distance education. *The American Journal of Distance Education, 15*(1), 37–41.

Kinash, S., Crichton, S., & Kim-Rupnow, W. S. (2004). A review of 2000–2003 literature at the intersection of online learning and disability. *The American Journal of Distance Education, 18*(1), 5–19.

Knowles, M. S. (1980). *The modern practice of adult education*. Englewood Cliffs, NJ: Cambridge Adult Education Prentice Hall Regents.

Kolb, D. (1981). Learning styles and disciplinary differences. In A. W. Chickering (Ed.), *The modern American college*. San Francisco: Jossey-Bass.

Kortering, L., McClannon, T., & Braziel, P. (2005). What algebra and biology students have to say about universal design for learning. *National Center for Secondary Education and Transition Research to Practice Brief, 4*, 2.

Langley-Turnbaugh S. J., Blair, M., & Whitney, J. (2013). Increasing accessibility of college STEM courses through faculty development in UDL. In S. Burgstahler (Ed.), *Universal design in higher education: Promising practices*. Seattle: DO-IT, University of Washington. Retrieved from http://www.washington.edu/doit/increasing-accessibility-college-stem-courses-through-faculty-development-universal-design-learning

Lightfoot, E., & Gibson, P. (2005). Universal instructional design: A new framework for accommodating students in social work courses. *Journal of Social Work Education, 41*(2), 269–277.

Lombardi, A. R., Murray, C., & Gerdes, H. (2011). College faculty and inclusive instruction: Self-reported attitudes and actions pertaining to universal design. *Journal of Diversity in Higher Education, 4*(4), 250–261.

Mason, C., & Orkwis., R. (2005). Instructional theories supporting universal design for learning—Teaching to individual learners. In Council for Exceptional Children (Ed.), *Universal design for learning: A guide for teachers and education professionals*. Upper Saddle River, NJ: Pearson/Merrill Prentice Hall.

McGuire, J. M., Scott, S. S., & Shaw, S. F. (2003). Universal design for instruction: The paradigm, its principles, and products for enhancing instructional access. *Journal of Postsecondary Education and Disability, 17*(1), 11–21.

Merriam-Webster Dictionary. (n.d.). Framework. In *Merriam-Webster's Collegiate Dictionary*. Chicago: Encyclopedia Britannica Company. Retrieved from http://www.merriam-webster.com/dictionary/framework

Minkler, J. E. (2002). ERIC review: Learning communities at the community college. *Community College Review, 30*(3), 46–63. Retrieved from http://crw.sagepub.com/cgi/content/abstract/30/3/46

Mino, J. (2004). Planning for inclusion: Using universal instructional design to create a learner-centered community college classroom. *Equity & Excellence in Education, 37*(2), 154–160.

Moriarty, M. A. (2007). Inclusive pedagogy: Teaching methodologies to reach diverse learners in science instruction. *Equity and Excellence in Education, 40*(3), 252–265.

National Council on Disability. (2004). *Design for inclusion: Creating a new marketplace*. Washington, DC: Author. Retrieved from http://www.ncd.gov/newsroom/publications/2004/online_newmarketplace.htm

Nesset, V., & Large, A. (2004). Children in the information technology design process: A review of theories and their applications. *Library and Information Science Research, 26*(2004), 140–161.

Office of Postsecondary Education. (n.d.). *Demonstration projects to ensure students with disabilities receive a quality higher education*. Washington, DC: U.S. Department of Education. Retrieved from http://www.ed.gov/programs/disabilities/index.html

O'Loughlin, M. (1992). Rethinking science education: Beyond Piagetian constructivism toward a sociocultural model of teaching and learning. *Journal of Research in Science Teaching, 29*(8), 791–820.

Orkwis, R., & McLane, K. (1998). *A curriculum every student can use: Design principles for student access*. ERIC/OSEP Topical Brief. Reston, VA: ERIC/OSEP Special Project. (ERIC Document Reproduction Service No. ED423654). Retrieved from http://eric.ed.gov/ERICDocs/data/ericdocs2sql/content_storage_01/0000019b/80/16/e9/bd.pdf

Osborne, J. (1996). Beyond constructivism. *Science Education, 80*(1), 53–82.

Ouellett, M. L. (2004). Faculty development and universal instructional design. *Equity and Excellence in Education, 37*, 135–144.

Pearson, E., & Koppi, T. (2006). Supporting staff in developing inclusive online learning. In M. Adams & S. Brown (Eds.) *Towards Inclusive Teaching in Higher Education* (pp. 56–66). London: Routledge.

Phillips, A., Terras, K., Swinney, C., and Schneweis, C. (2013). Online disability accommodations: Faculty experiences at one public university. *Journal of Postsecondary Education and Disability, 25*(4), 346–366. Retrieved from http://www.ahead.org/publications/jped/vol_25

Pliner, S., & Johnson, J. (2004). Historical, theoretical, and foundational principles of universal instructional design in higher education. *Equity and Excellence in Education, 37*, 105–113.

Poore-Pariseau, Cindy. (2013). Universal design in assessments. In S. Burgstahler (Ed.), *Universal design in higher education: Promising practices*. Seattle: DO-IT, University of Washington. Retrieved from http://www.washington.edu/doit/universal-design-assessments

Quality Matters. (n.d.). *Higher Ed Program–Rubric*. Retrieved from https://www.qualitymatters.org/rubric

Rangin, H. (2011). How to guide for creating accessible online learning. *CANnect*. Retrieved from http://projectone.cannect.org

Reich, C., Price, J., Rubin, E., & Steiner, M. (2010). *Inclusion, disabilities, and informal science learning: A CAISE inquiry group report*. Washington, DC: Center for Advancement of Informal Science Education (CAISE).

Roberts, K. D., Park, H. J., Brown, S., & Cook, B. (2011). Universal design for instruction in postsecondary education: A systematic review of empirically based articles. *Journal of Postsecondary Education and Disability, 24*(1), 5–15.

Roberts, J. B., Crittenden, L. A., & Crittenden, J. C. (2011). Students with disabilities and online learning: A cross-institutional study of perceived satisfaction with accessibility compliances and services. *Internet and Higher Education, 14*(4), 242–250.

Rose, D. H., Harbour, W. S., Johnston, C. S., Daley, S. G., & Abarbanell, L. (2006). Universal design for learning in postsecondary education: Reflections and principles and their applications. *Journal of Postsecondary Education and Disability, 19*(2), 135–151.

Rose, D. H., & Meyer, A. (2002). *Teaching every student in the digital age: Universal design for learning*. Alexandria, VA: Association for Supervision and Curriculum Development.

Rose, D. H., Meyer, A., & Hitchcock, C. (Eds.). (2005). *The universally designed classroom: Accessible curriculum and digital technologies*. Cambridge, MA: Harvard Education Press.

Santangelo, T., & Tomlinson, C. A. (2009). The application of differentiated instruction in postsecondary environments: Benefits, challenges, and future directions. *International Journal of Teaching and Learning in Higher Education, 20*(3), 307–323.

Savidis, A. & Stephanidis, C. (2005). Developing inclusive e-learning and e-entertainment to effectively accommodate learning difficulties. *SIGACCESS Accessibility and Computing, 83*, 42–54.

Schelly, C. L., Davies, P. L., & Spooner, C. L. (2011). Student perceptions of faculty implementation of Universal Design for Learning. *Journal of Postsecondary Education and Disability, 24*(1), 17–30.

Schmetzke, A. (2001). Online distance education: "Anytime, anywhere" but not for everyone. *Information Technology and Disabilities, 7*(2). Retrieved from http://www.rit.edu/~easi/itd/itdv07n2/axel.htm

Scott, S., McGuire, J., & Shaw, S. (2003). Universal design for instruction: A new paradigm for adult instruction in postsecondary education. *Remedial and Special Education, 24*(6), 369–379.

Seale, J. K. (2014). *E-learning and disability in higher education. Accessibility research and practice*. London: Routledge, Taylor & Francis.

Shaw, S. F., & Scott, S. (2003). New directions in faculty development. *Journal of Postsecondary Education and Disability, 17*(1), 3–9.

Silver, P., Bourke, A., & Strehorn, K. C. (1998). Universal instructional design in higher education: An approach for inclusion. *Equity & Excellence in Education, 31*(2), 47–51.

Smith, R. E., & Buchannan, T. (2012). Community collaboration: Use of universal design in the classroom. *Journal of Postsecondary Education and Disability, 25*(3), 271–279.

Soldner, L., Lee, Y., & Duby, P. (1999). Welcome to the block: Developing freshman learning communities that work. *Journal of College Student Retention, 1*(2), 115–129.

Souma, A., & Casey, D. (2008). The benefits of universal design for students with psychiatric disabilities. In S. Burgstahler & R. Cory (Eds.). *Universal design in higher education: From principles to practice* (pp. 97–104). Cambridge, MA: Harvard Education Press.

Stein, E. (2013, May 14th). *Chisel a teaching masterpiece: A MiddleWeb blog*. Retrieved from http://www.middleweb.com/7574/chisel-a-teaching-masterpiece

Svinicki, M. D. (1999). New directions in learning and motivation. *New Directions for Teaching and Learning, 80*, 5–27.

Svinicki, M. D., & Dixon, N. M. (1987). The Kolb model modified for classroom activities. *College Teaching, 35*, 141–146.

Tanenbaum, A. S. (1988). *Computer networks* (2nd ed.). Upper Saddle River, NJ: Prentice Hall, Inc.

Tomlinson, C. A. (2001). *How to differentiate instruction in mixed-ability classrooms* (2nd ed.). Alexandria, VA: Association for Supervision and Curriculum Development.

Wooldridge, B. (1995). Increasing the effectiveness of university/college instruction: The results of learning style research into course design and delivery. In R. R. Simms and S. J. Sims (Eds.), *The importance of learning styles* (pp. 49–68). Westport, CT: Greenwood Press.

Xu, D., & Jaggars, S. S. (2014). Performance gaps between online and face-to-face courses: Differences across types of students and academic subject areas. *The Journal of Higher Education, 85*(5), 633–659.

Zeff, R. (2007). Universal design across the curriculum. *New Directions for Higher Education, 137,* 27–44.

This chapter is based on work supported by the U.S. Department of Education Office of Postsecondary Education (grant numbers P333A990042, P333A020044, and P333A050064) and the National Science Foundation (grant numbers CNS-1042260 and HRD-0833504). Any opinions, findings, and conclusions or recommendations are those of the author and do not necessarily reflect the policy or views of the federal government, and you should not assume its endorsement.

3

Universal Design of Instruction in Postsecondary Education
A Literature Review of Empirically Based Articles

Kelly D. Roberts
Maya Satlykgylyjova
Hye-Jin Park

This chapter reports on nineteen research-based articles published in peer-reviewed journals that focus on the application of universal design (UD) principles in higher education. The focus of these articles is specific to "intervention" studies, meaning those that applied UD in higher education, collected outcome data, and reported on results associated with learning and instruction. The findings fit into two primary areas: (1) research that investigated the use of UD principles as applied to course/instructional design and the impact on students' perceptions and performance, and (2) research that investigated professional development (PD) on UD provided to educators and their subsequent use of UD principles and impact on student outcomes.

Postsecondary education is becoming exceedingly more diverse (Higher Education Research Institute, 2006); thus there is a need for instruction to be responsive to this diversity. As described in Chapter 2 of this book, the UD paradigm shows promise for addressing all diversity characteristics, including the multiple ways in which people learn. Aligned with this approach, reports in the literature suggest that increasing numbers of faculty in higher education are applying UD principles in their courses (e.g., Aguiree & Duncan, 2013; Ashman, 2010; Bigelow, 2012; Black, Weinberg, & Brodwin, 2014). They are also recognizing that the UD approach benefits all students, not just those with disabilities or other special learning needs (Higbee, 2009). UD is also being applied to noninstructional offerings of postsecondary institutions, including student services, physical spaces, and technology as shared in other chapters of this book. Likewise, multiple authors have investigated the impact of UD training on teacher candidates and, in some cases, the impact of this instruction in K–12 settings (Courey, Tappe, Siker, & LePage, 2013; Frey, Andres, McKeeman, & Lane, 2012; McGhie-Richmond & Sung, 2013).

Various frameworks have been developed for applying UD to teaching and learning. In Chapter 2, universally designed teaching (UDT), universal design for learning (UDL), universal design for instruction (UDforI), universal design of instruction (UDI), and universal instructional design (UID) are presented as frameworks for applying UD principles to teaching and learning. Each framework, to some degree, is based upon the seven general UD principles designed for products and environments developed by the Center for Universal Design (CUD) at North Carolina State University (1997). For example, the Center for Applied Special Technology (CAST) created three new principles of UDL for applying UD to curriculum development and delivery: multiple means of representing information, multiple means of action and expression, and multiple means of engagement (CAST, 2012). The UDI framework, created by collaborators in projects hosted by the DO-IT Center (n.d.) at the University of Washington, embraces the combined set of UD and UDL principles (Burgstahler, 2015) in order to address a wider range of factors that impact learning than are covered by UDL alone (e.g., the design of the physical environment of a classroom or lab); it operationalizes the principles into instructional practices to addresses class climate, interaction, physical environments and products, delivery methods, information resources and technology, feedback and assessment, and accommodations.

In 2011, Roberts, Park, Brown, and Cook published a review of the literature on the use of UD in higher education and reported on only eight empirically based articles published from 2000 through 2009. This chapter reports on nineteen research-based articles published in peer-reviewed journals that focus on the application of UD principles to postsecondary instruction from January 1, 2000, through September 30, 2014. The underlying intention is to provide readers with evidence-based practices they can apply in their own higher education settings.

METHODS

The search terms used to identify intervention studies in published articles that applied UD to instruction in higher education are: (a) UDI (to refer to UD *of* instruction and UD *for* instruction) and universal design instruction; (b) UDL and universal design learning; (c) UID and universal instructional design; (d) UD and universal design; (e) postsecondary education; (f) college; (g) university; and (h) higher education. The prepositions (e.g., the *for* in universal design *for* learning) were not used in searches in order to be most inclusive, as the number of articles found when the prepositions were not used was greater than when the prepositions were used.

The search terms were used to search for articles in four electronic databases that specialize in housing educational research: ERIC, PsychInfo, Academic Search Complete, and Education Research Complete. The articles found were then reviewed to determine which met the inclusion criteria. An article included in the study: (a) was published between January 1, 2000, and September 30, 2014; (b) was research-based (i.e., research using quantitative, qualitative, or mixed methods); (c) was published in

TABLE 3.1   The Number of Peer-Reviewed Articles Published Between January 1, 2000, and September 30, 2014, on UDL, UDI, UID, or UD in Postsecondary, College, University, or Higher Education Settings

Search Terms	ERIC		Academic Search Complete		PsychInfo		Education Research Complete	
	Initial	*Final*	*Initial*	*Final*	*Initial*	*Final*	*Initial*	*Final*
U D L Postsecondary	22	5	5	0	1	0	23	2
College	23	3	24	2	12	0	59	1
University	20	0	79	1	39	0	145	2
Higher Education	32	0	11	0	5	0	29	1
U D I Postsecondary	16	0	5	0	5	0	11	0
College	16	0	11	0	4	0	19	0
University	7	0	21	0	14	0	35	0
Higher Education	20	0	7	0	4	0	10	0
U I D Postsecondary	14	1	7	0	1	0	7	0
College	11	0	7	0	2	0	16	0
University	6	0	12	0	4	0	26	0
Higher Education	20	0	6	0	1	0	13	0
U D Postsecondary	65	1	19	0	7	0	65	0
College	72	0	125	0	43	0	146	0
University	51	0	496	0	156	0	311	0
Higher Education	92	0	39	0	13	0	78	0

a peer-reviewed journal; (d) reported research that applied UD to instruction and/or learning in postsecondary, college, university, or higher education (i.e., had an intervention and collected data on the impact); and (e) was published in English. Table 3.1 presents the number of articles located through the various searches. The first column, "Initial," shows the number of articles initially retrieved from the electronic search of each database with each combination of search terms.

The abstracts for the articles in the "Initial" pool were screened. Those that clearly did not meet the inclusion criteria were screened out. Each of the remaining articles was fully examined to determine if it met the inclusion criteria. Duplicate articles across the four search engines were included only once. The number of articles determined to meet the inclusion criteria is presented in the second column, "Final."

RESULTS

The search and analysis identified a total of nineteen articles that met the inclusion criteria. They primarily addressed two categories, as summarized in Tables 3.2 and 3.3. Table 3.2 summarizes the research that investigated the use of UD principles as applied to course/instructional design and the impact on students' perceptions and performance, and Table 3.3 summarizes research that investigated professional development on UD provided to educators and their subsequent use of UD principles and possible impact on student outcomes. These are broad categories, and some articles fit under both; in those cases, they were included in the table that was the best fit. The tables are organized by year of publication, author, objectives of the study, methodology, and summary of the findings.

DISCUSSION

The results of this literature review suggest that the amount of research on the application of UD to instruction in higher education has increased since 2000. Whereas only four articles meeting the inclusion criteria were found during the seven-year period from 2000 through 2007, fifteen were found during the seven-year period from 2008 through September 30, 2014. This increase in the number of research-based articles is aligned with the literature in general, which includes increasing numbers of articles on UD in higher education, most of which are not research-based and do not apply an intervention, as indicated in the search results provided in Table 3.1.

The sample size median was approximately 65 and ranged from a low of 4 students interviewed in the Kumar and Wideman study (2014) to a high of 1,223 students completing post-surveys in the Schelly, Davies, and Spooner study (2011). The average sample size was approximately 147.

The primary methodology of the articles that met the inclusion criteria was qualitative, including action research. Only one study used a true experimental design and included random assignment of subjects to the control and intervention groups (Spooner, Baker, Harris, Ahlgrim-Delzell, & Browder, 2007). Two other studies (Tzivinikou, 2014; Davies, Schelly, & Spooner, 2013) used quasi-experimental pre-post designs.

Category One Research: Use of UD Principles

The research reported in category one—that which investigated the use of UD principles as applied to course/instructional design and related impact on students' perceptions and performance—is supportive of the use of UD principles in higher education as applied to instruction. The majority of the studies were related to course/instructional design (Parker, Robinson, & Hannafin, 2007–2008; Simonchelli & Hinson, 2008; Basham, Lowrey, & deNoyelles, 2010; Bongey, Cizaldo, & Kalnbach, 2010; Ragpot, 2011; Rao & Tanners, 2011; Smith, 2012; Zhong, 2012; Catalano, 2014; He, 2014; Kumar & Wideman, 2014; Tzivinikou, 2014). This focus dealt with how instructors can modify their course design by using strategies that apply UD principles and the impact of this approach on student learning and/or perceptions.

Overall, the findings from the research-based studies that applied UD to course/instructional design indicated that students had improved perceptions of the course, increased satisfaction, increased social presence, and enhanced success (e.g., Tzivinikou, 2014; Schelly, Davies, & Spooner, 2011; Kumar & Wideman, 2014). Students also reported that they felt more confident, in control of their own learning process, and empowered to make personal choices to best support their own learning (e.g., Kumar & Wideman, 2014; He, 2014).

TABLE 3.2   Articles Investigating the Use of UD Principles as Applied to Course/Instructional Design and the Impact on Students' Perceptions and Performance

Year, Authors	Objective(s)	Methodology	Findings
2007–2008, Parker, Robinson, & Hannafin	Investigate the effects of a redesigned core course aligned with UDI	Qualitative action research conducted with 114 students with data collected from students' online interactions and course evaluations	Students' online interactions, their satisfaction, and course evaluations supported UDI.
2008, Simonchelli & Hinson	Examine whether world history course design modifications, according to UDL, have an impact on students' attitudes or performance	One-to-one interviews with 5 students, 2 who indicated they had learning disabilities	Results were mixed. There were technical problems with audio lectures, which, when used, were not considered useful; the discussion board was reported useful; text-to-speech software use was encouraged but it was not used by any participants.
2010, Basham, Lowrey, & deNoyelles	Explore the UDL framework for course design as a basis for a bi-university computer-mediated communication collaborative project	Qualitative study with 78 students with data collected through a rubric for the online presentation, discussion board, chat logs, and course evaluation	The application of the UDL framework was important to the overall course design; using UDL as a foundational framework to build computer-mediated communication into the instructional design encouraged student participation and improved instructor ratings.
2010, Bongey, Cizaldo, & Kalnbach	Explore the efficacy of UDL features applied in an online biology course	Action research with 116 students with data collected through surveys, follow-up interviews, student usage statistics, and points earned on tests	UDL tools were widely applauded by most students; 2 students strongly disagreed on the usefulness of the intervention.
2011, Ragpot	Apply UD to the means by which students can demonstrate their knowledge by allowing multiple assessment options	Qualitative action research with an unspecified number of students with students' work and their response to the multimodal manner of conducting assessment analyzed	Different approaches to assessment created opportunities for students to engage with the curriculum content in a variety of ways; taught students a different way of looking at assessment in general and also made them think about how they would approach assessment in their own classrooms.
2011, Rao & Tanners	Explore the reactions of students to UDL features of a graduate-level online course	Case study with 25 students completing surveys, with 6 of these students purposefully selected for interviews	Students reported positive experiences with the course, including clarity in course expectations and options in text formats, and identified effective instructional strategies and effective asynchronous and synchronous technology elements.
2012, Smith	Explore faculty's use of a UDL framework to design and deliver an introductory graduate research methods course and assess student perspectives of this approach	Action research, using mixed methods, with 80 students, with data collection including a survey on UDL practices, multiple informal conversations, observations, and participation in some class sessions and online blogs	A statistically significant relationship between UD practices and student interest and engagement was found.

(continued on next page)

TABLE 3.2 (continued) Articles Investigating the Use of UD Principles as Applied to Course/ Instructional Design and the Impact on Students' Perceptions and Performance

Year, Authors	Objective(s)	Methodology	Findings
2012, Zhong	Assess student response to UDL principles applied to library instruction	Quantitative survey study with 50 students about their learning styles and instructional effectiveness as related to UDL principles	In a post-survey, the majority of students reported benefiting from UDL-integrated instruction.
2014, Catalano	Explore value of UD practices for students when applied in a distance education course	Qualitative study where 7 students with disabilities experienced a UDL-adapted online course and provided feedback on it via in-depth interviews	Common themes included the need for: clear expectations; frequent interaction with the professor; the provision of audio for all tutorials/PowerPoints; the provision of rubrics for all assignments; a detailed syllabus with due dates; feedback on assignments, discussion board posts, and papers; an invitation to meet in person at least once and/or a video introduction of the instructor; answer all emails in a timely manner; different due dates throughout the week for different assignments to help with time management.
2014, He	Use UDL in an online teacher education course to enhance learner confidence to teach online	Case study on a UDL-based online teacher education course with 24 teacher candidates, with survey results and statistics collected through the online learning management system	The intervention improved teacher candidates' confidence and self-efficacy in teaching and learning online. They considered pacing and flexibility as benefits and lack of face-to-face interactions with instructor as a concern.
2014, Kumar & Wideman	Apply UDL to course design	Case study with 50 students that included student interviews and the perspective of the instructor (the first author) and a disability service provider (the second author)	Students responded very positively to the course design and reported increased flexibility, social presence, reduced stress, and enhanced success. Students also felt more in control of their own learning process and empowered to make personal choices to best support their own learning. The instructor had increased satisfaction. There was a noticed reduction in the need for interventions from the disability services department.
2014, Tzivinikou	Explore student evaluation of a study guide with UDL principles applied	Quantitative, quasi-experimental study with repeated measure with 60 students, without a control group	In the student evaluation of a study guide with UDL modification, student responses on the subcategories for representation, perception, language and symbols, and comprehension increased statistically significantly.

TABLE 3.3   Articles Investigating Professional Development (PD) on UD Provided to Educators, Subsequent Use of UD Principles, and Impact on Outcomes for Students

Year, Author(s)	Objectives	Methodology	Summary of Findings
2005, Zhang	Initiate and implement UDL theory and provide PD for K–12 in-service, preservice, and teacher educators	Qualitative study with 69 educators that included participant reflections	Teachers lacked educational technology skills. A needs-based survey was administered prior to planning PD activities. Both teachers and faculty reported value regarding the application of UDL principles. Sustained and focused PD activities proved effective in university faculty's and schoolteachers' academic growth and expanded use of technologies.
2007, McGuire-Schwartz, & Arndt	Prepare early-childhood teacher candidates in the planning and delivery of UD lessons and conduct research on the effectiveness of such lessons	Study 1: Qualitative, action research conducted by 36 teacher candidates to implement a UDL strategy during their student teaching	UDL strategies improved learning and accessibility for both struggling and non-struggling students.
		Study 2: Qualitative, action research conducted by 5 teacher candidates who were introduced to the principles of UDL and designed UDL lesson plans during their first practicum	UDL strategies improved student learning and engagement while meeting diverse student needs and making education more inclusive and effective.
2007, Spooner, Baker, Harris, Ahlgrim-Delzell, & Browder	Investigate the effects of a 1-hour UDL training on lesson plan development of special and general educators in a college classroom	Quantitative, true experimental study with 72 graduate and undergraduate students in 4 classes, randomly assigned to control and experimental groups with a rubric used to "judge" lesson plans and a pre-post survey used to measure representation, expression, and engagement scores	The results suggest that teachers need to be informed about UDL to develop lesson plans. Pre-test and post-test scores found that the teachers in the experimental group improved their lesson plan development at a greater rate than those in the control group.
2008, Izzo, Murray, & Novak	Provided PD for faculty and administrators and conducted a field test of the impact	Mixed-methods study 1: A survey of 271 faculty and TAs, with focus groups held with 92 of them, to assess the instructional climate for students with disabilities	UDL was identified as the most needed training topic. Thus, a web-based, self-paced PD was developed and piloted.
		Mixed-methods study 2: A survey to evaluate the pilot testing of PD with 98 faculty and administrators	Faculty and administrators reported that the PD was effective in increasing their comfort in meeting the instructional needs of students with disabilities.

(continued on next page)

TABLE 3.3 (continued)   Articles Investigating Professional Development (PD) on UD Provided to Educators, Subsequent Use of UD Principles, and Impact on Outcomes for Students

Year, Author(s)	Objectives	Methodology	Summary of Findings
2011, Moon, Utsching, Todd, & Bozzorg	Evaluate programmatic interventions (including faculty PD) to enhance postsecondary STEM education	Mixed-methods study with 15 longitudinal instructors with data collected from classroom observations to assess the accessibility of classroom and laboratory instruction; feedback forms and focus groups to collect data on workshop outcomes; surveys and online journal reflections completed by instructors; data was also collected on performance and demographics of students with disabilities enrolled in project-affiliated courses and through student-completed surveys	Positive feedback was reported regarding group-based learning and class materials.
2011, Schelly, Davies, & Spooner	Test the effectiveness of instructor PD on subsequent course delivery modifications implemented and the impact on students assessed (instructors were PhD-level graduate students)	Pre-post design with 5 instructors who were provided training and their 1,362 students; with 1,223 of the students responding to the post-survey	After training instructors on the use of UDL, students reported a significant increase in the use of UDL strategies by instructors; 6 out of 14 questions on UDL had effect sizes that suggest the improvement was meaningful.
2013, Davies, Schelly, & Spooner	Explore student perceptions of instructor teaching methods, where instructors in the intervention group received UDL PD.	Quasi-experimental study with pre-post survey with 6 instructors in the intervention group teaching a total of 1,164 students (with 386 students completing both pre- and post-surveys) and 3 instructors in a control group with 646 students (204 students completing both pre- and post-surveys)	Students' perceptions of instruction, as measured through a survey, suggested that UDL PD had a significant positive effect on teaching methods.

Included in this category is one study (Ragpot, 2011) that specifically investigated UDL as applied to assessment. In this study, students were provided the opportunity to demonstrate their understanding of course content through nontraditional means of assessment, such as posters and plays. This study was conducted at the University of Johannesburg, where Ragpot indicated that many students enter the university with an underdeveloped competence in academic English. She argues that a multimodal approach to assessment provided students with the opportunity to draw on atypical modes to express what they had learned while they were still becoming acquainted with academic language.

However, while most studies reported positive impacts, Simonchelli and Hinson (2008) reported mixed results when they investigated student attitudes and performance after students participated in a course that applied UDL principles. These mixed results were at least partly due to technology difficulties; the students were to use audio lectures but, because the technology did not always work, they struggled to access these lectures. In addition, the instructors recommended the use of text-to-speech software, but the student participants did not use it. However, the participants did find the discussion board useful. This is important to note, as unforeseen technology issues and access to information can greatly hinder access to universally designed activities and thus reduce effectiveness and increase frustration.

Likewise, Bongey, Cizaldo, and Kalnbach (2010) reported mixed results. They investigated the use of a supplemental website that applied UDL principles for an online biology course and compared student usage and perceptions with students in the same course who did not have access to the supplemental site. The authors reported that, although the use of the supplemental website resulted in students' perceptions of added value, the UDL-enhanced site did not lead to improved grades. This result led the authors to conclude that there may be a "sweet spot," or optimal blend of tools and approaches, that can be used to support student learning.

Only one study (Catalano, 2014), with a sample of seven, focused specifically on students with disabilities, while two others (Simonchelli & Hinson, 2008; Bongey, Cizaldo, & Kalnbach, 2010) each conducted interviews with two student participants with disabilities. The limited research specific to students with disabilities may be indicative of educators recognizing the benefits of UD for all students. However, in these studies the impact of UD on students with disabilities, as well as other population subsets, was not specifically investigated further to ascertain if certain UD practices work better for individuals under particular conditions (e.g., what works for an individual with a visual impairment may not be effective for an individual who is an English language learner).

Category Two Research: UD Professional Development

The second primary category of research—that which investigated PD on UD provided to educators and their subsequent use of UD principles and possible impact on student outcomes—focuses on instructors (Zhang, 2005; McGuire-Schwartz & Arndt, 2007; Spooner, Baker, Harris, Ahlgrim-Delzell, & Browder, 2007; Izzo, Murray, & Novak, 2008; Moon, Utsching, Todd, & Bozzorg, 2011; Schelly, Davies, & Spooner, 2011; Davies, Schelly, & Spooner, 2013). In general, the results of these studies demonstrate that UD training for higher education instructors increased the application of UD principles in their courses. The majority of these studies reported on student perceptions. For example, Schelly, Davies, and Spooner (2011) found that only a few hours of instructor training resulted in better student perceptions regarding the use of UD principles. They also reported that training and the subsequent increased use of UD principles by instructors might enhance the learning experiences of all students, including those with disabilities. Similarly, in 2013, Davies, Schelly, and Spooner conducted a pre-post intervention study, with the intervention being professional development on UD for instructors. The study compared student perceptions of instructor teaching methods measured by responses to a questionnaire that asked about UD practices, completed before and after six instructors received training. The results were compared to those of a control group of students taking the same course in a different section where the three instructors did not receive training. Students in the courses where the instructors received PD reported a significant increase in faculty applying the UD principle of multiple means of representation. This included presenting materials in multiple formats, using instructional videos, and using well-organized and accessible materials. Likewise, Moon et al. (2011) reported on the results of fifteen instructors who received training on accessible teaching methods aligned with UD principles. Their students provided positive feedback in response to group-based learning and class materials, with a majority suggesting that group testing continue. However, not all students responded positively to the group testing, reporting a dysfunctional group as the reason.

The research reviewed had a focus on UD as a tool to benefit *all* students, with respect to gaining better access and understanding of course materials and otherwise fully benefiting from the learning environment, as opposed to *only* students with disabilities. Of the nineteen articles that met the inclusion criteria, only three specifically focused on UD applications for students with disabilities (Catalano, 2014; Moon et al. 2011; Spooner et al., 2007). This finding is relevant to the field in that UD is intended to benefit all learners but historically tended to be associated with improving learning outcomes for individuals with disabilities. This finding is also aligned with published articles that reported on the perceptions of UD in higher education by faculty and instructors (e.g., Cook, Rumrill, & Tankersley, 2009; Dallas, Sprong, & Upton, 2014; Ginsberg & Schulte, 2008; Lombardi & Murray, 2011; Seok, Kinsell, DaCosta, & Tung, 2010). While these articles did not meet the inclusion criteria, as they did not report on the application of UD in higher education, the fact that numerous articles reported on faculty perceptions of UD use in higher education suggests increased interest in the subject.

Other Findings

In addition to the articles that met the search criteria and are presented in Tables 3.2 and 3.3, researchers noted that the initial search identified numerous articles where higher education faculty trained preservice teachers on UD strategies to apply the strategies in preK–12 settings (e.g., Courey et al., 2013; Evans, Williams, King, & Metcalf, 2010; Frey et al., 2012; McGhie-Richmond & Sung, 2013; Theoharis & Causton-Theoharis, 2011; Williams, Evans, & King, 2012). These articles were not included in Tables 3.2 and 3.3, as their focus was not on teaching and learning outcomes in higher education settings. However, it is important to note that each of these articles found that preservice teachers who received instruction on UD had improved outcomes in areas such as lesson plan design and student engagement. It is also notable that teacher education instructors are using UD principles in their instruction. They are recognizing the strengths of UD and how it can benefit all students.

RECOMMENDATIONS

In order for higher education faculty to apply the principles of UD, the principles need to be operationalized into practices. Concrete examples can be useful for faculty new to the UD approach. Based upon the research-based journal articles reported in this chapter, a few examples are suggested in the paragraphs that follow.

With respect to teaching students, an inclusive statement on the syllabus is an easy step that can help students feel welcomed and included (Davies, Schelly, & Spooner, 2013). It opens the door for all students struggling with the course, or feeling that they might struggle with the course, to approach the instructor. An example of an inclusive statement is: "The instructor is committed to making this course fully accessible to all students. If you have questions or concerns about the course readings or requirements, please contact the instructor. If you have a documented disability, you are also encouraged to contact the disability support office to request accommodations."

Student participants, in the reported studies, indicated specific practices as being important and/or effective for them (Parker, Robinson, & Hannafin, 2007–2008; Kumar & Wideman, 2014; Moon et al., 2011; Ragpot, 2011; Davies, Schelly, & Spooner, 2013; Tzivinikou, 2014). The practices they reported include the following:

- Course expectations are clearly presented in the syllabus and aligned with the course content.
- Directions are clear and include step-by-step instructions.
- Learning activities are clearly aligned with course objectives.
- The instructor responds promptly to all e-mails and other communications.
- Students have choices—for example, a choice of completing several small assignments or a final exam; the option of doing group or individual work; and a choice of due dates for assignments.
- The instructor provides prompt feedback on drafts of assignments.
- There are choices in assessment measures.
- A study guide or an outline of the content to be covered is provided in advance.
- There are rubrics for each graded assignment.
- Practical and applied learning activities are included in the course.
- Material is presented in multiple formats.
- The instructor highlights key information after showing a video.

The results of the literature review suggest that the provision of professional development on UD principles and guidelines to higher education instructors has potential for improving postsecondary education outcomes for all students (Davies, Schelly, & Spooner, 2013; Izzo, Murray, & Novak, 2008; Moon et al., 2011; Spooner et al., 2007; Zhang, 2005). A suggestion to help instructors improve their curricula is to have groups of instructors review others' course materials and provide feedback on clarity and organization. In some cases it might be reasonable to have students do this as well. The research findings support the following as components of instructor training:

- presenting information in multiple formats;
- providing prompt feedback to students on assignments;
- providing opportunities for active engagement in learning such as small-group work;
- using guided learning techniques, such as providing an outline of what will be included in a lecture;
- helping instructors to provide choice to students;
- summarizing key concepts before, during, and immediately following instruction;
- using rubrics to provide structure on the expectations of assignments; and
- using clearly organized and accessible materials, including technology that is accessible to all students and works with minimal effort.

There is a need for more resources for faculty. The DO-IT Center, at the University of Washington, devised a list of ways to operationalize UD principles. Some examples include checklists for class climate, interaction, physical environments, and products; delivery methods; information resources and technology; feedback and assessment; and accommodation (Burgstahler, 2015). This is an admirable start and one that practitioners should build upon while also conducting research on each operationalized principle.

LIMITATIONS

In any review of published articles, there is always a chance that articles that meet the inclusion criteria were missed. In our case, this includes the fact that only four data-based search engines were used in the search. In addition, there may be articles that are research-based and investigated the use of UD principles but used terms other than those used in our search and thus were not reviewed in this study. While these limitations are associated specifically with the search, another limitation lies with the findings: the majority of the studies did not use rigorous research designs. This is to be expected for a field in the infant stage of development, implementation, and the conduct of research.

Another noteworthy point is that the journal article search, using the named search terms, did not find any research-based articles that focused on applying UD principles in the noninstructional spheres of higher education, such as physical access, student services, and information technology. This lack of published research articles indicates that this is an area in need of study.

Lastly, the current published research strives to show the benefits of UD practices for students overall, but does not contribute much to the understanding of how UD practices can benefit specific groups. To date, researchers have primarily sought to determine the benefits of UD to a particular collection of students in a course, not to students with the great variety of characteristics that UD purports to address. By definition, UD *does* require that faculty consider the needs of all *potential* students, including those from underserved populations, such as students with disabilities. When researchers look only at the average results of students enrolled in a specific course that is taught using UD practices, they cannot report on whether the practices have benefited students with a variety of characteristics unless the study is designed to capture the diverse characteristics of the student body studied, as well as whether some groups benefit more than others and if students with different characteristics in a future class would benefit from the methods employed. For example, a faculty member could apply some UD practices in a distance learning course and report that they benefit students in the class as a whole, but some of these practices could be inaccessible to students with certain types of disabilities or unusable by English language learners if there were no students with these characteristics in the course included in the study. Thus, the results of the study would not indicate that the instructor has proactively ensured an accessible and usable course for *all* potential students.

FUTURE RESEARCH

While the number of research studies on UD applications in higher education has increased, the field is open to the conduct of new research as well as the replication of existing studies to begin to validate the current findings. This recommendation includes the conduct of large-scale randomized control trials, as the majority of the research is qualitative with relatively small sample sizes. For future research, the authors of this chapter encourage researchers to explore the potential impact of UD broadly (i.e., outcomes for all students in the course), and more specifically by collecting outcome data on students with specific characteristics who are enrolled in a course. By disaggregating a sample, one can begin to test the benefits of a particular UD practice for a particular group of students, such as students with certain types of disabilities. This ties into the need for research that investigates usability—that is, to test whether the UD practices being applied are usable and accessible to students with a specific characteristic (e.g., visually impaired or English language learners).

There is a need for research that ties UD practices to brain function. For example, if a student with a math learning disability is provided instruction that is heuristic in nature versus delivered via lecture, how does the brain respond?

There is a need for research about very specific UD strategies and the impact of choice on student success. For example, one section of a course could complete all assignments in groups. Results could be compared to a section of the course where half of the assignments were completed as a group and the other half individually. These two sections could then be compared to a third section where students were provided the choice of doing group work or individual work. This study could test multiple hypotheses. For example, did students in the section of the course provided with a choice perform better, deliver higher quality assignments, earn better grades, demonstrate a greater increase in knowledge of course content, and express greater satisfaction with the course when compared to the two other groups? Researchers could also develop questions to assess the social and environmental aspects of the participants in the various sections of the course. The sample could be disaggregated to determine if there are specific groups of students who perform better under one condition. Another possible research study could involve multiple sections of the same online course where students are pooled and then randomly assigned to the control or intervention group. The intervention course could investigate operationalized UD principles such as providing guided notes, allowing students to choose their due dates, and giving students the option of completing several small assignments instead of a final exam. Data on the outcomes for each group would be collected and analyzed.

CONCLUSION

While the research on UD use in higher education is not extensive, the number of research-based articles published in the literature has increased. This is a start in verifying that UD has a place in higher education and that the application of UD has potential for improving student learning outcomes. The research also suggests that increasing numbers of faculty members are recognizing that UD is not just beneficial for students with disabilities but potentially for all students. The literature review reported in this chapter further supports the need to operationalize the use of UD principles in postsecondary education, and to conduct research on these operationalized processes. This is evident in the number of articles that reported on general perceptions (e.g., whether the instructor uses multiple means of representation) as opposed to specific outcomes (e.g., increases in student learning in a course that used specific multiple means of representation, such as a recorded lecture along with a transcript of the lecture and guided notes, compared to the same course using lecture only). Such efforts will help inform instructors as to specifics that are beneficial to students.

REFERENCES

Aguiree, R. T. P., & Duncan, C. (2013). Being an elbow: A phenomenological autoethnography of faculty-student collaboration for accommodations. *Journal of Teaching in Social Work, 33*, 531–551. doi:10.1080/08841233.2013.827611

Ashman, A. (2010). Modeling inclusive practices in postgraduate tertiary education courses. *International Journal of Inclusive Education, 14*(7), 667–680.

Basham, J. D., Lowrey, K. A., & deNoyelles, A. (2010). Computer mediated communication in the universal design for learning framework for preparation of special education teachers. *Journal of Special Education Technology, 25*(2), 31–44.

Bigelow, K. E. (2012). Designing for success: Developing engineers who consider universal design principles. *Journal of Postsecondary Education and Disability, 25*(3), 211–225.

Black, R. D., Weinberg, L. A., & Brodwin, M. G. (2014). Universal design for instruction and learning: A pilot study of faculty of instructional methods and attitudes related to students with disabilities in higher education. *Exceptionality Education International, 24*(1), 48–64.

Bongey, S. B., Cizaldo, G., & Kalnbach, L. (2010). Blended solutions: Using a supplemental online course site to deliver universal design for learning (UDL). *Emerald Group Publishing Limited, 27*(1), 4–16. doi:10.1108/10650741011011246

Burgstahler, S. (2015a). *Equal access: Universal design of instruction.* Seattle: University of Washington. Retrieved from http://www.washington.edu/doit/equal-access-universal-design-instruction

Catalano, A. (2014). Improving distance education for students with special needs: A qualitative study of students' experiences with an online library research course. *Journal of Library & Information Services in Distance Learning, 8*, 17–31. doi:10.1080/1533290X.2014.902416

Center for Applied Special Technology (CAST) (2012). *Universal Design for Learning Guidelines—Version 2.0.* Retrieved from http://www.udlcenter.org/aboutudl/udlguidelines

Center for Universal Design (CUD). (1997). *The principles of universal design.* Raleigh: North Carolina State University. Retrieved from http://www.ncsu.edu/ncsu/design/cud/about_ud/udprinciples text.htm

Cook, L., Rumrill, P. D., & Tankersley, M. (2009). Priorities and understanding of faculty members regarding college students with disabilities. *International Journal of Teaching and Learning in Higher Education, 21*(1), 84–96.

Courey, S. J., Tappe, P., Siker, J., & LePage, P. (2013). Improved lesson planning with universal design for learning (UDL). *Teacher Education and Special Education, 36*(1), 7–27.

Dallas, B. K., Sprong, M. E., & Upton, T. D. (2014). Post-secondary faculty attitudes toward inclusive teaching strategies. *Journal of Rehabilitation, 80*(2), 12–20.

Davies, P. L., Schelly, C. L., & Spooner, C. L. (2013). Measuring the effectiveness of universal design for learning intervention in postsecondary education. *Journal of Postsecondary Education and Disability, 26*(3), 195–220.

Disabilities, Opportunities, Internetworking, and Technology Center (DO-IT). (n.d.). *DO-IT.* Retrieved from http://www.washington.edu/doit/

Evans, C., Williams, J. B., King, L., & Metcalf, D. (2010). Modeling, guided instruction, and application of UDL in a rural special education teacher preparation program. *Rural Special Education Quarterly, 29*(4), 41–48.

Frey, T. J., Andres, D.K., McKeeman, L. A., & Lane, J. J. (2012). Collaboration by design: Integrating core pedagogical content and special education methods courses in a preservice secondary education program. *The Teacher Educator, 47*, 45–66.

Ginsberg, S. M., & Schulte, K. (2008). Instructional accommodations: Impact of conventional vs. social constructivist view of disability. *Journal of the Scholarship of Teaching and Learning, 8*(2), 84–91.

He, Y. (2014). Universal design for learning in an online teacher education course: Enhancing learners' confidence to teach online. *MERLOT Journal of Online and Teaching, 10*(2), 283–298.

Higbee, J. L. (2009). Implementing universal instructional design in postsecondary courses and curricula. *Journal of College Teaching and Learning, 6*(8), 65–77.

Higher Education Research Institute. (2006). *The American freshman, forty-year trends: 1966–2006.* Los Angeles: University of California, Los Angeles, Graduate School of Education & Information Studies.

Izzo, M. V., Murray, A., & Novak, J. (2008). The faculty perspective on universal design for learning. *Journal of Postsecondary Education and Disability, 21*(2), 60–72.

Kumar, K. & Wideman, M. (2014). Accessible by design: Applying UDL principles in a first year undergraduate course. *Canadian Journal of Higher Education, 44*(1), 125–147.

Lombardi, A. R., & Murray, C. (2011). Measuring university faculty attitudes toward disability: Willingness to accommodate and adopt Universal Design principles. *Journal of Vocational Rehabilitation, 34*, 43–56. doi:10.3233/JVR-2010-0533

McGhie-Richmond, D., & Sung, A. N. (2013). Applying Universal Design for Learning to instructional lesson planning. *International Journal of Whole Schooling, 9*(1), 43–59.

McGuire-Schwartz, M. E., & Arndt, J. S. (2007). Transforming universal design for learning in early childhood teacher education from college classroom to early childhood classroom. *Journal of Early Childhood Teacher Education, 28*(2), 127–139.

Moon, N. W, Utschig, T. T., Todd, R. L., & Bozzorg, A. (2011). Evaluation of programmatic interventions to improve postsecondary STEM education for students with disabilities: Findings from Sci-Train University. *Journal of Postsecondary Education and Disability, 24*(4), 331–349.

Parker, D. R., Robinson, L. E., & Hannafin, R. D. (2007-2008, Winter). "Blending" technology and effective pedagogy in a core course for preservice teachers. *Journal of Computing in Teacher Education, 24*(2), 61–66.

Ragpot, L. (2011). Assessing student learning by way of drama and visual art: A semiotic mix in a course on cognitive development. *Education As Change, 15*(S1), S63–S78.

Rao, K., & Tanners, A. (2011). Curb cuts in cyberspace: Universal instructional design for online courses. *Journal of Postsecondary Education and Disability, 24*(3), 211–229.

Roberts, K. D., Park, H. J., Brown, S., & Cook, B. (2011). Universal design for instruction in postsecondary education: A systematic review of empirically based articles. *Journal of Postsecondary Education and Disability, 24*(1), 4–14.

Schelly, C.L., Davies, P. L., & Spooner, C. L. (2011). Student perceptions of faculty implementation of universal design for learning. *Journal of Postsecondary Education and Disability, 24*(1), 17–30.

Seok, S., Kinsell, C., DaCosta, B., & Tung, C. K. (2010). Comparison of instructors' and students' perceptions of the effectiveness of online courses. *The Quarterly Review of Distance Education, 11*(1), 25–36.

Simonchelli, A., & Hinson, J. M. (2008). College students' with learning disabilities personal reactions to online learning. *Journal of College Research and Learning, 38*(2), 49–62.

Smith, F. G. (2012). Analyzing a college course that adheres to the universal design for learning (UDL) framework. *Journal of the Scholarship of Teaching and Learning, 12*(3), 31–61.

Spooner, F., Baker, J. N., Harris, A. A., Ahlgrim-Delzell, L., & Browder, D. M. (2007). Effects of training in universal design for learning on lesson plan development. *Remedial and Special Education, 28*(2), 108–116. doi:10.1177/07419325070280020101

Theoharis, G., & Causton-Theoharis, J. (2011). Preparing pre-service teachers for inclusive classrooms: Revising lesson-planning expectations. *International Journal of Inclusive Education, 15*(7), 743–761.

Tzivinikou, S. (2014). Universal design for learning—application in higher education: A Greek paradigm. *Problems of Education in the 21st Century, 60*, 156–166.

Williams, J., Evans, C., & King, L. (2012). The impact of universal design for learning instruction on lesson planning. *The International Journal of Learning, 18*(4), 213–222.

Zhang, Y. (2005). A collaborative professional development model: Focusing on universal design for technology utilization. *ERS Spectrum, 23*(3), 32–38.

Zhong, Y. (2012). Universal design for learning (UDL) in library instruction. *College & Undergraduate Libraries, 19*, 33–45. doi:10.1080/10691316.2012.652549

4

Universal Design for Learning in Postsecondary Education
Reflections on Principles and Their Application

Jenna W. Gravel
Laura A. Edwards
Christopher J. Buttimer
David H. Rose

Written by the teaching staff of the course T-560: Meeting the Challenge of Individual Differences, at the Harvard Graduate School of Education, this chapter reflects on potential applications of universal design for learning (UDL) in university courses, illustrating major points with examples. The authors emphasize the ongoing developmental nature of the course and the UDL principles as tools or guidelines for postsecondary faculty, rather than a set of definitive rules. UDL is proposed as a way to address diversity and disabilities in higher education classrooms by shifting the burden of being flexible and responsive from the student to the curriculum.

The first version of this chapter, published in 2008, was written by the teaching staff of a university course at Harvard's Graduate School of Education (Rose, Harbour, Johnston, Daley, & Abarbanell, 2008). Six years later, most of that staff have earned their doctorates and are now teaching and researching in ways that advance the field of universal design for learning (Wendy Harbour teaches at Syracuse; Sam Johnston and Sami Daley are both exemplary researchers and developers at the Center for Applied Special Technology [CAST]). But in 2008, this teaching team considered themselves very much novices in the application of UDL at the postsecondary level. And they were not alone in that regard. Although the UDL framework was already familiar to many educators in K–12 education, its application to higher education had not gathered much momentum.

Six years later, the entire teaching staff has changed (with the exception of Rose), and there are new authors for this updated version (Gravel, Edwards, and Buttimer). As we updated this chapter for the present edition, we found that there are many other changes. For one thing, there is much wider interest in UDL at the college and university level. Some of that new interest stems from the Higher Education Act of 2010, which first defined and recommended the practice of UDL for college and university faculty. Another important stimulant was the emergence of innovative and thoughtful faculty in various university campuses, who are bringing UDL to a much wider postsecondary audience (UDL on Campus, n.d.).

There is an additional aspect that has changed: the course itself. In this chapter, we will concentrate on some of the newer practices that have changed our teaching (happily) over the last couple of years. Our course is still far from exemplary, but it is getting better as we more consistently apply UDL principles to our own practice. In what follows, we will attempt to illustrate the principles of UDL through progress in our own course, and we thankfully acknowledge that we have learned a great deal from others in this field.

For those not yet familiar with the UDL framework, we recommend *Universal Design for Learning: Theory and Practice* (Meyer, Rose, & Gordon, 2014). It is available in multiple print and online versions, the latter entirely free of charge. That book, like UDL itself, is a specialized application of the broad approach of universal design. What differentiates UDL from universal design in general is its focus specifically on learning and teaching (rather than accessibility, for example). Because of that focus, the UDL framework is based upon advances in two fields: the learning sciences (especially modern cognitive neuroscience) and the use of modern networked learning technologies.

There are three principles that underlie UDL in practice:

- provide multiple means of representation;
- provide multiple means of action and expression; and
- provide multiple means of engagement.

Each of these principles is expressed in three research-based guidelines that can be viewed in Figure 4.1.

THE APPLICATIONS OF UDL IN A UNIVERSITY COURSE

In this section we describe our semester-long course called T-560: Meeting the Challenge of Individual Differences, offered at the Harvard Graduate School of Education (HGSE). In the 2014 academic year, forty-seven graduate students were registered (mostly education master's students). The students who take the course are diverse in background and interests, and a significant number have cross-registered from other colleges (e.g., law, public health) or other universities (e.g., the Massachusetts Institute of Technology). In general, however, the majority of students come from three areas within HGSE: human development (especially those interested in mind, brain, and education), technology in education, and teaching and curriculum development.

FIGURE 4.1 CAST's Universal Design for Learning Guidelines

I. Provide Multiple Means of **Representation**	II. Provide Multiple Means of **Action and Expression**	III. Provide Multiple Means of **Engagement**
1: Provide options for perception 1.1 Offer ways of customizing the display of information 1.2 Offer alternatives for auditory information 1.3 Offer alternatives for visual information	4: Provide options for physical action 4.1 Vary the methods for response and navigation 4.2 Optimize access to tools and assistive technologies	7: Provide options for recruiting interest 7.1 Optimize individual choice and autonomy 7.2 Optimize relevance, value, and authenticity 7.3 Minimize threats and distractions
2: Provide options for language, mathematical expressions, and symbols 2.1 Clarify vocabulary and symbols 2.2 Clarify syntax and structure 2.3 Support decoding of text, mathematical notation, and symbols 2.4 Promote understanding across languages 2.5 Illustrate through multiple media	5: Provide options for expression and communication 5.1 Use multiple media for communication 5.2 Use multiple tools for construction and composition 5.3 Build fluencies with graduated levels of support for practice and performance	8: Provide options for sustaining effort and persistence 8.1 Heighten salience of goals and objectives 8.2 Vary demands and resources to optimize challenge 8.3 Foster collaboration and community 8.4 Increase mastery-oriented feedback
3: Provide options for comprehension 3.1 Activate or supply background knowledge 3.2. Highlight patterns, critical features, big ideas, and relationships 3.3 Guide information processing, visualization, and manipulation 3.4 Maximize transfer and generalization	6: Provide options for executive functions 6.1 Guide appropriate goal-setting 6.2 Support planning and strategy development 6.3 Facilitate managing information and resources 6.4 Enhance capacity for monitoring progress	9: Provide options for self-regulation 9.1 Promote expectations and beliefs that optimize motivation 9.2 Facilitate personal coping skills and strategies 9.3 Develop self-assessment and reflection
Resourceful, knowledgeable learners	**Strategic, goal-directed learners**	**Purposeful, motivated learners**

Source: CAST (2011). *Universal design for learning guidelines version 2.0.* Wakefield, MA: Author.

Many students interested in disabilities and special education also take the course, although there are (unfortunately) no particular degree programs or concentrations in those subjects at Harvard University.

In previous years, enrollment for this course typically soared to close to one hundred students, an enrollment that is quite large for HGSE. This large class size presented several challenges to the teaching team. We struggled to develop the necessary individual relationships with students that make the learning process meaningful. Further, the course was confined to one of the few spaces on campus that could accommodate our high enrollment, an auditorium-style classroom. The layout of this room is designed for lecture-based classes and offers little flexibility for collaborative work. Each semester, these challenges troubled us. On the one hand, we wanted to enroll as many students as possible in an effort to support students' understanding of diverse learners and to grow the field of UDL. On the other hand, we felt as though the large class size limited our flexibility and our ability to effectively model UDL through the design of the course. We began to acknowledge that our reliance on lecture stood in stark contrast to the kinds of instructional practices we were advocating.

Thus, in the 2012–2013 academic year, we made a drastic change. After ten years of unlimited enrollment, we capped the course at fifty students. We hoped that this more intimate class size would provide us the freedom to begin reenvisioning the course: to design new scaffolds for developing relationships among and between students and the teaching team, to move away from our overreliance on a lecture format, and to develop a learning environment that more actively encouraged students to construct their own knowledge, collaborate, create, and reflect. We hope that this opportunity to experiment with different pedagogical approaches within a smaller class size will ultimately allow us to expand the course again as we gain skills and confidence in our approach.

It has only been two years since we made this sweeping change, and the course is still very much in experimental mode. We are continually learning from our successes and failures and working together to develop ways to make improvements. Thus, we acknowledge that T-560 is not a perfect demonstration of UDL. Many aspects of the course would fail to meet any standard for UDL. Like UDL itself, the course is a work in progress, not a destination. We offer our observations merely as travelers on a journey, and we look forward to your suggestions as fellow travelers. Furthermore, we encourage readers not to take our observations as rules or steps to follow. UDL emerges differently in different contexts. The ideas here are a set of starter tools, not a complete vision, and we expect to learn a great deal as we travel ahead and incorporate additional advice, research, and experiences.

Goals of T-560

The largely implicit goal of T-560 has been to teach information and ideas about applying cognitive and affective neuroscience to the education of diverse students. Its methods in the past were primarily traditional, including lectures and readings that were selected to transfer facts and ideas from the instructor and authors to eager (and sometimes not so eager) students.

Over time, especially over the past two years, the course content migrated somewhat, as did its instructional methods, and finally its goals. The teaching team has continuously collaborated to ensure that the principles and practices associated with UDL are reflected in the design of the course itself. The current course description reads as follows:

> The challenge and opportunity of individual differences confront every teacher, administrator, and curriculum designer. To meet that challenge and to capitalize on that opportunity, educators are typically equipped with media and materials that are "one size fits all" and that have been designed primarily for a narrow and elusive group of "regular" students. In this course, we will explore an alternative approach—universal design for learning (UDL)—that creates curricula and learning environments that are designed to achieve success for a much wider range of student abilities and disabilities. To do that, the UDL approach takes advantage of advances in two fields: (1) the cognitive neuroscience of learning and individual differences and (2) the universal design of educational technologies and multimedia. This course will explore recent advances in both of these fields through appropriate readings and through media construction exercises designed to prepare and support participants to optimize the challenge of individual differences through universal design for learning.

With this basic information about the outline of the course, it is instructive to consider its goals from a UDL perspective, including consideration of three aspects of the goals following the three primary principles of UDL.

First, there is the obvious goal: teaching *content*. In our case, the core content is the principles and practices of UDL but also includes foundational knowledge about cognitive and affective neuroscience, learning in the brain, individual differences in the way our brains learn, as well as the limits and strengths of various educational media for teaching and the ways in which they can be individualized. This goal of developing students' understanding has remained fairly consistent over the last decade; however, the ways in which we aim to meet this goal have changed. The first principle of UDL reminds us that content must be represented in multiple ways in order for learning goals to be achieved for a wide range of students. Thus, we have worked as a team to more fully incorporate this principle into the design of the course through new methods that will be described shortly.

Second, the UDL framework reminds us that it is not enough for students simply to acquire information; they must also have some way to express and to reflect upon what they have learned and some way to apply that information as usable knowledge. Only in its expression is knowledge made useful. Thus, the goals for the course must have an expressive component: students must know how to apply the information they have learned in authentic settings, including the kinds of work they will likely perform during their lives ahead. The second principle reminds us that there must be multiple means for expressing their knowledge. Offering multiple means of action and expression has been a strength of the course over the years; yet, as described below, we have recently refined this goal so as to include an even richer array of options for students to act on and to express their learning.

Third, the UDL framework reminds us that there is an affective component to reaching any goal. While the explicit goals of a course tend to focus on the first two principles—the knowledge students will learn and the skills to express that knowledge—the third is even more critical. Students will never use knowledge they do not care about, nor will they practice or apply skills they do not find valuable. Therefore, the course also has an affective goal. Certainly we want students to be motivated and engaged fully in learning the content, but we also want them to be eager to apply what they know and to leave the course wanting to learn even more. In the past, we felt that this affective goal was the weakest aspect of the course. As members of the teaching staff, we have always informally assessed student engagement through observation during classes and discussions, through a mid-semester survey, as well as through formal written course evaluations mandated by HGSE. Yet ongoing evaluation of engagement and motivation was a continual challenge. As noted above, we felt that we fell short in developing meaningful relationships with many students in the course. We also fell short in encouraging students to develop meaningful relationships with one another. Further, we believed that we could do more in terms of supporting students to become more self-reflective—to more proactively assess their learning, their confusions, and their motivations. When redesigning the course, we challenged ourselves to confront these weaknesses associated with the affective goal. Although we have certainly not fully addressed all of the challenges posed by this goal, we feel that we have come closer by applying the new pedagogical approaches described below.

Lectures and Their Alternatives: The Universal Design for Learning Perspective

One of the most obvious changes in the last two years has been a reduction in the centrality of lectures as the core of teaching the course. Classes used to meet once a week for two or three hours where the main activity for students was listening to a lecture. (An additional discussion section, often optional, met once a week.)

There are many reasons that lectures still dominate university teaching in general and the previous design of our course in particular. And, to be honest, the lectures were very popular—they were the reason that most students took the course. Done well, lectures capture the enormous expressive power of the human voice, and optimize the social cohesion of group storytelling. But lectures have very significant limitations as an instructional medium for most students, and especially significant limitations, even barriers, for others.

For some students (especially those who are deaf, who have specific weaknesses in language processing, or who are English language learners) lectures are largely inaccessible in their raw form. For many others they raise barriers stemming principally from high demands on linguistic and cognitive abilities, including memory, attention, and the amount of background knowledge they assume. These inherent barriers pushed us to move away from the lecture format and to diversify the pedagogical approaches used in the course. Now, we use lecture (usually thirty to forty minutes) only as a way to "kick off" the class. Typically, the purpose of this introductory lecture is to stimulate engagement, to highlight critical challenges or obstacles, to provide necessary background knowledge, to demonstrate models or best practices, and to prepare students for turning their knowledge into action. Yet we are fully aware that this lecture, abbreviated as it may be, still presents barriers to learners. Therefore, we continue to draw from the multiple strategies that we have used in the past to overcome the limitations and differential demands that lectures present, as we will now describe.

First, in recognition of the first principle of UDL, we give alternative representations of the lectures. Several types of options are provided, differing in the kinds of problems they seek to address, the ease of implementation, and the kinds of technologies they require (from no-tech to high-tech). For example, the lecture's content is made available in alternate sensory modalities. The speaker verbally describes any visuals, and the university provides sign language interpreters whenever there is a student or teaching fellow who is deaf in the class. Good interpreters capture not only the semantics of what they hear but also—through body movements, facial expressions, and gestures—the affect and stress.

Second, we video-record each lecture in its entirety and post that video on the course website, where it can be accessed at any time. This recording of the lecture is much more accessible than the live version for many students. Students for whom English is a second language or who have a language-based disability, for example, find the video version superior because it can be reviewed to fill in gaps, stopped and started to repeat difficult segments, and even replayed in its entirety. For students with attentional weaknesses, the online video presentation is helpful because it allows them to segment the larger whole of the lecture into manageable chunks. In truth, however, the lecture videos are not used that much by the typical student in T-560. They are important for a very few students (including students who miss class) but are far too time-consuming, low in quality, and passive for most. It is interesting and important to note, for example, that in spite of all lectures being available online (and thus very convenient for viewing at any time and any place), students overwhelmingly come to class anyway.

Third, and perhaps most interestingly, we collect student notes from the lecture and display them for everyone in the course. This may seem both time-consuming and redundant, especially in light of the online video availability, but we have found this simple technique to be enormously beneficial and a wonderful example of the unexpected advantages of universal design for learning. While it is possible to have volunteers or paid note takers as an accommodation for students with disabilities, we have found these unsatisfactory in many instructive ways. In brief, "professional" note takers are typically first-time students in the course, and their own skills at making sense of the content are highly variable. Since their background knowledge, interests, and learning preferences often differ considerably from the student for whom they are taking notes, paid or volunteer note takers' notes are often poorly aligned to the student's needs. Instead, we have hit on a very simple alternative. Each week, several students (in our case, two or three per lecture) volunteer to take notes on the lecture, including whatever discussion happens. The volunteers then post their notes on the social networking platform that we use for the course, making the notes available to everyone, regardless of their disability or lack thereof. Though the notes are not graded, they are included as part of a student's participation in the course.

There are several unexpected benefits of this note-taking process. First, the notes are more universally designed than the lecture itself; that is to say, different students capture and express very different content from the lecture, and they represent it in very different ways. In addition, despite being ungraded, students are highly engaged with the notes, responding to student notes through the course's online social networking platform and using them as examples during class lecture. The variance in T-560 notes is astonishing. Some students post notes that are almost perfect linear outlines of the lecture. Some of these notes are very short and succinct with bullet outlines only, while others are much longer, more expressive, and expansive. Others are different in kind. For example, some students do not outline the talk at all and are much more anecdotal than taxonomic, capturing more of the stories of the lecture than its structure. That is only the beginning of the variation. Some students take very graphic notes instead of ones that rely primarily on text. Their notes range from doodles that accompany text, to heavy use of illustration and visual highlighting that clarify and connect parts of the text, to notes that are literally superimposed on the PowerPoint slides of the lecture, to full-scale visual representations of the main ideas and concepts in the lecture that have almost no words, just labels. The latter are often a big hit with other students who immediately find these notes a strong complement to the outline view.

A second benefit derives from the public posting of these notes. Students, seemingly already engaged with the notes, recognize that their notes are about to become public to their peers. As a result, they often enhance the notes in various ways: by bringing in additional information, commentary, or questions; adding images or drawings; adding multimedia (like video or sound); or preparing the notes in a particularly cogent and clear way. We have never requested this kind of enhancement. Instead, there is a natural contagion of enthusiasm among the note takers, who view notes from the previous lecture as a way of preparing to take their own. In fact, they learn to take better notes by informally mentoring each other.

Last, the point of universal design quickly becomes clear to every student, as the kinds of notes they take and what they learn from a given lecture often differ greatly from those of their classmates. Even though the lecture ostensibly conveys the exact same content for all students, its reception is highly variable; students perceive, understand, and prioritize their learning in a range of ways. This diversity is often especially interesting (and a big relief) to students who have been told they cannot take notes because of a disability (e.g., having a learning disability or brain injury, being deaf or hard of hearing). Though they may initially dread this aspect of the course because of preexisting beliefs about what constitutes good or acceptable notes, they often quickly realize that their notes will be as good as their classmates' notes. Years ago, one student told a T-560 teaching fellow that she felt more like a true member of the class, learned a lot about herself, and gained new insights into her learning disability and what it meant for her learning, simply because of the T-560 note-taking system.

Thus far we have talked about three different representations of the lecture: an alternative sensory presentation, like American Sign Language; a reviewable alternative in the form of online videos; and multiple notes shared among students. There are actually many other ways to provide alternative means of support within a lecture; PowerPoint slides that use visuals (rather than text) are often a vital way to offer students alternate representations that emphasize structure, proportion, relationships, and emphasis while providing explicit landmarks to guide students in the overall progress of the lecture.

These and other means are used to make lectures more accessible to a wide variety of students. But none of these alternatives actually address a more general problem: the weaknesses of lectures as a medium for learning. While lectures are often entertaining, illuminating, and engaging, they privilege passive information transfer over active and constructive learning. As a result, they are good for some kinds of learning, but not for others. In T-560, the weaknesses of lectures became more and more apparent as we migrated from a course *about* learning and its differences to a course about *doing* or practicing UDL—designing multimedia curricula for all students, teaching in classrooms where there is a wide range of individual differences, and creating schools that optimize rather than minimize learner variability. To prepare students for *doing* these kinds of things, lectures are not a particularly effective medium. More than anything, that realization changed the ways in which we use lectures in T-560.

During the last two years, lectures have been drastically reduced in favor of "hands-on and minds-on" activities where students are actively engaged in designing or creating artifacts that express and activate what they are learning. As noted above, each class typically begins with a thirty- to forty-minute lecture. Following that mini-lecture, students adjourn to a different space, which we refer to as "the lab," for collaborative work rather than listening to a lecture. Here they engage—in teams—in one or more structured and scaffolded activities related to the topic of the day. Those activities give them a chance—with supervision—to put their learning into practice and to evaluate what they know and can do. Support is provided by the teaching team (all of us) and by colleagues in their particular working groups. Often the group work is interrupted by a brief demonstration or mini-lecture that seems particularly relevant to their work or provides an opportunity to challenge or support students in deepening their practice. After a couple hours of such guided and mentored activities—including breaks—the group as a whole is reconvened in the lecture hall in order to reflect on what we have learned (or failed to learn).

For example, one day the class focused on how to prepare texts that would address common linguistic barriers. The lecture focused on recent work in the cognitive science of reading comprehension and what kinds of language impediments and barriers interfere with comprehension across a range of individual differences and disabilities. Following the lecture, the students travelled to the lab where teams were given a specific passage of text and were asked to analyze its "readability." (Web-based readability checkers were identified and demonstrated for their use.) After comparing different tools for readability measurement, the teams were asked to discuss and to summarize what they learned by comparing different automated readability checkers.

Following that, they were asked to work as teams to "reduce" the readability demands of the passage as much as they could by making only seven changes in the text. Repeated measurement allowed them to independently monitor their own progress in reducing text complexity but also to understand the key elements of what makes passages difficult to comprehend (at least as measured by these instruments). Once the teams had finished their analyses (and the competition for most effective alteration of readability) and compared their results and observations, we adjourned back to the lecture hall to discuss and reflect on what all the groups had learned about how to manipulate (and how *not* to manipulate) the demands of text complexity for readers. The class concluded with a whole-class reflection on their observations during lab. Especially important were their observations about the limitations of this kind of formulaic "reduction" in text complexity—and why UDL typically avoids such "dumbing down" of texts in favor of approaches that "smarten up" texts by providing helpful alternatives (like voice-assisted reading or embedded vocabulary definitions) instead.

That is roughly how classes have been conducted over the last two years.

Textbooks and Universal Design for Learning

Printed books and other texts are not a promising foundation for UDL because they are inherently inflexible. The product of mass production, books are designed with a uniform display and identical content for every student. Print is a technology that is particularly difficult to modify to meet the needs of many students with disabilities. As a result, books as they are presently delivered create barriers rather than opportunities for many students. Nevertheless, they are popular in universities (and we like them for their virtues, not their liabilities), so in T-560 we use books. For the most part, we use books in typical ways, but not in uniform ways.

This year, for example, we had a brand new textbook to use: *Universal Design for Learning: Theory and Practice* (Meyer, Rose, & Gordon, 2014). This book comes in multiple versions. There is a traditional print version available at the bookstore and library. But the "native version" of the book was created, and delivered, digitally. That native book has many UDL features inherent in its design (e.g., all of the text reads itself aloud; there are embedded videos throughout; there are many options for display, for differential content, and for vocabulary and comprehension supports). There is an especially accessible version online, best for students with visual disabilities, now also in EPUB 3 format. For some students, the print version is more convenient, more readable in the long run, and more familiar. Many of the students in this class are adult graduate students, immigrants to the land of digital books instead of natives. However, many other students, not just those with disabilities, choose to read the UDL version entirely online. These students, including those with dyslexia or those who are blind, for example, do not find that the print version is more convenient, more readable, or more comfortable. For them, it is much better to read the book online using a talking browser. Other students, like those with attention deficit disorder (ADD) or attention deficit/hyperactivity disorder (ADHD) and/or those who are computer-savvy, prefer the online book because they enjoy exploring the format, especially embedded links, which foster connections to relevant material that may not be as easy to access through a print version. One student reported that he never read any of the text, but chose to access the book's content entirely through the embedded videos.

What was most interesting this year was the large number of students who used multiple versions; that is, they bought the print version and used it some of the time, but used one of the digital versions at other times and for other purposes. UDL works at the individual level as well!

But not all of the readings for T-560 are available in such accessible versions yet. As a result, some students still approach the disability services office to scan the printed books into digital versions that they can use. This is an unfortunate, time-consuming, and expensive workaround to overcome the limitations of print, but our course demands much less of these services as more of our readings are available with proper options. One thing that has worked in our favor is that course readings are increasingly available online, where they are usually natively much more accessible (and handy). In 2004, the U.S. Department of Education endorsed, both houses of Congress passed, and President Bush approved a revision of the Individuals with Disabilities Education Act (IDEA) that included a new policy: the National Instructional Materials Accessibility Standard (NIMAS). NIMAS stipulates that publishers must provide a digital source file of their printed textbooks to a national repository at the time print versions are distributed. Furthermore, states must distribute accessible versions of those source files to their students in a timely fashion. NIMAS is valuable because it specifies the format (an XML base with DAISY tags) in which those textbooks must be provided. This makes it vastly faster and easier to generate many types of accessible and digital versions, and the format is consistent for all publishers and for all states and districts.

Officially, NIMAS applies only to preschool, elementary, and secondary education. However, the popularity of NIMAS among states and publishers alike has led many colleges and state systems, as well as publishers, to consider adopting the NIMAS standard for postsecondary use as well. Although these ideas have yet to be implemented in any formal or systemic way, we believe that there will be readily available textbooks in both print and digitally accessible versions in the near future. One important advancement at HGSE has been the provision of course readings in digital as well as printed versions.

Social Networking and Universal Design for Learning

Text and textbooks are a limited presentation medium. In the T-560 course, we try to include a richer set of media as alternatives. The simplest expansion of media comes from using the Web as a tool for both course organization and as an alternative means of class participation.

In the most recent iterations of T-560, all course-related online activity took place on a private social networking platform, Ning. For the purposes of course organization, Ning serves as a frame that holds the syllabus, assignment deadlines and instructions, class videos, student-submitted class notes, PowerPoint slides for lectures, and other relevant resources, such as model assignments from past years or links to related web materials. The use of an interactive website has several obvious advantages over traditional paper syllabi; a multimedia syllabus contains not only the text readings for the week but also the websites and other media resources, all available for easy access through simple clicks of a mouse. Students may also use the course website to navigate seamlessly between core course materials and external websites that contain additional representations of the topic for the week or scaffolds and supports for student learning.

As an example, one of the course mini-lectures draws heavily on understanding optical illusions. While there are typical examples of illusions in the textbooks, there are several extraordinary websites devoted entirely to understanding illusions. These websites have extensive collections with accompanying explanations. Moreover, the range of illusions is far more comprehensive and dramatic than those available in print. For example, illusions of movement or sound cannot be captured in text. During the mini-lecture, which is always done with a live connection to the Web, some of the more dramatic illusions are exhibited and discussed; students may easily navigate to these resources via the syllabus or PowerPoint slides on the course website if they wish to view the illusions on their own computers, or explore further examples at their own pace before, during, or after class. Additionally, digital presentation of typically paper-based materials, such as the course syllabus, enables our diverse students to access the course content and information in the formats that are best suited to their needs (e.g., by utilizing a computer's text-to-speech, zooming, or color/contrast modification functions). Such uses of contemporary media in the course are mildly engaging for some students, but essential for relevance and comprehensive understanding for others, particularly those who were born in a different generation from their professors.

Beyond course organization, however, the use of a social networking platform as a course website enables class participation and resource sharing in a manner that is better aligned with the varied ways in which twenty-first-century individuals create and share knowledge. The Ning platform allowed student users to create profile pages to which they could link images, videos, blog posts, and other materials as a means of introducing themselves to other class members, organizing personal resources, and interacting around course topics at their own convenience. Rather than writing reading responses, students create weekly blog posts about the course materials that they explore, and they are able to learn from each other's work and learning processes by browsing relevant tags, topics, and profile pages. Teaching fellows and students can develop discussion groups and topic pages to share resources and to discuss subtopics of particular interest within the course. The use of a social networking platform also greatly facilitates organization and communication between class members who are working together on semester project assignments; group pages specific to these projects are used for student communication about the projects, as well as a venue for submitting multimedia deliverables. Students and teaching fellows can even create event pages to notify each other about relevant community events, and class members can indicate and coordinate attendance through these venues.

Despite all its advantages, the use of a social networking platform for class organization and communication is not without its drawbacks. Given the range of ages, generations, and experiences represented in a graduate-level course, some students have found the social networking component of the course forced and/or difficult to navigate. Given each student's ability to contribute to the online community of the course, the number of resources available for perusal can also quickly become overwhelming. A wealth of user-contributed resources may also distract from the main learning goals of the class, if not well moderated. Finally, despite the promise of digital platforms for enhancing the accessibility of material for a variety of learners, the specific platform used in T-560 has not functioned well with some common screen readers. Thus, in future iterations of the course, the teaching team plans to switch to a more accessible web platform, with tools that do a better job of organizing, customizing, and streamlining the information to which each end user is exposed. Additionally, while the population of students remains heterogeneous with regards to their degree of comfort with digital media, it might be necessary to continue to provide traditional alternatives or supplements to online materials and resources where possible.

Assessment and Scaffolding Methods for the Course

It is not enough, of course, to use the framework of UDL only when considering how to present and teach methods, information, or skills. It is also essential to consider UDL as a framework to guide the design of another critical element of instruction: assessment. In considering assessment, we will focus on two UDL principles: providing multiple means of action and expression and providing multiple means of engagement.

There are many assessment techniques, the choice of which should be aligned with and constrained by the goals of the course. In our course, we want to develop students who not only can recognize UDL in practice but can also express that knowledge in action. Whether they are designing a curriculum or workshop, choosing from among a number of available curricular options, or preparing to teach a single unit or lecture, we need to know whether they can effectively apply what they have learned. Is it usable knowledge? Administering multiple-choice tests or essay questions is not likely to be an adequate measure of those abilities, nor is writing a traditional paper about how they might apply what they have learned. Instead, we seek to create an opportunity for students to engage in extended apprenticeships—within a supportive community of practice—where members can build and test the knowledge and skills required for leadership in the growing field of UDL.

Two years ago, we decided to create an entirely new form of assessment for the course: a semester-long project that challenges students to collaborate, create, take risks, and reflect throughout the thirteen weeks of the course. We ask students to form teams of four to five members and to develop an educational intervention of their choice that supports robust disciplinary thinking within a particular content area *for all students*, including those students who have been typically underserved or marginalized in traditional educational environments. Dividing up responsibilities optimally, each team must work together to create a final product that consists of four interrelated parts: (1) a working prototype or highly detailed mock-up of the intervention; (2) a multimedia "brochure" or video that introduces the intervention and highlights the specific UDL features that are embedded into its design; (3) a research white paper that underscores the need for the intervention and provides the research and evidentiary basis for the inclusion of the specific UDL features; and (4) an implementation guide that provides a plan for effective integration into real settings and provides guidance, resources, and strategies for teachers, students, and parents. Over the past two years, there has been a remarkable diversity in terms of the content areas, the age ranges, and the contexts addressed by the teams' projects. Past projects range from an online platform designed to support religious educators in applying the principles of UDL, to a smartphone app to guide students and teachers in learning at Harvard's Museum of Natural History, to a UDL arts-focused day camp for kids.

Given the complexity of this project, we draw from the UDL principles of multiple means of action and expression and multiple means of engagement to offer a range of scaffolds to support both individual and team learning. First, we hold a "mixer" during the first class to support students in getting to know one another and in finding potential teammates. We also encourage students to use social media (again, we used Ning) as an additional way to connect with peers and to form teams made up of individuals with diverse areas of expertise—diverse enough to encompass all four deliverables of the semester project. Once teams are formed, each team is assigned a teaching fellow to serve as the team's "contact person" and to offer individualized support throughout the semester. We also provide numerous models of past projects, making sure to emphasize to the students that these "exemplars" are not meant to constrain their thinking but to inspire them as to the kinds of interventions that are possible. Finally, the semester project is "chunked" into a sequence of deliverables over the course of the semester that lead up to the final product. The first deliverable asks students to reflect on the barriers they have encountered in their own learning in order to begin brainstorming a potential intervention that will feel relevant and meaningful. The second deliverable asks teams to identify their top two ideas for an intervention. The third deliverable asks teams to submit a first draft of the project, and the fourth deliverable asks teams to submit a second draft that responds to advice and suggestions from their peers and their teaching fellow.

Each of these deliverables embeds options for action and expression as well as engagement. Teams have opportunities to express their ideas through multiple media; they can choose to develop the components of their projects using tools that range from PowerPoint, VoiceThread, or CAST's UDL BookBuilder to more complex tools such as Apple's development platform or XML Mastermind. The "chunking" nature of the deliverables also scaffolds teams' executive function by supporting planning and goal setting. Further, the series of deliverables offers the teaching team multiple opportunities to monitor and assess teams' progress along their path to their final product. Rubrics are used for the first and second drafts as well as for the final product to ensure that the learning goals and objectives are explicit and to provide teams with the feedback they need to challenge their thinking and to fully develop their ideas. After the submission of the second draft, teams are also paired up to engage in "consultation sessions" where one team presents their intervention and the other team offers feedback regarding its strengths and weaknesses. Yet, along with these numerous opportunities to receive feedback from the teaching team and from peers, we also embed opportunities for students to monitor and to reflect on their *own* learning as individuals and as teams. Therefore, along with the submission of the first draft, the second draft, and the final project, teams are asked to evaluate their work using the deliverable rubrics, and each team member is also asked to submit an individual reflection. The individual reflection prompt asks students to consider the aspects of the course and/or the project that are working well for them as well as the ways that the teaching team could better support their learning.

This semester-long project requires extensive collaboration and communication among group members. Much like the real world, teams consist of individuals who bring very different strengths (and even weaknesses) to the challenge. Therefore, we set out to scaffold not only the development of students' projects but also the development of students' teams. To do this, we used what we call the *group learning assessment rubric*. The goal of the group learning assessment rubric is to scaffold students throughout the *process* of working together in groups, which we believe leads to higher-quality final *products*. Two of the teaching fellows had taken Professor Richard Elmore's course at HGSE, Supporting Teachers for Instructional Improvement. In his class, students work in small groups throughout the semester, and they are given a rubric to assess and push their learning over time. The teaching fellows felt that the

Figure 4.2 One Team's Group Learning Assessment Rubric.

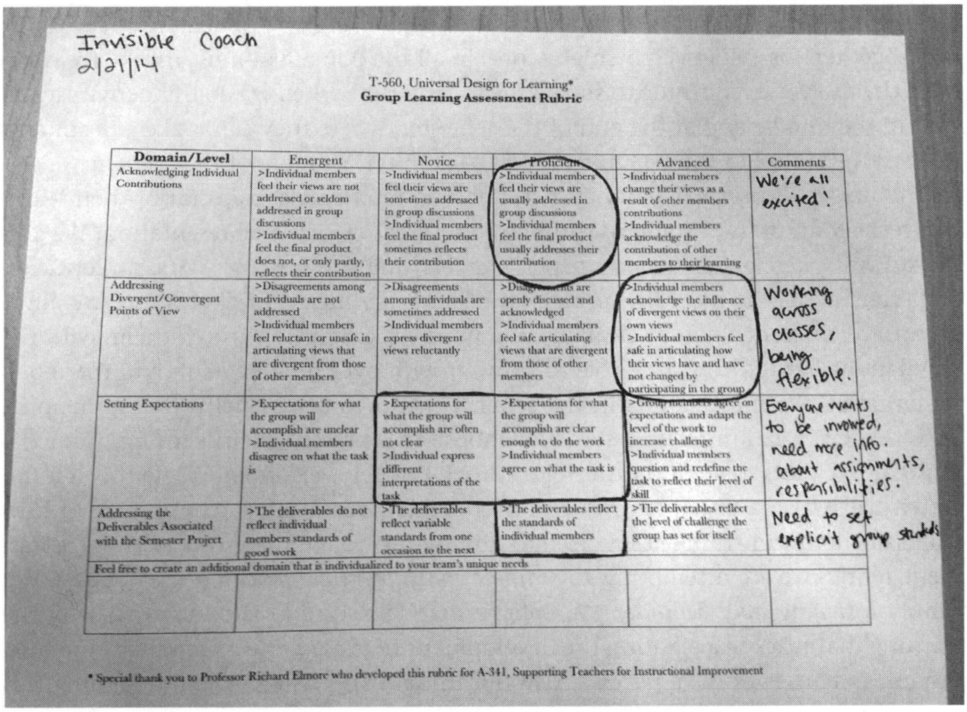

Invisible Coach
2/21/14

T-560, Universal Design for Learning*
Group Learning Assessment Rubric

Domain/Level	Emergent	Novice	Proficient	Advanced	Comments
Acknowledging Individual Contributions	>Individual members feel their views are not addressed or seldom addressed in group discussions >Individual members feel the final product does not, or only partly, reflects their contribution	>Individual members feel their views are sometimes addressed in group discussions >Individual members feel the final product sometimes reflects their contribution	>Individual members feel their views are usually addressed in group discussions >Individual members feel the final product usually addresses their contribution	>Individual members change their views as a result of other members contributions >Individual members acknowledge the contribution of other members to their learning	We're all excited!
Addressing Divergent/Convergent Points of View	>Disagreements among individuals are not addressed >Individual members feel reluctant or unsafe in articulating views that are divergent from those of other members	>Disagreements among individuals are sometimes addressed >Individual members express divergent views reluctantly	>Disagreements are openly discussed and acknowledged >Individual members feel safe articulating views that are divergent from those of other members	>Individual members acknowledge the influence of divergent views on their own views >Individual members feel safe in articulating how their views have and have not changed by participating in the group	Working across classes, being flexible.
Setting Expectations	>Expectations for what the group will accomplish are unclear >Individual members disagree on what the task is	>Expectations for what the group will accomplish are often not clear >Individual express different interpretations of the task	>Expectations for what the group will accomplish are clear enough to do the work >Individual members agree on what the task is	>Group members agree on expectations and adapt the level of the work to increase challenge >Individual members question and redefine the task to reflect their level of skill	Everyone wants to be involved, need more info. about assignments, responsibilities.
Addressing the Deliverables Associated with the Semester Project	>The deliverables do not reflect individual members standards of good work	>The deliverables reflect variable standards from one occasion to the next	>The deliverables reflect the standards of individual members	>The deliverables reflect the level of challenge the group has set for itself	Need to set explicit group standards
Feel free to create an additional domain that is individualized to your team's unique needs					

* Special thank you to Professor Richard Elmore who developed this rubric for A-341, Supporting Teachers for Instructional Improvement

Adapted from Professor Richard Elmore's Group Learning Assessment Rubric.

learning rubric in that class could be adapted to the new group learning format of T-560, and they reached out to Professor Elmore, who agreed to let them use it.

The group learning assessment rubric consists of four domains: (1) Acknowledging Individual Contributions; (2) Addressing Divergent/Convergent Points of View; (3) Setting Expectations; and (4) Addressing the Deliverables Associated with the Semester Project (R. H. Elmore, personal communication, January 30, 2013). We also provide space on the rubric for teams to create a fifth domain that can be individualized to their unique needs. In planning the course, the teaching team identifies three key points during the thirteen-week semester when teams will assess themselves using the rubric: shortly after teams form in Week 4, after the submission of the first draft in Week 6, and after the submission of the second draft in Week 9. During each of these weeks, teams are given forty-five minutes to take a snapshot of their learning as a group. Students score themselves on each of the domains using a four-point scale ranging from *emerging* (the lowest score) to *advanced* (the highest score).

The most important part of conducting the activity is to first ask students to individually assess how they think their teams have performed thus far using the rubric. Then, we ask students to come together as a group to discuss their scores and develop one consensus rubric. Because team members will likely have different scores in their individual assessments, they have to discuss and negotiate their scores for the consensus rubric, pointing to evidence and examples of work the team has done (or not) to justify their scores. This process often forces teams who are struggling with interpersonal tensions—tensions that exist in any group learning situation—to confront those issues, rather than allowing them to lay dormant until it is too late (e.g., a week before the project is due). On the other side of the spectrum, teams that start out working well together—as evidenced by high scores in all the domains—must think of ways to push themselves to continue to show growth over time when we do this activity again toward the middle and at the end of the semester, where they can make adjustments and strategize should they stagnate or fall back in one or more of the domains.

The final part of the activity asks students to represent a snapshot of their learning in the four (or five) domains through some form of visual representation. We give the students large pieces of chart paper, markers, and stickers (e.g., stars, smiley faces) and, consistent with the UDL principles of multiple means of expression, we allow groups to represent the four domains in any way that makes sense to them, with the stipulation that they must be able to show growth over time by adding to the representation at two more points in the semester. Also consistent with UDL principles, we see large variation in how students choose to represent their learning, from traditional X-Y plots to steps on the Yellow Brick Road, for example. While this is a fun activity, it is also a visual reminder to both students and the teaching team of how teams are doing and where they need to improve. Through the group learning assessment rubric, we are attempting to *scaffold and support group learning*, as opposed to simply *assigning group learning*. We believe that this scaffold is one reason why the learning that takes place during the development of these projects as well as the final products themselves have far exceeded our initial expectations when designing this assignment.

FIGURES 4.3, 4.4, & 4.5   Three Teams' Visual Representations of Their Learning at Different Points in the Semester. (Recreations of Student Work, Courtesy of the Authors.)

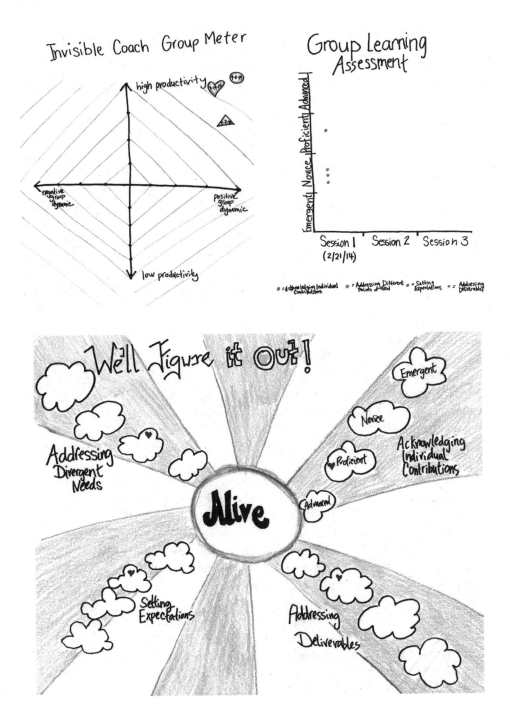

Affect and Engagement in T-560

From a UDL standpoint, there is a final concern: Does the course succeed affectively, engaging the students? Does it engage different kinds of students? Is that engagement sustained in changes in practice? Overall, there are indications that the course engages a reasonably broad range of students. For one thing, the course is quite popular. This is especially notable because it requires a considerable amount of work in difficult subjects, it is not required for any degree concentration, and there is no special education major at Harvard. What attracts students?

We believe that one of the significant attractions of the class is its attempt to respond to individual differences, providing multiple ways of presenting information and allowing students to respond. Of particular importance, especially for adult learners, is the ability to make choices (e.g., Cordova & Lepper, 1996). In the course, as we have noted, students experience choice in almost every arena: choices in the texts they read, the kinds of media they prefer to learn from, the media mix they use for their projects, the format for discussions, the amount of support they prefer, and the ways to interact with materials. For some students there are still too few choices, and for some there are too many. But overall, the very fact of choice is a tremendous source of attraction and motivation in the course.

There is a second way that choice is important: in terms of the faculty and teaching fellows. Because there are multiple means of interaction in the course, there are choices for the teaching team as well. Throughout the course, we emphasize the different areas in which we members of the teaching staff each have strengths and weaknesses (e.g., content areas, web design, pedagogical strategies). This *distributed intelligence* eliminates the onerous effects of having to be everything to everyone. It also models for students the value of collaborative teaching and learning. To some extent, the members of the teaching team choose the kinds of interactions with which they are most comfortable, and at times they choose situations in which they will be challenged to learn relatively new information or skills with the support of other instructional staff, placing them in the best positions to succeed and feel engaged.

However, given the inherent diversity among students and teaching team members in our course, it is not possible to successfully engage everyone all of the time. When poring over students' individual reflections, mid-semester surveys, and end-of-semester surveys, we inevitability find conflicting opinions. Some students relish the opportunity to post reflections on social media and comment on their peers' posts, while other students find the weekly posts forced and mechanical. Some students ask for more lecture time, while other students ask for more time engaged in the hands-on "labs." Some students appreciate the way in which the semester project rubrics clarify the goals and expectations, while other students feel as though the rubrics constrain their creativity. These conflicting opinions even exist among members of our teaching team. Some of us are concerned that we offer teams too much feedback and support on their semester projects, while others are concerned that we need to do more. Some of us contend that we need to integrate even more choice into the design of the course, while others warn that too much choice may feel overwhelming to students. Yet it is precisely this multiplicity of perspectives that makes the course the success that it is. This diversity of feedback among students and teaching team members pushes us to continually develop, test, balance, and refine new options and alternatives to embed into the design of the course in an effort to ensure that all of our learners find meaningful ways to engage in our semester-long journey together.

CONCLUSIONS AND RECOMMENDATIONS

As we look back at the previous version of this chapter, we recognize that there have been significant changes in the practices of this course, and we recognize that we have not come far enough. But we also recognize that there have been significant changes in our beliefs about the course and our students. In the earlier version there was a residual tendency to identify the "problems" we need to address as stemming from characteristics of the individuals in our course—problems that arise from the individual student's particular abilities and disabilities.

In the conclusion to that previous chapter, we attempted to "balance" that view by explicitly recognizing that the problems we were addressing stem not just from characteristics of individual students but also from characteristics of the environments in which they were required to learn. We concluded: "Right now, we believe that universities place too much emphasis on the disabilities in students and not enough on the disabilities in the learning environment. Accommodations and access issues are largely addressed on an individual basis rather than at the level of courses, departments, or universities" (Rose et al., 2008). This is still true, sadly.

Yet, after rereading the previous chapter in order to prepare this updated version, we feel uncomfortable with this "balanced" conclusion; this perspective continues to place *some* emphasis on the individual student. As our thinking about the course and about UDL in general has evolved over the past six years, we now find ourselves in favor of a much more aggressive, *unbalanced* stance: It is our learning environments, first and foremost, that are disabled. Addressing the disabilities in the learning environment is the proper and ethical approach that we as postsecondary educators must take. Only that approach will make courses that are better not just for students with disabilities, but for all students.

Finally, it is worth highlighting the increasing availability of resources for faculty interested in integrating UDL into their teaching practices. As noted in the introduction to this article, there are a number of faculty members at postsecondary institutions engaged in reenvisioning their courses through a UDL lens (including Emiliano Ayala at Sonoma State, Brett Christie in the California State System, Fran Smith at George Washington University, the STAR team of the University of North Carolina school system, Richard Jackson at Boston College, Matt Marino at the University of Central Florida, Maya Israel at the University of Illinois, and Jamie Basham at the University of Kansas). While they will each rightly have their unique take on how and where UDL might fit into their course design and instructional practice, a central resource for faculty to consult on UDL practices within higher education is now freely available to the field through the UDL on Campus website (UDL on Campus, n.d.), a website created by the Open Professionals Education Network with funding by the Bill & Melinda Gates Foundation.

REFERENCES

Cordova, D. I., & Lepper, M. R. (1996). Intrinsic motivation and the process of learning: Beneficial effects of contextualization, personalization, and choice. *Journal of Educational Psychology, 88*(4), 715–730.

Meyer, A., Rose, D. H., & Gordon, D. (2014). *Universal design for learning: Theory and practice.* Wakefield, MA: CAST Professional Publishing. Retrieved from http://udltheorypractice.cast.org (free registration required).

Rose, D. H., Harbour, W. S., Johnston, C. S., Daley, S. G., & Abarbanell, L. (2008). Universal design for learning in postsecondary education: Reflections on principles and their application. In S. Burgstahler & R. Cory (Eds.), *Universal design in higher education: From principles to practice* (pp. 45–59). Cambridge, MA: Harvard Education Press.

UDL on Campus. (n.d.). *Postsecondary Institutions with UDL Initiatives.* Retrieved from http://udloncampus.cast.org/page/policy_udl_initiatives

---

The earliest version of this chapter was published as Rose, D. H., Harbour, W. S., Johnston, C. S., Daley, S. G., & Abarbanell, L. (2006). Universal design for learning in postsecondary education: Reflections on principles and their application. *Journal of Postsecondary Education and Disability, 19*(2), 135–151.

5

The Faculty Perspective
Implementation of Universal Design in a First-Year Classroom

Jeanne L. Higbee

The author of this chapter illustrates the implementation of universal instructional design (UID) in a first-year experience course by providing specific examples of essential components, multiple formats for conveying information and assessing learning, and other principles of UID. Benefits and challenges for the faculty member are also addressed.

Universal instructional design (UID) (Bowe, 2000; Goff & Higbee, 2008a, 2008b; Higbee, 2003; Higbee & Goff, 2008; Silver, Bourke, & Strehorn, 1998) is a means for providing equity in access to higher education for all students by encouraging faculty to rethink their teaching practices to create curricula and courses that include all learners. Although initially many postsecondary educators perceived that the focus of UID was access for students with disabilities, the intent of this theoretical model is to consider all possible students who might be taking a course and then design the course accordingly. All students benefit. In implementation, as in theory, it becomes clear that when this approach to course development is taken, students from other historically underrepresented populations are also likely to experience a more welcoming learning environment (Higbee, 2009, 2014). Thus, UID has gradually gained notice as a tool for social justice and multicultural postsecondary education (Barajas & Higbee, 2003; Duranczyk & Higbee, 2012a; Duranczyk, Myers, Couillard, Schoen, & Higbee, 2013; Hackman & Rauscher, 2004; Higbee & Barajas, 2007; Higbee, Duranczyk, & Ghere, 2008; Johnson, 2004; Johnson & Fox, 2003). It is imperative that educators implementing UID consider the broad range and multiple intersections of students' diverse social identities rather than focusing only on disability. It is this notion of inclusion for all that prompted the use of the term *universal*. Within the context of UID, *universal* refers not to "one size fits all"; rather, it prompts universal access to learning for all students, including students with disabilities. The purpose of this chapter is to illustrate the implementation of UID in a first-year experience course, including the benefits for students as well as the rewards and challenges for the faculty member.

UNIVERSAL INSTRUCTIONAL DESIGN AS AN ALTERNATIVE TO INDIVIDUAL ACCOMMODATIONS

Research indicates that faculty members continue to perceive barriers to providing academic accommodations for students with disabilities. Particularly at research universities, where faculty are more likely to be rewarded for the quantity of their publications and grant income than the quality of their teaching, barriers have included lack of time, resources, and institutional support (Kalivoda, 2003; Smith, 1997). Some faculty members continue to express skepticism about the fairness of providing accommodations for students despite the documentation of their disabilities, especially when considering those that are hidden, such as psychological disabilities, attention deficit/hyperactivity disorder (ADHD), and learning disabilities (Kalivoda, 2003; Williams & Ceci, 1999). Rather than asking faculty to make exceptions for students with disabilities, UID proposes that strategies that might previously have been considered accommodations (e.g., extra time on tests) for students with disabilities are instead made available to all students. As a result, UID enables all students to learn more effectively and to earn grades that reflect their knowledge. Although implementing UID in a course may require additional planning time up front, often the outcome is a net savings of time for the faculty member because of the decrease in individual requests for accommodations by students with disabilities.

COMPONENTS OF UNIVERSAL INSTRUCTIONAL DESIGN

Components of UID, which are based on the work of Chickering and Gamson (1987), include (a) creating welcoming classrooms; (b) determining the essential components of a course; (c) communicating clear expectations; (d) providing constructive feedback; (e) exploring the use of natural supports for learning, including technology, to enhance opportunities for all learners; (f) designing teaching methods that consider diverse learning styles, abilities, ways of knowing, and previous experience and background knowledge; (g) creating multiple ways for students to demonstrate their knowledge; and (h) promoting interaction among and between faculty and students (Fox & Johnson, 2000; Opitz & Block, 2006). This chapter illustrates the implementation of each of these components in a course offered by the Department of Postsecondary Teaching and Learning (PSTL) at the University of Minnesota–Twin Cities, PSTL 1086: The First-Year Experience. Although PSTL 1086 has since been replaced by a first-year inquiry course (Lee, Williams, & Kiliberia, 2012; Lee, Williams, Shaw, & Jie, 2014) and a separate first-year experience course for student-athletes (Higbee & Schultz, 2012, 2013), many of the strategies implemented more than ten years ago are still in use.

In order to accommodate greater numbers of students, PSTL 1086 met for fifty minutes per week as a large lecture section facilitated by a tenured faculty member, and for one hundred minutes per week in small discussion sections of no more than twenty students facilitated by professional academic advisors. Thus, in describing UID implementation in PSTL 1086, this chapter can provide ideas for large lecture courses as well as more intimate learning settings.

Creating a Welcoming Classroom

Unfortunately, as at many large institutions, the lecture hall in which PSTL 1086 was typically taught did not necessarily convey the sense of a welcoming learning space to students as they entered. To assist in alleviating this barrier to effective teaching and learning, on the first day of lecture, the faculty member and advisors stood at the entrances to the lecture hall to welcome students as they came through the door and would continue to chat informally with students until it was time for class to start. This practice was particularly important for the tenured faculty member, who attended some—but not all—of the weekly discussion sections; it enabled her to address students by name, even when enrollments exceeded one hundred students. The class began with formal introductions of the teaching staff, including calling attention to e-mail addresses and phone numbers provided in the syllabus. Although the faculty member did not go over the syllabus point by point, she did call students' attention to important policies and procedures and "performed" (Pedelty, 2008) or read aloud the syllabus statement related to accommodations for students with disabilities. The following paragraph from the PSTL 1086 syllabus incorporated all the content of the institution's standard syllabus statement, but it also included a values statement on the part of the faculty member:

> I believe strongly in providing reasonable accommodations for students with documented disabilities on an individualized and flexible basis. The University's Disability Resource Center (DRC) determines appropriate accommodations through consultation with the student. Please contact me and your discussion section leader at the beginning of the semester to work out the details of accommodations. If you have a documented disability and have not as yet met with staff in the DRC, I strongly encourage you to do so at your earliest convenience. To make an appointment, call . . .

In the discussion sections this material was repeated, and students were asked to complete a "student information sheet" that included the question "Is there anything that I should be aware of that might have an impact on your participation in this course (examples: a documented disability, absences for religious observances, or athletic competitions representing the institution)? If so, please describe." Choosing to disclose a disability is a difficult decision for some students (Alexandrin, Schreiber, & Henry, 2008; Henning, 2007; *Uncertain Welcome*, 2002). The student information sheets, which the advisor collected individually as the students left the room at the end of discussion, enabled students to disclose more privately than by approaching an instructor before or after class, often when surrounded by other students. It also took some of the responsibility for follow-up off the student and placed it on the advisor. Given differences between high school and college in the procedures for securing accommodations, it is important for first-semester freshmen with disabilities to develop self-advocacy skills (Higbee & Kalivoda, 2008), but it is unlikely that all students will have these skills when they first walk in the door. In fact, I believe that communication skills should be a focus of any first-year experience course like PSTL 1086.

Another important aspect of creating a welcoming learning environment is to assure students that their voices will be heard. Even in the lecture portion of PSTL 1086, there was very little lecture per se. Immediately after the brief review of key components of the syllabus on the first day, students were engaged in conversations about their reasons for going to college and the purpose of higher education (Schultz & Higbee, 2007). The students first worked in dyads and triads and then chose whether to share their ideas with the class as a whole.

Even in a large lecture class, learning individual students' names has become more manageable with the advent of digital photography and the provision of student ID photos by the university via the faculty member's electronic class list. By referring to the ID photos frequently during the initial weeks of class, the faculty member was able to begin linking faces with names in order to call on students by name. For faculty at institutions where digital ID photos are not provided automatically, the ease of taking photos with a digital camera or mobile device as students enter on the first day of class can also facilitate linking names to faces in the classroom. Especially at larger institutions, letting students know that they are more than a number plays a critical role in making students feel welcomed—a key principle of UID—and encouraging further interaction.

Determining Essential Components

Considerations in determining essential components include the purpose of the course, intended outcomes, instructional methods for achieving these outcomes, and types of evaluation to be used (Fox & Johnson, 2000). Although the process of learning is important, essential components should focus on learning outcomes. Not all students learn in the same ways; what is important is that they *do learn*. Essential components of a course can vary widely, depending in part on whether the course is a prerequisite for subsequent courses or a requirement in a program governed by specific professional standards, such as those of the allied health professions (Casey, 2007; Sharby & Roush, 2008). For PSTL 1086, which did not have to conform to these types of standards, but which required consistency of content and the grading rubric across sections, the essential components of the course were reflected in the following course objectives:

- Explore the purpose of higher education
- Establish individual goals and objectives
- Examine issues of importance to all first-year college students
- Explore how diversity enhances educational and life experiences
- Examine students' responsibility for their own learning
- Introduce the many educational opportunities and resources available at the University of Minnesota
- Begin the career planning process
- Perfect time management skills
- Develop study strategies to enhance academic success

- Improve critical skills in thinking and problem solving
- Provide a venue for practicing oral and written communication skills
- Assess and reduce sources of stress

The content of both the lectures and the material presented in discussion sections in PSTL 1086, as well as the nature of the course assignments and methods of evaluation, reflected these essential components. At the end of the semester students were asked to rate on a scale of 1 to 10 the extent to which the course was successful in achieving each of its objectives (Higbee, Lee, Bardill, & Cardinal, 2008).

Communicating Clear Expectations

It is critical that course expectations are communicated in writing by means of the course syllabus and then reinforced via various forms of communication between instructors and students. PSTL 1086 used criterion-referenced grading; final grades were determined through a point system, with a total of one thousand points available. The grading rubric was presented in the syllabus, but students also received a "summary of assignments" form that listed each assignment by due date and the maximum number of points the student could earn for that assignment. This form also provided a blank column where the student was to record the number of points earned. During the third week of class all students received an e-mail message explaining how they could calculate their course grade in the form of a percentage as of that point in the semester, as well as how to do so in future weeks, by dividing the number of points they had earned by the number possible to date. Examples were provided. This material was also covered briefly in lecture that week. Thus, students were taught how to track their own progress in this and any other course that uses a point system. Students were encouraged to contact the faculty member or the advisor teaching their discussion section if they had any questions. Grading rubrics were also provided for individual assignments, with a greater emphasis on content than on mechanics but with some points for organization, grammar, and so on because development of effective written communication skills was an objective of the course.

Today many of these practices implemented in PSTL 1086 can be accomplished via course websites, yet faculty do not always take advantage of the technological resources available to them or point out to students how they can track their progress in the electronic gradebook. Keeping grading systems simple (e.g., using numerical rather than letter grades and point totals that can easily be converted to percentages) can benefit both the instructor and the students.

Providing Constructive Feedback

Throughout the course, students in PSTL 1086 received numerous types of feedback from both the faculty member and the advisors teaching the discussion sections. The faculty member responded to each student every week via her comments on the open-ended short-answer and essay-style study guides and "question cards." Upon entering each lecture, students picked up a colored index card (a different color each week) and responded to a question posted on the screen at the front of the room. Examples of weekly questions included the following:

- What are the top three reasons (in priority order) why you are attending college? (Schultz & Higbee, 2007)
- How do you feel about college mathematics? Why? In your opinion, how important is mathematics for college graduation or for your preparation for your career and life after college? Why?
- How do *you personally* benefit from the diversity of the student body at the University of Minnesota?
- What adjective best describes your first semester in college? Why?

The responses to these questions provided key insights into student progress, not just in PSTL 1086, but in other courses and nonacademic areas as well. Advisors found this strategy extremely beneficial as a supplement to the institution's early alert system.

The faculty member also used these question cards instead of scanning university IDs for taking attendance in lectures, thus reducing congestion at the entrance to the lecture hall. Although attendance technically was not required, it was emphasized that research conducted in both PSTL courses and other venues demonstrated that students who attend class earn higher grades (Higbee & Fayon, 2006; Higbee, Schultz, & Goff, 2006; Moore, 2003, 2004; Moore, Jensen, Hatch, Duranczyk, Staats, & Koch, 2003; Thomas & Higbee, 2000). And, although there was no penalty for not attending class, the only opportunity for extra credit in the course was perfect attendance (20 points) or missing only one class meeting (10 points), whether discussion or lecture.

After returning the midterm and final exams—which occurred at the next discussion section meetings or, for some sections, on the same day as the test—the faculty member provided an answer key that listed both the correct answer and where in the text or lecture handouts the answer could be found. This is one of those strategies that benefits the faculty member as well as the student; students cannot debate the answers when the source of the material is so clearly spelled out. The advisors graded students' reflection papers and other writing assignments, commenting on both content and style. For oral presentations and small-group projects, students also received feedback from their peers. Students also benefit from the process of giving feedback: they learn to think critically and shape comments to be constructive rather than punitive, which is an important life skill.

Feedback on the student's progress in the course was also provided via the University of Minnesota's midsemester report process, which all PSTL faculty and instructional staff members were required to complete for each first-year student enrolled in their classes. Typical information provided in these reports, which were generated electronically and sent to each student via e-mail, included the student's current grade in the course, the percentage of the course work completed, the student's attendance record, and any individually constructed comments on the student's progress. There was also a checklist that enabled the instructor to indicate if the student (a) should make an appointment to see the faculty member or advisor, (b) needed to attend more regularly, (c) was missing assignments, or (d) should consider dropping the course. Even if students were not tracking their own performance, upon receiving the midsemester report they should have had a clear picture of where they stood in the course.

Using Natural Supports

When natural supports for learning are described, the emphasis is frequently on technological supports (Duquaine-Watson, 2008; Fox & Johnson, 2000), which can take the form of course websites and other Internet resources, smart classrooms, and the use of mobile devices. For students with disabilities, these supports may also include a wide variety of assistive technologies, from listening devices to screen readers (Knox, Higbee, Kalivoda, & Totty, 2000; Totty & Kalivoda, 2008; Kalivoda, Totty, & Higbee, 2009). For PSTL 1086, the faculty member maintained regular communication with all students in the class via e-mail messages sent at least once per week. This practice also encouraged the students to be in frequent contact with the faculty member and assisted her in becoming better acquainted with the students individually. The faculty member made a habit of approaching students when they came for lectures and following up on e-mail conversations in person.

For PSTL 1086, the most significant natural support may have been the weekly study guides created by the faculty member. The primary purposes of the study guides were to (a) assist the student in learning how to navigate the text and determine what was important, (b) facilitate engagement with the text that went beyond memorization of facts and figures to application of course content to the student's individual experience, and (c) provide a mechanism for reviewing for the midterm and final exams. Although many textbooks, including the one used in PSTL 1086, provide publisher-generated study guides, by creating her own study guides the faculty member ensured a richer understanding of the course content. Printed copies of the study guides were distributed each week in lecture while also provided electronically via e-mail and on the course website. All other faculty-generated instructional materials—from PowerPoint slides as a backup for taking notes (although PowerPoint was used infrequently in this course) to handouts and assessment tools—were also available to students electronically and sent out again as e-mail attachments during the weeks before the midterm and final exams, with a reminder of what to study. At the end of the semester, students not only completed the university's standard faculty evaluation form, they also ranked the helpfulness of the study guides and other natural supports.

Considering Diverse Learning Styles and Abilities

Within PSTL 1086, students completed four assessments related to learning styles, each of which approached the topic in a different way. Through the combination of large and small class meetings, the faculty member and advisors teaching PSTL 1086 were able to use a wide variety of teaching styles to help address the usual diversity in the learning preferences of students, most of whom did not believe that they learn best through reading textbooks and listening passively to lectures (Higbee, Ginter, & Taylor, 1991). In both lecture and discussion, film clips were used frequently to illustrate course topics. In the discussion sections, small-group exercises, such as games and simulations (Ghere, 2003; Hatch, Ghere, & Jirik, 2008), enhanced the learning of students who preferred experiential learning and of those who learn best when interacting with others. The final course evaluation asked students whether the course had been successful in addressing individual learning styles and ways of knowing.

Enabling Students to Demonstrate Knowledge in Multiple Ways

Students earned points for a broad range of assignments, including (a) weekly question cards; (b) study guides; (c) a wide variety of self-assessments, including some provided in the course text (Gardner, Jewler, & Barefoot, 2007); (d) attendance at a campus event of the student's choice, approved by the discussion leader; (e) participation in a community service project; (f) reflection papers and other writing assignments; (g) an oral presentation; (h) a small-group multimedia project; and (i) the midterm and final examinations. Not only did this breadth of assignments allow students to demonstrate their knowledge in multiple ways, but it also prepared them for divergent expectations in future courses.

Each of the two exams consisted of fifty true-false, multiple choice, and matching items. Most students completed the test within twenty or twenty-five minutes. However, all students were given the full class period of fifty minutes to complete the test. This is the equivalent of providing all students with extended time. This practice benefits students who read more slowly, those with test anxiety, and those who are not native speakers of English, as well as students with disabilities. However, many students with learning disabilities, ADHD, and other disabilities that often warrant extended time on tests may also benefit from taking exams in less distracting environments and may qualify for an accommodation, like individually administered exams. After the practice of providing "double time" was instituted in PSTL 1086, 100% of the students with disabilities taking the class chose to remain in lecture for test days rather than be segregated for separate administration of the exams. In other words, although given the opportunity, students did not choose to make use of a standard accommodation that, over time, not only segregated them from other students but also was likely to inadvertently breach the confidentiality of students with invisible disabilities. The students with disabilities who could have taken the exams individually also earned grades that were not significantly lower than those of students without disabilities and in some cases were significantly higher.

Promoting Interaction

As already discussed, both the faculty member and the advisors working with PSTL 1086 used a wide array of mechanisms built into the course to encourage interaction with and among students. In some cases, the weekly question cards provided opportunities for students to pose questions that they might not have felt comfortable asking aloud, or that they might not have thought to ask, such as those on the following prompt used the Friday before the midterm exam:

> What concerns do you have about the midterm exam? What further questions can I answer for you? I will read these cards over the weekend, type up your questions (no names, I promise!), and provide answers to the whole class via e-mail.

When guest speakers on topics like human sexuality, financial planning, or diversity presented during lecture, students also received a white index card as they entered the room and were prompted to write down any questions they might have for the speaker without having to identify themselves. This practice benefited many students, including students with disabilities, students who were not native speakers of English, students who were shy, and students who had questions they considered embarrassing but to which they desperately needed answers. Often the speaker did not have time within the lecture period to answer all the questions posed, but these individuals were thoughtful in providing written responses during the following week; these responses were sent to the entire class via e-mail.

Implementing UID in Distance Education

Distance education has made postsecondary courses and services much more accessible for some students with disabilities (Duranczyk & Higbee, 2012b; Higbee, Duranczyk, & Buturian, 2011), and many large-enrollment first-year courses are now offered online. The UID strategies implemented in PSTL 1086 are easily adapted for online instruction. Best practices in distance education include creating introductions to the faculty member, the course, and each unit; encouraging students to use different modalities to introduce themselves to other participants; involving students in developing guidelines for online discussions; providing clear expectations, directions, timelines, and grading rubrics; posting a wide range of resources to enhance student understanding; and considering multiple methods for students to demonstrate their learning. Many faculty members have their course websites ready long before the online course begins. In some ways distance education forces faculty members to think about all possible participants in the course in advance in a way that may not be necessary when teaching face-to-face.

When preparing materials for the course website, the faculty member should ensure that all documents are accessible by screen reader (Duranczk et al., 2013). Using the Styles tool in a word processing program like Microsoft Word establishes levels of headings and other navigational cues that assist students who are blind or have low vision, while also helping all students understand how the document is organized and what the instructor considers most important. When developing presentations for posting online, it is also important that the faculty member consider accessibility. Even if the final format of the presentation will be Prezi, creating it first in PowerPoint provides a linear record accessible by screen reader. PowerPoint includes an accessibility check and steps for ameliorating access problems. Meanwhile, a number of resources (e.g., Camtasia) are available for adding voice to presentations that otherwise would be accessible only by sight. Similarly, providing captioning ensures access for students who cannot hear. However, engaged online learning also includes the opportunity for students to share with one another, and it may not be reasonable to expect students to caption all of their work. On the other hand, all students can benefit from learning to speak more slowly and clearly in situations like developing films for platforms like YouTube, which provides captioning that can be quite accurate if the speaker has articulated words with care. It is instructive for students to view the built-in captioning of their own videos. Furthermore, it is not difficult to edit YouTube captions as necessary; this is a skill students may find useful in the future. Another option is to have students create a script for their videos before recording, which may strengthen the quality of their finished product, and then provide a transcript. However, this practice does not allow a student who is deaf to watch and read simultaneously, thus preventing that student from accessing the information in a single viewing as other students in the class would.

Although it may appear that distance education poses additional accessibility challenges for both instructors and students, in fact these same issues should be addressed with face-to-face teaching but are too often ignored. As higher education institutions serve increasingly diverse populations of students, creating more inclusive teaching and learning environments is critical (Higbee, 2009, 2014).

THE FACULTY PERSPECTIVE: BENEFITS AND CHALLENGES OF UNIVERSAL INSTRUCTIONAL DESIGN

Implementing UID benefits the teacher as well as the student. Although some students with disabilities will still need individual accommodations (e.g., a sign language interpreter or a text on tape), in planning a course using UID the faculty member often reduces the need for individual accommodations, thereby saving time in the long run. Frequently, the faculty member does not have advance notice of the accommodation needs of students with disabilities enrolled in a course prior to the first day of class, when some—but not all—students with disabilities provide a letter from the institution's disability resources office. At that point there is little time to prepare accommodations like alternative test formats or additional forms of the tests for separate administration. Although students may be encouraged to contact faculty members earlier, some students are hesitant to do so until they can meet with the faculty member in person and gauge the teacher's response to them and their disability (*Uncertain Welcome*, 2002).

One of the challenges of implementing UID is trying to predict the needs of potential students. In twenty-nine years of teaching at large public research universities, the faculty member for PSTL 1086 has taught only two students who are blind. During recent decades it has become much easier to acquire videos with captioning for students who have hearing impairments and for whom written English is easier to comprehend than spoken English, and faculty can generally count on the availability of the technology needed to view the films in the classroom or online. Faculty members can caption the videos they create themselves in YouTube and can use resources like Amara to caption other YouTube videos for which the "instant" captioning is not accurate. But it is still problematic to request in advance that all videos be described for students who have visual impairments, when no students who are blind may ever enroll in the course, and it may divert resources from the teachers and students who need them most. One solution is to select clips from films that are already available with oral description (Media Access Group, n.d.). Local cable television providers may also have information on descriptive services for films on demand and television programs.

Thus, many of the challenges to implementing UID can be relatively easy to overcome if the faculty member is aware of available resources. Professional development in the areas of universal design and UID can enhance the likelihood that faculty members will perceive the advantages of designing courses that are fully accessible to all students. To the extent possible, it is helpful if faculty receive training from other faculty who are in the same or similar disciplines and can provide concrete examples for implementation in that disciplinary area (e.g., in the chemistry laboratory, in student-teacher placements, in web pages that illustrate accounting ledger pages). Professional development opportunities are also important for learning center staff members, academic advisors, career counselors, and others who provide services for students (Goff & Higbee, 2008b; Higbee & Mitchell, 2009).

EVALUATION

As previously noted, the PSTL 1086 instructor augmented institutional evaluation processes with her own assessment instruments, which were designed to determine whether the course was meeting its objectives and implementing UID successfully and the extent to which students found class activities, guest speakers, and assignments helpful. In another, similar first-year course taught by the instructor, the mean rating for implementation of each of the UID principles ranged from 9.6 out of 10 ($n = 31$) for "The required course content was appropriate" (related to essential components) to 9.9 out of 10 ($n = 31$) for three of the eight items: (a) "Dr. _____ created a respectful and welcoming learning environment"; (b) "Dr. _____ provided timely, clear, and accurate feedback"; and (c) "Dr. _____ used multiple teaching strategies (e.g., short lecture, discussion, films, small-group exercises)" (Higbee et al., 2008). The faculty member also achieved high marks for her overall teaching ability on the institution's standard evaluation of teaching and recently received the institution's most prestigious teaching award.

RESPONDING TO CRITICS: CONSIDERING CULTURAL DIFFERENCES

As Hackman (2008) pointed out, one of the weaknesses of UID is that it does not consider culture or other aspects of social identity. When disability is approached from a social justice perspective (Evans, 2008), the role of culture is important—whether disability culture, Deaf culture, or a facet of the cultural heritage of the individual student that may not appear to be directly related to disability. For example, to understand the learning challenges of students in Africa who are albino, exploring the intersection of culture and disability is critical (Osifuye & Higbee, 2014). A new pedagogical model—integrated multicultural instructional design (IMID)—has built on UID to consider not just *how* we teach and support and assess learning, but also *what* we teach (Duranczyk & Higbee, 2012a; Higbee, 2014; Higbee, Duranczyk, & Buturian, 2011; Higbee & Goff, 2013; Higbee, Goff, & Schultz, 2012; Higbee, Schultz, & Goff, 2010; Schultz & Higbee, 2011). For example, including disability in the "diversity mix" in a freshman seminar (Lor, Holmen, Song, Loyle-Langholz, Higbee, & Zhou, 2013; Song, Loyle-Langholz, Higbee, & Zhou, 2013) had a profound impact on students: course participants embraced the role of disability ally, and two first-year students worked with the instructor to develop their final papers into related publications (Clinton & Higbee, 2011; Higbee, Katz, & Schultz, 2010). But what is most important is that implementation of IMID ensures that disability—or any other aspect of social identity—is not viewed as a label that singularly defines an individual.

CONCLUSION

In 1997, Hodge and Preston-Sabin edited a book titled *Accommodations—Or Just Good Teaching?* In many respects, UID could be construed as simply good teaching. But creating universally designed courses and curricula requires intentionality and thorough advance planning. Even the most naturally gifted lecturer is not necessarily a good teacher if other aspects of the course (e.g., electronic supports) do not meet the needs of students. Faculty members who implement UID gain in many ways, not just because they know that they are making their courses more accessible to all students but often in the form of better teaching evaluations and recognition for excellence in teaching as well.

REFERENCES

Alexandrin, J. R., Schreiber, I. L., & Henry, E. (2008). Why not disclose? In J. L. Higbee & E. Goff (Eds.), *Pedagogy and student services for institutional transformation: Implementing universal design in higher education* (pp. 377–392). Minneapolis: Regents of the University of Minnesota, Center for Research on Developmental Education and Urban Literacy. Retrieved from http://www.cehd.umn.edu/passit/docs/PASS-IT-Book.pdf

Barajas, H. L., & Higbee, J. L. (2003). Where do we go from here? Universal design as a model for multicultural education. In J. L. Higbee (Ed.), *Curriculum transformation and disability: Implementing universal design in higher education* (pp. 285–290). Minneapolis: University of Minnesota, General College, Center for Research on Developmental Education and Urban Literacy. Retrieved from http://www.cehd.umn.edu/CRDEUL/books-ctad.html

Bowe, F. G. (2000). *Universal design in education—Teaching nontraditional students.* Westport, CT: Bergin & Garvey.

Casey, D. A. (2007). Students with psychological disabilities in allied health sciences programs. In J. L. Higbee, D. B. Lundell, & I. M. Duranczyk (Eds.), *Diversity and the postsecondary experience* (pp. 87–102). Minneapolis: Regents of the University of Minnesota, Center for Research on Developmental Education and Urban Literacy. Retrieved from http://www.cehd.umn.edu/passit/docs/PASS-IT-Book.pdf

Chickering, A. W., & Gamson, Z. F. (1987). Seven principles for good practice in undergraduate education. *AAHE Bulletin, 39*(7), 3–7.

Clinton, L., & Higbee, J. L. (2011). The invisible hand: The power of language in creating welcoming postsecondary learning experiences. *Journal of College Teaching and Learning, 8*(5), 11–16. Retrieved from http://www.cluteinstitute.com/ojs/index.php/TLC/article/view/4253/4324

Duquaine-Watson, J. M. (2008). Computing technologies, the digital divide, and "universal" instructional methods. In J. L. Higbee & E. Goff (Eds.), *Pedagogy and student services for institutional transformation: Implementing universal design in higher education* (pp. 437–449). Minneapolis: Regents of the University of Minnesota, Center for Research on Developmental Education and Urban Literacy. Retrieved from http://www.cehd.umn.edu/passit/docs/PASS-IT-Book.pdf

Duranczyk, I. M., & Higbee, J. L. (2012a). Constructs of integrated multicultural instructional design for undergraduate mathematical thinking courses for nonmathematics majors. *Journal of Mathematics & Culture, 6*(1), 148–177.

Duranczyk, I. M., & Higbee, J. L. (2012b). Designing distance education for access and equity: Structure and content. *Proceedings of the 28th Annual Conference on Distance Teaching & Learning.* Madison: Regents of the University of Wisconsin System.

Duranczyk, I. M., Myers, K. A., Couillard, E. K., Schoen, S., & Higbee, J. L. (2013). Enacting the spirit of the United Nations Convention on the Rights of Persons With Disabilities: The role of postsecondary faculty in ensuring access. *Journal of Diversity Management, 8*(2), 63–72. Retrieved from http://www.cluteinstitute.com/ojs/index.php/JDM/article/view/8232/8269

Evans, N. J. (2008). Theoretical foundations of universal instructional design. In J. L. Higbee & E. Goff (Eds.), *Pedagogy and student services for institutional transformation: Implementing universal design in higher education* (pp. 11–23). Minneapolis: Regents of the University of Minnesota, Center for Research on Developmental Education and Urban Literacy. Retrieved from http://www.cehd.umn.edu/passit/docs/PASS-IT-Book.pdf

Fox, J. A., & Johnson, D. (2000). *Curriculum transformation and disability workshop facilitator's guide.* Minneapolis: University of Minnesota, General College and Disability Services.

Gardner, J. N., Jewler, A. J., & Barefoot, B. O. (2007). *Your college experience* (7th ed.). Boston: Thomson Wadsworth.

Ghere, D. L. (2003). Best practices and students with disabilities: Experiences in a college history course. In J. L. Higbee (Ed.), *Curriculum transformation and disability: Implementing universal design in higher education* (pp. 149–161). Minneapolis: University of Minnesota, General College, Center for Research on Developmental Education and Urban Literacy. Retrieved from http://www.cehd.umn.edu/CRDEUL/books-thegcvision.html

Goff, E., & Higbee, J. L. (Eds.). (2008a). *Pedagogy and student services for institutional transformation: Implementation guidebook for faculty and instructional staff.* Minneapolis: Regents of the University of Minnesota, College of Education and Human Development. Retrieved from http://www.cehd.umn.edu/passit/docs/guidebook-2.pdf

Goff, E., & Higbee, J. L. (Eds.). (2008b). *Pedagogy and student services for institutional transformation: Implementation guidebook for student development programs and services.* Minneapolis: Regents of the University of Minnesota, College of Education and Human Development. Retrieved from http://www.cehd.umn.edu/passit/docs/guidebook-1.pdf

Hackman, H. W. (2008). Broadening the pathway to academic success: The critical intersection of social justice education, critical multicultural education, and universal instructional design. In J. L. Higbee & E. Goff (Eds.), *Pedagogy and student services for institutional transformation: Implementing universal design in higher education* (pp. 26–48). Minneapolis: Regents of the University of Minnesota, Center for Research on Developmental Education and Urban Literacy. Retrieved from http://www.cehd.umn.edu/passit/docs/PASS-IT-Book.pdf

Hackman, H. W., & Rauscher, L. (2004). A pathway to success for all: Exploring the connections between universal instructional design and social justice education. *Equity & Excellence in Education, 37*(2), 114–123.

Hatch, J. T., Ghere, D. L., & Jirik, K. N. (2008). Empowering students with severe disabilities: A case study. In J. L. Higbee & E. Goff (Eds.), *Pedagogy and student services for institutional transformation: Implementing universal design in higher education* (pp. 393–403). Minneapolis: Regents of the University of Minnesota, Center for Research on Developmental Education and Urban Literacy. Retrieved from http://www.cehd.umn.edu/passit/docs/PASS-IT-Book.pdf

Henning, G. (2007). What happens if others find out? *About Campus, 12*(3), 26–29.

Higbee, J. L. (Ed.). (2003). *Curriculum transformation and disability: Implementing universal design in higher education.* Minneapolis: University of Minnesota, General College, Center for Research on Developmental Education and Urban Literacy. Retrieved from http://www.cehd.umn.edu/CRDEUL/books-ctad.html

Higbee, J. L. (2009). Student diversity. In R. Flippo & D. Caverly (Eds.), *Handbook of college reading and study strategies research* (2nd ed.; pp. 67–94). New York: Routledge, Taylor & Francis Group.

Higbee, J. L. (2014). Creating inclusive learning experiences: Integrating developmental education and social justice education. In J. L. Higbee (Ed.), *The profession and practice of learning assistance and developmental education: Essays in memory of Dr. Martha Maxwell* (pp. 243–265). Boone, NC: Council of Learning Assistance and Developmental Education Associations and the National Center for Developmental Education.

Higbee, J. L., & Barajas, H. L. (2007). Building effective places for multicultural learning. *About Campus, 12*(3), 16–22.

Higbee, J. L., Duranczyk, I. M., & Buturian, L. (2011). Implementing integrated multicultural instructional design in blended courses. *Proceedings of the 27th Annual Conference on Distance Teaching & Learning.* Madison: Regents of the University of Wisconsin System.

Higbee, J. L., Duranczyk, I. M., & Ghere, D. (2008). Institutional transformation: From multicultural awareness to integrated multicultural instructional design. In F. Ferrier & M. Heagney (Eds.), *Higher education in diverse communities: Global perspectives, local initiatives* (pp. 60–65). London: European Access Network and Higher Education Authority of Ireland.

Higbee, J. L., & Fayon, A. K. (2006). Attendance policies in developmental education courses: Promoting involvement or undermining students' autonomy? *Research & Teaching in Developmental Education, 22*(2), 71–77.

Higbee, J. L., Ginter, E. J., & Taylor, W. D. (1991). Enhancing academic performance: Seven perceptual styles of learning. *Research & Teaching in Developmental Education, 7*(2), 5–10.

Higbee, J. L., & Goff, E. (2008). *Pedagogy and student services for institutional transformation: Implementing universal design in higher education.* Minneapolis: Regents of the University of Minnesota, Center for Research on Developmental Education and Urban Literacy. Retrieved from http://www.cehd.umn.edu/passit/docs/PASS-IT-Book.pdf

Higbee, J. L., & Goff, E. (2013). Widening participation through integrated multicultural instructional design. In K. Bridges, J. Shaw, & I. Reid (Eds.), *Inclusive higher education: An international perspective on access and the challenge of student diversity* (pp. 41–55). Faringdon, Oxfordshire, UK: Libri.

Higbee, J. L., Goff, E., & Schultz, J. L. (2012). Promoting retention through the implementation of integrated multicultural instructional design. *Journal of College Student Retention, 14*(3), 291–310.

Higbee, J. L., & Kalivoda, K. S. (2008). The first-year experience. In J. L. Higbee & E. Goff (Eds.), *Pedagogy and student services for institutional transformation: Implementing universal design in higher education* (pp. 245–253). Minneapolis: Regents of the University of Minnesota, Center for Research on Developmental Education and Urban Literacy, Retrieved from http://www.cehd.umn.edu/passit/docs/PASS-IT-Book.pdf

Higbee, J. L., Katz, R. E., & Schultz, J. L. (2010). Disability in higher education: Redefining mainstreaming. *Journal of Diversity Management, 5*(2), 7–16. Retrieved from http://www.cluteinstitute.com/ojs/index.php/JDM/article/view/806/790

Higbee, J. L., Lee, P. H., Bardill, J., & Cardinal, H. (2008). Student evaluations of the effectiveness of implementing universal instructional design. In J. L. Higbee & E. Goff (Eds.), *Pedagogy and student services for institutional transformation: Implementing universal design in higher education* (pp. 367–375). Minneapolis: Regents of the University of Minnesota, Center for Research on Developmental Education and Urban Literacy. Retrieved from http://www.cehd.umn.edu/passit/docs/PASS-IT-Book.pdf

Higbee, J. L., & Mitchell, A. A. (2009). *Making good on the promise: Student affairs professionals with disabilities.* Washington, DC: ACPA—College Student Educators International and University Press of America.

Higbee, J. L., & Schultz, J. L. (2012). Taking a pulse: Student-athletes' descriptors for their first semester of college. *Journal of College Teaching & Learning, 9*(4), 253–260.

Higbee, J. L., & Schultz, J. L. (2013). Responding to the concerns of student-athletes enrolled in a first-year experience course. *Contemporary Issues in Education Research, 6*(2), 155–162.

Higbee, J. L., Schultz, J. L., & Goff, E. (2006). Attendance policies in developmental education courses: The student point of view. *Research & Teaching in Developmental Education, 23*(1), 78–85.

Higbee, J. L., Schultz, J. L., & Goff, E. (2010). The pedagogy of inclusion: Integrated multicultural instructional design. *Journal of College Reading and Learning, 41*(1), 49–66.

Hodge, B. M., & Preston-Sabin, J. (1997). *Accommodations—Or just good teaching? Strategies for teaching college students with disabilities.* Westport, CT: Praeger.

Johnson, J. R. (2004). Universal instructional design and critical (communication) pedagogy: Strategies for voice, inclusion, and social justice/change. *Equity & Excellence in Education, 37*, 145–153.

Johnson, D. M., & Fox, J. A. (2003). Creating curb cuts in the classroom: Adapting universal design principles to education. In J. L. Higbee (Ed.), *Curriculum transformation and disability: Implementing universal design in higher education* (pp. 7–21). Minneapolis: University of Minnesota, General College, Center for Research on Developmental Education and Urban Literacy. Retrieved from http://www.cehd.umn.edu/CRDEUL/books-ctad.html

Kalivoda, K. S. (2003). Creating access through universal instructional design. In J. L. Higbee, D. B. Lundell, & I. M. Duranczyk (Eds.), *Multiculturalism in developmental education* (pp. 25–34). Minneapolis: University of Minnesota, General College, Center for Research on Developmental Education and Urban Literacy. Retrieved from http://www.cehd.umn.edu/CRDEUL/pdf/monograph/4-a.pdf

Kalivoda, K. S., Totty, M. C., & Higbee, J. L. (2009). Appendix E: Access to information technology. In J. L. Higbee, & A. A. Mitchell (Eds.), *Making good on the promise: Student affairs professionals with disabilities* (pp. 226–232). Washington, DC: ACPA—College Student Educators International and University Press of America.

Knox, D. K., Higbee, J. L., Kalivoda, K. S., & Totty, M. C. (2000). Serving the diverse needs of students with disabilities through technology. *Journal of College Reading and Learning, 30*(2), 144–157.

Lee, A., Williams, R. D., & Kilaberia, R. (2012). Engaging diversity in first-year college classrooms. *Innovative Higher Education, 37*(3), 199–213.

Lee, A., Williams, R. D., Shaw, M., & Jie, Y. (2014). First year students' perspectives on intercultural learning. *Teaching in Higher Education. 19*(5), 543–554.

Lor, K., Holmen, A., Song, D., Loyle-Langholz, A., Higbee, J. L., & Zhou, Z. (2013). Exploring diversity through the lens of popular culture in a freshman seminar. *Proceedings of the Clute Institute International Conference on Academic Research.* Littleton, CO: The Clute Institute.

Media Access Group at WGBH. (n.d.). *Accessible DVDs.* Retrieved from http://main.wgbh.org/wgbh/pages/mag/resources/accessible-dvds.html

Moore, R. (2003). Students' choices in developmental education: Is it really important to attend class? *Research & Teaching in Developmental Education, 20*(1), 42–52.

Moore, R. (2004). Does improving developmental education students' understanding of the importance of class attendance improve students' class attendance and academic performance? *Research & Teaching in Developmental Education, 20*(2), 24–39.

Moore, R., Jensen, M., Hatch, J., Duranczyk, I., Staats, S., & Koch, L. (2003). Showing up: The importance of class attendance for academic success in introductory science courses. *American Biology Teacher, 65*(5), 325–329.

Opitz, D. L., & Block, L. S. (2006). Universal learning support design: Maximizing learning beyond the classroom. *Learning Assistance Review, 11*(2), 33–45.

Osifuye, S., & Higbee, J. L. (2014). African university students' perspectives on disability access. *Journal of Diversity Management. 9*(2), 1–10. Retrieved from http://www.cluteinstitute.com/ojs/index.php/JDM/article/view/8969/8935

Pedelty, M. (2008). Making a statement. In J. L. Higbee & E. Goff (Eds.), *Pedagogy and student services for institutional transformation: Implementing universal design in higher education* (pp. 79–85). Minneapolis: Regents of the University of Minnesota, Center for Research on Developmental Education and Urban Literacy. Retrieved from http://www.cehd.umn.edu/passit/docs/PASS-IT-Book.pdf

Schultz, J. L., & Higbee, J. L. (2007). Reasons for attending college: The student point of view. *Research & Teaching in Developmental Education, 23*(2), 69–76.

Schultz, J. L., & Higbee, J. L. (2011). Implementing integrated multicultural instructional design in management education. *American Journal of Business Education, 4*(12), 13–21.

Sharby, N., & Roush, S. E. (2008). The application of universal instructional design in experiential education. In J. L. Higbee & E. Goff (Eds.), *Pedagogy and student services for institutional transformation: Implementing universal design in higher education* (pp. 305–320). Minneapolis: Regents of the University of Minnesota, Center for Research on Developmental Education and Urban Literacy. Retrieved from http://www.cehd.umn.edu/passit/docs/PASS-IT-Book.pdf

Silver, P., Bourke, A., & Strehorn, K. C. (1998). Universal instructional design in higher education: An approach for inclusion. *Equity & Excellence in Education, 31*(2), 47–51.

Smith, K. L. (1997). Preparing faculty for instructional technology: From education to development to creative independence. *Cause/Effect, 20*(3), 36–44.

Song, D., Loyle-Langholz, A., Higbee, J. L., & Zhou, Z. (2013). Achieving course objectives and student learning outcomes: Seeking student feedback on their progress. *Contemporary Issues in Education Research, 6*(3), 1–10.

Thomas, P. V., & Higbee, J. L. (2000). The relationship between involvement and success in developmental algebra. *Journal of College Reading and Learning, 30*(2), 222–232.

Totty, M. C., & Kalivoda, K. S. (2008). Assistive technology. In J. L. Higbee & E. Goff (Eds.), *Pedagogy and student services for institutional transformation: Implementing universal design in higher education* (pp. 473–478). Minneapolis: Regents of the University of Minnesota, Center for Research on Developmental Education and Urban Literacy. Retrieved from http://www.cehd.umn.edu/passit/docs/PASS-IT-Book.pdf

Uncertain welcome: Student perspectives on disability and postsecondary education [Video]. (2002). Minneapolis: University of Minnesota, General College and Disability Services. Retrieved from http://mediamill.cla.umn.edu/mediamill/display/70826

Williams, W. M., & Ceci, S. J. (1999, August 6). Accommodating learning disabilities can bestow unfair advantages. *Chronicle of Higher Education*, B4–B5.

6

Universal Design of Instruction
Reflections of Students

Imke Durre
Michael Richardson
Carson Smith
Jessie Amelia Shulman
Sarah Steele

The coauthors of this chapter, who have a variety of disabilities themselves, share insights from past and present postsecondary experiences regarding the benefits to students of universal design of instruction. Their insights can help professors design their courses to be engaging for all students.

Most literature about the application of universal design to instruction has been written by researchers and practitioners. In contrast, this chapter explores universal design of instruction (UDI) from the student point of view. The coauthors—five successful current and former students who have disabilities with respect to mobility, hearing, vision, learning, and attention—present experiences and insights into the application of UDI. They share their perspectives in the form of responses to a checklist of strategies for the application of UDI. This checklist was originally developed through a literature review and input from participants in the *DO-IT Prof* project, funded by the U.S. Department of Education Office of Postsecondary Education (OPE) and directed through Disabilities, Opportunities, Internetworking, and Technology (DO-IT) at the University of Washington (DO-IT, 2006). It was then updated through an iterative process that was conducted within two more OPE-funded projects, *DO-IT Admin* (DO-IT, 2007) and *AccessCollege* (DO-IT, 2015). The checklist has been modified based on input from project team members, professionals from postsecondary institutions who field-tested earlier versions. This working document continues to be updated with feedback from administrators, educators, students, and other stakeholders. The current version of the checklist can be found in the publication *Equal Access: Universal Design of Instruction* on the DO-IT website (Burgstahler, 2015).

The content of this chapter is organized into the following sections, which mirror the original UDI checklist categories:

- Class climate
- Interaction
- Physical environments and products
- Delivery methods
- Information resources and technology
- Feedback
- Assessment
- Accommodation

Examples of specific strategies are provided under each category in a format similar to the checklist itself. Coauthor perspectives are included as bulleted items under each strategy; a comment that applies to multiple strategies, for the sake of expedience, is included only once. The coauthors hope their feedback will provide guidance not only to DO-IT as they continue to update the checklist but also to instructors who wish to apply universal design in their courses, to educators who provide professional development to faculty, and to service providers who work directly with students and their instructors.

CLASS CLIMATE

Adopt practices that reflect high values with respect to both diversity and inclusiveness.

Welcome everyone. Create a welcoming environment for all students. Encourage the sharing of multiple perspectives. Demonstrate and demand mutual respect.

- When people feel respected, they are more likely to view themselves as valuable members of the student body than when they feel disrespected. The feeling of belonging that is fostered by mutual respect can help retain students in a class or program.

Avoid stereotyping. Offer instruction and support based on student performance and requests, not simply on assumptions that members of certain groups (e.g., students with certain types of disabilities or from a specific racial/ethnic group) will automatically do well or poorly or require certain types of assistance.

- I don't expect professors to have great knowledge about my disability. I see my role as simply articulating the accommodations I need to do my best work.
- My approach has always been to keep the discussion about my disability professional. The objective of the discussion is to arrange appropriate accommodations, not to discuss the validity of my disability. The disability services documentation I give the faculty before this discussion helps to keep the meeting on track.

Be approachable and available. Learn students' names. Welcome questions in and outside of class, seek out a student's point of view, and respond patiently. Maintain regular office hours, encourage students to meet with you, and offer alternatives when student schedules conflict with those hours; consider making a student-instructor meeting a course requirement. Be available for online communication as well.

- Being approachable and available to all students allows the student with a disability to feel like an equal part of the class. Rather than being the only student whose name the professor knows, they are simply one of *many* students whose names the professor knows.
- Students are positively motivated when a professor calls on them by name. If they feel known, not anonymous, they feel encouraged to participate in class. This benefits the individual as well as the entire class by invigorating the discussion so real learning can take place.
- Even in large classes, when I visit a professor during office hours and she remembers my name and the history of my previous visits, it has impact.
- Some professors say they have office hours but rarely encourage students to come. Too often students are afraid to look dumb in front of the professor. If the instructor makes more of an overture, more students will come to seek deeper knowledge and build a productive academic relationship with the professor.
- It is also very helpful if the professor has five or ten minutes to spend after class to address individual student questions informally. Some students might not feel comfortable going to office hours but do not have a problem asking a quick question after class. This is particularly convenient for students who use sign language interpreters or captioning services in class because they have ready access to interpretation at that time.

Motivate all students. Use teaching methods and materials that are motivating and relevant to students with diverse characteristics, such as age, gender, and culture.

- In a differential equations course I took, the professor actually had a hearing impairment. It was really interesting to watch how he explained this to the students and integrated classroom accommodations to facilitate his teaching. Because of his experience and openness, I felt he was very approachable in terms of requesting accommodations and flexible in his teaching approach.

Address individual needs in an inclusive manner. Both on the syllabus and in class, invite students to meet with you to discuss disability-related accommodations and other learning needs. Avoid segregating or stigmatizing any student by drawing undue attention to a difference (e.g., disability) or sharing private information (e.g., a specific student's need for an accommodation) unless the student brings up the topic in front of others. Remind students of their role in making requests early and contributing to a positive relationship. Communicate effectively with teaching assistants (TAs) about student accommodations.

- Many professors advise on the course syllabus that students with disabilities should make an office appointment if they need to discuss accommodations. This gesture makes students feel more comfortable about approaching the professor.
- Our campus disability service protocol for requesting accommodations asks students to meet and discuss needed accommodations with faculty members. I have always felt this was an important process in terms of self-advocacy, as well as a way to add clarity and set coursework off on the right foot.

- When instructors address individual needs in a confidential manner, this encourages students to come forward with specific needs, thus increasing their chances of reaching their full potential in the class.
- It is important for students to recognize their roles in making requests early and otherwise developing positive relationships with faculty by applying skills in self-advocacy and problem solving.
- Being flexible is a good skill to have in the self-advocacy tool kit. I usually initiate my accommodation request with the primary course instructor. In the Physics department I worked with the course program director for exam accommodations. When I took courses in the Psychology and Mathematics departments, I would often take exams in a department conference room.
- There were occasional instances when I arranged my accommodations with the course faculty, but the TA wasn't informed. This happened in a chemistry course, where I was instructed to return to a TA mailbox an exam I took at disability services. When the TA found the exam in her box, I was accused of cheating and not turning in my exam at the end of class. This was frustrating and demeaning. The incident was resolved after I explained to the TA that I had a disability and had arranged accommodations with the professor. I told the TA I was following the professor's instructions and if there was a concern, he should be consulted.

INTERACTION

Encourage regular and effective interactions between students and the instructor and ensure that communication methods are accessible to all participants.

Promote effective communication. Employ interactive teaching techniques. Face the class, speak clearly, use a microphone if your voice does not project adequately for all students, and make eye contact with students. Consider requiring a meeting with each student. Supplement in-person contact with online communication. Use straightforward language, avoid unnecessary jargon and complexity, and use student names in electronic, written, and in-person communications.

- Several of my professors required a student-instructor meeting. Those who did this tended to develop a strong rapport with their students. Personal connections are an important part of learning for many students.
- Effective communication is crucial. Most students default to using e-mail, which is an accessible form of communication for most students, including those with disabilities. Phone and in-person meetings are also used to coordinate work between students.
- Although e-mail is technically accessible to most students, it is important for an instructor to understand that there are students for whom written communication is less efficient than verbal communication. The use of e-mail should not replace the availability of the instructor after class and during office hours.
- For prearranged appointments with my instructor, I am usually able to secure a sign language interpreter. However, there are times when I may want to communi-

cate with the instructor on short notice. It is helpful when the instructor is open to regular communication through e-mail.

Make interactions accessible to all participants. For example, use a telephone conference only if all students can participate, given their abilities to hear, speak, and meet, and their schedule constraints. Also, require that small groups communicate in ways that are accessible to all group members. Be flexible regarding interaction strategies.

- Professors who are approachable and have some knowledge of disability issues can help make a student comfortable by suggesting an alternative communication strategy, if needed.
- E-mail is an accessible method of communication for many students with disabilities. It also provides the best options for students and faculty with conflicting schedules.

Encourage cooperative learning. Assign group work for which learners must support each other and employ different skills and roles. Encourage different ways for students to interact with each other (e.g., in-class discussion, group work, and Internet-based communication). Ensure full participation by insisting that all students participate; facilitate their participation as needed.

- Group work can make it possible for students with disabilities to build on their strengths. For example, a student who has a mobility impairment and cannot perform the physical manipulations required in an assignment can take on a different role, such as reading the instructions or taking notes with a laptop computer equipped with assistive technology.
- To ensure the active participation of everyone, an instructor asked all students in a group, including one who was deaf, to select communication strategies and task assignments so that everyone was able to participate.

PHYSICAL ENVIRONMENTS AND PRODUCTS

Ensure that facilities, activities, materials, and equipment are physically accessible to and usable by all students, and that all potential student characteristics are addressed in safety considerations.

Ensure physical access to facilities. Use classrooms, labs, workspaces, and fieldwork sites that are accessible to individuals with a wide range of physical abilities.

- In an organic chemistry lab, many of the tasks involved fine motor skills and students needed to stand for the duration of three- to four-hour lab sessions. The professor could have addressed these issues through UDI.

Arrange instructional spaces to maximize inclusion and comfort. Arrange seating to encourage participation, giving each student a clear line of sight to the instructor and visual aids and allowing room for wheelchairs, personal assistants, sign language interpreters, captionists, and assistive technology. Minimize distractions for students with a range of attention abilities (e.g., put small groups in quiet work areas). Work within constraints to make the environment as inclusive as possible. Encourage administrators to apply UD principles in facility design and renovation.

- A clear line of sight is particularly important when an oral interpreter or sign language interpreter is present.
- Ideally, seats with sufficient room for wheelchairs and assistive technology are scattered around the room, so that each student can choose a seat that is comfortable and maximizes learning.

Ensure that everyone can use equipment and materials. Minimize nonessential physical effort and provide options for operation of equipment, handles, locks, cabinets, and drawers from different heights, with different physical abilities, with one hand, and by right- and left-handed students. Use large print to clearly label controls on lab equipment and other educational aids, using symbols as well as words. Provide straightforward, simple oral and printed directions for operation and use.

- It is helpful when instructors put students who have complementary skills in each group.

Ensure safety. Develop procedures for all students, including those who are blind, deaf, or wheelchair users. Label safety equipment in simple terms, in large print, and in a location viewable from a variety of angles. Consider the impact of specific disabilities on emergency procedures. Provide safety instructions, as well as instructions for specific equipment, in writing prior to class. Repeat printed directions orally.

- When safety instructions are provided in electronic format before class, it gives students who rely on computers for access a chance to familiarize themselves with the instructions ahead of time and refer back to them as needed.
- Quite often, laboratory work includes the use of hazardous materials and substances. For people who are deaf or hard of hearing, it is imperative that oral instructions on safe handling and disposal of materials are also supplemented with instructions in a printed format.

DELIVERY METHODS

Use multiple instructional methods that are accessible to all learners.

Select flexible curricula. Choose textbooks and other curriculum materials that address the needs of students with diverse abilities, interests, learning styles, preferences, and other characteristics. When possible, use curriculum materials that are well organized, emphasize important points, provide references for gaining background knowledge, include comprehensive indices and glossaries, and have chapter outlines, study questions, and practice exercises. Consider technology-based materials that provide prompting, feedback, opportunities for multiple levels of practice, background information, vocabulary, and other supports based on student responses.

- Using technology is often the best approach to making learning more flexible. Students find it helpful when a course instructor makes good use of a course website for the course syllabus, calendar, and other materials.

- It is important that web-based materials be offered in a format that is accessible, particularly to students who are blind and using text-to-speech technology, which can only access web content that is in text-based format. For example, often PDF documents cannot be read by students who are blind and using speech- or braille-output technology. Text-based materials are accessible to these students and also more convenient to those using word-finding features to locate specific passages.
- A search engine course I took had one of the worst course web pages I have ever used. The web page consisted of a long, single page that listed course policies, materials, and resources and required excessive scrolling. It was very difficult for any student to use. Materials were easily buried, and there were no chapters or navigational controls. What is interesting is that the informatics program, like many other departments, provides templates for course websites, so that students do not need to acclimate themselves and learn how to use a new website every quarter. I am not sure why the professor chose not to use the template. These templates also provide an e-mail address that can be used to give anonymous feedback to the course instructor.

Make content relevant. Put learning in context. Incorporate multiple examples and perspectives with respect to specific concepts to make them relevant to individuals with diverse characteristics such as age, ability, gender, ethnicity, race, socioeconomic status, and interests.

- A portion of the informatics course work is borrowed from the library science field. In many of our theory-based courses, we would read a number of seminal papers. These readings were valuable to me because the teachers would go to great lengths to augment them with discussions of historic significance by providing real-world examples.
- The ability of instructors to relate the subject matter to their own experience helps students understand both the material and its importance.
- One of my favorite classes was Computer-Supported Collaborative Work. This class was based on a lot of theory; every article we read cited a real-world case study. It was easy for students to relate what they were learning to something they had experienced in a job or internship.
- The university can benefit students by hiring staff with diverse backgrounds and perspectives so that a college education as a whole can be seen as a mosaic of different and authentic perspectives.

Provide cognitive supports. Summarize major points, give background and contextual information, deliver effective prompting, and provide scaffolding tools (e.g., outlines, class notes, summaries, study guides, and copies of projected materials with room for taking notes) and other cognitive supports. Deliver these materials in printed form and in a text-based electronic format. Provide opportunities for gaining further background information, vocabulary, and different levels of practice with variable levels of support. Encourage and support students to develop their own scaffolding materials.

- When they are made available online before a course begins, outlines or notes can be used by students to prepare for the first class session. Providing such materials is particularly helpful in courses without textbooks.

- I find it very helpful when professors make copies of their PowerPoint slides available to students in electronic and paper format. Without them, I was stressed during class and too focused on taking down all the material in my notes that was covered in the PowerPoint slides. As a result, I didn't participate in class discussions, and I think it may have distracted me from the lecture.
- I learn most effectively from generating and organizing my own outline, notes, and study guides. I learn best and make sense of the material when I read the text, process the information, and then think about it again as I formulate and compose my notes. Although it is time-consuming, I prefer to write my notes by hand because I am a very kinesthetic person and physically writing out notes, instead of typing, helps to reinforce material in my brain. These personalized notes are also very important when I refer back to the material because they are often written to emphasize material that I struggled with.

Provide multiple ways to gain knowledge. Keep in mind that learning styles and levels of familiarity with background material vary among students. Use multiple modes to deliver content; when possible allow students to choose from multiple options for learning; and motivate and engage students. Consider lectures, collaborative learning options, small-group discussions, hands-on activities, Internet-based communications, online review materials, educational software, fieldwork, and so forth.

- For those who do not catch the concept the first time, a second mode of presentation can enhance the understanding of that concept.

Deliver instructions clearly and in multiple ways. Provide instructions both orally and in printed form. Ask for questions and have students repeat directions and give feedback.

- There is a certain amount of stress associated with receiving only verbal instructions for a homework assignment or paper. Though I take detailed notes, I can never be sure I have recorded all the instructions correctly. Providing a written document (either paper-based, electronic, or both) and supplementing it with a verbal explanation is most helpful to all students.
- Most students are not familiar enough with the objective of an assignment when it is first introduced to formulate all the questions they may have. It is helpful when professors provide their e-mail addresses, a class list, or a message board for students to ask questions on their own as they arise.

Make each teaching method accessible to all students. Consider a wide range of abilities, disabilities, interests, learning styles, and previous experiences when selecting instructional methods. Provide the same means of participation to all students—identical when possible, equivalent when not. Vary teaching methods.

- Supplementing a lecture with visuals and printed materials, such as a lecture outline, not only benefits a student who is deaf or hard of hearing but also provides a richer experience for all students. This idea is great in theory but more difficult to realize in practice.

- Part of the student's role is learning to adapt to different delivery methods; this will serve them well in the work world.
- Some instructors continue to lecture with their back to the class while writing on the whiteboard. This makes it impossible for me to lip-read and follow what is being written. If an instructor can take the time first to write and then face the class, not only would it be easier for me but also the eye contact and face-to-face engagement would be much more engaging for all students.
- I agree that instructors should not be discussing things while facing the board, but it is also important that they clearly verbalize what they are writing while they are writing, so that students who are visually impaired are able to take accurate notes. This is particularly important in scientific courses where an accurate verbalization of mathematical expressions and verbal descriptions of illustrations are critical to the visually impaired student's ability to follow along in class.

Use large visual and tactile aids. Use manipulatives to demonstrate content. Make visual aids as large as is feasible (e.g., use large, bold fonts on uncluttered overhead displays and use a computer to enlarge microscope images).

- Large visual and tactile aids help students with limited vision, as well as those who are visual and tactile learners. Students and instructors should also be aware of the availability of photocopy machines and technology that can produce materials in a larger size when needed.

INFORMATION RESOURCES AND TECHNOLOGY

Ensure that course materials, notes, and other information resources are engaging, flexible, and accessible for all students.

Select materials early. Choose printed materials and prepare a syllabus early to allow students the option of beginning to read materials and work on assignments before the course begins. Allow adequate time to arrange for alternate formats, such as books in audio format or in braille, which, for textbooks, can take longer than a month.

- It is important for the faculty to be organized so that students can buy their textbooks and prepare for the class. I typically contact professors the week before, or the first week of, the quarter to arrange course accommodations. I have found if I contact professors earlier, they have either not completed their syllabi or are still grading finals from the previous quarter.
- I took a usability engineering course for which no textbooks were originally required. On the first day of class, however, it was announced that course textbooks were not going to be made available for purchase through the bookstore, and instead, students would need to make their own arrangements. The timing of the announcement did a huge disservice to students. Many were without textbooks until the fourth week of the quarter because of the variability of shipping options from online distributors.

Use multiple, redundant presentations of content that use multiple senses. Use a variety of visual aids and manipulatives.

- I had a biology teacher who brought in models of animals and plants that helped illustrate concepts.
- Professors who augment their lectures by writing information on the board or in overhead visuals are very helpful to some students.

Provide all materials in accessible formats. Select or create materials that are universally designed. Use textbooks that are available in a digital, accessible format with flexible features. Provide the syllabus and other teacher-created materials in a text-based, accessible electronic format. Use captioned videos and provide transcriptions for audio presentations. Apply accessibility standards to websites.

- Simply stated, students with disabilities benefit from access to the same software, textbooks, websites, and other materials their nondisabled peers use.
- While taking a program management course, which had a heavy emphasis on Microsoft Project, I used the web-based software tutorials provided by the textbook publisher. This was a really helpful tool.
- My experience has taught me that accessible design happens or does not happen at the publishing house, which bundles CD and web resources with books. Faculty may choose accessible resources but still teach in an inaccessible way.
- I have found that even when accessibility standards are applied to departmental websites, they are frequently not imposed on course websites, which are thrown together during the first week of the quarter.
- In many classes at larger colleges and universities, TAs are responsible for managing course websites and class materials. I think it is critical that an instructor work closely with the TA to address accessibility standards and ensure consistent accessibility of materials.
- Instructors sometimes link web media content, such as web-based video clips. To accommodate students with hearing impairments, instructors may want to determine beforehand if the clip is captioned or if transcripts are available.

Accommodate a variety of reading levels and language skills, when appropriate, given the goals of the course. Present content in a logical, straightforward manner and in an order that reflects its importance. Avoid unnecessary jargon and complexity and define new terms when they are presented. Create materials in simple, intuitive formats that are consistent with the expectations and needs of students with a diverse set of characteristics.

- Faculty need to remind themselves that there are students in the class for whom English is not a first language and that opportunities to reduce language complexity will benefit everyone.
- Deaf students who use American Sign Language as their primary language may find jargon and complex vocabulary especially confusing. Just as important, sign language interpreters may have a difficult time interpreting such vocabulary to a deaf student. A valuable universal design strategy in this situation is for the instructor to give the interpreters as well as the students a list of complex terms, vocabulary,

and concepts to be used in the class. Ideally this is done before the beginning of the course so that interpreters have time to strategize the best way to convey content to deaf students and all students have an opportunity to plan ahead.

Ensure the availability of appropriate assistive technology. If computer or science labs are used, ensure that assistive technology for students with disabilities is available or can be readily acquired.

- My campus had a lab with a number of software and hardware products. Although I am most comfortable using accessible technology on my own personal machine, where my preferences can be saved, I have used text-to-speech software with headphones in the campus labs.

FEEDBACK

Provide specific feedback on a regular basis.

Provide regular feedback and corrective opportunities. Allow students to turn in parts of large projects for feedback before the final project is due. Give students resubmission options to correct errors in assignment or exams. Arrange for peer feedback when appropriate. Solicit feedback from students regarding course effectiveness.

- I took a systems analysis course in which we received all our grades at the end of the quarter. This was a source of frustration and hindered my learning. I received no feedback during the course that could have been used to improve my work.
- For any report writing in technical fields, professors should be aware of the revision process and apply it appropriately.
- There is a benefit to group work and collaboratively building on the ideas of your peers, but peer feedback should not reduce the need for faculty to review student work. Instructors should keep in mind that some student feedback can be valuable, but frequently other students don't take the exercise seriously and provide meaningless feedback.
- Professors should encourage discussion and actually incorporate student feedback and comments into their course design and content.
- One professor asked for feedback in the middle of the quarter, not just about his own performance but also about how students felt the class was progressing. I did not see a notable change in his style, but the intent was greatly appreciated.

ASSESSMENT

Regularly assess student progress using multiple accessible methods and tools, and adjust instruction accordingly.

Set clear expectations. Keep academic standards consistent for all students, including those who require accommodations. Provide a syllabus with clear statements of course expectations, assignment descriptions, and deadlines, as well as assessment methods and dates. Include a straightforward grading rubric.

- It is helpful if a syllabus and grading rubric are presented to students on day one of a class and posted in an accessible format on a course website. Academic standards should be consistent for all students, including those with disabilities.

Provide multiple ways to demonstrate knowledge. Assess group and cooperative performance as well as individual achievement. Consider using traditional tests with a variety of formats (e.g., multiple choice, essay, short answer), papers, group work, demonstrations, portfolios, and presentations as options for demonstrating knowledge. Give students choices in assessment methods when appropriate. Allow students to use information technology to complete exams.

- I have a great deal of respect for professors who choose written answers over multiple-choice answers. It shows that they are willing to evaluate our unique thoughts, not just what we crammed in the night before.
- I think choices in assessment methods can work, but grading fairness is a huge issue if several methods are offered.

Monitor and adjust. Assess students' background knowledge and current learning regularly, informally (e.g., through class discussion), and/or formally (e.g., through frequent, short exams), and adjust instructional content and methods accordingly.

- I like it when instructors show an interest in how students are grasping content and adjust their teaching accordingly.

Test in the same manner in which you teach. Ensure that a test measures what students have learned and not their ability to adapt to a new format or style of presentation.

- It is helpful when the instructor provides some advance indication of which type of test the students should expect.

Minimize time constraints when appropriate. Plan for variety in students' ability to complete work by announcing assignments well in advance of due dates. Allow extended time on tests and projects, unless speed is an essential outcome of instruction.

- Just as a professor should use good judgment in giving appropriate time to complete an assignment, the student should be able to budget time to meet a variety of deadline assignment "styles."

ACCOMMODATION

Plan for accommodations for students whose needs are not met by the instructional design.

Know how to arrange for accommodations. Know campus protocols for getting materials in alternate formats, rescheduling classroom locations, and arranging for other accommodations for students with disabilities. Make sure that assistive technology can be made available in a computer or science lab in a timely manner. Ensure that the course experience is equivalent for students with accommodations.

- I don't expect a professor to be an expert about my disability; that's my job. What I do expect is that the professor will have a professional conversation with me and facilitate arrangements for my accommodations.

- One instructor offered to teach me verbal concepts of synoptic meteorology that other students learned by completing weather maps. When I asked him a few months before the beginning of the class what he thought might be the best way for me to participate in this highly visual work, he offered me the approach of weekly one-on-one meetings. I very much appreciated his willingness to go out of his way to help me learn the material in a manner that was effective for me.
- I have been very accommodating to instructors and willing to do whatever it takes, within reason, to succeed in class. I think I am successful with this because I provide the professor with my own accommodation ideas rather than asking them how they might suit my needs.
- If students take an exam in a classroom setting, they are allowed to ask the faculty and TAs questions. This is harder to do when a student is taking an exam in a disability services testing facility. To remedy this inequality, professors have included in the exam packet delivered to disability services written instructions and announcements that they plan to make to the entire class. One chemistry professor graciously called the disability services office in the middle of my exam to give me the opportunity to ask any questions. It meant a lot that he took my needs into account and made this extraordinary effort.
- In a physical oceanography class I took, the directions of the various currents and explanations for these directions were discussed in class, described in a textbook, and illustrated with maps. To reinforce understanding of the material, students were given the homework assignment of completing a map of the ocean currents. The instructor and I modified this assignment to accommodate my blindness, and instead I was quizzed orally about the locations and directions of the various currents. This arrangement provided me with an equivalent way of demonstrating my knowledge about the subject.

CONCLUSION

Students with disabilities do not always agree on the best practices for UDI. Overall, however, they make it clear that universal design strategies represent good teaching practice and minimize the need for specific accommodations. Important considerations are to create an environment that is welcoming and accessible to all students, employ a variety of teaching strategies, and ensure that each one is accessible to all students. Others are to make effective use of accessible information technology, make sure that course materials can be provided in accessible formats, ensure that products and environments are physically accessible and safe for everyone, interact often and in a variety of ways with students, assess students in multiple and accessible ways, and be prepared to provide accommodations to make learning activities fully accessible to students with disabilities. The disabled student services office, the instructor, and the student all have specific roles to play to ensure equal access to instruction for all students. All students benefit when universal design strategies are employed. Universally designed instruction is good instruction.

REFERENCES

Burgstahler, S. (2015). *Equal access: Universal design of instruction*. Seattle: University of Washington. Retrieved from http://www.washington.edu/doit/equal-access-universal-design-instruction

Disabilities, Opportunities, Internetworking, and Technology (DO-IT). (2006). *DO-IT Prof: A project to help postsecondary educators work successfully with students who have disabilities*. Seattle: University of Washington. Retrieved from http://www.washington.edu/doit/do-it-prof-project-help-postsecondary-educators-work-successfully-students-who-have-disabilities

DO-IT. (2007). *DO-IT Admin: A project to help postsecondary campus services administrators work successfully with students who have disabilities*. Seattle: University of Washington. Retrieved from http://www.washington.edu/doit/do-it-admin-project-help-postsecondary-student-services-administrators-work-successfully-students

DO-IT. (2012). *AccessCollege: Systemic change for postsecondary institutions*. Seattle: University of Washington. Retrieved from http://www.washington.edu/doit/accesscollege-systemic-change-postsecondary-institutions

The content of this chapter was developed under grants from the U.S. Department of Education Office of Postsecondary Education (grant numbers P333A990042, P333A020044, and P333A050064). However, this content does not necessarily represent the policy of the Department of Education, and you should not assume endorsement by the federal government.

7

The Benefits of Universal Design for Students with Psychological Disabilities

Al Souma
Deb Casey

The authors of this chapter discuss barriers to the learning process for students with psychological disabilities and suggest ways that applying universal design (UD) strategies can reduce these barriers as they enhance learning for all students. They offer practical suggestions for classroom teaching, assessment, and alternative assignments.

As coordinators of accommodations for students with disabilities, it has been our observation that most faculty are dedicated to teaching students theoretical and practical content without discrimination. However, they are continually challenged to create environments in which all students can achieve academic success. Accommodation requests to increase physical and sensory access in the classroom for students with disabilities are generally provided without objection. Examples of these accommodations include adjusting the height of a table for a wheelchair user, bringing in an oversized chair for a person large in stature, hiring an interpreter for a student who is deaf, and moving the location of a class when a student with mobility impairment is unable to access a classroom with entrance barriers. Requests for the removal of such physical and sensory barriers for individuals with disabilities are typically seen by faculty as reasonable.

During our tenure at various colleges and universities, however, we have spent many hours in consultation, workshops, and meetings with colleagues who question the justification for accommodations for students with disabilities that do not lend themselves to immediate visual identification, commonly referred to as *invisible disabilities*. Examples of invisible disabilities include learning disabilities, brain injuries, attention deficit disorders, and psychological disabilities. Over the past decade, the number of students with disabilities in postsecondary education has increased; it is estimated that 11% of undergraduate students enrolled in postsecondary institutions have a disability (Casey & Larsen, 2015). This trend increases the need for faculty members to learn strategies for effectively teaching these students. Universal design of instruction holds promise for addressing this need, while simultaneously improving the learning environment for other students.

In this chapter, we discuss barriers to the learning process for students with psychological disabilities and suggest UD strategies faculty members may employ that benefit students with psychological disabilities and others who have diverse learning abilities. Our experience suggests that a UD approach benefits students with and without disabilities, creates a productive and inclusive experience for everyone, and minimizes the need for additional accommodations for students with disabilities. Applying UD strategies in class provides "alternative teaching methods for individuals with different backgrounds, learning style abilities, and disabilities" and gives students flexible methods to learn materials and reflect knowledge (Center for Applied Special Technology [CAST], 2006, p. 2). The examples in this chapter affirm the application of UD principles for diverse learners.

PSYCHOLOGICAL DISABILITIES ON CAMPUS

Colleges throughout the country are reporting a marked increase in students with mental health disabilities, also referred to as psychiatric disabilities (Eudaly, 2002). These broad terms are used to describe multiple mental health issues that vary in intensity and duration. A specific condition may have a biochemical origin, environmental origin, or a combination of both. One survey revealed a rise in the number of students taking psychiatric medication, from 9% in 1994 to 24.5% in 2003–2004 (Gallagher, 2004). Learners with psychological disabilities may face educational challenges (Souma, Rickerson, & Burgstahler, 2012) that include those related to one or more of the following functional limitations:

- difficulty screening out environmental stimuli
- difficulty sustaining concentration and stamina
- difficulty handling time pressures and multiple tasks
- difficulty interacting with others
- fear of approaching authority figures, such as instructors or teaching assistants
- difficulty responding to change
- difficulty responding to negative feedback
- severe test anxiety

Students with psychological disabilities with whom we have worked have used one or more of the following accommodations:

- tape recorders
- note takers
- consistent feedback from faculty members
- extended test-taking time
- testing in a quiet room

- testing in alternative formats
- written assignments to replace oral assignments
- oral assignments to replace written assignments

A negative aspect of providing traditional accommodations for specific students is the implication of an inherent dysfunction in the way these individuals learn without consideration of problems in the way the content is taught. In addition, accommodations often have the unintended consequence of singling out individual learners.

As educators critically assess the manner in which their instruction is delivered and learning is assessed, they may begin to appreciate the issues faced by students with psychological disabilities as learning differences. As explained by experts at CAST, "Recent research in neurosciences shows that each brain processes information differently. The way we learn is as individual as DNA or fingerprints" (CAST, n.d.).

UNIVERSAL DESIGN AND INSTRUCTION

A model that shows promise in designing effective teaching, learning, and work-based learning environments in the academic setting is UD. This approach puts high value on full inclusion, accessibility, and usability for all students (Burgstahler, 2015; Sinski 2014). Through the application of UD principles in classroom and clinical environments, faculty help all students without having to make major modifications to curriculum or clinical experiences for individual students.

UD emerged in the architectural field, and for over a decade it has been studied in the fields of education and technology (CAST, 2006; Kalivoda, 2003). Researchers and practitioners have shown how academic content and materials developed in alternative formats, as well as diverse teaching strategies, can offer a host of benefits to students because they allow learners to customize and engage with instructional content in ways suited to their diverse learning styles and abilities (Abell, Bauder, & Simmons, 2004; Brown & Augustine, 2000; Burgstahler & Gleicher, in press; Casey-Powell, 2007). The conceptual framework of UD offers faculty and students new teaching and learning possibilities, as well as inclusive academic support provisions for students with disabilities.

Characteristics of universally designed instruction (Post-Secondary Academic and Curriculum Excellence [PACE], 2002) include the following:

- The essential components of the course are clearly defined.
- Prerequisite courses, knowledge, and skills are identified.
- Expectations are communicated clearly.
- The physical environment is accessible and conducive to learning.
- The climate encourages and supports interaction.
- Instructional methods recognize student diversity.
- Technology enhances instruction and increases accessibility.
- A variety of mechanisms for demonstrating knowledge are available.
- Feedback is clear, prompt, and frequent.
- Good study habits are encouraged and supported.

UD is designed to benefit students with disabilities, as well as those for whom English is a second language, nontraditional students, students uncomfortable with computer technology, and international students. "All learners, but especially those with learning disabilities, attention deficits, developmental disabilities, or affective difficulties, may encounter barriers when instructional materials are not designed in a flexible manner" (CAST, 2006). "Universal design education goes beyond accessible design for people with disabilities to make all aspects of the educational experience more inclusive for students, parents, staff, faculty, administrators, and visitors with a great variety of characteristics" (Burgstahler, 2015). Applying UD principles to teaching, assignments, and assessments promotes the greatest amount of learning and offers all students opportunities to express their knowledge without adaptation or retrofitting of lectures, assignments, or assessment practices. The end result is to reduce the need for traditional accommodations for students with psychological and other disabilities.

Chickering and Gamson (1987) suggest the following best practices for instruction, consistent with UD:

- encouraging student-faculty contact
- encouraging cooperation among students
- encouraging active learning
- giving prompt feedback
- emphasizing time on task
- communicating high expectations
- respecting diverse talents and ways of learning

UNIVERSAL DESIGN STRATEGIES THAT BENEFIT STUDENTS WITH PSYCHOLOGICAL DISABILITIES

The rising numbers of students with invisible disabilities in postsecondary education increases the importance of employing teaching practices that address the diverse needs of these students. The adoption of UD strategies benefits all students, but it may particularly benefit students with psychological disabilities and reduce their need for accommodations. In this section we point out how UD strategies might benefit students with psychological disabilities.

Classroom Teaching Strategies and Universal Design

Typical content delivery methods in the classroom require students to listen and take notes simultaneously, grasp key concepts quickly, listen attentively to long periods of verbal input, and negotiate interpersonal social relationships with other students. Some or all of these activities may prove especially challenging for a student with a psychological disability. Table 7.1 includes strategies that apply UD principles for the benefit of a student with a psychological disability in the classroom.

TABLE 7.1   Classroom Teaching: Universal Design Practices That Benefit Students with Psychological Disabilities

Issue Faced by a Student with a Psychological Disability	Universal Design Strategies That Benefit This Student and Others
Student may not be aware of accommodation options available.	Include course syllabus statement of accommodation (e.g., "If you need accommodations based on a documented disability, please contact Disability Support Services.").
Student may not be able to take notes while listening to a lecture.	Consider posting class notes on a website, or assign students to post notes; be sure that they are in a text-based accessible format.
Student may feel isolated from instructor and peers.	Strengthen faculty and student interactions by learning the names of students, encouraging office visits, personalizing feedback on student assignments, and mentoring. Encourage healthy student relationships by creating learning communities or study groups and modeling healthy exchanges when talking to students.
Student may not initially grasp key concepts introduced later in the lecture.	Present new concepts at the beginning of class using blackboards/whiteboards, and review them before the lecture.
Student may struggle to absorb information delivered in a single learning modality.	Consider the use of visual aids, hands-on learning, and electronic aids that underscore main ideas. Simulations, role-playing, structured exercises, and challenging discussions can also enhance learning.
The delivery of information is affected by the instructor's manner and pace of speech, as well as how the instructor is physically positioned in the classroom.	Face the class, speak in a direct manner, and make eye contact. Pace speech in a manner that promotes comprehension and observation of student facial expressions of understanding and confusion.
Student may need guidance when preparing for exams.	Consider holding optional review sessions for students before exams or after the completion of chapters, major topics, or important concepts.

Testing Strategies and Universal Design

Faculty members typically assess student learning with quizzes, unit tests, midterms, and final exams. A student's complete course grade might be based on the results of one or two written exams. Exams often include true/false, multiple-choice, matching, and/or short-answer essay formats. Unfortunately, some students may have a grasp of course content not measured by one or more of these exam formats. Students who think more globally may have a wider perspective on a topic but may not be able to identify, for example, the year a particular bill was signed into legislation. Similarly, a student may not remember what year Social Security was implemented under President Roosevelt but understand clearly what led up to this historic event.

TABLE 7.2   Testing Strategies: Universal Design Practices That Benefit Students with Psychological Disabilities

Potential Learning Style of a Student with a Psychological Disability	Types of Assessments to Complement Student Learning Styles
Expressive learner. A student may exhibit test anxiety during paper-and-pencil testing. This learner may perceive test-taking as overwhelming, and a test may be too narrow in focus to allow the student to express comprehension.	Alternative methods of expressing knowledge include portfolios, student verbal presentations, written research assignments completed at home, peer- and self-evaluations, or individual creative projects agreed on by student and instructor. Group presentations as an alternative to, or in addition to, written exams can also be built into an assessment.
Team or group support learner. Group learning is effective for a student who needs to discuss course content to learn material and demonstrate learning.	Case study analysis by individuals or groups may be an effective assessment strategy.
Collaborative learner. A student may work well in peer-to-peer teaching and learning activities.	Instructors may employ group-testing strategies in which grades are determined, in part, by the collective efforts of students.
Reflective learners. A student may work well writing independently and in self-reflective experience of course content.	Journaling about how theories apply to concepts taught in class may be an effective assessment method.
Technology-competent learner. One-to-one computer time may be most effective for a student who works better alone and/or without distraction.	Web-based assessment programs provide an interactive option for testing learning and conceptual understanding of processes and procedures.

Other challenges posed by standard exams for students with psychological disabilities may occur when a student is experiencing sleep deprivation, panic attacks, or unpleasant side effects of a new medication regimen. The student may be forced to miss an exam completely due to a medical emergency. UD strategies can be effective in assessing the knowledge of students with a wide variety of learning styles and abilities, including those with psychological disabilities. Offering a variety of alternative assessment strategies allows a student to express ideas and concepts in ways best suited to each student. Table 7.2 illustrates a number of ways diverse learners, including those who have psychological disabilities, can be assessed.

Class Assignments and Universal Design

The traditional oral method of teaching challenges students who are unable to focus on lectures 100% of the time. Faculty members may want to consider offering assignments inside and outside the classroom that apply UD principles. Through activities that include some degree of peer-to-peer or hands-on interaction, students with psychological disabilities can focus more directly and engage in ways that are more meaningful to them. In-class writing assignments to be handed in by the end of a class session cause a tremendous amount of anxiety for some students. Students with psychological disabilities report that their level of anxiety greatly increases when they

TABLE 7.3   Class Assignments: Universal Design Practices That Benefit Students with Psychological Disabilities

Issues Faced by a Student with a Psychological Disability	Alternative Assignments
Auditory teaching is a passive activity that may not engage the student.	In-class debating Case studies and discussion Brainstorming Cooperative learning projects
Producing written work in class may not reflect a student's best work.	In-class writing that can be taken home and refined.

cannot take an assignment home to rework and better represent their thinking. Over the years, students have informed us that their reason for dropping a class was related to having to complete in-class writing assignments, citing anxiety about spelling, sentence structure, and other issues. Table 7.3 gives examples of UD strategies for assessment that might benefit a student with a psychological impairment.

CONCLUSION

Universally designed teaching practices can have a positive academic impact on students with psychological disabilities, just as they enhance the learning environment for other students. The UD approach recognizes that all learners have unique skills, interests, and learning styles. UD strategies presented in this chapter include those for presenting information in the classroom, assessing student knowledge, and designing class assignments. Such applications of UD can lead to the need for fewer individual accommodations for students with psychological or other disabilities. Clearly, UD holds promise for creating a positive and healthy institutional climate of inclusion, promoting access and success, and demonstrating a commitment to nondiscrimination.

REFERENCES

Abell, M., Bauder, D., & Simmons, T. (2004). Universally designed online assessments: Implications for the future. *Information Technology and Disability, 10*(1). Retrieved from http://itd.athenpro.org/volume10/number1/abell.html

Brown, P. J., & Augustine, A. (2000). *Summary of the findings of the 1999–2000 screen reading field test: Inclusive comprehensive assessment system.* Newark: University of Delaware, Education Research and Development Center. Retrieved from http://udspace.udel.edu/handle/19716/2329?mode=full

Burgstahler, S. E. (2015). *Universal design of instruction: Definition, principles, guidelines, and examples.* Seattle: University of Washington. Retrieved from http://www.washington.edu/doit/universal-design-instruction-udi-definition-principles-guidelines-and-examples

Burgstahler, S. E., and Gleicher, R. (in press). Applying universal design to address the needs of post-secondary students on the autism spectrum. *Journal of Postsecondary Education and Disability.*

Casey, D., & Larsen, D. (2015). Serving diverse student populations in the community college. In A. Tull, L. Kuk, & P. Dalpes (Eds.), *Handbook for student affairs in community college.* Sterling, Virginia: Stylus Publishing, LLC.

Casey-Powell, D. A. (2007). Students with psychological disabilities in allied health sciences programs: Enhancing access and retention. In J. L. Higbee, D. B. Lundell, & I. M. Duranczyk (Eds.), *Diversity and the postsecondary experience* (pp. 87–102). Minneapolis: University of Minnesota, Center for Research on Developmental Education and Urban Literacy.

The Center for Applied Special Technology (CAST). (n.d.). *What is universal design for learning?* Wakefield, MA: Author. Retrieved from http://www.cast.org/udl/index.html

CAST. (2006). *Universal design for learning: Frequently asked questions.* Wakefield, MA: Author. Retrieved from http://www.ode.state.or.us/initiatives/elearning/nasdse/udlfaqs.pdf

Chickering, A. W., & Gamson, Z. F. (1987). *Seven principles for good practice in undergraduate education.* Washington, DC: American Association for Higher Education (ERIC Document Reproduction Service No. ED282491).

Eudaly, J. (2002). *A rising tide: Students with psychiatric disabilities seek services in record numbers.* (Monograph No. 8N). Washington, DC: George Washington University HEATH Resource Center.

Gallagher, R. (2004). *National survey of counseling centers directors.* Alexandria, VA: International Association of Counseling Services.

Kalivoda, K. S. (2003). Creating access through universal instructional design. In J. L. Higbee, D. B. Lundell, & I. M. Duranczyk (Eds.), *Multiculturalism in developmental education* (pp. 25–34). Minneapolis: University of Minnesota, Center for Research on Developmental Education and Urban Literacy.

Post-Secondary Academic and Curriculum Excellence (PACE). (2002). *Universal design: Applications in postsecondary education.* Little Rock: University of Arkansas. Retrieved from http://www.ualr.edu/pace/udcd/intro.html

Sinski, J. (2014). Classroom Strategies for Teaching Veterans with Post-Traumatic Stress Disorder and Traumatic Brain Injury. *Journal of Postsecondary Education and Disability, 25*(1), 87–95.

Souma, A., Rickerson, N., & Burgstahler, S. (2012). *Psychiatric disabilities in postsecondary education: Universal design, accommodations, and supported education.* Seattle: DO-IT, University of Washington. Retrieved from http://www.ncset.hawaii.edu/institutes/mar2004/papers/pdf/Souma_revised.pdf

8

Universal Design for Learning Intervention in Postsecondary Education

Results from Two Effectiveness Studies

Craig L. Spooner
Patricia L. Davies
Catherine L. Schelly

This chapter is a synthesis of two studies, both published previously in the Journal of Postsecondary Education and Disability (Davies, Schelly, & Spooner, 2013; Schelly, Davies, & Spooner, 2011), that measured the impact of providing training to university instructors on the principles and implementation methods of universal design for learning (UDL). Data not previously published have been included to represent the full scope of research conducted at Colorado State University by the ACCESS Project.

With its emphasis on diversity, inclusion, multimodal learning, and technology, universal design in higher education (UDHE) holds the potential to ameliorate some of higher education's most pressing challenges, including low rates of persistence, retention, and degree completion. UDHE is the offspring of universal design (UD), a philosophy and set of principles pertaining to architecture and product design, whose own origin and development can be traced back to the disability rights movement of the 1970s, 1980s, and especially the 1990s, following passage of the Americans with Disabilities Act (ADA, 1990; Center for Universal Design, 2012; Fair Housing Act, 1988; Institute for Human Centered Design, 2012; Rehabilitation Act, 1973). UDHE shares the UD goal of creating accessible products and environments. However, whereas UD originally concerned itself with the *built environment*, UDHE focuses on the higher education *learning environment*, where it strives to eliminate barriers that impact teaching and learning (Burgstahler, 2008).

Several frameworks have emerged for the application of UDHE. As presented in Chapter 2 of this book, they include *universal design of instruction* (Burgstahler, 2015), *universal design for instruction* (McGuire, Scott, & Shaw, 2006), *universal instructional design* (Higbee & Goff, 2008), and *universal design for learning* (Center for Applied Special Technology, 2009; Hall, Meyer, & Rose, 2012). These frameworks differ in their scope and other particulars, but share a common thread: proactive planning and the inclusive design of instruction, course materials, and learning environments to meet the varied needs of students. The framework used in the studies reported in this chapter is universal design for learning.

Embraced originally by K–12 educators, UDL has become increasingly popular among college and university instructors, who see it as "a conceptual and philosophical foundation on which to build a model of teaching and learning that is inclusive, equitable, and guides the creation of accessible course materials" (Schelly, Davies, & Spooner, 2011, p. 18). Just as architects and designers have discovered that UD "proactively builds in features to accommodate the range of human diversity" (McGuire & Scott, 2006, p. 173), so college educators are finding that UDL helps guide the selection of teaching strategies and the design of course materials that support the diverse learning needs of today's students (Burgstahler, 2008). According to David Rose, one of UDL's founders, "UDL puts the tag 'disabled' where it belongs—on the curriculum, not the learner. The curriculum is disabled when it does not meet the needs of diverse learners" (Council for Exceptional Children, 2011).

As described by the Center for Applied Special Technology, or CAST (2009), UDL practices are those techniques of instruction that apply one or more of the three UDL principles: (1) multiple means of representation (giving learners various ways of acquiring information and knowledge); (2) multiple means of student action and expression (providing learners alternative ways of demonstrating what they know); and (3) multiple means of student engagement (tapping into learners' interests, challenging them appropriately, and motivating them to learn). The three UDL principles map onto three groups of neural networks—recognition, strategic, and affective—that, through their interaction, create a model of cognition that helps explain how the brain works during learning episodes (Hall, Meyer, & Rose, 2012).

Despite numerous appeals in the literature for more research data to help evaluate UDHE's proposed benefits in the context of postsecondary education (Edyburn, 2010; Izzo, Murray, & Novak, 2008; Rose, Harbour, Johnston, Daley, & Abarbanell, 2006), only a handful of such studies have been published. Two systematic reviews of the literature have been conducted to identify empirical studies of UDHE—one in 2011 (Roberts, Park, Brown, & Cook), and the other in 2014 (Rao, Ok, & Bryant). The authors of this chapter also conducted their own extensive literature review.

From these reviews, four articles emerged that (1) were conducted in a postsecondary learning environment, and (2) attempted to measure the effects of training instructors on the principles and implementation techniques of UDL (Davies, Schelly, & Spooner, 2013; McGuire-Schwartz & Arndt, 2007; Schelly, Davies, & Spooner, 2011; Spooner, Baker, Harris, Delzell, & Browder, 2007). Two of these articles—herein referred to as "Study One" (Schelly, Davies, & Spooner, 2011) and "Study Two"

(Davies, Schelly, & Spooner, 2013)—were written by the authors of this chapter. Study One and Study Two describe research that was conducted at a large public university that attempted to measure the effectiveness of UDL instructor training as a means of increasing the use of inclusive, universally designed teaching practices. What follows are descriptions of these two studies and their implications for future research.

STUDY ONE (SCHELLY, DAVIES, & SPOONER, 2011)

The primary goal of Study One was to measure the effect of UDL training on the classroom teaching behavior of university instructors. In addition, the research team (hereafter referred to in the first person plural for the sake of brevity and clarity) wanted to test national estimates of the number of college-aged students with disabilities and the percentages of students in that group who seek, and choose not to seek, support from their campus disability services office.

The design of the study began with a search for a viable research model upon which to build. We discovered an exemplary, though unpublished, study conducted between 2002 and 2003 at the University of Guelph in Ontario, Canada. That study assessed "the extent of UID (Universal Instructional Design) implementation" and "whether student academic self-efficacy and affective states improved as a result" (Yuval, Procter, Korabik, & Palmer, 2004, p. 1). Like our colleagues at the University of Guelph, we sought to evaluate the impact of UDHE training. However, we chose UDL as the framework for defining accessible, inclusive instruction.

Research and Training Design

To accomplish our research goal, we needed to (1) operationalize the three UDL principles into a set of observable, measurable teaching practices, linked as closely as possible to commonly acknowledged good teaching practices in higher education; (2) create a UDL student questionnaire designed to measure student perceptions of the training's effects; and (3) develop a training program. We identified a collection of teaching strategies that conformed to the principles of UDL, along with efficient techniques for creating universally designed course materials, taking care that they would reflect the spirit of UD by being accessible and beneficial to all students, including students with a variety of disabilities. We used technology, as appropriate, to enrich the learning environment with opportunities for multimodal learning. We made special efforts to use UDL strategies and techniques that were relevant to a broader conversation that was already taking place on our campus and in higher education generally—a conversation centered on improving undergraduate learning and engagement in order to increase rates of retention, persistence, and, ultimately, degree completion. We expected that placing UDL in the broader discussion of teaching and learning would ensure its influence on the redesign of the curriculum for years to come. Thus, the UDL practices identified for the study related to other widely accepted best practices, such as

- the seven principles for good practice in undergraduate education (Chickering & Ehrmann, 1996; Chickering & Gamson, 1987, 1999)

- adult learning theories, which include andragogy (Knowles, 1975, 1980), self-directed learning (Cross, 1981; Knowles, 1975), and transformational learning (Cranton, 2002; Freire, 1970; Mezirow, 2000)
- student engagement (Bean, 2011; Zhao & Kuh, 2004)
- critical thinking (Kurfiss, 1988; Tsui, 2002)

Such were the requirements for selecting the UDL methods and techniques used in our research. These, in turn, were used to develop the pre-/post-survey instrument that would measure the degree to which these methods and techniques were manifested in the classroom. Likert statements used in the questionnaire were crafted to correspond to single UDL principles. For example, the statement, "The instructor presents information in multiple formats (e.g., lecture, text, graphics, audio, video)," corresponded to the first UDL principle of multiple means of representation. Teaching behaviors related to the second UDL principle, multiple means of student expression, were captured in the statement, "Students in this course are allowed to express their comprehension of material in ways besides traditional tests and exams (e.g., written essays, projects, portfolios)." Other Likert statements were developed to portray the third principle of UDL related to student engagement. For example: "In this course I feel interested and motivated to learn," "I feel challenged with meaningful assignments," and "The instructor expresses enthusiasm for topics covered in class."

Although the goal of pairing statements to their corresponding UDL principles was largely achieved, it became apparent that many good teaching practices address multiple principles simultaneously. For example, the statement mentioned previously, "The instructor presents information in multiple formats (e.g., lecture, text, graphics, audio, video)," relates to multiple means of representation, but also to multiple means for student engagement.

The new survey instrument was pilot-tested one semester prior to the beginning of data collection, and the feedback we received prompted us to add two Likert statements and refine the wording of several others. In the end, the survey consisted of twenty-seven statements, twenty-four of which pertained to UDL teaching strategies and employed a five-point Likert scale, from "0 = strongly disagree" to "5 = strongly agree." The final three questions focused on grade expectation, disability identification, and self-referral to the campus disability services. The survey was designed to be brief so that it could be completed in class. The questionnaire is included in our original article (Schelly, Davies, & Spooner, 2011, p. 23).

While the UDL questionnaire was being developed, we conducted focus groups with instructors who were teaching large, undergraduate "gateway" courses. Discussions in these meetings led us to select a target course for our research, Introduction to Psychology, because it was a prerequisite for nearly all undergraduate students and had high enrollment, with approximately sixteen hundred students per semester. The course offered another advantage as well: it was taught by a small cadre of instructors—PhD-level graduate students who had been selected by their department for teaching fellowships based on demonstrated teaching excellence—who met weekly under the supervision of an assistant professor to discuss issues of pedagogy. It was during five of these weekly meetings that our research team conducted the one-hour UDL training interventions.

Training topics included general disability information, such as legislation related to disabilities in higher education and the systems in place at our university for providing accommodations, the principles and history of UDL, and techniques for implementing each of the three UDL principles while developing teaching strategies and course materials. In addition to this face-to-face training, we created a series of online tutorials about how to create universally designed instructional materials in Word, PowerPoint, PDF, HTML, and e-text. These tutorials explained the accessibility barriers commonly found in electronic course materials and how to avoid them.

Research Participants and Results

In the spring of 2007, the surveys were distributed to 1,615 students enrolled in nine sections of Introduction to Psychology prior to the initiation of instructor training (the pre-survey) and again at the end of the semester (the post-survey). Of those, 1,362 students (84%) filled out the pre-survey and 1,223 students (76%) filled out the post-survey. Across all of the sections, the percentage of students who completed the surveys varied from 68% to 98% for the pre-survey, and from 51% to 93% for the post-survey. The remarkable response rate provided the power necessary to achieve significant results regarding student perceptions of changes in their instructors' teaching behaviors following structured training on UDL principles and techniques. Although achieving statistical significance was more likely with the power that resulted from a large number of respondents, we interpreted the results with caution by adjusting for multiple statistical analyses, considering effect sizes, and verifying that the significant changes obtained were consistent with the UDL training that was provided.

Respondents reported significant and meaningful changes on at least six of the twenty-four UDL items on the questionnaire. Student responses suggested that two general strategies presented in the training had the most impact on instructors' teaching behavior. The first was presenting concepts in multiple ways and offering course materials in a variety of formats. The second was summarizing key concepts before, during, and immediately following instruction. The instructors appeared to incorporate these UDL strategies into their teaching almost immediately following the training sessions.

Of the 1,362 students who completed the pre-survey, 1,330 responded either "yes" or "no" to the question "Do you have a disability?" Of the 106 students who answered "yes" (approximately 8%), only 23 (22%) had contacted the university's student disability services office to seek supports or accommodations. Of the 1,223 students who completed the post-survey, 1,195 answered the disability question, 98 (again, approximately 8%) reported having a disability, and 20 of those 98 (2%) said they had contacted the disability services office. The percentage of students reporting a disability in our study was consistent with, but somewhat lower than, the national estimate of approximately 11% (National Center for Education Statistics, 2008; National Council on Disability, 2003; U.S. Government Accountability Office, 2009). However, of students who reported they had disabilities, only 20% sought accommodations or otherwise identified themselves to the university as having a disability, which was remarkably lower than the 40% reported in previous research (Wagner, Newman, Cameto, Garza, & Levine, 2005).

Limitations

The research design did not include a control group to confirm that the reported changes in teaching behavior between the beginning and the end of the semester were due to the UDL intervention. Even without the training, instructors' teaching strategies may have improved over the course of the semester, perhaps due to their increased confidence and familiarity with the class. Other limitations of this study were related to the content and format of the questionnaire. For example, the survey items did not specifically ask students to identify teaching strategies they found to be most engaging, even though providing multiple means of engagement is a critical UDL principle and much of the instructor training provided during the study addressed this topic. In addition, the five-point Likert scale format resulted in some "ceiling effects," meaning that responses were compressed at the top of the scale ("agree" or "strongly agree"). This ceiling effect made the survey less sensitive to identifying changes in teaching practices, especially for instructors who began the semester already employing some of the UDL principles.

Discussion

The results of this first study strongly suggested that UDL training for higher education instructors was effective at increasing the use of universally designed teaching practices. Students indicated that instructors used significantly more UDL strategies following the UDL training than before the training was administered.

STUDY TWO (DAVIES, SCHELLY, & SPOONER, 2013)

Between the spring of 2008 and fall of 2010, our team carried out a new, more robust study on the outcomes of UDL training. Based on our previous work, Study Two introduced a quasi-experimental design—the first study of this type that we could find reported in the literature.

Research Design

Improvements to the research design made from the first to the second study are summarized as follows:

- A control group was added to allow comparison of results.
- The survey instrument was modified and expanded in three ways:
    - Additional Likert statements, especially in the area of student engagement, were added to better reflect the three UDL principles.
    - The five-point Likert scale was expanded to eleven points to improve its sensitivity to change (Darbyshire & McDonald, 2004).
    - Open-ended questions were added to capture student perceptions of teaching strategies they found engaging and helpful for learning.

- Questions were added to the end of the questionnaire to request additional student demographic data. The new questions asked what percentage of class sessions the respondent had attended for that course, if the syllabus included a statement about disability-related accommodations, the respondent's level of familiarity with campus resources for students, what grade the respondent expected to receive in the course, the student's status (including employment status and year in college), and the amount of time it took to complete the questionnaire.

Because the number of questionnaire items nearly doubled from the first to the second study, from twenty-seven to fifty, it was no longer feasible to administer the questionnaire in the classroom. The instrument was converted from a paper questionnaire, which students filled out in class, to an online questionnaire, which students could complete at any time within a specified seven-day period using the university's online course management system. Care was taken to ensure that the questionnaire was formatted to be accessible to all students, including those with disabilities. Offering the questionnaire in an online format increased its accessibility, as students could now fill it out using a variety of technologies whenever they had Internet access. A copy of this instrument is included in the original publication of the results of this study (Davies, Schelly, & Spooner, 2013).

Research Participants and Results

Instructors who participated in the second study once again consisted of PhD candidates who had been selected by the Department of Psychology for demonstrated teaching excellence. None of the participants had been involved in or exposed to the previous study, although all were mentored by the same assistant professor. Participants in both groups—intervention and control—attended the same number of weekly one-hour teaching seminars, although only those belonging to the intervention group received the five, one-hour UDL trainings.

The six instructors in the intervention group taught a total of nine psychology sections, with a total enrollment of 1,164 students. Of these, 622 students (approximately 53%) completed the pre-questionnaire and 421 students (approximately 36%) completed the post-questionnaire. A total of 386 students (approximately 33%) completed both the pre- and post-questionnaires. The participants in the control group included three instructors teaching six psychology sections, in which 646 students were enrolled. Of these, 276 students (approximately 43%) filled out the pre-questionnaire and 223 students (approximately 35%) filled out the post-questionnaire. A total of 204 students (approximately 32%) filled out both the pre- and post-questionnaires. As expected, online delivery resulted in a lower response rate when compared to our previous study, because students were no longer a "captive audience" as they completed the instrument.

Responses from students who had completed both the pre- and post-questionnaires (386 in the intervention group and 204 in the control group) were analyzed. At the time of the pre-questionnaire, 9.3% of the students ($n = 57$) in the intervention group reported having a disability, while 9.5% of the students ($n = 27$) in the control group said the same. The results of the second study confirmed those of the first:

UDL training had a significant effect on students' perceptions of instruction, as measured by the questionnaire. Teaching strategies that were most significantly impacted by the UDL training included (a) presenting material in multiple formats, (b) relating key concepts to the larger objectives of the course, (c) providing an outline at the beginning of each lecture, (d) summarizing material throughout each class session, (e) highlighting key points of an instructional video, (f) using instructional videos, and (g) using well-organized and accessible materials.

These strategies correspond to several key aspects of UDL. For example, presenting material in multiple formats, using instructional videos as well as printed materials, and using well-organized and accessible materials all exemplify the UDL principle of multiple means of representation. The four remaining items that showed improvement—relating concepts to the overall course objectives, providing an outline at the beginning of class, summarizing throughout the session, and highlighting key points of an instructional video—can also be considered a type of representation, specifically a type of communication characterized as "clarity," which is defined as the process by which an instructor stimulates the comprehension of course content and thought processes of the students through structured verbal and nonverbal communication (Chesebro & McCroskey, 2001).

Interestingly, a few of the UDL strategies were perceived by students in both the intervention and control groups to increase over the course of the semester. For example, students in both groups reported they were more actively engaged in learning and that their instructors expressed their personal enthusiasm more at the end of the semester than at the beginning. Students also reported that the feedback provided on assignments was more helpful and instructive at the end of the semester. Active learning, instructor enthusiasm, and prompt feedback, while not tied directly to the UDL principles, are widely acknowledged as effective techniques for increasing student engagement (Brigham, Scruggs, & Mastropieri, 1992; Carlisle & Phillips, 1984; Chickering & Gamson, 1999). We interpreted these results to mean that the familiarity and rapport that develops between students and instructors across the duration of a course are important factors in the improvement of certain UDL-related teaching strategies.

By comparing responses of participants in the intervention group with those in the control group, our results suggest that effective communication, which is likely to evolve naturally between instructors and students over the course of a semester, may contribute to the use of UDL teaching and learning strategies. To varying degrees, the three principles of UDL—multiple means of representation, multiple means of student action and expression, and multiple means of student engagement—are all dependent on effective communication. UDL training should therefore emphasize the importance of effective communication, such as clarity.

In Study Two we also examined student persistence and successful course completion, although these data were not reported in that publication (Davies, Schelly, & Spooner, 2013). Among students in the control group, 94.6% successfully completed the course, while 5.4% did not. In the intervention group, 96% of students successfully completed the course, compared to 4% who did not. Cross-tabulation analysis indicated there was not a significant difference between the intervention and control groups in the proportion of students who successfully completed the course and those who did not. However, when we examined persistence for students who reported a disability, the cross-tabulation analysis resulted in a significant difference between students with disabilities in the intervention group compared to the students with disabilities in the control group ($\chi2 = 4.13$, $p = .04$). For students with disabilities in the control group, 80% completed the course and 20% did not. For students with disabilities in the intervention group, 95.7% completed the course and 4.3% did not. The results of this study suggest that students with disabilities in a course where the instructor receives UDL training are more likely to successfully complete the course than students with disabilities in a course where the instructor did not receive this training (Roll, Davies, & Schelly, 2015).

Limitations

The instrument used in this study relied on student perceptions of their instructors' implementation of UDL. Future research in this area should include other outcome measures, such as in-class observations of instructors' performance, which would provide additional information about the actual implementation of UDL strategies (Yuval et al., 2004).

A second limitation was the length of the survey instrument (fifty items), and the fact that it was electronically delivered. It is conceivable that students found it burdensome to complete. Subsequent research should look closely at shortening the instrument, which may facilitate a higher response rate. That said, electronic questionnaires support efforts to "go green," and respond to contemporary students' preferred method of communication (Greenhow, Robelia, & Hughes, 2009). They are also, at least potentially, more accessible.

A third limitation relates to the pre-intervention characteristics of the instructor-participants, who were doctoral students and as such were at a different stage of professional development than full-time faculty. It is possible that UDL training for graduate teaching assistants may not be generalizable to UDL training for full-time faculty. Future studies should include both full-time faculty and graduate teaching assistants. In addition, the instructors competitively applied for the teaching positions and were capable instructors before participating in the study. It is therefore possible that student perceptions of their teaching skills would have been quite positive even without the UDL training.

DISCUSSION AND RECOMMENDATIONS FOR FUTURE RESEARCH

UDL appears to hold great promise in higher education, not only as a leveling force for students with disabilities, but also as a way for colleges and universities to retain and successfully graduate students who are increasingly diverse, nontraditional, and therefore more "at risk." Despite this promise, the literature on UDHE is "long on principles and 'best practices,' but short on empirical evidence of its benefits" (Schelly et al., 2011, p. 18). The two published studies reported in this chapter begin to provide evidence on the effectiveness of using UDHE to improve learning for all students.

It is recommended that future research focus on instructors who are at varied levels of competence and experience. Future research should examine instructor characteristics (for example, experience) and techniques at baseline. Accordingly, instructor characteristics can be treated as covariate variables and differential changes in teaching/learning methodologies used by instructors in an intervention group compared to a control group. The results of Study Two, which employed a quasi-experimental design, emphasize the importance of using control groups when examining the effectiveness of UDL training. Quasi-experimental studies are essential for research in higher education because they do not require random assignment, meaning that enrollment in courses need not be manipulated in order for applied research to be conducted.

CONCLUSIONS

The two studies reported in this chapter suggest that as little as five hours of group instruction on the use of UDL principles and teaching strategies can increase the implementation of those strategies. The addition of a control group in Study Two suggested that the increased use of universally designed teaching practices was a direct result of the training the instructors received. Changes in instructors' implementation of UDL strategies, based on student survey responses, were compared between those who received UDL training and a control group of instructors who did not. Students enrolled in courses in which their instructors received training reported a positive change in instructors' use of UDL strategies, especially those strategies related to the principle of multiple means of representation. Students in both the intervention and control groups reported a positive change in engagement, which indicates that some effective teaching and learning strategies may emerge across a semester regardless of instructor training. UDL training was also positively correlated with increased likelihood that a student with a disability would successfully complete the course. Collectively, these two studies provide evidence that instructor training is an effective way to promote universally designed teaching practices in postsecondary education.

REFERENCES

Americans with Disabilities Act of 1990, as amended, 42 U.S.C § 12101 et seq. (1990).

Bean, J. C. (2011). *Engaging ideas: The professor's guide to integrating writing, critical thinking, and active learning in the classroom*. San Francisco: Jossey-Bass.

Brigham, F. J., Scruggs, T. E., & Mastropieri, M. A. (1992). Teacher enthusiasm in learning disabilities classrooms: Effects on learning and behavior. *Learning Disabilities Research & Practice, 7*(2), 68–73.

Burgstahler, S. E. (2008). Universal design in higher education. In S. E. Burgstahler & R. C. Cory (Eds.), *Universal design in higher education: From principles to practice* (pp. 3–20). Cambridge, MA: Harvard Education Press.

Burgstahler, S. E. (2015). *Universal design of instruction (UDI): Definition, principles, guidelines, and examples*. Seattle: University of Washington.

Carlisle, C., & Phillips, D. A. (1984). The effects of enthusiasm training on selected teacher and student behaviors in preservice physical education teachers. *Journal of Teaching in Physical Education, 4*(1), 164–175.

Center for Applied Special Technology. (2009). *What is universal design for learning?* Retrieved from http://www.cast.org/research/udl/index.html

Center for Universal Design. (2012). *About universal design: Universal design history.* Retrieved from http://www.ncsu.edu/www/ncsu/design/sod5/cud/about_ud/udhistory.htm

Chesebro, J. L., & McCroskey, J. C. (2001). The relationship of teacher clarity and immediacy with student state receiver apprehension, affect, and cognitive learning. *Communication Education, 50*(1), 59–68. doi:10.1080/03634520109379232

Chickering, A. W., & Ehrmann, S. C. (1996). Implementing the seven principles: Technology as lever. *American Association for Higher Education Bulletin, 49*(2), 3–6.

Chickering, A. W., & Gamson, Z. F. (1987). Seven principles for good practice in undergraduate education. *AAHE Bulletin*, 3–7.

Chickering, A. W., & Gamson, Z. F. (1999). Development and adaptations of the seven principles for good practice in undergraduate education. *New Directions for Teaching & Learning, 80*, 75.

Council for Exceptional Children. (2011). *New guidelines for universal design for learning provide a roadmap for educators and educational publishers.* Retrieved from http://www.cec.sped.org/AM/Template.cfm?Section=Home&CAT=none&CONTENTID=10573&TEMPLATE=/CM/ContentDisplay.cfm

Cranton, P. (2002). Teaching for transformation. *New Directions for Adult & Continuing Education, 2002*(93), 63–71.

Cross, K. P. (1981). *Adults as learners. Increasing participation and facilitating learning.* San Francisco: Jossey-Bass.

Darbyshire, P., & McDonald, H. (2004). Choosing response scale labels and length: Guidance for researchers and clients. *Australasian Journal of Market Research, 12*(2), 17–26.

Davies, P. L., Schelly, C. L., & Spooner, C. L. (2013). Measuring the effectiveness of universal design for learning intervention in postsecondary education. *Journal of Postsecondary Education and Disability, 26*(3), 195.

Edyburn, D. L. (2010). Would you recognize universal design for learning if you saw it? Ten propositions for new directions for the second decade of UDL. *Learning Disability Quarterly, 33*(1), 33–41. doi:10.1177/073194871003300103

Fair Housing Act, as amended, 42 U.S.C § 3601 et seq. (1988).

Freire, P. (1970). *Pedagogy of the oppressed.* New York: Herder and Herder.

Greenhow, C., Robelia, B., & Hughes, J. E. (2009). Learning, teaching, and scholarship in a digital age. Web 2.0 and classroom research: What path should we take now? *Educational Researcher, 38*(4), 246–259.

Hall, T. E., Meyer, A., & Rose, D. H. (2012). An introduction to universal design for learning: Questions and answers. In T. E. Hall, A. Meyer, & D. H. Rose (Eds.), *Universal design for learning in the classroom: Practical applications* (pp. 1–8). New York: Guilford Press.

Higbee, J. L., & Goff, E. (2008). *Pedagogy and student services for institutional transformation: Implementing universal design in higher education.* Minneapolis: Regents of the University of Minnesota, Center for Research on Developmental Education and Urban Literacy. Retrieved from http://www.cehd.umn.edu/passit/docs/PASS-IT-Book.pdf

Institute for Human Centered Design. (2012). *History of universal design.* Retrieved from http://www.humancentereddesign.org/universal-design/history-universal-design

Izzo, M. V., Murray, A., & Novak, J. (2008). The faculty perspective on universal design for learning. *Journal of Postsecondary Education and Disability, 21*(2), 60–72.

Knowles, M. S. (1975). *Self-directed learning: A guide for learners and teachers.* New York: Association Press.

Knowles, M. S. (1980). *The modern practice of adult education from pedagogy to andragogy.* Wilton, CT: Association Press.

Kurfiss, J. G. (1988). *Critical thinking: Theory, research, practice, and possibilities.* ASHE-ERIC Higher Education Report No. 2. Washington DC: Eric Clearinghouse on Higher Education.

McGuire-Schwartz, M. E., & Arndt, J. S. (2007). Transforming universal design for learning in early childhood teacher education from college classroom to early childhood classroom. *Journal of Early Childhood Teacher Education, 28*(2), 127–139.

McGuire, J. M., & Scott, S. S. (2006). An approach for inclusive college teaching: Universal design for instruction. *Learning Disabilities: A Multidisciplinary Journal, 14*(1), 21–32.

McGuire, J. M., Scott, S. S., & Shaw, S. F. (2006). Universal design and its applications in educational environments. *Remedial and Special Education, 27*(3), 166–175.

Mezirow, J. (2000). Learning to think like an adult: Core concepts of transformation theory. In J. Mezirow (Ed.), *Learning as transformation: Critical perspectives on a theory in progress* (pp. 3–33). San Francisco: Jossey-Bass.

National Center for Education Statistics, U.S. Department of Education. (2008). *Table 231: Number and percentage of students enrolled in postsecondary institutions, by level, disability status, and selected student characteristics: 2003–04.* Washington, DC: National Center for Education Statistics. Retrieved from http://nces.ed.gov/programs/digest/d08/tables/dt08_231.asp.

National Council on Disability. (2003). *People with disabilities and postsecondary education—position paper.* Washington, DC: Retrieved from http://www.ncd.gov/publications/2003/Sept152003

Rao, K., Ok, M. W., & Bryant, B. R. (2014). A review of research on universal design educational models. *Remedial and Special Education, 35*(3), 153–166. doi:10.1177/0741932513518980

The Rehabilitation Act of 1973, 29 U.S.C § 701 (1973).

Roberts, K. D., Park, H. J., Brown, S., & Cook, B. (2011). Universal design for instruction in postsecondary education: A systematic review of empirically based articles. *Journal of Postsecondary Education and Disability, 24*(1), 5–15.

Roll, M. C., Davies, P. L., & Schelly, C. L. (2015). *Universal design for learning: Implications for students with disabilities in higher education.* Manuscript in preparation.

Rose, D. H., Harbour, W. S., Johnston, C. S., Daley, S. G., & Abarbanell, L. (2006). Universal design for learning in postsecondary education: Reflections on principles and their application. *Journal of Postsecondary Education and Disability, 19*(2), 135–151.

Schelly, C. L., Davies, P. L., & Spooner, C. L. (2011). Student perceptions of faculty implementation of universal design for learning. *Journal of Postsecondary Education and Disability, 24*(1), 17–28.

Spooner, F., Baker, J. N., Harris, A. A., Delzell, L. A., & Browder, D. M. (2007). Effects of training in universal design for learning on lesson plan development. *Remedial & Special Education, 28*, 108–116.

Tsui, L. (2002). Fostering critical thinking through effective pedagogy: Evidence from four institutional case studies. *Journal of Higher Education, 73*(6), 740–763.

U.S. Government Accountability Office. (2009). *Higher education and disability: Education needs a coordinated approach to improve its assistance to schools in supporting students.* (GAO-10-33). Washington, DC: U.S. Government Accountability Office. Retrieved from http://www.gao.gov/new.items/d1033.pdf

Wagner, M., Newman, L., Cameto, R., Garza, N., & Levine, P. (2005). *After high school: A first look at the postschool experiences of youth with disabilities. A report from the national longitudinal transition study-2 (nlts2).* Washington, DC: Office of Special Education Programs, U.S. Department of Education. Retrieved from http://files.eric.ed.gov/fulltext/ED494935.pdf

Yuval, L., Procter, E., Korabik, K., & Palmer, J. (2004). *Evaluation report on the universal instructional design project at the university of guelph.* Ontario, Canada: University of Guelph.

Zhao, C.-M., & Kuh, G. D. (2004). Adding value: Learning communities and student engagement. *Research in Higher Education, 45*(2), 115–138. doi:10.1023/B:RIHE.0000015692.88534.de

The content of this chapter is based on work supported by the U.S. Department of Education, Office of Postsecondary Education (grant numbers P333A050015 and P333A080026). Any opinions, findings, and conclusions or recommendations are those of the authors and do not necessarily reflect the policy or views of the federal government, and the reader should not assume its endorsement.

9

Incorporating Universal Design into Administration Courses

A Case Study

Karen A. Myers

For universal design (UD) to be understood and utilized by faculty and student affairs professionals, educational preparation programs must address this concept through disability awareness, pedagogical practices, and experiential learning. As a result, future educators will be prepared to utilize universal instructional design (UID) in their classes, and future student affairs professionals will be prepared to use universal design in their programs and services. In her preparation programs, the author incorporates UID into her classes and teaches universal design to current and future higher education faculty and student affairs practitioners. In this chapter, she shares her experiences in infusing UID into professional preparation programs and other efforts that promote the understanding and application of universal design.

> People will forget what you said, people will forget what you did, but people will never forget how you made them feel.
>
> —*Bonnie Jean Wasmund*

Applying UD in education supports my goal as an educator to foster understanding and appreciation of human differences while helping people recognize the importance of civility and inclusion. Teaching UD to students who will be developing and teaching their own courses is a rewarding experience. Teaching UD while modeling universal instructional design practices as I teach is an exhilarating experience. As a professor in a graduate higher education/student affairs preparation program, I am in the "exhilaration" stage and thrilled to be there. I use a multimodal approach to helping future teachers and practitioners learn how to apply UD in their classes, curricula, services, programs, and daily work. In this chapter, I share my journey in applying UID in my teaching, infusing UD content into professional preparation programs, and empowering students to promote disability awareness and the application of UD through course projects that have a lasting impact. It is my hope that my experiences will stimulate ideas for how others can promote the application of UD on their campuses.

BACKGROUND

According to the U.S. Census Bureau's 2000 report, the number of college students with disabilities made up approximately 9% of the undergraduate population. More current statistics reveal that approximately 11% of college students have reported a diagnosed and documented disability (United States Department of Education, National Center for Education Statistics [ED NCES], 2012). The percentage of high school graduates with disabilities matriculating to college has increased from 3% in 1978 to 19% in 1996, and the number of students with disabilities attending colleges and universities has more than tripled over the last thirty years, from 3% in 1978 to 9% in 1998 and 11% in 2008 (Snyder & Dillow, 2010; ED NCES, 2006; U.S. Census Bureau, 2010). Nondiscrimination laws have opened the doors of higher education to students with disabilities who may never have considered college a viable option. These students are engaging in graduate and undergraduate programs, accessing student services, participating in campus clubs and organizations, living in residence halls, working in libraries and labs, and participating in institutional events. Despite the fact that legislation prohibiting discrimination against people with disabilities was enacted years ago in Section 504 of the Rehabilitation Act of 1973 and the Americans with Disabilities Act (ADA) of 1990, recently updated in the Americans with Disabilities Act Amendments Act (ADAAA) of 2008, and expanded in the 21st Century Communications and Video Accessibility Act (CCVA) of 2010, knowledge of disability issues and sensitivity about inclusion are lacking on our campuses and in our communities (Higbee & Mitchell, 2009; Myers, Lindburg, & Nied, 2013). UD provides an approach for helping future faculty, practitioners, and university administrators address these issues.

In the first edition of this book, I wrote that anecdotal evidence continues to suggest that UD is not a significant part of the curriculum and professional development plan at my current institution. When I first began teaching UD principles, the only student in my class who was familiar with the concept prior to the class was the university's disability services provider. Today, I am pleased to report that many of my students and student affairs colleagues have not only heard of UD principles, but have also incorporated them in their daily work. That is the good news. As I conduct campus-wide, regional, and national seminars on related issues, however, it is apparent to me that few faculty, teaching assistants, and other higher education professionals have heard about UD. Although UDI has been presented, written about, and discussed for many years (e.g., Burgstahler & Cory, 2008; Duranczyk, Myers, Couillard, Schoen, & Higbee, 2013; Higbee, 2012; Myers, Lindburg, & Nied, 2013; Silver, Bourke, & Strehorn, 1998), UD applications appear to be a well-kept secret on many college campuses.

I work at Saint Louis University, a religious-affiliated private research university in the Midwest with an enrollment of nearly fourteen thousand (approximately eighty-eight hundred undergraduate and fifty-one hundred graduate students). Founded in 1818, the institution offers degrees in the fields of law, medicine, natural and health sciences, social sciences, business, education, aviation, technology, and the humanities. The Higher Education Administration Graduate Program is housed in the College of Education and Public Service. The program offers a master's degree in student personnel administration and a PhD in higher education administration. The Higher Education Administration faculty work closely in a collaborative team with faculty who teach in other programs in the same College, including Educational Leadership, Curriculum and Instruction, Teacher Education, Educational Foundations, and Disability Education. In support of its mission, the university welcomes diversity in its faculty, staff, and students—diversity in racial, religious, and ethnic backgrounds; abilities; and beliefs. It fosters a community of learners and promotes social justice and service to others. This philosophy of inclusion is a natural fit with the intentions of UD.

MY JOURNEY WITH UD

When I first arrived at Saint Louis University nine years ago, my teaching responsibilities included courses in higher education curricula, organization, administration, and leadership; student personnel administration; student development theory; college environment and culture; and college teaching. Recent additional responsibilities include serving as director of the Higher Education Administration Program, coordinator of the Higher Education Administration internships, and director of The Ability Institute, which serves to address multiple aspects of equity and inclusion in higher education and society. The Ability Institute houses *Allies for Inclusion: The Ability Exhibit,* an award-winning national traveling exhibit (http://www.slu.edu/theabilityexhibit), and the Ability Ally Initiative, a disability ally training program, both of which were created by students in the Higher Education Administration program. Given this opportunity to educate future postsecondary faculty and practitioners, I made a conscious decision at the outset to incorporate UD into every course I taught. Not only do I educate students about UD principles and applications, but I also model UID by implementing competency-based learning and other instructional practices as well as in-class and online delivery methods. Through UD, I strive to eliminate barriers in the classroom and provide equal access for all students to all information, employing "pedagogical curb cuts" (Ben-Moshe, Cory, Feldbaum, & Sagendorf, 2005).

In 2006, I began developing and teaching a course called Disability in Higher Education and Society, which is discussed more fully later in this chapter. I first discussed the idea of incorporating UID in every class with the department chairperson, not only to inform him about UID but also to gain his support. This type of communication with our College's dean has continued throughout a university-wide reorganization and under our College's new structure. Building on informal communication with colleagues in the College and at other institutions and with current graduate students, I developed an academic plan as to how I would utilize, model, teach, and, in the process, spread the word about UD. As a result of intentional communication with the director of the university's Center for Transformative Teaching and Learning (CTTL; formerly the Center for Teaching Excellence), I now partner with the Center, utilizing its expertise in my college teaching course and other courses by inviting CTTL staff to my classes as guest speakers. One of the many pleasant outcomes of this partnership is that the CTTL director is now the instructor for our Higher Education Administration College Teaching course. In turn, I present campus-wide workshops on disability awareness, policies, rights and responsibilities, communication, ally development, and UD. I model UID in the workshops, using large-print handouts, open-captioned videos, multiple delivery methods, and various instructional strategies. I provide coaching (i.e., guiding) and scaffolding (i.e., incorporating hints and tips) to the participants as they apply UID techniques and processes to various scenarios. When participants leave the educational setting, they should be able to reflect on their performance in the educational experience workshop, reflect on what they have learned about UID, articulate that knowledge in their own work and provide reasons for their decisions, and explore new opportunities to use UID as they apply various strategies and observe their effects.

For more than ten years, I consulted on disability issues and studied UD. As director of disability services and an adjunct faculty member in a student affairs graduate program at a midwestern regional institution, I developed a course on disability in higher education at the urging of my graduate students. They wanted to learn more about communicating with students with disabilities, a topic other curricula did not cover. The course addressed disability law, policies, procedures, responsibilities, language, communication, disability types and models, and UD. It emphasized the provision of barrier-free classrooms and other facilities. Years later, as director of disability services at a large public research institution on the West Coast, I contributed to a book chapter on integrating disability into professional preparation programs (Evans, Herriott, & Myers, 2009). This opportunity motivated me to revise and update the original course to address two essential topics: viewing disability through a social construct lens and utilizing UID through modeling, teaching, and experiential exercises.

An insatiable desire ensued among my colleagues to spread the word about incorporating disability issues into the higher education curriculum. The disability course and sample modules of it were shared at national, state, and local venues. In my role as chair of the standing committee on disability for the American College Personnel Association (ACPA)–College Student Educators International, I collaborated with the commission for professional preparation programs to cultivate interest in the infusion of disability information into graduate programs nationwide. This collaboration led to a research project. The purposes of this study were to determine (1) how much graduate students know about disability inclusion and (2) if students were interested in enrolling in a course designed around disability issues. I developed a questionnaire to assess graduate student interests and needs regarding the infusion of a disability course or disability modules into existing program curricula. The survey asked seven questions, including one that identified the student's current degree program. The final question was open-ended, allowing the participants to list any other courses they would like added to their curriculum. Chairpersons and program coordinators of selected graduate programs were asked, via e-mail, to send the questionnaire to their students. Students received an introductory e-mail message from me explaining the purpose of the survey.

I sent surveys to twenty-nine higher education/student affairs professional preparation programs throughout the United States (with names obtained from the ACPA website) and to four selected colleges (approximately twenty graduate programs) within my home institution. Of the 784 respondents, 67% were enrolled in master's programs and 33% in doctoral programs. Fifty-seven percent (57%) of the respondents expressed interest in enrolling in the proposed disability course. Of these, 24% preferred an online course, 32% preferred a classroom course, and 44% would take either. Seventy-one percent (71%) of the respondents saw a need for this type of course in their degree programs. Regarding course requirements, 57% said that it should be an elective course, 27% believed it should be a module within an existing course, and 13% reported that it should be required. When asked about their knowledge of disability issues in higher education, 53% believed that students with disabilities do not fully participate in higher education, and 62% said they do not know what steps to take to ensure that students with disabilities can fully participate in higher education. These responses revealed an interest in and need for disability-related education.

My next step was to offer a three-week online noncredit course, Disability and Student Development, through ACPA's e-Learning Series. I designed, developed, and implemented this online course using UID, with a component of the course addressing UD. My co-instructor and I insisted on modeling UID throughout the entire course. During course preparation we learned about the accessibility capabilities of Blackboard, an online course development program, and of JAWS, screen-reader software commonly used by people who are blind. This online course served as a precursor to the national seminar, Enhancing Learning for Students with Disabilities: The Intersection of Disability Studies and Student Development Theories, which was offered in spring 2006 at the National Center for Higher Education in Washington, DC. The three-day seminar was one of the most edifying experiences of my career. It was there that I gleaned essential information to be used in my new course, which was offered as a result of my research project conducted in winter 2006.

INCORPORATION OF UD IN COURSES AND MODULES

Supported by the results of my research study, I was allowed to develop and offer an experimental course through our Higher Education Administration Graduate Program. The three-credit course, Disability in Higher Education and Society, initially was designed as a hybrid class in which students met twenty-four hours face-to-face and twenty-one hours online using Blackboard. Since its inception as a hybrid class, the course has also been offered 100% online and 100% on-site. The course continues to be offered as a requirement for the master's program in student personnel administration and as a popular elective in the doctoral program in higher education administration. In preparation for teaching this course, I enrolled in a seven-week non-credit online course on Competency Assessment in Distributed Education (CADE). The CADE model is a "backward design approach from competencies to evidence to tasks . . . [which] makes the assessment of student competencies within designed tasks explicit from the start" (Association of Jesuit Colleges and Universities, 2004, p. 1). With my disability course as the CADE assignment, my first task was to develop strategic, procedural, and factual knowledge competencies. Strategic knowledge competencies are complex thinking strategies and processes that students will utilize during the class and in their lives beyond the classroom. One strategic knowledge competency for the disability course is the following: "Students will learn strategies to create an environment that fosters inclusiveness." This strategic competency is complemented by the following procedural knowledge competency: "Students will learn techniques for incorporating UD into academic and student services environments." Evidence of student mastery for this strategic competency is that students are able to use techniques for structuring educational settings in accordance with suggested UD practices. Through the CADE process, I developed competencies; evidence for student mastery; instructional tasks to reveal the evidence; course modules; instructional strategies using the Cognitive Apprenticeship model; and a timeline for designing, developing, and implementing the hybrid course. My integration of CADE and UID practices in the course demonstrates how UD can be combined with other teaching approaches and methodologies adopted in a course.

Additional preparation for me included participation in an online seminar, Low-Tech Strategies to Incorporate Technology into Teaching, offered through the university's CTTL. Based on Chickering and Gamson's seven principles for good practice in undergraduate education (1991), the seminar addressed best practices for using technology, such as streaming videos, PowerPoint with audio, and web-based discussion boards, both in and out of the classroom. It was particularly helpful to those of us who were technology novices and timid about using it in our classes. This seminar gave me confidence and encouragement—so much so that I incorporated a podcast into my syllabus the following semester, and, more recently, have incorporated Tegrity, FuzeBox, and Google Plus in addition to cofacilitating with the CTTL a faculty workshop entitled Getting Started in Designing Accessible Course Materials. Now *that* is progress. In applying technological tools, I modeled UID in ensuring that resulting practices were accessible to all of my potential students.

Instructional resources that are well received by students in the course and in classes utilizing modules include videos, handouts, and online materials offered by the Disabilities, Opportunities, Internetworking, and Technology (DO-IT) Center at the University of Washington (DO-IT, n.d.a.) and the University of Minnesota's Pedagogy and Student Services for Institutional Transformation (PASS IT) program, both of which provide guidelines for implementing UD in higher education (PASS-IT, n.d.). A particularly rich resource, DO-IT's AccessCollege website, tailors disability- and UD-related content to specific stakeholder groups through the Faculty Room, the Student Services Conference Room, the Board Room, the Student Lounge, and the Center for

Universal Design in Education. These focused websites provide stimulating and useful streaming videos, publications, readings, and resource links relevant to postsecondary faculty, student services personnel, high-level administrators, and students, along with a center that covers all applications of UD to educational environments (DO-IT, n.d.b). PASS IT offers books, guidebooks, videos, and other tools to faculty and student affairs professionals for designing and implementing UD in higher education settings. Respecting the guidelines of these and other resources, the Disability in Higher Education and Society course and modules utilize UID in multiple ways, including: course notes and readings in accessible online formats; large-print handouts; multimodal course instruction, delivery methods, and resources; open-captioned videos; individual and group work; and an online discussion board. During the first week of each course offering, I assess Visual, Aural, Reading/Writing, and Kinesthetic (VARK) learning styles with the VARK learning style inventory (VARK, n.d.), and students provide me with their expectations of the course. Armed with this valuable information, I can apply UID as planned, but also modify my strategies to better fit the learning styles, needs, and expectations of the students. I integrate UID practices with other approaches to teaching that I embrace. For example, UID works comfortably with the constructivist model of teaching, in which students are encouraged and expected to construct their own meaning and take responsibility for their own learning.

Modules addressing disability and UD have also been incorporated into other courses offered at the university (e.g., Law in Higher Education, Curriculum in Higher Education, Student Personnel Administration, Student Development Theory, Counseling and Diversity, Teacher Education) and for professional development (e.g., CTTL seminars, student affairs staff development sessions, human resources leadership institutes). Particularly useful in the student affairs sessions (as mentioned above) are DO-IT's UD for student services materials (DO-IT, 2007–2014) and PASS IT guidebooks and instructional materials (Goff & Higbee, 2008a; Higbee & Goff, 2008).

Gauging Success

Formative and summative evaluations are used throughout the Disability in Higher Education and Society course. At the end of many class sessions, students respond in writing to the following questions: "When were you most engaged in today's class? When were you least engaged in today's class?" From time to time, I also use "Three Checks and a Wish," a quick and easy assessment idea suggested by one of my students (R. Von der Hyde, personal communication, March 2006). Students write down three lessons learned that session and one topic they wish could be covered by the end of the course or be improved when the course is offered again. Both of these exercises give me immediate feedback to which I can respond in a timely fashion. They allow me to keep my finger on the pulse of the class and, accordingly, make changes in current and future courses. Students are asked to complete an online midterm evaluation, which I use for my own edification and to make curricular adjustments, as I deem necessary.

Students also complete an online final evaluation conducted by the academic department. I use these final assessment results to improve the course the next time it is offered. Although students report they enjoy the flexibility of an online class, their feedback indicates they experience more personal development and positive change through face-to-face classes and discussions with the instructor, guest speakers, and classmates. Seminar and workshop participants (faculty, staff, and students) provide feedback via evaluation forms at the end of each professional development session. I use constructive criticism to improve and enhance future presentations.

Course Projects and Their Long-Term Impact

The Disability in Higher Education and Society course has become a springboard for critical inquiry and constructive thinking about equity throughout all social strata. I require students to complete a three-hour service-learning component and a final major project. To fulfill these requirements, students are asked to serve in a capacity that is related to disability and to develop a practical and usable product promoting disability education, respectively. The service-learning component of the course provides students with an opportunity to immediately address barriers for people with disabilities. They must think constructively about how to limit or omit restrictive practices and how to work collaboratively with other professionals to enhance services and programs in higher education, with specific regard to disability awareness and UD.

Through the project assignment, students have developed and implemented the award-winning *Allies for Inclusion: The Ability Exhibit*, a unique universally designed traveling exhibit intended to promote the inclusion of people with disabilities by demonstrating respect for others, comfort during interactions, and awareness of disability issues. Through ten interactive stations (one of which focuses specifically on UD) and using a multimedia approach, the exhibit offers suggestions for becoming disability allies and educators. This student project, which began as an end-of-semester PowerPoint presentation four years ago, has now become a national traveling exhibit hosted by over forty institutions. Following the *Ability Exhibit*'s inception, all students enrolled in the Disability in Higher Education and Society course are required to contribute to the continuation and enhancement of the exhibit.

Another recent outcome of the course is the Ability Ally Initiative (AAI), which provides training to institutions that wish to create more inclusive campus environments for people with disabilities. As a professional development tool, the AAI seeks to apply the spirit of the law by educating participants on topics that include person-first language, UD, effective communication, case studies, and other interactive activities. The AAI, initially funded by a United Way grant awarded to a student in my class, has been hosted by several institutions in the U.S. and has been used as professional development training for counselors and academic advisors. The AAI has been developed for the international community as well and was presented at the University of Ghana in 2014 and at St. Joseph's University in Bangalore, India, in 2014.

A third development from the course is the initiation of the K–12 edition of the AAI and the *Ability Exhibit*, beginning with a preK–1 edition piloted last year. Graduate students and staff continue to develop the AAI to meet its unique and diverse participant populations.

LESSONS LEARNED AND ONGOING WORK

My UID modeling and UD instruction have received high marks from learners. Students, faculty, and staff appear genuinely interested in the topic and are pleased to know they can participate proactively in ally development and the UD movement. They enjoy applying what they have learned to the scenarios presented to them in classes and other instructional sessions, and they enthusiastically collect examples and samples of UD practices and application areas. On campus, I lead a UD-focused community of practice for individuals interested in teaching and modeling UID principles and in developing and conducting UD educational initiatives to transform institutional student services and pedagogy campus-wide.

In addition to participating in UD training opportunities and accessing valuable resources developed by leaders in the field, being involved in the CADE pedagogically based workshop was an important stop in my journey in applying UD. It gave me an opportunity to develop the hybrid course and modules using the backward design approach, which focuses first on the learner and the learner's competencies before developing instructional methods. Much time was spent pondering the question: "What do you want students to be able to do beyond the classroom?" This type of thinking shifts attention from learning outcomes for the class to learning outcomes for life.

Future plans at my institution are to continue to provide face-to-face and online seminars on applications of UD for faculty, teaching assistants, and student affairs administrators and practitioners through CTTL and student development workshops. Also planned are sessions on UD for university administrators and continued courses and modules on UD infused into the curriculum in Higher Education Administration and other programs in the College of Education and Public Service and beyond.

In the past several years, I have collaborated with experts in UD to present sessions at international conventions. It has been my experience that faculty, administrators, staff, and students are more receptive now to the idea of designing their courses, programs, and services for all students utilizing UID, rather than focusing exclusively on accommodations for students with disabilities. Marketing UD seminars, classes, and other training options by relating them to diversity or multicultural inclusion rather than disability inclusion "puts more people in the seats." By focusing on inclusion of *all* students, we are taking the spotlight off persons with disabilities and putting it where it should be: on society as a whole. We are asking society (e.g., members of the campus community) to effect change by incorporating UD into their lives, work, classes, and services. We are not asking persons with disabilities to change to fit our agenda; rather, we are asking the institution to create an environment that fosters total inclusion. With universal design, we all benefit.

CONCLUSION

My experiences in infusing UD principles into my teaching practices and course content have been rewarding and exhilarating. It is my hope that sharing them here will encourage others to incorporate UD into their research and practices in order to make higher education more inclusive. One vital and valuable lesson I have learned in my thirty-year career in higher education is to give credit where credit is due. My work in ability ally development and universal instruction design would not be possible if it were not for the many colleagues and students who supported my goals and played vital roles in disability education endeavors. In particular, I would like to credit and thank Dr. Jeanne Higbee, Dr. Sheryl Burgstahler, Dr. Rebecca Cory, Dr. Gerard Fowler, Dr. Ann Rule, Alisha Abbot, Amy Brinkely, Anne Marie Carroll, A. J. Friedhoff, Kate Goedde, Matthew Sullivan, and Maureen Wikete Lee in addition to the hundreds of students who dedicated their time, energy, talents, and creativity into the development, promotion, and implementation of the Ability Institute, the *Ability Exhibit*, and the Ability Ally Initiative. Without their interest, passion, and devotion in developing allies and building inclusive welcoming environments, my accomplished goals would be hopeful dreams.

REFERENCES

21st Century Communications and Video Accessibility Act of 2010, Public Law 111–260 (2010). Retrieved from http://www.gpo.gov/fdsys/pkg/PLAW-111publ260/html/PLAW-111publ260.htm

Allies for Inclusion: The Ability Exhibit (2014). Retreived from Saint Louis University website: http://www.slu.edu/x45782.xml

Americans with Disabilities Act of 1990, 42 U.S.C.A. § 12101 *et seq* (1990). Retrieved from http://www.ada.gov/archive/adastat91.htm

Americans with Disabilities Act Amendments Act of 2008, Public Law 110–325, 42 U.S.C. § 12102 (2008). Retrieved from http://www.law.georgetown.edu/archiveada/documents/ADAAACR9.17.08.pdf

Association of Jesuit Colleges and Universities. (2004). *Competency assessment in distributed education.* Washington, DC: Author.

Ben-Moshe, L., Cory, R., Feldbaum, M., & Sagendorf, K. (Eds.). (2005). *Building pedagogical curb cuts: Incorporating disability in the university classroom and curriculum.* Syracuse, NY: Graduate School, Syracuse University.

Burgstahler, S., & Cory, R. (Eds.). (2008). *Universal design in higher education: From principles to practice.* Cambridge, MA: Harvard Educational Press.

Chickering, A., & Gamson, Z. (Eds.). (1991). *Applying the seven principles for good practice in undergraduate education.* San Francisco: Jossey-Bass.

Disabilities, Opportunities, Internetworking, and Technology (DO-IT). (n.d.a). *DO-IT resources.* Seattle: University of Washington. Retrieved from http://www.washington.edu/doit/resources-5

DO-IT. (n.d.b). *AccessCollege: Postsecondary education and students with disabilities.* Seattle: University of Washington. Retrieved from http://www.washington.edu/doit/programs/accesscollege

DO-IT. (2007–2014). *Applying universal design to specific student service units.* Seattle: University of Washington. Retrieved from http://www.washington.edu/doit/programs/center-universal-design-education/postsecondary/universal-design-student-services/applying

Duranczyk, I. M., Myers, K. A., Couillard, E. K., Schoen, S., & Higbee, J. L. (Fall 2013). Enacting the spirit of the United Nations Convention on the Rights of Persons with Disabilities: The role of postsecondary faculty in ensuring access. *Journal of Diversity Management, 8*(2), 63–72.

Evans, N., Herriott, T., & Myers, K. (Spring 2009). Integrating disability into the diversity framework of our professional preparation and practice. In J. Higbee & A. Mitchell (Eds.), *Making good on the promise: Student affairs professionals with disabilities.* Lanham, MD: University Press of America.

Goff, E., & Higbee, J. L. (Eds.). (2008a). *Pedagogy and student services for institutional transformation: Implementation guidebook for student development programs and services.* Minneapolis: Regents of the University of Minnesota by its College of Education and Human Development, University of Minnesota.

Goff, E., & Higbee, J. L. (Eds.). (2008b). *Pedagogy and student services for institutional transformation: Implementation guidebook for faculty and instructional staff*. Minneapolis: Regents of the University of Minnesota by its College of Education and Human Development, University of Minnesota.

Higbee, J. L. (2012). Creating a culture of inclusion: Respectful, intentional, reflection teaching. Expanding the frame—Applying universal design in higher education, Part III. *ACPA Developments 10*(3). Retrieved from http://www.myacpa.org/publications/developments/volume-10-issue-3

Higbee, J. L., & Goff, E. (Eds.). (2008). *Pedagogy and student services for institutional transformation: Implementing universal design in higher education*. Minneapolis: The Regents of the University of Minnesota, Center for Research on Developmental Education and Urban Literacy, College of Education and Human Development, University of Minnesota.

Higbee, J., & Mitchell, A. (Eds.), (2009). *Making good on the promise: Student affairs professionals with disabilities*. Lanham, MD: University Press of America.

Myers, K., Lindburg, J., & Nied, D. (2013). *Allies for Inclusion: Students with Disabilities. ASHE Higher Education Report*, 39(5). San Francisco: Jossey-Bass.

Pedagogy and Student Services for Institutional Transformation (PASS IT) (n.d.). PASS-IT publications, videos, and training materials. Minneapolis: University of Minnesota. Retrieved from http://www.cehd.umn.edu/passit/

Section 504 of the Rehabilitation Act of 1973, as amended. 29 U.S.C. § 794 *et seq.*

Silver, P., Bourke, A., & Strehorn, K. C. (1998). Universal instructional design in higher education: An approach for inclusion. *Equity and Excellence in Education, 2*, 47–51.

Snyder, T., & Dillow, S. (2010). *Digest of Education Statistics 2009* (NCES 2010-013; Table 231). Washington, DC: National Center for Education Statistics, Institute of Education Sciences, United States Department of Education.

United States Census Bureau. (2000). *Disability*. Retrieved from www.census.gov/prod/2003pubs/c2kbr-17.pdf

United States Census Bureau. (2010). *Disability*. Retrieved from http://www.census.gov/people/disability/

United States Department of Education, National Center for Education Statistics (ED NCES). (2006). *Profile of Undergraduates in U.S. Postsecondary Education Institutions: 2003–2004. With a Special Analysis of Community College Students (NCES 2006184), Section 6*. Retrieved from http://nces.ed.gov/pubsearch/pubsinfo.asp?pubid=2006184

United States Department of Education, National Center for Education Statistics (ED NCES). (2012). *Digest of Education Statistics, 2011* (2012–001), Chapter 3. Retrieved from http://nces.ed.gov/pubs2012/2012001.pdf

Visual, Aural, Read/Write, Kinesthetic (VARK) Learn Limited. *VARK: A guide to learning styles* (n.d.). Christchurch, New Zealand. Retrieved from http://www.vark-learn.com

10

Universal Design of Assessment

Leanne R. Ketterlin-Geller
Christopher J. Johnstone
Martha L. Thurlow

Universal design is a concept that has been applied to the design of assessments in K–12 education. It originated in architecture but has promising educational applications, including postsecondary assessment design. This chapter defines and describes universal design of assessment (UDA), its challenges for application in postsecondary education, and several specific approaches that make its application feasible in postsecondary institutions. Conclusions are based on UDA possibilities in postsecondary education along with theoretical linkages to K–12 education. The authors recommend steps to take toward designing assessments for classroom use, as well as other tasks and assessments that improve access for all students.

Higher education administrators and faculty in the United States are challenged to consider the ways in which their institutions are accessible to the increasingly wide variety of students who attend them. Because of major legislation, such as Section 504 of the Rehabilitation Act of 1973 and the Americans with Disabilities Act of 1990 (including its reauthorization in 2008, which expanded the definition of disability), colleges and universities are required to remove barriers that might deprive qualified persons with disabilities from the opportunity to succeed in postsecondary education. "Accessibility" for a college student with a disability might include anything from physical access to a dormitory to learning and testing accommodations in the classroom.

Because postsecondary students with disabilities are a heterogeneous group, some colleges and universities have adopted a "universal design" approach to meeting the needs of their students. Universal design, originally applied in the field of architecture, is defined as "the design of products and environments to be usable by all people, to the greatest extent possible, without the need for adaptation or specialized design" (Mace, n.d.). In the case of postsecondary education, universal design of environments and learning is especially relevant because only students who disclose their disabilities receive specialized services (Banerjee & Thurlow, 2012; Bierwert, 2002). It is likely that there are students who have diagnosed disabilities or other learning and physical challenges who do not receive any formal services in postsecondary education because they have not self-identified. For these students, applying the principles of universal design in assessment might ameliorate this situation.

In this chapter we discuss some of the challenges that higher education faculty might encounter when designing assessments and then present several approaches to applying the philosophy of universal design when assessing students in postsecondary educational settings. *Assessment*, broadly defined, is any tool used to evaluate students or to provide data for making adjustments in teaching and learning processes (Roberts & McInnerney, 2006). UDA draws on the philosophy of access to all, but also recognizes that assessments must discriminate between students who have mastered the content and those who have not. Given the purpose of assessments, implementing UDA principles must maintain the validity of the interpretations made from the test results. Evidence to document the comparability of the outcomes is challenging to obtain in postsecondary institutions where assessments are often instructor-developed and non-normed. However, applying UDA principles to such assessments may improve accessibility for all students without reducing content complexity or difficulty. In this chapter, we highlight the utility of UDA principles developed for K–12 large-scale assessments for designing accessible assessments in postsecondary settings.

Thompson, Johnstone, and Thurlow (2002) developed *Elements of Universally Designed Assessments* to guide the design of K–12 large-scale assessments (see also Johnstone, Altman, & Thurlow, 2006). They include seven elements:

1. Inclusive assessment population (e.g., all populations who might take an assessment are considered during assessment development)
2. Precisely defined constructs (i.e., intended material or skills to be tested are transparent)
3. Accessible, nonbiased items (i.e., test items should not be biased against particular populations)
4. Amenability to accommodations (e.g., the test design should allow for the use of accommodations)
5. Simple, clear, and intuitive instructions
6. Comprehensible language
7. Maximum legibility (in both print and graphics)

Dolan, Hall, Banerjee, Chun, and Strangman (2005) and Hall, Strangman, and Meyer (2003) approached UDA from the perspective of technology enhancements to assessment. These researchers viewed UDA as a mechanism for choice and built-in accommodation in assessment. They advocated for multiple means of information retrieval and multiple opportunities for expression (e.g., voice-activated technology to reduce barriers to students who have writing disabilities and screen readers to reduce barriers for students who struggle reading print); their work can be applied to the design of postsecondary assessments (Rose, Harbour, Johnston, Daley, & Abarbanell, 2006). The Center for Applied Special Technology's (CAST) flexible and multimodal approaches to assessment align well with learning preferences and multicultural education theories, which guide instructional design in contemporary postsecondary education (Johnson & Fox, 2003).

Interpretations of UDA differ but are common in the assumption that accessibility and validity are the hallmarks of high-quality assessments. Such assessments require that designers discriminate between the actual content they want to test and other nonconstruct information or skills that may act as barriers to students (Ketterlin-Geller, Yovanoff, & Tindal, 2007). Such interpretations are reinforced in the American Educational Research Association (AERA), American Psychological Association (APA), and National Council on Measurement in Education's (NCME) *Standards for Educational and Psychological Testing* of 2014. These standards call for accessibility and fairness to be fundamental considerations in testing, and to be factored into the process of assessment design and interpretation. UDA research and the 2014 *Test Standards*, however, say little about assessments that are designed by individual teachers for class-specific goals. Therefore, UDA research (which is largely focused on large-scale assessment in K–12 schools) needs to be interpreted carefully within the context of postsecondary education.

CHALLENGES FOR UNIVERSAL DESIGN OF ASSESSMENT IN POSTSECONDARY EDUCATION

Assessments serve many purposes in the postsecondary environment. Test scores are used to evaluate students' proficiency in course-specific learning objectives, identify students' readiness for advanced courses, and determine whether students have reached specific competencies in core content areas. In many cases, course instructors are responsible for designing and implementing the assessments (e.g., topical quizzes or performance tasks). Assessments used to make decisions that impact multiple courses or departments may require input from faculty teams within an academic department (e.g., common final exams) or across multiple academic units (e.g., placement exams). Because these decisions often have high stakes, there is increased pressure to develop high-quality assessments that are appropriate for all students, including students with disabilities.

In recent years, designing assessments for use in postsecondary settings has gotten easier and more complex at the same time. With the seemingly ubiquitous access to technology on college campuses, many new assessment options exist. Learning management systems (LMSs) such as Blackboard and Moodle are available on most campuses and offer faculty members an efficient system for delivering, scoring, and reporting test results directly to students. Electronic portfolio tracking systems such as TaskStream allow academic programs and departments to collect, evaluate, and store students' work products. There are also a plethora of on-demand classroom-response systems such as clickers and text-message polling systems that allow instructors to gather and evaluate real-time data about students' understanding. With these and other technology-based systems facilitating the assessment delivery and scoring process, faculty members, academic departments, and postsecondary institutions have ready access to student performance data. However, without careful attention to the accessibility of these assessments for all students, the data may not support the goals of improving postsecondary outcomes and systems.

Importantly, many LMSs that incorporate online teaching and assessment tools merely provide a platform for student engagement. Such platforms have the potential to engage and provide accessibility support for a variety of students, but are analogous to architectural elevators, curb cuts, and signage. If such features are not deployed in a way that considers both the intended construct of the assessment and the validity of the interpretations of the results, they are merely tools that replicate previous practices in new ways. In short, even though there is increased access to student performance data, the content of the assessments still rests in the hands of the test developer (e.g., individual faculty members or faculty teams). Academic programs that prepare faculty members (typically PhD and EdD programs) rarely contain coursework focused on how to teach and assess in postsecondary settings; thus, many faculty members have limited formal training in designing tests and assignments. Moreover, campuses that offer instructional support through an instructional technology office or centers for teaching and learning often focus on designing instructional materials, integrating technology into instruction, or refining classroom-management techniques. Still, little attention is paid to creating assessment tools. In some cases, course textbooks provide assessment resources, but these materials are often limited in depth and breadth of the content covered, may be created by item writers (as opposed to the textbook authors), and rarely report on the technical quality of the materials. Faculty members are left with few resources other than their past experience in designing tests and their expertise in the area.

Knowledge of assessment and test development techniques is critical for designing appropriate assessments. In the context of supporting students with disabilities, test developers need to identify the skills and knowledge that are targeted by the test and those that are not. *Target skills* are the knowledge, skills, and abilities that form the basis of the decisions the test developer will be making. For example, if a botany instructor is administering an assessment to determine which students in her class have reached the minimum level of competency in their understanding of the form and function of cellular structures, the target skills for her assessment will include aspects of the form and function of plant cell structures.

Even though assessments are designed to measure target skills, many other skills may be unintentionally tested. These skills often are referred to as *access skills* because they are needed to *access* the intended construct and may influence students' capacity to demonstrate their knowledge, skills, and abilities in the targeted content. Shinn and Ofiesh (2012) describe the cognitive demands associated with accessing a test as language comprehension, visual spatial skills, and academic fluency (e.g., reading, writing, mathematical skills), and note that these cognitive demands also interact with skills needed to generate output, such as long-term retrieval and visual motor integration. Working memory, attention, and processing speed also influence postsecondary students' interaction with tests.

Access skills are especially prevalent in performance assessments that require students to integrate many supplemental skills when demonstrating their knowledge. In the botany assessment described above, access skills might include the students' ability to interpret diagrams, express their knowledge in writing, and perform a host of other skills that depend on the structure and format of the actual test. For students with diverse characteristics—including students with disabilities, students whose first language is not English, and students who struggled for a variety of reasons in high school—access skills often limit their ability to demonstrate their content area knowledge. If a student's performance on an assessment is influenced by these access skills, the score may not accurately reflect his knowledge, skills, and abilities in the targeted content. Hence, the decisions that will be made based on the data will be invalid. In some settings and classrooms, target and access skills are easily conflated, posing challenges for assessment design. This may be especially true for institutions focused on access (e.g., community colleges). Schuck and Larson (2003) posited that UDA is relevant in community college classrooms, where students often have diverse characteristics, such as differing levels of language proficiency, and may be more likely to need remedial classes than students in four-year universities (Shults, 2001).

Access skills can be supported through accommodations for specific students with self-reported disabilities. However, postsecondary students with disabilities are often reluctant to request accommodations for fear of being socially stigmatized or of losing independence, or because of previous frustrations with postsecondary disability services' or faculty members' implementation of accommodations (Marshak, Van Wieren, Ferrell, Swiss, & Dugan, 2010). Along with characteristics of the postsecondary institution itself, students' attitudes about accommodations have been found to be a significant predictor of their willingness to request accommodations (Barnard-Brak, Davis, Tate, & Sulak, 2009). Because research on the use of accommodations in postsecondary settings indicates that students with disabilities most often need accommodations to access assessments (Schreuer & Sachs, 2014), students' hesitation to request accommodations may compromise the accuracy of their results. To circumvent these barriers and support access for all students, assessments can be intentionally designed to incorporate the principles of universal design.

UDA AND POSTSECONDARY EDUCATION: THEORETICAL AND PRACTICAL APPROACHES

To develop an assessment that addresses both validity and accessibility concerns, instructors are faced with the challenge of identifying the intended target skills, the access skills necessary to be successful on the assessment, and accessibility approaches to support students' demonstration of their knowledge, skills, and abilities. For the latter, many features of UDA approaches that emerged from K–12 education are applicable in postsecondary education. For example, the qualities of UDA that Thompson, Johnstone, & Thurlow (2002) described can serve to meet the needs of a wide variety of postsecondary students if the assessments are amenable to accommodations; have simple, clear, and intuitive instructions and procedures (see also AERA, APA, & NCME, 2014); have maximum readability and comprehensibility (see also Hanson, Hayes, Schriver, LeMahieu, & Brown, 1998); and have maximum legibility (Schriver,

1997). Similarly, the characteristics of UDA that allow for students to use different modalities for the input and output of information described by Dolan et al. (2005) and Hall, Strangman, & Meyer (2003) can be clearly applied in postsecondary educational settings.

Technology can also facilitate access to assessments as well as support the implementation of the principles of UDA in postsecondary settings. Technology-based assessments may make accommodations easier to implement, allow students to access assistive technology (e.g., screen readers and speech recognition software), and enable students to customize their learning environment to support readability and legibility. However, some technology-based assessment tools may pose unique access barriers for students. For example, students with visual impairments may have difficulty accessing multimedia embedded in assessments. Similarly, on-demand classroom response systems (e.g., clickers) require students to generate responses within a narrow time frame; some students with disabilities may find this challenging. When implementing technology-based assessments, faculty should evaluate possible access barriers for students with disabilities, and consider the utility of alternate mechanisms of assessment.

Finally, recent research and development in postsecondary education points to promising practices that can support access. Fox, Hatfield, and Collins (2003) evaluated a "Curriculum Transformation and Design" training program for university faculty that focused on the principles of Universal Instructional Design and approaches to make classrooms and programs more inclusive. Other learning goals for the training program included helping faculty learn about recent legislation, assistive technology, and local resources, as well as develop a personal action plan for supporting students with disabilities in their courses. As a result of the training, 26% of respondents made changes in their teaching and assessment efforts to improve access. The most common form of accessibility changes made by instructors was to provide additional time for assessments to all students and to provide more frequent assessments throughout the semester (e.g., from four to six examinations) with fewer questions (e.g., from ten to eight items per test). Other changes included shifting from multiple-choice tests to essay exams, providing the topic in advance of writing assignments, and incorporating simulations (Ghere, 2003). Some instructors noted that they were becoming more focused on performance assessments in their classrooms rather than relying solely on exams to evaluate student learning (Hatfield, 2003). Although some researchers have found that many faculty are still at the beginning stages of learning about universal design rather than implementing it (LaRocco & Wilken, 2013), others have found that when faculty implement universal design, there are many positive outcomes, including positive student interest and engagement (Smith, 2012).

CAST's "accessibility through flexibility" approach—incorporating multiple mechanisms for students to demonstrate their knowledge, skills, and abilities—may reach a wide variety of students, not just those with disabilities. For example, James Banks (2000, p. 12) noted, "Evaluating the progress of students from diverse racial, ethnic, and social-class groups is complicated by differences in language, learning styles, and cultures. Hence, the use of a single form of assessment will likely further disadvantage students from particular social classes and groups."

To minimize the effects of deficits in access skills and to provide instructors with a more accurate understanding of students' target knowledge, skills, and abilities, instructors can ask themselves a series of questions about their assessments and then make adjustments as needed. These questions include the following:

- Are the instructions on this assessment easy for students to understand?
- Is the layout of the assessment easy to navigate?
- Are items formatted consistently throughout the assessment?
- Is the language I am using in the assessment appropriate for the students in my classroom? Will students understand the vocabulary associated with information not directly related to the coursework?
- Is the print large and legible enough for *all* students to read? Are diagrams clear and consistent with text?
- Can the assessment be taken in a variety of formats without changing the accessibility of the information (e.g., paper, computer-based)?
- Can a potential allowable accommodation for a student be used on this assessment without changing the constructs of what I am testing?

Answering these questions affirmatively supports students' access to the tested content. However, in the event that instructors cannot answer these questions in the affirmative, we offer several approaches to consider as they develop more accessible assessments. When considering designing assessments to incorporate UDA principles, it is important that instructors focus on supporting students' access to the targeted content; changes that are made to improve access should not change the targeted knowledge, skills, and abilities that the test was intended to measure.

UNIVERSAL DESIGN OF ASSESSMENT APPROACHES FOR HIGHER EDUCATION

Applying elements of universal design to assessments in higher education and other postsecondary settings may be challenging for some faculty members. However, several specific approaches can make it feasible for UDA to be applied in postsecondary institutions. The following steps can start you on your way toward applying universal design elements to your own assessments.

Determine the decision you will make based on the students' scores. There are many reasons why we give assessments. We may want to get a quick snapshot of students' understanding of the day's learning objective. We may want to determine students' background knowledge on a topic before we introduce new material. We may want to evaluate students' ability to apply their knowledge to a new situation. We may want to assign a course grade. There are seemingly endless reasons for administering an assessment. Carefully considering what you will do with the data will help you make other decisions about the content and format of the assessment.

Clearly articulate the target skills you want to assess. After you have identified the decision you want to make, identify the knowledge, skills, and abilities you want to evaluate in your students. Are you assessing students' understanding of a specific topic area (e.g., forms and functions of plant cell structures), or are you interested in their ability to demonstrate a process (e.g., application of the scientific method)? To what level of depth are you expecting students to demonstrate their understanding (e.g., reiteration of factual knowledge, illustration to a novel example, synthesis of multiple sources)? By carefully thinking about the target skills you want to assess, you can determine which type of assessment will allow students to demonstrate their knowledge, skills, and abilities.

Think about how students can best demonstrate their target skills in a way that will help you make the decisions you want. Keep in mind that the role of assessment in postsecondary education is usually to make decisions about students' level of mastery of a specific content area. Based on the decision you want to make and the target skills you want to assess, you may decide that students can best demonstrate their knowledge, skills, and abilities through written tests, papers, presentations, demonstrations, observation of students actually performing a task, interviews, and so on. Rose and colleagues (2006) describe their rationale for requiring postsecondary students to demonstrate their knowledge by creating an online performance assessment, noting that the online environment allows students to incorporate multimedia as well as efficiently share their work with other students. You may want to seek assistance from your instructional technology office or center for teaching and learning to help you understand the different types of tasks.

Identify the access skills students will need to successfully demonstrate their knowledge, skills, and abilities in the targeted content on the type of task you selected. Identify skills students need in order to complete the test or assignment that are *not* skills about which you are making decisions. It may be helpful to work with the disabilities services office on your campus to identify access skills that might impact the accuracy of scores for students with disabilities and specific changes that may be necessary if diversity of access skills exists.

For example, you are assigning an in-class essay about conditions leading to the Vietnam War, and you want to measure students' content knowledge and how they synthesize information from multiple sources; however, you may *not* be interested in the spelling capabilities of students or the speed at which they complete the task. In this example, you might agree that students could bring a dictionary or use a computer with spell-checking software to complete the test. Also, time might be extended for students who cannot accurately display their knowledge within the typical time frame. These testing conditions should be determined in advance of the testing session to make sure they do not change the intended construct of the test. This analysis also helps you clarify which skills really are important to your decision making and which ones are not. Providing these UDA testing conditions will benefit all students and minimize the need for accommodations for students with disabilities. However, if specific students need additional approved accommodations to support the skills about which you will not be making decisions, provide them. Research on the effects of accommodations has supported this approach, in which students with disabilities receive differential benefit from the use of accommodations they need, confirming that the accommodations are not providing an unfair benefit but instead meeting a need created by the students' disabilities (Sireci, Scarpati, & Li, 2005).

Know your student population. Although providing multiple means of demonstrating knowledge is a hallmark of UDA test development, knowledge of student characteristics is helpful in designing an assessment that will be accessible to all students. For example, performance assessments may be more relevant (and more accessible) to students in professional fields than traditional assessments (e.g., tests that rely on selected response or short-answer constructed response options). At the same time, traditional assessment may have accessibility features built in (e.g., computer accessible, untimed) to minimize the need for accommodation.

Design an assessment that will allow you to make the decisions you want to make. Consider the different options you have for designing and delivering the assessment, including the use of technology. Determine what will be the most efficient option for you and your students, and will provide accurate and reliable data for making decisions. Determine how you can incorporate multiple means of expression to support accessibility for all students (Rose et al., 2006).

Explicitly state the expectations for students. Provide straightforward and clear instructions for accomplishing the tasks on the assessment. Provide multiple modalities through which expectations are described (e.g., directions, rubric, listed steps). Remember that you want to make a decision about what students know and can do on the tested content, not whether or not the students understood the directions. Consider asking some colleagues or advanced students to review the directions and provide feedback. You can tell a lot about the clarity of your directions by asking someone to repeat to you what they understand and how they would go about completing the tasks.

Design the scoring system based on the decisions you want to make and the type of assessment you designed. Tell students which skills you will and will not be evaluating. The scoring system you employ to generate data from the assessment should align with the purpose of the assessment, the content you are assessing, and the types of tasks students will be completing. You may score some tasks dichotomously (e.g., correct or incorrect) because there is only one correct answer. You may score other tasks by assigning partial credit to each response because there are varying degrees of correctness. Other tasks require you to make a judgment about the response based on specific criteria (e.g., rating scale, categorical rubric). Students should understand how their responses will be scored, and what aspects of their responses will be evaluated. For example, if you are not trying to measure grammatical skills, do not include them on the rubric. However, if you are trying to make multiple decisions that go beyond mastery of the content of your course, such as readiness to advance to the next course or general development of advanced skills (e.g., writing, critical thinking), then consider designing rubrics for these skills.

In some cases, you may decide that you want to provide feedback on some skills but do not want to formally evaluate them. Some programs have competencies that may be evaluated over time; providing students with formative feedback on the development of their proficiency can be informative without being evaluative. For example, many graduate programs evaluate students' ability to communicate in writing. There may be a formal mechanism to evaluate this competency, but providing informal feedback throughout the program may support students' development of proficiency.

Evaluate your assessment. Because you will use the results of your assessments to make a decision (e.g., design your instruction, assign a grade, recommend remediation), it is important that your assessments generate accurate and reliable data for all students, including students with disabilities. Before you give an assessment, ask your colleagues or advanced students to review the assessment to provide feedback on the appropriateness of your assessment for making the decisions you want to make. Ask for feedback on the accessibility of the assessment. After you give the assessment, evaluate the quality of the data (e.g., examine measures of central tendency and dispersion). Evaluate the reliability of the results statistically and anecdotally (i.e., did the students whom you expected to score well actually score well?). These observations will allow you to make improvements for future versions of the assessment.

CONCLUSIONS: MOVING TOWARD ACCESSIBILITY IN ASSESSMENTS FOR ALL STUDENTS

The changing nature of students in postsecondary education environments heightens the importance of accurate information about the meaning of universal design as it applies to assessments and the importance of applying some elements of universal design immediately and additional ones as understanding grows. Discussion of universal design should expand as the diversity of the student body expands (e.g., U.S. Government Accountability Office, 2011). In addition to students who have physical and sensory disabilities, postsecondary institutions now have increasing numbers of students who have learning disabilities, psychological disabilities, autism spectrum disorders, attentional challenges, and other disabilities that are not necessarily visible. These students have access needs, too. Understanding the elements of universal design and the approaches outlined in this chapter will help in designing assessments and assignments that improve access for all students.

Besides the push to apply UDA because of the increasing diversity of the student body, other pressures encourage its application. Increasingly, students with disabilities have moved through a K–12 education system in which accommodations have been provided frequently. They are accustomed to obtaining the accommodations they need and to participating in assessments designed to allow them to show what they know in diverse ways (Banerjee & Thurlow, 2012). In addition, states' large-scale assessment systems have been "encouraged" by federal laws to conform to the principles of universal design (Individuals with Disabilities Education Improvement Act, 2004; No Child Left Behind Act, 2001). Further, students who receive accommodations during classwork or on homework assignments should expect the same accommodations to be present during assessments (if they are not built into the assessment itself).

An important way forward is to provide faculty and staff with development opportunities to understand assessment practices and how to create accessible assessments (Gradel & Edson, 2009). Such activities may take place in faculty preparation programs, but also may be sponsored by instructional technology offices or centers for teaching, disability services offices, or academic units. For example, in 2003, the General College and Disability Services office at the University of Minnesota trained a cohort of faculty on Universal Design for Instruction (see Higbee, 2003). Further training in this area is warranted in postsecondary institutions, especially given the shift from paper-and-pencil-based to computer-based instruction and assessment systems. The inevitable move to technology-based teaching, learning, and assessment in postsecondary education requires more sophistication about ways to improve accessibility for students with disabilities without compromising the content being assessed. Typically, technology can minimize the influence of access skills (e.g., computers can support spelling and print reading), but by its nature, technology presents topics differently from other sources of delivery and therefore needs careful scrutiny to ensure fidelity to the content being tested.

Finally, there is a need for research on the effects of applying UDA principles to assessments and assignments in postsecondary education classes. Higher-education settings, with their lack of standardization from institution to institution and instructor to instructor, will require creative approaches to understanding the effects of universal design on course assessments. Research may consist of a series of classroom-based case studies or may draw from universal design elements applied to large-scale admission or placement tests. Both approaches may help determine how accessibility is constructed with adult learners. As instructors continue to grapple with designing accessible assessments to support valid interpretations, we encourage researchers in the field to use the principles of universal design of assessment developed for K–12 large-scale assessments to articulate elements of UDA for postsecondary education that reflect the unique characteristics of these settings.

REFERENCES

American Educational Research Association, American Psychological Association, & National Council on Measurement in Education. (2014). *Standards for educational and psychological testing.* Washington, DC: American Educational Research Association.

Americans with Disabilities Act of 1990. 42 U.S.C.A. § 12101 *et seq.*

Americans with Disabilities Act Amendments of 2008. Pub. L. No 110–325, 122 Stat.3553 (2008).

Banerjee, M., & Thurlow, M. (2012). Using data to find common ground between secondary and postsecondary accommodations for students with disabilities. In C. Secolsky & D. B. Denison (Eds.), *Handbook on measurement, assessment, and evaluation in higher education* (pp. 553–568). New York: Routledge.

Banks, J. (2000). *Diversity within unity: Essential principles for teaching and learning in a multicultural society.* Seattle: Center for Multicultural Education, University of Washington.

Barnard-Brak, L., Davis, T., Tate, A., & Sulak, T. (2009). Attitudes as a predictor of college students requesting accommodations. *Journal of Vocational Rehabilitation, 31,* 189–198.

Bierwert, C. (2002). *Making accommodations for students with disabilities: A guide for faculty and graduate student instructors* (CRLT Occasional Paper No. 17). Ann Arbor: Center for Research on Learning and Teaching, University of Michigan.

Dolan, R. P., Hall, T. E., Banerjee, M., Chun, E., & Strangman, N. (2005). Applying principles of universal design to test delivery: The effect of computer-based read-aloud on test performance of high school students with learning disabilities. *Journal of Technology, Learning, & Assessment, 3*(7).

Fox, J. A., Hatfield, J. P., & Collins, T. C. (2003). Developing the Curriculum Transformation and Disability (CTAD) Model. In J. L. Higbee (Ed.). *Curriculum transformation and disability: Implementing universal design in higher education* (pp. 23–40). Minneapolis: University of Minnesota, General College, Center for Research on Developmental Education and Urban Literacy.

Ghere, D. L. (2003). Best practices and students with disabilities: Experiences in a college history course. In J. L. Higbee (Ed.), *Curriculum transformation and disability: Implementing universal design in higher education* (pp. 149–162). Minneapolis: University of Minnesota, General College, Center for Research on Developmental Education and Urban Literacy.

Gradel, K., & Edson, A. J. (2009). Putting universal design for learning on the higher ed agenda. *Journal of Educational Technology Systems, 38*(2), 111–121.

Hall, T., Strangman, N., & Meyer, A. (2003). *Differentiated instruction and implications for UDL implementation.* Retrieved from http://www.cast.org/system/galleries/download/ncac/DI_UDL.pdf

Hanson, M. R., Hayes, J. R., Schriver, K. A., LeMahieu, P. G., & Brown, P. J. (1998). *A plain language approach to the revision of test items.* Paper presented at the annual meeting of the American Educational Research Association, San Diego, CA.

Hatfield, J. P. (2003). Perceptions of Universal (Instructional) Design: A qualitative Examination. In J. L. Higbee (Ed.), *Curriculum transformation and disability: Implementing universal design in higher education* (pp. 41–58). Minneapolis: University of Minnesota, General College, Center for Research on Developmental Education and Urban Literacy.

Higbee, J. L. (2003). *Curriculum transformation and disability: Implementing universal design in higher education.* Minneapolis: University of Minnesota, General College, Center for Research on Developmental Education and Urban Literacy. Retrieved from http://www.cehd.umn.edu/CRDEUL/books-ctad.html

Individuals with Disabilities Education Improvement Act of 2004. 20 U.S.C. § 1400 *et seq.*

Johnson, D. M., & Fox, J. A. (2003). Creating curb cuts in the classroom. Adapting universal design principles. In J. L. Higbee (Ed.), *Curriculum transformation and disability: Implementing universal design in higher education* (pp. 7–22). Minneapolis: University of Minnesota, General College, Center for Research on Developmental Education and Urban Literacy.

Johnstone, C. J., Altman, J., & Thurlow, M. (2006). *A state guide to the development of universally designed assessments.* Minneapolis: University of Minnesota, National Center on Educational Outcomes.

Ketterlin-Geller, L. R., Yovanoff, P., & Tindal, G. (2007). Developing a new paradigm for conducting research on accommodations in mathematics testing. *Exceptional Children, 73*(3), 331–347.

LaRocco, D. J., & Wilken, D. S. (2013). Universal design for learning: University faculty stages of concerns and levels of use: A faculty action-research project. *Current Issues in Education, 16*(1), 1–15.

Mace, R. (n.d.). *About UD (universal design).* Retrieved from http://www.ncsu.edu/ncsu/design/cud/about_ud/about_ud.htm

Marshak, L., Van Wieren, T., Ferrell, D. R., Swiss, L., & Dugan, C. (2010). Exploring barriers to college student use of disability services and accommodations. *Journal of Postsecondary Education and Disability, 22*(3), 151–163.

No Child Left Behind Act of 2001. 20 U.S.C. § 6301 *et seq.*

Rehabilitation Act of 1973. 29 U.S.C. § 794–794a.

Roberts, T., & McInnerney, J. (2006). *Assessment in higher education.* Retrieved from http://ahe.cqu.edu.au/introduction.htm

Rose, D. H., Harbour, W. S., Johnston, C. S., Daley, S. G., & Abarbanell, L. (2006). Universal design for learning in postsecondary education: Reflections on principles and their applications. *Journal of Postsecondary Education and Disability, 19*(2), 135–151.

Schreuer, N., & Sachs, D. (2014). Efficacy of accommodations for students with disabilities in higher education. *Journal of Vocational Rehabilitation, 40,* 27–40.

Schriver, K. A. (1997). *Dynamics in document design: Creating text for readers.* New York: Wiley.

Schuck, J., & Larson, J. (2003). Community Colleges and Universal Instructional Design. In J. L. Higbee (Ed.), *Curriculum transformation and disability: Implementing universal design in higher educa-*

tion (pp. 59–70). Minneapolis: University of Minnesota, General College, Center for Research on Developmental Education and Urban Literacy.

Section 504 of the Rehabilitation Act of 1973, as amended. 29 U.S.C. § 6301

Shinn, E., & Ofiesh, N. S. (2012). Cognitive diversity and the design of classroom tests for all learners. *Journal of Postsecondary Education and Disability, 25*(3), 227–245.

Shults, C. (2001, June). *Remedial education: Practices and policies in community colleges.* (Research Brief). Retrieved from http://www.aacc.nche.edu/Publications/Briefs/Pages/rb06052001.aspx

Sireci, S. G., Scarpati, S. E., & Li, S. (2005). Test accommodations for students with disabilities: An analysis of the interaction hypothesis. *Review of Educational Research, 75*(4), 457–490.

Smith, F. G. (2012). Analyzing a college course that adheres to the universal design for learning (UDL) framework. *Journal of the Scholarship of Teaching and Learning, 12*(3), 31–61.

Thompson, S. J., Johnstone, C. J., & Thurlow, M. L. (2002). *Universal design applied to large scale assessments* (Synthesis Report 44). Minneapolis: University of Minnesota, National Center on Educational Outcomes. Retrieved from http://cehd.umn.edu/NCEO/OnlinePubs/Synthesis44.html

U.S. Government Accountability Office. (2011). *Higher education and disability: Improved federal enforcement needed to better protect students' rights to testing accommodations* (GAO-12-40). Washington, DC: Author.

PART 3

Universal Design of Student Services and Physical Spaces in Higher Education

In Part 3, Sheryl Burgstahler provides an overview and then other chapter authors share perspectives and strategies for applying universal design principles to student service units and physical spaces. The chapters detail how such practices can make all institutional offerings welcoming to, accessible to, and usable by all students, faculty, staff, and visitors.

Universal Design in Higher Education

Instruction	Services	Information Technology	Physical Spaces
Class climate	Planning, policies, & evaluation	Procurement, development policies, & procedures	Planning, policies, & evaluation
Interaction	Physical environments & products	Physical environments & products	Appearance
Physical environments & products	Staff	Staff	Entrances & routes of travel
Delivery methods	Information resources & technology	Input, output, navigation, & manipulation	Fixtures & furniture
Information resources & technology	Events	Compatibility with assistive technology	Information resources & technology
Feedback & Assessment			Safety
Accommodation			Accommodation

Source: S. Burgstahler (2015). *Applications of universal design in education.* Seattle: University of Washington. Retrieved from http://www.washington.edu/doit/applications-universal-design-education

11

Universal Design of Student Services
From Principles to Practice

Sheryl E. Burgstahler

The author of this chapter describes challenges faced by students with disabilities accessing student services on postsecondary campuses. These services include recruitment and admissions, registration, financial aid, recreation, advising, and counseling services; computer, engineering, and science labs; tutoring and learning centers; libraries; housing and residential life; and student organizations. She also shares a framework for applying universal design (UD) to make any student service unit more welcoming to, accessible to, and usable by all students. The framework includes guidelines, practices, a process, and resources.

Here is a math problem: In an ongoing effort to improve services, a registration officer invited a group of nine university students to discuss their experiences registering for courses. One of the participants requested a sign language interpreter for the meeting. Later, the office accountant looked at the interpreting bill and remarked, "Wow, $80 for one student! That's expensive." The registration officer said, "Oh, no, the cost was only $8 per person; ten of us participated in the discussion." The registration officer's response embodies a view that considers the interpreting service to be of value to each participant in the group—interpreting what others are saying for the benefit of the student who is deaf and interpreting what that student is saying for the benefit of others. Too often, individuals, like the accountant in this story, consider the interpreter as providing a service only to the student who is deaf. The view of the registration officer is consistent with the author of this chapter's experience giving presentations overseas. When she gives a talk in Japan, language interpreters are always present. It is clear that the interpreters are provided so that everyone in the room can engage in a conversation. If the UD paradigm were fully embraced, more people would think of sign language interpreters in this way.

The student service officer described in this example clearly values equity and social integration. If access and inclusion issues are dealt with in a systemic way throughout the unit, everyone who interacts with the service's staff and resources will have a positive experience. UD holds promise as a paradigm for setting goals, developing processes, and then implementing inclusive practices within student service units.

STUDENT SERVICES AND UNIVERSAL DESIGN

Institutions of higher education offer a range of student services that may include libraries, admissions and registration offices, student housing, career centers, computer labs, tutoring and learning centers, food services, and student organizations. These services play important roles in the academic, social, and career success of postsecondary students (Seidman, 2005). As campuses are becoming more diverse with respect to such characteristics as gender, age, race, ethnicity, culture, sexual orientation, veteran status, physical and sensory abilities, learning styles, reading ability, and native language, the effectiveness of student services for a diverse audience is increasing in importance.

If a student service goal with respect to diversity is that everyone who needs to use the service can do so comfortably and efficiently (Burgstahler, 2015, p. 1), staff would want to ensure that everyone can

- feel welcome,
- get to the facility and maneuver within it,
- communicate effectively with support staff,
- access the content in printed materials and electronic resources, and
- fully participate in events and other activities.

UD can guide efforts to make a student service welcoming to, accessible to, and usable by everyone. As explained in Chapter 1 of this book, UD has a rich history in architecture and commercial product development and, more recently, in instructional design. Ronald Mace coined the term *universal design* and defined it as "the design of products and environments to be usable by all people, to the greatest extent possible, without the need for adaptation or specialized design" (The Center for Universal Design, 2008). In its application to postsecondary campus units, UD means that services are designed not just for the average or typical user but for people with a broad range of abilities, disabilities, ages, learning styles, native languages, cultures, sexual orientations, and other characteristics. It is important to keep in mind that students (as well as staff) may be diverse with respect to such skills as reading, vision, hearing, mobility, and communication. Preparing a service that will be accessible to them may make it more usable by others and minimize the need for special accommodations.

Although there is no federal mandate to apply UD to a student service in higher education, civil rights laws cannot be ignored. For example, virtually all U.S. postsecondary institutions are covered entities under Section 504 of the Rehabilitation Act of 1973, the Americans with Disabilities Act of 1990, and the Americans with Disabilities Act Amendments Act of 2008. These laws prohibit discrimination against individuals with disabilities. With respect to student service units, no otherwise qualified students with disabilities should be excluded from participation in programs or activities or be denied access to resources offered to others solely by reason of their disabilities (U.S. Department of Justice, 2005). Being proactive in making a campus unit accessible to students with a wide variety of disabilities goes a long way toward the ultimate goal of UD to be inclusive of everyone.

Students with disabilities have reported difficulties in accessing housing, financial aid, and other services (National Council on Disability, 2003). Published research and practice highlight specific barriers students face in tutoring centers (Higbee & Eston, 2003), counseling services (Uzes & Connely, 2003), libraries (Schmetzke, 2001), residential living (Wisbey & Kalivoda, 2003), and computer labs (Thompson, 2008). Sheppard-Jones, Krampe, Danner, & Berdine (2002) identified staff needs for information about hiring students with disabilities, providing accessible transportation and parking, including accessible technologies in libraries, and ensuring physical access to campus units for students with disabilities. Burgstahler and Moore (2009) discussed fourteen focus groups with a total of seventy-two student service personnel, and thirteen focus groups with a total of fifty-three postsecondary students with disabilities. Participants identified access problems encountered by students with disabilities when they attempted to use student services, as well as potential solutions to these problems. Students reported incidents where staff did not know how to accommodate their disabilities and where they felt disrespected. Results of the study suggest a need to increase the comfort level of student service personnel in working with students who have disabilities, as well as their knowledge and skills regarding disabilities (particularly those that are not obvious), the rights and responsibilities of students and institutions, accommodation strategies, issues unique to specific units, and available resources.

Reports of applying accessible and UD to student service units, though not plentiful, have appeared in the literature (e.g., Ashmore & Kasnitz, 2014; Higbee & Mitchell, 2009; Kroeger & Schuck, 1993; Myers, Lindberg, & Nied, 2013; Sheppard-Jones et al., 2002; Staeger-Wilson & Sampson, 2012; Uzes & Connely, 2003; Wisbey & Kalivoda, 2003). These publications suggest a growing interest in the application of UD to student services. The Disabilities, Opportunities, Internetworking, and Technology (DO-IT) Center at the University of Washington, building on its earlier grant-funded work in the area of UD of instruction, expanded its development of guidelines, practices, resources, and training into the student services arena with funding from the U.S. Department of Education Office of Postsecondary Education (OPE). As summarized by Robbin Zeff (2007, p. 41),

> DO-IT's work demonstrates that universal design is needed not only in all aspects of learning and instruction, but in every touch point in higher education. Perhaps the previous work in universal design in higher education has focused too narrowly on instruction. The path to further adoption and implementation should traverse the entire campus.

The following sections in this chapter describe DO-IT's framework for the application of UD to student service units. Much of the work that led to the framework was undertaken by the leadership team of disability services personnel, faculty, and administrators from campuses that were engaged in DO-IT's OPE-funded UDHE initiative.

A PROCESS FOR UNIVERSAL DESIGN OF A STUDENT SERVICE

UD is a process as well as a goal. Keys to applying UD principles when designing a new student service or upgrading an existing one are to plan ahead and keep the diversity of the campus population in mind at each design phase. The following steps outline a process for the application of UD to a student service unit (Burgstahler, 2015, pp. 1–2). They are adapted from the more general process presented in Chapter 1 and are also summarized in Figure 11.1.

1. *Identify the service.* Select a student service (e.g., library, tutoring center, career services office). Consider the purpose of the campus unit, specific services and resources provided, facility constraints, budget, and other issues that affect the range and delivery of services provided.

2. *Define the universe.* Describe the overall population and then consider the diverse characteristics of those who might potentially use the service (e.g., students and other visitors with diverse characteristics with respect to gender; age; size; ethnicity and race; native language; learning style; and abilities to see, hear, manipulate objects, read, and communicate).

3. *Involve consumers.* Involve people with diverse characteristics (as identified in Step 2) in all phases of the development, implementation, and evaluation of the service. Also, gain perspectives of students through diversity programs such as the campus disability services office.

4. *Adopt guidelines or standards.* Review research and best practices to identify specific strategies for the delivery of an effective service (e.g., best practices for housing and food services, career services, a tutoring center, or other services as identified in Step 1). Create or select existing universal design guidelines and standards for the service (e.g., DO-IT, n.d.a). Integrate UD practices with other best practices within the field of service.

5. *Apply guidelines or standards.* Apply UD strategies in concert with other best practices, both identified in Step 4, to the overall design of the service, all subcomponents of the service, and all ongoing operations (e.g., procurement processes, staff training) to maximize the benefit of the service to students with the wide variety of characteristics identified in Step 2.

6. *Plan for accommodations.* Develop processes to address accommodation requests (e.g., arrangements for a sign language interpreter) from individuals for whom the design of the service does not automatically provide access. Promote the process through the service's website, publications, and/or signage.

7. *Train and support.* Tailor and deliver ongoing training and support to student service staff.

FIGURE 11.1   A Process for the Application of Universal Design for Student Services

8. *Evaluate.* Include UD measures in the evaluation of the service, evaluate the service with a diverse group of students, and make modifications based on their feedback. Provide ways to collect ongoing input from service users (e.g., through online and printed instruments and communications with staff).

The following section suggests UD guidelines and practices that can be identified in Step 4 and then applied to create a welcoming, accessible, and usable student service in Step 5.

GUIDELINES AND PRACTICES FOR APPLYING UNIVERSAL DESIGN TO STUDENT SERVICES

The application of UD can help administrators ensure that everyone can comfortably use all aspects of a service. As a result of the engagement of twenty-three campuses nationwide in a project funded by OPE, on-site and online training materials were created and freely distributed to guide student service personnel in being both (1) proactive in designing welcoming, accessible, and usable services (i.e., employing UD principles) and then (2) reactive in providing accommodations when needed by individual students with disabilities (Burgstaher, 2006, 2015; Burgstahler & Moore, 2013; DO-IT, 2008). Created in this project, tested on more than twenty campuses, and refined from the results of a nationwide survey of student service personnel (DO-IT, n.d.b), a checklist of UD strategies for student service units continues to be maintained by the DO-IT Center. Organized around guidelines for six application areas—planning and evaluation, facility and environment, staff, information resources, computers and assistive technology, and events—the checklist operationalizes UD principles into practices relevant to student service units.

As project collaborators field-tested the original checklist for the UD of any service, student service organizations requested checklists that operationalized UD principles into practices tailored to their specific units. In response, the student service general checklist was modified and unique lists were created (DO-IT, n.d.a). They include checklists for

- recruitment and undergraduate admissions
- registration
- financial aid
- advising
- career services
- housing and residential life
- tutoring and learning centers
- computer labs
- science labs
- libraries

Although no single checklist can capture every issue to address in the design or redesign of a campus service, these publications provide a good starting point for administrators who wish to implement UD. All checklists are working documents; practitioners are encouraged to propose revisions to DO-IT and to modify them for their own use. Included below are categories of UD applications that are common to most of the student service checklists.

- *Planning, policies, and evaluation.* Consider diversity issues as you plan and evaluate services.
- *Physical environments and products.* Ensure physical access, comfort, and safety in an environment that is welcoming to visitors with a variety of abilities, racial and ethnic backgrounds, genders, and ages. (See Figure 11.2.)
- *Staff.* Make sure staff are prepared to work with all students.
- *Information resources and technology.* Ensure that publications and websites welcome a diverse group, content is accessible to all visitors, and technology in the service area is accessible to everyone.
- *Events.* Ensure that everyone can participate in events sponsored by the organization. (See Figure 11.3.)

Under each guideline, project leaders, with input from student service units on their campuses, developed specific practices for implementation of that guideline. These guidelines and practices serve to operationalize UD principles so that they can be more easily applied to service units. Table 11.1 provides examples of these practices. Project team members report that initial training is important and that UD can be implemented in incremental steps. Additionally, their experiences suggest that measurable change toward the UD of a student service unit often requires ongoing staff training and support, encouragement, and systematic monitoring.

As reflected in the checklists, an essential skill for student service staff is to be able to communicate effectively with all students. The following suggestions provide

FIGURE 11.2   A student accesses the student service publications from a seated position.

FIGURE 11.3   A wheelchair user participates in mock interviews with potential employers.

TABLE 11.1   Universal Design of Student Services

Universal Design Guidelines	Examples of Universal Design Applied to a Student Service
1. *Planning, policies, and evaluation.* Consider diversity issues as you plan and evaluate services.	• Include students with disabilities in planning and review processes and advisory committees. • Consider accessibility issues in procurement processes. • Address disability-related issues in evaluation methods.
2. *Physical environment.* Ensure physical access, comfort, and safety within an environment that is inclusive of people with a variety of abilities, racial and ethnic backgrounds, genders, and ages.	• Be sure there are ample high-contrast, large-print directional signs to and throughout the office. • Keep aisles wide and clear for wheelchair users and protruding objects removed or minimized for the safety of users who are visually impaired.
3. *Staff.* Make sure staff are prepared to work with all students.	• Ensure that all staff members are familiar with disability-related accommodations, including alternate document formats and procedures for responding to requests for accommodations, such as sign language interpreters.
4. *Information resources and technology.* Ensure that publications and websites welcome a diverse group and content is accessible to everyone.	• In key publications, include a statement about a service commitment to access and procedures for requesting disability-related accommodations. • Ensure that web resources adhere to accessibility guidelines or standards. • For student service units that use computers as information resources, ensure that commonly used assistive technology is available.
5. *Events.* Ensure that everyone can participate in events sponsored by the organization.	• Ensure that events are located in wheelchair-accessible facilities and that information about how to request disability-related accommodations is included in promotional materials.

Source: S. Burgstahler. (2015). *Equal access: Universal design of student services.* Seattle: University of Washington.

some general guidance in this regard (Honolulu County Committee on the Status of Women, 1998):

• Don't single out a person's sex, race, ethnicity, or other personal traits or characteristics (such as sexual orientation, age, or a disability) when it has no direct bearing on the topic at hand. In other words, don't create or promote stereotypes based on unavoidable human characteristics.
• Be consistent in your description of members of a group: don't single out women to describe their physical beauty, clothes, or accessories or note a disabled person's use of an aid, or refer to the race of the only minority in a group unless it is at that individual's request.
• Keep in mind that inclusive language is for general cases. Direct requests by individuals take precedence over general rules.

Specifically, administrators should make sure that staff members are trained to support individuals with diverse abilities, respond to specific requests for accommodations in a timely manner, and know whom to contact if they have disability-related questions. To provide guidance in this area, the DO-IT publication *Equal Access: Uni-*

TABLE 11.2   Hints for Communicating with Individuals Who Have Disabilities

Treat people with disabilities with the same respect and consideration with which you treat others. There are no strict rules when it comes to relating to people with disabilities, but here are some helpful hints.

General
- Ask people with disabilities if they need help before providing assistance.
- Talk directly to the person, not through the person's companion or interpreter.
- Refer to a person's disability only if it is relevant to the conversation. If so, mention the person first and then the disability. "A man who is blind" is better than "a blind man" because it puts the person first.
- Avoid negative descriptions of a person's disability. For example, "a person who uses a wheelchair" is more appropriate than "a person confined to a wheelchair." A wheelchair is not confining—it's liberating!
- Do not interact with a person's guide dog or service dog unless you have received permission to do so.

Blind or Low Vision
- Be descriptive. Say, "The computer is about three feet to your left," rather than "The computer is over there."
- Speak all the content presented with overhead projections and other visuals.
- When guiding people with visual impairments, offer them your arm rather than grabbing or pushing them.

Learning Disabilities
- Offer directions/instruction both orally and in writing. If asked, read instructions to individuals who have specific learning disabilities.

Mobility Impairments
- Sit or otherwise position yourself at the approximate height of people sitting in wheelchairs when you interact.

Speech Impairments
- Listen carefully. Repeat what you think you understand and then ask the person with a speech impairment to clarify and/or repeat the portion that you did not understand.

Deaf or Hard of Hearing
- Face people with hearing impairments so they can see your lips. Avoid talking while chewing gum or eating.
- Speak clearly at a normal volume. Speak louder only if requested.
- Use paper and pencil if the person does not read lips or if more accurate communication is needed.
- In groups, raise hands to be recognized so the person who is deaf knows who is speaking. Repeat questions from audience members.
- When using an interpreter, speak directly to the person who is deaf; when an interpreter voices what a person who is deaf signs, look at the person who is deaf, not the interpreter.

Psychiatric Impairments
- Provide information in clear, calm, respectful tones.
- Allow opportunities for addressing specific questions.

Source: S. Burgstahler. (2015). *Equal access: Universal design of student services.* Seattle: University of Washington.

versal Design of Student Services (Burgstahler, 2015), which includes the UD checklist, also provides the communication hints listed in Table 11.2.

The combined efforts of teams of postsecondary institutions who collaborated in DO-IT's UDHE initiative resulted in the creation and maintenance of multiple websites, with content tailored to the interests of specific stakeholder groups. The one designed for student service personnel—called The Student Services Conference Room—includes a collection of documents, checklists, and videos to help student service administrators and staff make their offerings welcoming, accessible, and useful to everyone. Also relevant here is the Center for Universal Design in Education, which disseminates information on all aspects of UD applied to educational settings. Consult any of these websites by selecting *AccessCollege* from the DO-IT website's programs page.

CONCLUSION

Campus services play important roles in the academic, social, and career success of postsecondary students. Therefore, promoting inclusive practices in these units is of critical importance. UD holds promise for making student service units welcoming to, accessible to, and usable by all students. Promising practices have been identified and implemented nationwide, but research studies are needed to further validate their efficacy. In the next chapter of this book, students with disabilities and student service practitioners share their experiences and recommendations with respect to the UD of student service units.

REFERENCES

Americans with Disabilities Act of 1990. 42 U.S.C.A. § 12101 *et seq* (2011).

Americans with Disabilities Act Amendments Act of 2008. 42 U.S.C.A. § 12101 note (2011).

Ashmore, J., & Kasnitz, D. (2014). Models of disability in higher education. In M. L. Vance, K. Parks, & N. Lipsitz (Eds.), *Beyond the Americans with Disabilities Act: Inclusive policy and practice for higher education*. Washington, DC: NASPA Student Affairs Administrators in Higher Education.

Burgstahler, S. (Ed.). (2006). *Students with disabilities and campus services: Building the team—Presentation and resource materials*. Seattle: University of Washington. Retrieved from http://www.washington.edu/doit/building-team-faculty-staff-and-students-working-together-presentation-and-resource-materials

Burgstahler, S. (2015). *Equal access: Universal design of student services*. Seattle: University of Washington. Retrieved from http://www.washington.edu/doit/equal-access-universal-design-student-services

Burgstahler, S., & Moore, E. (2009). Making student services welcoming and accessible through accommodations and universal design. *Journal of Postsecondary Education and Disability, 21*(3), 151–174. Retrieved from http://files.eric.ed.gov/fulltext/EJ831433.pdf

Burgstahler, S., & Moore, E. (2013). Development of a UD checklist for postsecondary student services. In S. Burgstahler (Ed.), *Universal design in higher education: Promising practices*. Seattle: DO-IT, University of Washington.

The Center for Universal Design (2008). *About UD*. Raleigh: North Carolina State University. Retrieved from http://www.ncsu.edu/ncsu/design/cud/about_ud/about_ud.htm

Disabilities, Opportunities, Internetworking, and Technology (DO-IT). (n.d.a) *Resources for student services staff*. Seattle: University of Washington. Retrieved from http://www.washington.edu/doit/programs/accesscollege/student-services-conference-room/resources/resources-student-services-staff

DO-IT. (n.d.b). Survey on universal design of student services. [Unpublished raw data.]

DO-IT. (2008). *DO-IT Admin: A project to help postsecondary student services administrators work successfully with students who have disabilities.* Seattle: University of Washington. Retrieved from http://www.washington.edu/doit/do-it-admin-project-help-postsecondary-student-services-administrators-work-successfully-students

Higbee, J. L., & Eaton, S. B. (2003). Implementing universal design in learning centers. In J. Higbee (Ed.), *Curriculum transformation and disability: Implementing universal design in higher education* (pp. 231–240). Minneapolis: University of Minnesota, Center for Research on Developmental Education and Urban Literacy.

Higbee, J. L., & Mitchell, A. Al (Eds.) (2009). *Making good on the promise: Student affairs professionals with disabilities.* Lanham, MD: America College Personnel Association and University Press of America.

Honolulu County Committee on the Status of Women. (1998). *Do's and don'ts of inclusive language.* Honolulu: Author.

Kroeger, S., & Schuck, J. (1993). *Responding to disability issues in student affairs.* San Francisco: Jossey-Bass.

Myers, K. A., Lindberg, J. J., & Nied, D. M. (2013). *Allies for inclusion: Disability and equity in higher education.* Hoboken, NJ: Wiley Periodicals, Inc.

National Council on Disability (2003). *People with disabilities and postsecondary education.* Position paper. Retrieved from http://www.ncd.gov/publications/2003/Sept152003

Rehabilitation Act of 1973. § 504, 29 U.S.C. § 794 *et seq* (2012).

Schmetzke, A. (2001). Web accessibility at university libraries and library schools. *Library Hi Tech, 19*(1), 35–49.

Seidman, A. (Ed.). (2005). *College student retention: Formula for student success.* Westport, CT: Praeger Publishers.

Sheppard-Jones, K., Krampe, K., Danner, F., & Berdine, W. (2002). Investigating postsecondary staff knowledge of students with disabilities using a web-based survey. *Journal of Applied Rehabilitation Counseling, 33*(1), 19–25.

Staeger-Wilson, K., & Sampson, D. H. (2012). Infusing just design in campus recreation. *Journal of Postsecondary Education and Disability, 25*(3), 247–252. Retrieved from http://files.eric.ed.gov/fulltext/EJ994289.pdf

Thompson, T. (2008). Universal design of computer labs. In S. Burgstahler & R. Cory (Eds.), *Universal design in higher education: From principles to practice* (pp. 107–175). Cambridge, MA: Harvard Education Press.

United States Department of Justice. (2005). *A guide to disability rights laws.* Washington, DC: U.S. Department of Justice, Civil Rights Division. Retrieved from http://www.ada.gov/cguide.pdf

Uzes, K. B., & Connelly, D. O. (2003). Universal design in counseling center service areas. In J. Higbee (Ed.), *Curriculum transformation and disability: Implementing universal design in higher education* (pp. 241–250). Minneapolis: Center for Research on Developmental Education and Urban Literacy, University of Minnesota.

Wisbey, M. E., & Kalivoda, K. S. (2003). Residential living for all: Fully accessible and "liveable" on-campus housing. In J. Higbee (Ed.), *Curriculum transformation and disability: Implementing universal design in higher education* (pp. 215–230). Minneapolis: Center for Research on Developmental Education and Urban Literacy, University of Minnesota.

Zeff, R. (2007). Universal design across the curriculum. *New Directions for Higher Education, 137*, 27–44.

The content of this chapter was developed under grants from the U.S. Department of Education Office of Postsecondary Education (grant numbers P333A020042, P333A020044, and P333A050064) and the National Science Foundation (grant numbers CNS-1042260 and HRD-0833504). However, this content does not necessarily represent the policy of the Department of Education, and you should not assume endorsement by the federal government.

12

Applications of Universal Design to Student Services

Experiences in the Field

Alice Anderson
Rebecca C. Cory
Pam Griffin
Patricia J. Richter
Scott Ferguson
Eric Patterson
Lacey Reed

In this chapter, four administrators describe how universal design was implemented in student services units on their campuses, and three students with disabilities share their experiences in using campus services. Access issues and solutions include those related to planning, policies, and evaluation; facilities; staff training; information resources; computer software; and campus events. Practitioners may find these insights useful as they design student services in higher education.

Student services are an important part of any institution of higher education. As campuses strive to become more competitive and respond to the pressure to address a spectrum of needs for students as whole, well-rounded people, administrators have created a variety of services to support them. These include residential life programs, counseling centers, and career centers, as well as niche services like minority student centers and support services for gay, lesbian, bisexual, and transgender students. One-time special programs, such as campus orientation or commencement and initiatives for first-year students, are also common in higher education. The application of universal design strategies holds promise for making all these programs and services welcoming, accessible, and usable for everyone, and articles in the literature have presented suggestions for the inclusive design of specific services (Goff & Higbee, 2008; Higbee & Eaton, 2003; Schmetzke, 2001; Thompson, 2008; Uzes & Connelly, 2003; Vance, Lipsitz, & Parks, 2014; Wisbey & Kalivoda, 2003).

The coauthors of this chapter share examples of challenges faced by students with a variety of disabilities as they access student services, as well as how some administrators have implemented universal design in aspects of their student services units. Student coauthors provide the perspectives of students with disabilities that affect sight, mobility, speech, learning, and social interaction. Other coauthors include members of a team of disability services and student life professionals from a diverse set of colleges and universities around the country. These professionals worked together to develop and promote practices that advance the implementation of universal design. They were part of the AccessCollege team, which was directed by the Disabilities, Opportunities, Internetworking, and Technology (DO-IT) Center at the University of Washington (UW). To meet their goal of preparing postsecondary faculty and administrators to fully include students with disabilities in their courses and service units (DO-IT, 2015), AccessCollege team members offered training in universal design and accommodations to faculty and staff on their campuses.

The topics discussed in this chapter are organized around a checklist that is included in the publication *Equal Access: Universal Design of Student Services* (Burgstahler, 2015). This checklist was developed and updated in two projects funded by the U.S. Department of Education (DO-IT, 2012) and continues to be improved. Focus groups composed of students with disabilities and student service providers contributed to the first draft of the checklist (Burgstahler & Moore, 2009). To validate the checklist, a large group of disability student services and career services personnel were asked to respond to a survey distributed nationwide. Analysis of the results shows that all areas of access referred to in the checklist are considered "important" or "highly important" by the majority of respondents (Burgstahler & Moore, 2013). Training materials were developed through these project activities (Burgstahler, 2005).

The coauthors of this chapter hope that their experiences will inspire other campuses to take concrete steps to ensure that student services benefit all students. Their comments are organized around the five subcategories of the current student services accessibility checklist:

- planning, policies, and evaluation
- physical environments and products
- staff
- information resources and technology
- events

PLANNING, POLICIES, AND EVALUATION

This section of the checklist asks the user to think about diversity while planning, creating policies, and evaluating programs. When universal design is used to inform the policies of an institution, the result is accessibility and usability for people with a wide range of characteristics.

One way universal design can inform institutional planning policies is by considering accessibility in the procurement process. Purchasing inaccessible products places a burden on some students. For example, a student who is blind said, "[I had a] programming instructor who expected me to use a software utility that was not accessible with screen readers and keyboard commands. I was frustrated." This student was unable to work independently with that software because accessibility was not considered when the software package was purchased. When an institution implements a policy requiring forethought about accessibility in the procurement process, it promotes access and usability for all members of the campus community. UW has such a policy; its purchasing officers added a requirement in contracts for web design stating that the resulting product must meet accessibility standards.

Policies that ensure timely responses to requests for accommodations can also make the campus more welcoming. For example, a student who is blind noted, "It frequently takes more time for students with disabilities to acquire [accessible] material." Encouraging faculty to prepare reading lists and order materials in advance is one step toward ensuring equal access for students with print-related disabilities (e.g., students who are blind, students with dyslexia). Institutions can be proactive by implementing policies that require accessibility. For example, at Kutztown University in Pennsylvania, the administration implemented a policy for on-campus events (Kutztown University, 2006):

> Meetings, events, programs, and activities that are open to the public or the Kutztown University campus community must be held in an accessible location. There may be attendees who need reasonable accommodation. The Room Scheduler system was remodeled so that currently inaccessible spaces will require a second approval before they can be scheduled. For other accommodations, the sponsor of an event, meeting or program will include on the promotional/invitational material a statement that asks for special needs to be made known ahead of time in order to allow a reasonable accommodation.

To implement this policy, the campus revamped the online room reservation system to indicate the level of accessibility of any space and removed from the automatic system the option to reserve spaces that are inaccessible to some people. This means that when someone reserves a room through this system, they are automatically reserving an accessible space. To reserve one of the inaccessible spaces on campus, an event planner must communicate with a staff member in the room reservation department. Before the space can be reserved, the event planner must confirm that the guest list is known and no one on the list requires a physically accessible space. This reservation system makes accessibility the default and inaccessibility the exception, thus ensuring that a space is accessible to everyone planning to attend an event. Additionally, reminding event planners to include a statement that invites requests for accommodations in their materials sends the message that people with disabilities are welcome. This example recognizes that universal design requires both proactive steps and a process for arranging accommodations when needed.

PHYSICAL ENVIRONMENTS AND PRODUCTS

The second section of the checklist reminds users that universal design principles can be implemented to make the facilities and the campus's social and cultural environment more welcoming to and usable by all campus community members, including people with disabilities. Discussions of physical access to campus are often limited to providing access for individuals who use wheelchairs. Universal design of physical spaces considers the wide variety of ways in which people may wish to use the space and the difficulties they may encounter when attempting to do so. For example, the design and layout of physical spaces should be intuitive, so that people who are visually impaired or have difficulty orienting themselves in space can easily find their way. One student on the autism spectrum gave this example about his campus:

> My community college has a road system that does not circle the campus in a way that is easy to follow. Roads around a college campus should be intuitive. That means it should be easy to find your way at each place along the way, even if you can't read the signs. The road was not marked clearly by a continuous line system or signs. In several places you could not tell which way to go to get back to the main entrance, or how to exit to get off campus. You would get stuck in a parking area and not know how to get out. This made it very difficult for people with processing or directional disabilities to figure out where to go. I use the Access bus, and often a new driver would get lost. It was almost impossible for the dispatcher to give them directions over the phone because the roads were not marked.

In this case, self-advocacy of the student, with the help of his mother, brought some resolution, explained as follows:

> The administration has posted some signs now that my mom and I brought it to their attention. They did not realize how difficult the old system was for people with disabilities. When they are finished with the major construction project they are working on, they have promised to paint a continuous line on the roadway that circles the campus.

The accessibility of routes of travel also affects students with visual impairments. As one student who is blind explained:

> On my campus, some areas are not very safe and accessible for students with visual impairments . . . especially when I have had to try and cross the parking lot in order to get to the library. I was relieved when my trainer from the State Commission for the Blind helped me find an accessible route.

The student also noted, "When people park their service vehicles on the walkways, this makes it harder for me to get to the library or science building without running the risk of ending up in the parking lot." Vigilance to remove physical barriers from campuses can help meet universal design goals for a welcoming and accessible environment. A student with a mobility impairment reminds us:

> Accessible restrooms are really important. Not only does there need to be enough room for a wheelchair to navigate, there also needs to be enough room for an assis-

tant, if needed. The handles on the door need to be universally accessible, too. Often the dispensers are mounted on the wall, too close to the hand bars, which make[s] it hard to grab the hand bars without banging your knuckles.

An easy way to improve the usability of all physical spaces is to install window blinds to reduce glare, especially on computer screens. Window blinds help students with visual impairments, but others benefit as well. As pointed out by one student, "The reduction of sensory input will allow autistic workers to concentrate with fewer sensory problems. This also includes the ability to control other light and sound in the workspace."

Additionally, the availability of quiet spaces can benefit visually impaired students who use talking computers, as well as students with learning disabilities or attention deficit disorders that make it difficult to focus. One student confirms the value of a space free of distractions: "I started utilizing the academic support center to do my studying. It is a quiet area with seats next to power outlets, so I can plug in my laptop."

Student service administrators should consider visual and auditory stimuli when planning student spaces. The reduction of sensory input may help many students pay attention to the task at hand. For example, a career center that is planning to incorporate computer workstations for students to use when searching for jobs may want to provide adjustable lighting at each station and reduce distractions through the use of cubicles, or some other space dividers, instead of open desks.

Additional space considerations for student service administrators include issues related to transportation and food services. One student offers these comments: "Student services organizations should be close to bus stops and train stations, so people with disabilities can get to and from the office using transit." That student also noted:

> It is important that cafeterias be accessible so that people with disabilities can see, reach, and choose the food, and then pay for it. Food choices also need to be accessible. Hardly anyone thinks about that. Offering food and drinks that are easy to open and eat is an important accessibility issue.

Student service offices can take a proactive stance in the improvement of facilities to make the campus accessible and welcoming. For example, the campus webmaster and other staff of Information Technology Systems and Services at the University of Minnesota–Duluth (UMD) collaborated to create an accessible campus map. Now students, faculty, staff, and campus visitors can look up this map on the Web to find accessible building entrances and elevators on campus. The map helps people plan their route of travel prior to a journey. It is especially helpful to individuals with mobility impairments—both permanent and temporary—and to those who fatigue easily or are carrying large items across campus.

The admissions office is often the first point of contact between a prospective student and the college or university; therefore, making it accessible is crucial for a campus that welcomes all prospective students. During a reception space remodel in one admissions office, it became apparent that a person could not see over the reception counter from a seated position. With the assistance of the facilities management office, admissions staff replaced the counter with a modular desk that accommodates a variety of counter heights. Now those who are seated and those who are standing can get the attention of staff behind the desk and use the surface to fill out forms. In allowing comfortable use by people with a broad range of physical sizes and abilities, this option is a good example of universal design.

Universal design can be applied to telephone communications as well. UMD worked with an outside contractor to install the first public videophone stations in northern Minnesota. The videophones provide a video-to-video connection, through which people who are deaf or hard of hearing can communicate by using American Sign Language or another means of visual communication. To call a hearing person, a deaf person can use a video relay service, in which an interpreter translates between sign and spoken word. With these systems in place, people who are deaf or hard of hearing can communicate easily and naturally with others; this contributes to a campus environment of access and inclusion.

STAFF

The next section on the checklist focuses on ensuring that staff members are prepared to help all students. One way to create a more welcoming campus is to have staff with diverse characteristics as role models for the student body. Colleges may consider ways to recruit people with disabilities in order to diversify their staff. Such steps require flexibility on the part of existing staff, but taking the time to hire a diverse staff can provide the institution with new perspectives and depth of skills. As one student pointed out:

> Because many people on the autism spectrum have high skill levels and positive attitudes toward work, it is important to consider them beyond the first impression when hiring because their abilities tend to make up for any minor social issues or lack of work experience.

Preparing staff to work with individuals with disabilities is as important as having an accessible physical environment. Staff should be ready to greet all community members who enter their offices (or contact them via phone or e-mail) and to respond to requests for accommodations. Because the quality of customer service provided to visitors is a critical component of creating a welcoming environment for students with disabilities, a list of communication hints is included in *Equal Access: Universal Design of Student Services* (Burgstahler, 2015) and in Chapter 11 of this book. Students with disabilities emphasize the need for college and university staff who are able to focus on their diverse interests and skills, not just their disabilities. One way to help students know that staff are open to working with people with disabilities is to include a statement in key publications that conveys the following:

> Our goal is to make all materials and services accessible to everyone. Please inform staff of accessibility barriers you encounter and request accommodations that will make activities and information resources accessible to you.

As one student reported:

> I think it is important for student services staff to publicly state their commitment to accessibility because that assertion may be difficult for people on the autism spectrum to understand if not in writing. A physical copy of information will help them more easily make use of resources.

In an effort to improve the ability of staff to work with students with disabilities, one campus streamlined the process of arranging a sign language interpreter by creating an accessible web-based form for interpreter requests. All staff on campus were informed of the new process and thus empowered to retain an interpreter more easily. Sharing information and streamlining processes for obtaining accommodations are examples of universal design that contribute to a welcoming and accessible campus.

INFORMATION RESOURCES AND TECHNOLOGY

The fourth section of the checklist focuses on ensuring that publications and websites welcome diverse groups, that information resources are available in accessible formats, and that technology in the service area is accessible to all visitors. Equal access to information is a key aspect of a universally designed campus. One visually impaired student explains:

> For a website to be accessible to people who are visually impaired, it needs to have text descriptions for each link and graphic. The more information available and accessible online, the better it is for me. Many classes have their syllabus online. In one class I took, the professor posted his notes online, including the test reviews, and that worked great.

Providing information in an accessible electronic format allows students to access it in their preferred way: by using a screen reader or braille, reading it on screen in the preferred size, or printing it in standard or large print.

An additional way to make websites and campus publications more accessible is to include pictures of people with disabilities engaged in campus life. Students often look through campus publications for images with which they can identify. Making sure that they find images of individuals with disabilities, and that those individuals are engaging with others on campus, can help to cultivate a welcoming environment. Alternative text in electronic versions of these publications should describe these visuals in such a way that individuals who are blind and using text-to-speech systems can access the visual content as well.

At the University of Wisconsin–Madison, the registrar's office is continually challenged to provide enrollment information, transcripts, and tuition rates in an accessible format for students with disabilities. To achieve their accessibility goals, they have implemented an online system using commercial software along with software built by the Division of Information Technology on campus. The registrar's office, along with the disabilities services office, wrote questions to include in the annual Students with Disabilities Survey to assess the accessibility of the online registration tools. As a result of the survey, problems with online registration were identified and addressed by the Division of Information Technology, thus improving the tools' accessibility to all students, regardless of levels of ability, mobility, age, or gender, and to those with slow network connections, older hardware, diverse software platforms, and small mobile devices.

Administrators should consider space issues for all potential service users, not just the average user. One student notes that she often works with an assistant and needs room for both of them to work at the computer at the same time. Many standard workstation spaces are too small to do this. Providing adequate space for both right- and left-handed users is also important.

UMD created an assistive technology (AT) team to ensure timely responses to AT requests from students. The team focuses on providing hardware and software solutions that allow people with disabilities to access the current information technology. The team is composed of representatives of key campus constituents: disability services, information technology, the library, and human resources. Together, they respond to requests for AT and have access to a budget from which to purchase software and pay technicians to install it. The team works with all campus computer labs to ensure that adjustable tables and at least one large monitor are available to students. To take the technology to the next level, the AT team participated in UMD's Transformational Leadership Program (TLP) to teach staff how to identify and prioritize opportunities for improvement, measure the effectiveness of current services and programs, analyze what can be done better, implement new solutions, and institutionalize improvements. This curriculum, taught by the TLP, is based on the process improvement methodology used at 3M, a corporate sponsor of UMD research and process improvement initiatives. These methodologies are incorporated in a checklist that focuses on the universal design of computing environments and can be found in the publication *Equal Access: Universal Design of Computer Labs* (Burgstahler, 2012).

UW created an Access Technology Center (ATC) into the largest general-use technology lab on campus. This strategy addressed the needs for a centralized resource for AT and universal design consultation *and* for students with disabilities to be able to work side-by-side with their peers. The ATC serves all UW students, faculty, and staff through this main facility and by supporting satellite workstations located in some departmental computing labs. These satellite stations are equipped with the most commonly used AT. When additional AT is needed for a specific student in a departmental lab, ATC staff arrange to purchase appropriate products using central funds allocated for this purpose. They also provide technical support to the department staff.

EVENTS

The final section of the universal design of student services checklist emphasizes the importance of ensuring that everyone can fully participate in the campus community. Wheelchair-accessible facilities, wide aisles, and adjustable-height tables are some important considerations in making events accessible to all participants. Campus safety is another important consideration for large and small events. One student reminds us:

Autistic individuals may need to see visually where to go in an emergency. Maps and evacuation plans must be able to be followed; otherwise, confusion may occur regardless of verbal instructions or practiced drills.

One institution that wanted to make its Welcome Week more welcoming to all new students used universal design principles to examine current practices and make more aspects of the orientation accessible. First, campus signage was examined to ensure that accessible entrances to buildings were easy to find and that there were large-print and braille signs in all buildings. Next, the school arranged the schedule for Welcome Week to be simple and predictable: academics in the morning, exploration of clubs and employment in the afternoon, and major social events in the evening. Each required session was repeated multiple times to allow students options to plan their own schedules and eliminate the likelihood of fatigue. Finally, all students were given a guide to Welcome Week, available in print, alternate formats, and online, allowing participants to access at their convenience the schedule of activities and session handouts. These universally designed improvements to the traditional Welcome Week activities created a more welcoming, accessible, and navigable program for all students.

CONCLUSION

Universal design can be applied to any product or environment. This chapter provides concrete examples of universal design actions that institutions of higher education have taken to improve their student services. These implementation strategies make campuses more welcoming and accessible to everyone. As the universal design of student services checklist was being field-tested, student service administrators requested checklists tailored to the unique needs of their service areas. In response, checklists were created for recruitment and undergraduate admissions, registration, financial aid, advising, libraries, computer labs, career services, and housing and residential life. They can be located, along with other useful information, in the Student Services Conference Room on the DO-IT website (DO-IT, n.d.).

REFERENCES

Burgstahler, S. (Ed.). (2005). *Students with disabilities and campus services: Building the team—Presentation and resource materials.* Seattle: University of Washington. Retrieved from http://www.washington.edu/doit/building-team-faculty-staff-and-students-working-together-presentation-and-resource-materials

Burgstahler, S. (2012). *Equal access: Universal design of computer labs.* Seattle: University of Washington. Retrieved from http://www.washington.edu/doit/equal-access-universal-design-computer-labs

Burgstahler, S. (2015). *Equal access: Universal design of student services.* Seattle: University of Washington. Retrieved from http://www.washington.edu/doit/equal-access-universal-design-student-services

Burgstahler, S., & Moore, E. (2009). Making student services welcoming and accessible through accommodations and universal design. *Journal of Postsecondary Education and Disability, 21*(3), 155–174. Retrieved from https://www.ahead.org/publications/jped/vol_21

Burgstahler, S., & Moore, E. (2013). Development of a UD Checklist for postsecondary student services. In S. Burgstahler (Ed.). *Universal design in higher education: Promising practices.* Seattle: DO-IT, University of Washington. Retrieved from www.uw.edu/doit/development-ud-checklist-postsecondary-student-services

Disabilities, Opportunities, Internetworking, and Technology. (DO-IT). (2012). *AccessCollege: Systemic change for postsecondary institutions*. Seattle: University of Washington. Retrieved from http://www.washington.edu/doit/accesscollege-systemic-change-postsecondary-institutions

DO-IT. (n.d.). *Resources for student services staff*. Seattle: University of Washington. Retrieved from http://www.washington.edu/doit/programs/accesscollege/student-services-conference-room/resources/resources-student-services-staff

Goff, E., & Higbee, J. L. (Eds.). (2008). *Pedagogy and student services for institutional transformation: Implementing universal design in higher education*. Minneapolis: Center for Research on Developmental Education and Urban Literacy, University of Minnesota.

Higbee, J. L., & Eaton, S. B. (2003). Implementing universal design in learning centers. In J. Higbee (Ed.), *Curriculum transformation and disability: Implementing universal design in higher education* (pp. 231–240). Minneapolis: University of Minnesota, Center for Research on Developmental Education and Urban Literacy.

Kutztown University. (2006). *Kutztown University policy 2006-305: Accessible meetings, events, programs*. Retrieved from http://www2.kutztown.edu/prebuilt/apps/policyregister/policy.aspx?policy=DIV-001

Schmetzke, A. (2001). Web accessibility at university libraries and library schools. *Library Hi Tech, 19*(1), 35–49.

Thompson, T. (2008). Universal design of computer labs. In S. Burgstahler & R. Cory (Eds.), *Universal design in higher education: From principles to practice* (pp. 107–175). Cambridge, MA: Harvard Education Press.

Uzes, K. B., & Connelly, D. (2003). Universal design in counseling center service areas. In J. Higbee (Ed.), *Curriculum transformation and disability: Implementing universal design in higher education* (pp. 241–250). Minneapolis: University of Minnesota, Center for Research on Developmental Education and Urban Literacy.

Vance, M. L., Lipsitz, N. E., & Parks, K. (2014). *Beyond the Americans with Disabilities Act: Inclusive policy and practice for higher education*. Washington, DC: National Association for Student Personnel Administration.

Wisbey, M. E., & Kalivoda, K. S. (2003). Residential living for all: Fully accessible and "livable" on-campus housing. In J. Higbee (Ed.), *Curriculum transformation and disability: Implementing universal design in higher education* (pp. 241–250). Minneapolis: University of Minnesota Center for Research on Developmental Education and Urban Literacy.

The content of this chapter was developed under a grant from the U.S. Department of Education Office of Postsecondary Education (grant numbers P333A020044 and P333A050064). However, this content does not necessarily represent the policy of the Department of Education, and you should not assume endorsement by the federal government.

13

Universal Design of Physical Spaces
From Principles to Practice

Sheryl E. Burgstahler

When universal design (UD) is applied to physical spaces, they are welcoming, accessible, and usable for people with a wide range of characteristics. History, strategies, and processes for applying UD to physical spaces in higher education are discussed in this chapter. This content can help administrators design inclusive campus environments.

Let's start with a test. When a student has only one choice for a place to sit in an auditorium, and it is not next to his friends, is it (1) because he uses a wheelchair or (2) because the space was not designed to be flexible? When a student cannot tell that an emergency alarm is blaring, is it (1) because she is deaf or (2) because the designer of the emergency alarm system neglected to provide a visual signal along with the audio warning signal? The second responses to these questions resonate with the universal design paradigm, because they suggest that a disabling condition may reside in the environment rather than within an individual.

Designers who apply UD to physical spaces anticipate the wide variety of abilities and other characteristics potential users might have, and they make design decisions that both serve the needs of the broadest audience and are reasonable under the given circumstances. When an existing space is not suitable for a specific user, UD advocates consider how the environment might be improved so that, even if an accommodation must be provided to address the current situation, the accessibility barrier could be removed for future users.

The field of UD can guide institutions of higher education as they strive to make their physical environments functional and comfortable for all students, employees, and visitors. To put the practice of UD in higher education into context, highlights from the history of UD of physical spaces are shared in the next section.

HISTORY OF UNIVERSAL DESIGN OF PHYSICAL SPACES

Many people have worked toward the goal of making physical spaces welcoming, accessible, and usable. Following are some of the most noteworthy.

Pioneering Work

Marc Harrison, professor of industrial engineering at the Rhode Island School of Design (RISD), was a pioneer in what eventually became known as UD. His experiences through years of rehabilitation after sustaining a brain injury as a child gave him insight and inspiration in his design of physical spaces that could be used efficiently by everyone, including those who have disabilities or are elderly. At the end of his career, he was part of a large team of RISD faculty and students that, in 1993, became engaged in the Universal Kitchen project to design kitchens that are efficient, user-friendly, and accessible to people with a wide range of abilities. The motivation for the project is described as follows (Rhode Island School of Design, n.d., p. 1):

> Spurred by the knowledge that routine kitchen tasks force people to bend, stoop, reach and lift—repeatedly compensating for weak design in uncomfortable ways— the team began with research. Making a succession of dinners together in typical kitchens, they used careful time/motion studies to document how inefficiencies in kitchen design require more than 400 discrete steps to make a simple dinner. Ultimately, the goal was to redesign the kitchen environment and help as many potential users as possible function independently—from the young to the old.

The Universal Kitchen team disassembled common elements of a kitchen (e.g., stovetops, ovens, refrigerators, dishwashers), studied ergonomics and human factors, and researched demographic trends. They generated thousands of innovative ideas, such as continuous wet surfaces, pop-up burners, countertop waste channels, retractable appliance cords, and modular refrigeration units. Each component, designed to be custom selected and arranged, included flexible features with respect to heights and depths that could be manually or automatically adjusted to an individual's "comfort zone" (Rhode Island School of Design, n.d., p. 1). Prototypes of the Universal Kitchen were exhibited at the Hagley Museum and Library in New York City (n.d.) and similar projects were displayed in other venues (e.g., Rhode Island School of Design, n.d.). The exhibitions served to increase interest in the design of environments within which people of all ages and abilities can function independently and comfortably. Together, they demonstrated that many accessibility barriers could be blamed on poor design, an observation in sharp contrast to the more traditional view that products and environments were inaccessible due to the limitations or "deficits" of specific individuals. Instead of looking for disabling conditions in the individual, these designers looked for disabling conditions in physical spaces.

Development of a Definition and Principles of Universal Design

Ronald Mace, an internationally known architect, product designer, educator, and wheelchair user, coined the term *universal design*. He defined UD as "the design of products and environments to be usable by all people, to the greatest extent possible, without the need for adaptation or specialized design" (The Center for Universal Design, 2008, p. 1). After four years of practicing conventional architecture, Mace helped create the first building code for accessibility in the United States. It became mandatory in North Carolina in 1973, served as a model for other states, and contributed to the passage of the U.S. Architectural Barriers Act of 1968. This act mandates that "buildings and facilities that are designed, constructed, or altered with Federal funds, or leased by a Federal agency, comply with Federal standards for physical accessibility" (U.S. Department of Justice, 2005, p. 19).

In 1989, Mace established the Center for Accessible Housing, currently known as the Center for Universal Design, at North Carolina State University. Under Mace's direction, the Center became a leader in UD research and practice with respect to products and the built environment. Its staff and collaborators created the seven principles of UD described in Chapter 1 of this book. Projects that Mace directed include the creation of universally designed house plans, thermostats, toilets, faucets, bathing units, and other products. At Designing for the 21st Century: An International Conference on Universal Design, held in New York in 1998, Mace delivered his last speech before his death later that year. In it, he shed light on the differences between assistive technology, barrier-free design, and UD. He explained that barrier-free design, or accessible design, is predominantly focused on removing architectural barriers for people with physical disabilities through adherence to building codes and regulations, such as architectural standards mandated by the Americans with Disabilities Act of 1990 (ADA) and its 2008 Amendments. In contrast, he said, UD defines the "user" more broadly (Reagan, 1998, p. 1):

> It's a consumer market driven issue. Its focus is not specifically on people with disabilities, but all *people*. It actually assumes the idea that everybody has a disability and I feel strongly that that's the case. We all become disabled as we age and lose ability, whether we want to admit it or not. It is negative in our society to say, "I am disabled" or "I am old." We tend to discount people who are less than what we popularly consider to be "normal." To be "normal" is to be perfect, capable, competent, and independent. Unfortunately, designers in our society also mistakenly assume that everyone fits this definition of "normal." This just is not the case.

Public Awareness and Advocacy for Removal of Environmental Barriers

A barrier-free movement began that included veterans injured in World War II and other individuals with disabilities and their advocates. It gained momentum during the civil rights movement of the 1960s and resulted in the enactment of public policies and legislation mandating accessible design, including the Architectural Barriers Act of 1968 (U.S. Department of Justice, 2005). More general civil rights legislation followed. Section 504 of the Rehabilitation Act of 1973 states that "no qualified individual with a disability in the United States shall be excluded from, be denied the benefits of, or be subjected to discrimination under any program or activity" (U.S. Department of Justice, 2005, p. 17) that receives federal financial assistance, which includes the vast majority of institutions of higher education. Further, Section 504 regulations address "reasonable accommodation for employees with disabilities; program accessibility; effective communication with people who have hearing or vision disabilities; and accessible new construction and alterations" (U.S. Department of Justice, 2005, p. 17).

Patricia Moore, an industrial designer and gerontologist, contributed to greater awareness of the need for UD of the built environment with her book *Disguised: A True Story* (Moore & Conn, 1984). In the book, Moore reported her experiences undertaking activities of everyday life when she disguised herself as an elderly woman and artificially limited her physical and sensory abilities. She encountered many barriers, including lights that could not be turned on, directions that could not be seen, steps that could not be negotiated, knobs that could not be turned, and doors that could not be pushed by people with limited strength, sight, hearing, and/or motor skills. The popularity of Moore's book, her appearances on television talk shows, and related articles in magazines and newspapers increased public awareness of the extent to which the traditional built environment is inaccessible to many people.

Moore emphasizes that the solution to inaccessible design is *not* to design multiple sets of products (e.g., one for those who are young, healthy, and physically fit; one for the elderly; one for those with a specific type of disability) but rather to design products that are flexible, making them suitable for people of all ages and abilities.

Many other educators and architects have promoted accessible, usable, and universal design. For example, from 1965 to 1993, James Pirkl, professor and chair of the Department of Design at Syracuse University, sensitized his students to the needs of people who are elderly and/or who have disabilities. In 1985, he pioneered the concept of *transgenerational design*, in which products and environments are designed to be compatible with physical and sensory changes associated with aging (Cooper-Hewitt National Design Museum, 1998).

The Baby Boomers

It has been predicted that the free market system will build demand for accessible products and environments because of "the graying of America": "an unprecedented demographic bulge in the United States, in which senior citizens comprise the fastest-growing segment of our society" (Moore & Conn, 1984, p. 158). Global aging is occurring even faster in Europe and Northeast Asia and expected to affect economic, social, and political systems worldwide (Stokes, 2014). This trend may contribute to the promotion of universally designed products and environments. Moore and Conn (p. 160) quote Canadian social critic Joel Garreau as somewhat cynically describing the situation in this way:

> Greed is a far more reliable and universal agent of change than is the urge to do good for your fellow man. The future of any great idea is always made more bright when it's found to be profitable.

The increasing size of the aging population—many members of which experience varying levels of physical, sensory, and cognitive limitations—and the desire of senior citizens to continue to live in single-family housing as long as possible have kindled interest in addressing issues beyond basic wheelchair accessibility to promote UD of physical spaces. One example is universal *smart home* design, which is defined as "the process of designing products and housing environments that can be used to the greatest extent possible for people of all ages, abilities and physical disabilities" (Schwab, 2004). As Gordon Mansfield, former deputy secretary of the U.S. Department of Veterans Affairs and chair of the Architectural and Transportation Barriers Compliance Board, explains (Community Resources for Independent Living, n.d., p. 4):

> Universal design is an approach to design that acknowledges the changes . . . everyone [undergoes] during his or her lifetime. It considers children, the elderly, people who are tall or short, and those with various disabilities. It addresses the lifespan of human beings beyond the mythical "average" person.

Legislation

Legislation throughout the world has contributed to the removal of physical barriers to the environment through curb cuts, elevators, bus lifts, elimination of unnecessary steps, and tactile floor markers. The Convention on the Rights of Persons with Disabilities addresses this issue and sets out a code of implementation. Article 20 requires that countries identify and remove barriers and ensure that people with disabilities can access the environment, transportation, and public facilities. In the U.S., the ADA and its 2008 Amendments increased public awareness of accessibility issues. The ADA "prohibits discrimination on the basis of disability in employment, State and local government, public accommodations, commercial facilities, transportation, and telecommunications" (U.S. Department of Justice, 2005, p. 1). The ADA requires that covered entities follow specific architectural standards in new construction and alterations of their facilities (United States Access Board, 2002). Some state laws mandate even higher standards for accessibility. Although the practice of ADA compliance focuses on a narrow range of issues (typically by employing barrier-free or accessible design), the ADA and other civil rights legislation have promoted the idea that product and facility designers should be proactive in considering users with a range of abilities rather than simply focusing on the average user.

UD goes beyond legal compliance for accessibility by addressing a broader range of user characteristics. Strategies and processes for applying UD are presented in the next sections of this chapter.

UNIVERSAL DESIGN GUIDELINES FOR PHYSICAL SPACES

UD addresses issues not only for individuals with disabilities but also for those who are short and tall, are excellent or poor readers, are right- or left-handed, speak a variety of native languages, and have other characteristics, only some of which are defined as disabilities. As in other applications of UD described in Chapter 1, UD of physical spaces can be measured on a continuum. For example, whereas including a ramp next to steps into a building is an example of accessible design, developing a sloping entrance into that building for all visitors to use is closer to the UD ideal because it does not unnecessarily segregate people who belong to specific groups. UD encompasses both accessible design, which primarily focuses on complying with standards so as to avoid creating barriers for individuals with physical disabilities, as well as usable design, ergonomics, and human factors, which more subjectively measure the capacity of a product or space to allow an individual to perform a task efficiently, safely, and comfortably (Iwarsson & Stahl, 2002).

The Center for Universal Design provides guidelines and technical assistance regarding UD in housing, commercial and public facilities, and outdoor environments. Other organizations have applied the principles of UD to create guidelines and checklists for the UD of specific physical spaces. For example, the American Association of Retired Persons (n.d.) has created checklists for UD of residential spaces that include strategies for entrances, interior circulation, storage, bathrooms, and kitchens. They suggest that a universally designed home include such features as an entry with no steps; main rooms on one level; thresholds that are flush with the floor; wide doorways and hallways; nonslip surfaces; lever door handles and faucets; grab bars by toilets; rocker light switches; appliances with large print on the controls; and lighting for walkways, closets, and work areas. Specific practices for universally designed interiors, landscapes, housing, and transportation systems are readily available in the literature (e.g., Preiser & Smith, 2011; Schwab, 2004; Steinfeld, 2012).

The author of this chapter reviewed existing guidelines and checklists for accessible and universal design to draft a list of strategies for the application of UD to physical spaces on postsecondary campuses. The strategies were reviewed by and updated with formative feedback from members of a team of administrators who engaged in DO-IT's UDHE initiative, a comprehensive set of projects focused on making all aspects of postsecondary institutions welcoming, accessible, and usable (DO-IT, 2012). Team members participating in the UDHE initiative, which was funded by the U.S. Department of Education Office of Postsecondary Education, represented a diverse set of institutions of higher education in more than twenty states. Table 13.1 displays examples of strategies for the UD of physical spaces identified in these projects (Burgstahler, 2012b, pp. 2–4).

Although UD guidelines are typically used to create a fully inclusive environment, UD considerations can also be applied where segregated spaces are desirable. For example, facilities typically include restrooms for men and for women. However, considering the diversity of a population that might use a large facility, there may be situations that require a restroom to accommodate mixed-sex groups and other individuals. Examples include a man who would like to accompany his young daughter to the restroom, an individual with a physical disability whose personal assistant is of the opposite sex, a person who is blind and prefers to navigate a smaller restroom space than is typical of large public restrooms, and someone whose physical characteristics and gender identity are not associated with a single sex. Consideration of such situations have led designers to offer male, female, and "family" or "gender-neutral" restrooms in airports and other large facilities. Depending on the size of its student body and of other groups that use its facilities, a campus may choose to offer family or gender-neutral restrooms.

TABLE 13.1   Universal Design of Physical Spaces

Categories	Examples of Universal Design Applied to a Physical Space
Planning, policies, and evaluation. Consider diversity issues as you plan and evaluate the space.	• Include people with diverse characteristics, including various types of disabilities, in planning processes. • Consider accessibility issues in procurement processes. • Address disability-related issues in evaluation methods.
Appearance. Design the space to foster a campus climate that is inclusive of all students, staff, faculty, and visitors.	• Create an environment that is appealing to those with a broad range of cultures, ages, abilities, and other characteristics.
Entrances, routes of travel. Make physical access welcoming and accessible to people with a variety of abilities, sizes, and ages.	• Ensure convenient, wheelchair-accessible parking spaces and routes of travel to facilities and within facilities. • Shelter entryways. • Install outdoor lights with motion sensors near entrances. • Provide sensors to automatically open exterior doors. • Use lever handles rather than knobs for doors. • Use gently sloping walks that are integrated into the design rather than steps and ramps that segregate individuals with physical disabilities. • Ensure that there are ample high-contrast, large-print directional signs to and throughout the physical space.
Fixtures, furniture. Provide fixtures and furniture that can be used by all employees, students, and visitors.	• Install levers for sink handles. • Use front-mounted, easy-to-operate controls on appliances and other equipment, with labels in large, high-contrast print. • Position electrical outlets and light switches (with dimmers) to be reached from standing or seated positions. • In classrooms, use furniture and fixtures that are adjustable in height and allow flexible arrangements for different learning activities and student groupings.
Information resources, technology. Ensure that information and technology is accessible to everyone.	• Position publications to be reachable from standing and seated positions. • Make sure directional and information kiosks are reachable from standing and seated positions.
Safety. Design the space to minimize the risk of injury.	• Use nonslip walking surfaces. • Install emergency systems that incorporate audio and visual warnings.
Accommodation. Develop a system for staff to address accommodation requests by individuals for whom the space design does not automatically provide access.	• Include procedures for requesting disability-related accommodations in signage, publications, and information kiosks.

Source: S. Burgstahler. (2012b). *Equal access: Universal design of physical spaces.* Seattle: University of Washington.

A PROCESS FOR UNIVERSAL DESIGN OF PHYSICAL SPACES

Key considerations to address when applying UD to a physical space at an institution of higher education are to plan ahead, to keep in mind the diversity of the campus community at all stages of a project, and to engage individuals with diverse characteristics in the planning process. The following steps, adapted from the more general process presented in Chapter 1 of this book, can be used when designing a new space or an upgrade of an existing space (Burgstahler, 2012a, pp. 1–2). They are also summarized in Figure 13.1.

1. *Identify the space.* Select a physical space (e.g., a student union building, dormitory, theater, athletic facility, classroom, or science lab). Consider the purpose of the space, location, dimensions, budget, and other issues that affect design.
2. *Define the universe.* Describe the overall population and then consider the diverse characteristics of potential members of the population who might use the space (e.g., students, staff, faculty, and visitors with diverse characteristics with respect to gender; age; size; ethnicity and race; native language; learning style; and abilities to see, hear, manipulate objects, read, and communicate).
3. *Involve consumers.* Consider and involve people with diverse characteristics (as identified in Step 2) in all phases of the development, implementation, and evaluation of the space. Also, gain the perspectives of potential users through diversity programs such as the campus disability services office.
4. *Adopt guidelines or standards.* Review research and practices to identify the most appropriate practices for the design of the type of space identified in Step 1. Identify universal design strategies to integrate with these best practices in architectural design.
5. *Apply guidelines or standards.* Apply UD strategies in concert with other best practices identified in Step 4 to the overall design of the physical space (e.g., aesthetics, routes of travel) and to all subcomponents of the space (e.g., signage, restrooms, sound systems, fire and security systems).

FIGURE 13.1   A Process for the Application of Universal Design for Physical Spaces

6. *Plan for accommodations*. Identify processes to address accommodation requests by individuals for whom the design of the space does not automatically provide access (e.g., cafeteria staff members should know how to assist customers who are blind). Tell potential users of the space how to request accommodations through signage, websites, and/or publications.

7. *Train and support*. Tailor and deliver ongoing training and support to staff who manage the physical space. Share institutional goals with respect to diversity and inclusion and practices for ensuring welcoming, accessible, and inclusive experiences for everyone using the space. Explain the reasoning behind design decisions, so that design integrity is maintained over time (e.g., make sure that staff know not to configure furniture in such a way that it creates physical barriers to wheelchair users).

8. *Evaluate*. Include universal design measures in periodic evaluations of the space, evaluate the space with a diverse group of users, and make modifications based on feedback. Provide ways to collect ongoing input from facility users (e.g., through online and printed instruments and signage that requests suggestions).

These steps can be adapted to any campus space. For example, the following steps could be taken to universally design a science lab.

1. *Identify and describe the science lab*. Consider the purpose of the space, location, dimensions, budget, and other issues that affect its design.

2. *Define the universe*. Consider all the students, faculty, staff, and others who might use the science lab and list their potential characteristics with respect to gender, size, age, race and ethnicity, physical and sensory abilities, and native language.

3. *Involve consumers*. Consider the perspectives of students and other individuals that reflect the diversity identified in Step 2. Include them in an advisory role and seek their perspectives in other ways, such as by viewing the video *Working Together: Science Teachers and Students with Disabilities* (Burgstahler, 2012d), in which high school students with a wide range of abilities recommend teaching strategies to science teachers.

4. *Adopt design guidelines or standards*. These include guidelines, standards, and checklists for applying UD to a science lab. Consult publications, websites, and practitioners for ideas on UD strategies to employ. For example, in Chapter 14 of this book, author Elisabeth Goldstein shares design suggestions that could be applied to a science lab. Other resources also provide specific guidance, such as the following (Burgstahler, 2012b, 2012c):

- Address safety procedures for students with a variety of sensory and mobility abilities, including the provision of visual lab warning signals.
- Make laboratory signs and equipment labels in large print, with high contrast.
- Make sure that the lab is accessible to a wheelchair user.
- Maintain wide aisles and keep the lab uncluttered.
- Incorporate an adjustable-height work surface for at least one workstation.

- Install a mirror above the location where demonstrations are typically given.
- Use lever controls instead of knobs.
- Install flexible connections to water, gas, and electricity.
- Buy lab products that can be used by students with a variety of abilities (e.g., plastic lab products instead of glass, tactile models, large-print diagrams, nonslip mats, support stands, beaker/object clamps, handles on beakers/equipment, surgical gloves to handle slippery items, and video cameras with computer/TV monitors to enlarge microscope images).
- Apply these UD practices in concert with other best practices used for the design of science labs.

5. *Apply design guidelines or standards.* Apply UD strategies in concert with other best practices identified in Step 4 to the overall design of the science lab (e.g., floor plan) and to all subcomponents of the space (e.g., signage, workstations, emergency systems).
6. *Plan for accommodations.* Make sure faculty members and lab assistants understand processes for addressing accommodation requests by individuals for whom the lab environment or activities are not fully accessible.
7. *Train and support.* Tailor and deliver ongoing training and support regarding access issues to faculty, staff, and lab assistants.
8. *Evaluate.* Include UD measures in the evaluation of the lab space, making efforts to gather input from individuals with diverse abilities. Provide ways for users to offer input (e.g., signage that requests suggestions from lab users for making the facility more accessible and comfortable to visitors).

EXAMPLES

A successful UD process was implemented when Missouri State University (MSU) created a campus recreation center with UD features (Staeger-Wilson & Sampson, 2012). It resulted from collaborative work among an architect, a disability resource professional, students with disabilities, and others serving on project committees. The third of six objectives for the design was that the facility "be designed, using universal design concepts, to be accessible to all individuals of the University community" (Staeger-Wilson & Sampson, 2012, p. 258). Through this type of engagement, students with disabilities can become part of a paradigm shift that focuses on equity and inclusion rather than minimum compliance.

Each summer, the DO-IT Center hosts a group of DO-IT Scholars in a residential program on the University of Washington campus. These high school students have a wide variety of disabilities and are attending the program to prepare for college. Every activity in the multiple-week program is universally designed—meals, dorm activities, field trips, recreational activities, computer labs (see Figure 13.2), science labs (see Figure 13.3), and more. The participants also learn about disabilities different than their own and how UD can make a more accessible and usable world for everyone. Some of them participate in follow-up activities to share this approach to design. For example, when the University of Washington developed a space for its newly

FIGURE 13.2 A computer lab in the DO-IT Scholars summer program is accessible to students with disabilities that impact mobility, hearing, sight, learning, and social skills.

funded Center for Sensorimotor Neural Engineering (n.d.), they engaged a focus group of DO-IT Scholar participants with a variety of disabilities to provide input to the architects designing the space. Their input was considered when the furniture and floor surfaces were selected and the floor plan arrangements were finalized.

FIGURE 13.3 A science experiment can be completed from a seated or standing position.

CONCLUSION

To some degree, most institutions of higher education understand their legal obligations to offer courses and services in physically accessible spaces; however, efforts must be made to ensure that more inclusive UD strategies are routinely applied. The pioneers and founders of UD envision a world in which products and environments are designed to be welcoming to, accessible to, and usable by people with a wide range of abilities and other characteristics. Developments in the areas of accessible design, ergonomics, human factors, and UD can provide guidance to administrators who wish to create inclusive opportunities for everyone who might use campus spaces. In the next chapter of this book, Elisabeth Goldstein shares examples of the application of UD to specific campus spaces.

REFERENCES

American Association of Retired Persons. (n.d.). *What is universal design?* Retrieved from http://www.aarp.org/families/home_design/universaldesign/a2004-03-23-whatis_univdesign.html

Americans with Disabilities Act of 1990. 42 U.S.C.A. § 12101 *et seq.*

Americans with Disabilities Act Amendments Act of 2008. 42 U.S.C.A. § 12101 note (2011)

Architectural Barriers Act of 1968. 42 U.S.C. §§ 4151 *et seq.*

Burgstahler, S. (2012a). *Equal access: Science and students with sensory impairments.* Seattle: University of Washington. Retrieved from http://www.washington.edu/doit/equal-access-science-and-students-sensory-impairments

Burgstahler, S. (2012b). *Equal access: Universal design of physical spaces.* Seattle: University of Washington. Retrieved from http://www.washington.edu/doit/equal-access-universal-design-physical-spaces

Burgstahler, S. (2012c). *Making science labs accessible to students with disabilities.* Seattle: University of Washington. Retrieved from http://www.washington.edu/doit/making-science-labs-accessible-students-disabilities

Burgstahler, S. (2012d). *Working together: Science teachers and students with disabilities.* Seattle: University of Washington. Retrieved from http://www.washington.edu/doit/working-together-science-teachers-and-students-disabilities

Center for Sensorimotor Neural Engineering. (n.d.). *Center for Sensorimotor Neural Engineering.* Seattle: University of Washington.

The Center for Universal Design. (2008). *About UD.* Raleigh: North Carolina State University. Retrieved from http://www.ncsu.edu/ncsu/design/cud/about_ud/about_ud.htm

Community Resources for Independent Living. (n.d.). *Universal design: Home for all ages.* Hayward, CA: Author. Retrieved from http://crilhayward.org/policies-advocacy/docs/UD-Brochure-2.pdf

Cooper-Hewitt National Design Museum. (1998). *Unlimited by design.* New York: Author. Retrieved from http://www.cooperhewitt.org/

DO-IT. (2012). *AccessCollege: Systemic change for postsecondary institutions.* Seattle: University of Washington. Retrieved from http://www.washington.edu/doit/accesscollege-systemic-change-postsecondary-institutions

Hagley Museum and Library. (n.d.). *The Marc Harrison collection.* Wilmington, DE: Author. Retrieved from http://www.hagley.org/A2193D.HTM

Iwarsson, S., & Stahl, A. (2002). Accessibility, usability and universal design—positioning and definition of concepts describing person-environment relationships. *Disability and Rehabilitation, 25*(2), 57–66.

Moore, P., & Conn, C. P. (1984). *Disguised: A true story.* Waco, TX: World Books.

Preiser, W., & Smith, K. H. (Eds.). (2011). *Universal design handbook* (2nd ed.). New York: McGraw-Hill Professional.

Reagan, J. (Ed.) (1998). *A perspective on universal design.* Presented at Designing for the 21st Century: An International Conference on Universal Design on June 19, 1998. Retrieved from http://www.ncsu.edu/ncsu/design/cud/about_us/usronmacespeech.htm

Rhode Island School of Design. (n.d.). *Designing the ultimate user-friendly kitchen.* Providence, RI: Author. Retrieved from http://www.risd.edu/Designing_Ultimate_User-Friendly_Kitchen/

Schwab, C. (2004). A stroll through the universal-designed smart home for the 21st century. *The Exceptional Parent, 34*(7), 24–28.

Section 504 of the Rehabilitation Act of 1973, as amended. 29 U.S.C. § 794.

Staeger-Wilson, K., & Sampson, D. H. (2012). Infusing just design in campus recreation. *Journal of Postsecondary Education and Disability, 25*(3), 247–252. Retrieved from http://files.eric.ed.gov/fulltext/EJ994289.pdf

Steinfeld, J. M. (2012). *Universal design: Creating inclusive environments.* Hoboken, NJ: John Wiley & Sons, Inc.

Stokes, B. (2014). *The countries that will be most impacted by aging population.* PEW Research Center. Retrieved from http://www.pewresearch.org/fact-tank/2014/02/04/the-countries-that-will-be-most-impacted-by-aging-population/

United States Access Board. (2002). *ADA accessibility guidelines*. Washington, DC: Author. Retrieved from http://www.access-board.gov/guidelines-and-standards/buildings-and-sites/about-the-ada-standards/background/adaag

United States Department of Justice. (2005). *A guide to disability rights laws*. Washington, DC: U.S. Department of Justice, Civil Rights Division. Retrieved from http://www.ada.gov/cguide.pdf

The content of this chapter was developed under grants from the U.S. Department of Education Office of Postsecondary Education (grant numbers P333A990042, P333A020044, and P333A050064) and the National Science Foundation (grant number HRD-0833504). However, this content does not necessarily represent the policy of the Department of Education, and you should not assume endorsement by the federal government.

14

Applications of Universal Design to Higher Education Facilities

Elisabeth Goldstein

Universal design principles can be readily applied to buildings and classrooms on campus. Specifically, universal design can be used to make gathering spaces, classrooms, labs, and student centers more accessible to students and the greater campus community through methods that promote equality, flexibility, and usability while simultaneously facilitating instruction, interaction, and learning. The author of this chapter explores the ways that a number of campuses have applied universal design to their spaces.

In the United States, each building project is required to follow accessibility guidelines mandated by the Americans with Disabilities Act of 1990 (ADA), which directs the minimum accessibility requirements for the built environment. Universal design is a concept developed by architect Ron Mace as "the design of products and environments to be usable by all people, to the greatest extent possible, without the need for adaptation or specialized design" (Mace, 2007, p. 1). Designing with the barrier-free considerations of universal design goes beyond making the built environment accessible to individuals with disabilities and makes it inclusive and equitable for everyone.

Promoting universal design of higher education campus grounds and facilities is particularly important since a widely diverse group of people (students, faculty, administration, alumni, visitors), with varying ages and physical and sensory abilities, makes up the campus community. A college campus is similar to a small city. Whether the campus is located in a rural or urban setting, there are spaces dedicated to housing, working, learning, retail, recreation, and social gathering that are available to all members of the campus community. The main function of the campus built environment is to provide places for all to learn, work, and live successfully. When designing campus grounds and facilities, one should be mindful of how its varied user groups travel throughout the campus, approach buildings, and work and live inside them.

FIGURE 14.1 Signage points to a wheelchair-accessible entrance that is located in a different location from the main building entrance. (Courtesy of the author.)

BUILDING ENTRANCES

The entry sequence to a building may be its most important feature. Approaching a building is an inherently communicative experience because it gives the first impression of the site and orients the visitor to the spaces within the rest of the facility. Building entrances are a high priority for universal design considerations. Entrances that meet accessibility codes are often located as an alternate entrance to a more prominent, noncompliant entrance. This design may technically provide access for all types of people to enter a building, but they will not share a common entry experience (Figure 14.1). An accessible entrance may be difficult to find if it is not located near the main entrance, and if a wheelchair user must separate from a group of friends or business colleagues to use an alternate entrance, it may make that person feel lower in status than the rest of the group (Bain, 1989). Those who do not use wheelchairs also benefit from a shared accessible entrance. Stairs are difficult to navigate for those using crutches (Figure 14.2), pushing strollers, and moving equipment or carrying luggage. While codes are useful to dictate a minimum threshold width and the rate of incline for a ramp, the designer and client institution should consider how the site conditions, building context, and desired user experience will allow for an optimally designed, barrier-free entrance for all user groups.

Erb Memorial Union Amphitheater, University of Oregon–Eugene

The Erb Memorial Union Amphitheater on the University of Oregon campus provides a good example of universal design because it is accessible for people of all abilities without providing separate travel routes for differently abled individuals. The amphitheater is sited within a plaza in front of the Erb Memorial Union Building (EMU), which is the student commons building and is centrally located on the University of

FIGURE 14.2   A student on crutches travels down a building's entry stair. (Courtesy of the author.)

Oregon campus. The EMU was built in 1950 and designed to be a place where students could gather and freely exchange ideas. In the 1970s, when the university experienced significant growth in enrollment, the EMU went through a series of renovations that changed the flow of traffic through the building, detracted from the aesthetics and accessibility of the spaces, and made it difficult for students to gather. In the late 1990s, to commemorate the Associated Student Government's one hundredth anniversary, the student body donated funds to restore the EMU to better fulfill its original mission and build a new gathering space in the form of an outdoor amphitheater.

The University of Oregon hired landscape architects Cameron McCarthy Gilbert & Scheibe and included groups of students, faculty, and staff in the design process (University of Oregon Planning Office, n.d.):

> [The amphitheater] was expressly designed with universal access in mind, and all of its areas are accessible by those in wheelchairs. Its main space is moved as far north as possible to take full advantage of the sun and to bring the activities as close as possible to the intersection [of two main arterials through campus].

One strength of the amphitheater's design is its placement into the site as the entrance for the EMU. The amphitheater itself is a physical symbol of the university's mission to provide a venue for the freedom of expression, and its location at the center of campus enhances the function of the building as a student commons. But it is the way that its paths are woven through the site and connect to the building that supports the university's mission to provide equality of opportunity. The amphitheater is formed by a series of stairs that wrap around a plaza and define its edge. While the amphitheater stairs can be used to reach the street from the plaza, they are deemphasized as a means of travel and are often used by those who want to sit and survey the action on the stage and plaza below.

The circulation through this space is mainly dictated by a sidewalk that follows the curve along the outside of the amphitheater and leads pedestrians to and from the EMU building. The sidewalk forks to form two gently sloping paths. The inner path slopes downward, providing access to the lower floor of the EMU as well as access into the plaza itself. The outer path slopes upward, bringing pedestrians to the upper level of the EMU. The gentle, even slope of the paths allows wheelchair users and those who are moving wheeled items to travel along the same route of travel as those who are not traveling with wheels.

These paths are also a barrier-free means of travel for pedestrians with visual impairments. Because the paths curve around the amphitheater with a broad turning radius, an individual with limited sight is not confronted with an abrupt change in direction of travel. There are no protruding objects within the path or along its edges to create unpredictable barriers, and its edges are accentuated by raised curbs so that the transition from the pedestrian path to the spaces beyond is easily detectable. In addition, the wide paths, gradual level changes, wide turning radius, and low landscaping beds offer expansive and clear sightlines of the plaza and amphitheater, which are a benefit to pedestrians with hearing loss (Kirschbaum et al., 2001).

By making the pathways accessible to everyone and creating an accessible main entrance, the designers allow all user groups to have the same opportunity to experience the plaza, enter two levels of the EMU facility, and engage in the activities that occur within the amphitheater.

CLASSROOMS

Classrooms on a college campus are typically used throughout the day by multiple instructors, who teach a variety of subjects and employ different pedagogical styles. Consequently, classrooms should be flexible and user-friendly to a broad audience. Classroom types range from small seminar-style rooms to lecture halls with a large seating capacity. With the increased use of media-enhanced tools and interactive learning models, the demands for flexibility in classrooms of all sizes are significant. A classroom designer must keep all potential instructors and students in mind and consider how to support the full range of activities that will occur within the space in order to create an inclusive classroom environment. A traditional classroom model is to place rows of fixed seats facing in one direction toward an instructor who lectures in front of a chalkboard. The more the classroom is designed to be fixed in place, the less accommodating it is to the wide variety of user groups who will use the space for learning. Also, the rigidity of a traditional classroom can make implementation of different methods of instruction difficult.

Large lecture hall–type classrooms typically utilize a tiered seating configuration to ensure clear sightlines and gain spatial efficiency within the building. With this type of seating configuration, a wheelchair user or someone who has difficulty navigating stairs must sit in a designated area of the classroom determined by the location of an accessible entrance. Ideally, the lecture hall should have entrances that allow wheeled access to the teaching area and multiple, if not all, seating levels of the classroom. Also, it is recommended that a total of at least 4% of the classroom seating area be available for wheelchair stations throughout the classroom, offering a choice of sight-lines that is comparable to those provided for people who do not use wheelchairs (Allen et al., 1996).

LeBaron Hall Auditorium, Iowa State University–Ames

As part of a campus-wide project to upgrade classrooms, Iowa State University reno-vated LeBaron Hall Auditorium, a tiered lecture hall with large seating capacity, to facilitate an interactive learning atmosphere that is often difficult to achieve in a tra-ditional classroom of its size. The design team included architects from Baldwin & White, KI furniture manufacturers, and specialists in educational studies, space man-agement, and technology services. The design team established goals for this class-room that included improving contact between the faculty member and students, facilitating active learning through group interaction, and promoting a social and collaborative atmosphere among students. They recognized that to achieve these goals, an inclusive classroom environment must be created that supports movement and encourages interaction and participation.

The renovated LeBaron Hall Auditorium has 363 seats and continues to use a tiered seating configuration, but the room was reconfigured to be wider than it is deep, so students seated in the back rows are not far from the front of the room. Sightlines were improved, so that students are more inclined to engage in classroom activities. There are wheelchair stations on the first, third, and sixth tiers, and an elevator out-side the classroom allows for access to all three levels. Each of the six seating tiers has two rows of seats, and the horizontal walkways between these rows are wide. These walkways allow for wheelchair passage and easy navigation by students and instruc-tors moving around the classroom as they participate in group activities. The wide spacing between the rows also accommodates a unique design feature of the seats themselves. The seats have a swivel function, with no "spring back to front" feature, which allows students sitting in one row to easily turn their seats to face the row behind them to engage in a group activity (see Figure 14.3).

Positive feedback from instructors and students using this classroom confirms that the classroom promotes an inclusive environment and active learning experience. Dr. Corly Brooke, professor and director of the Center for Excellence in Teaching and Learning, reports, "The best thing it does for my students is create community in the classroom. I can see all the students, and I can get them interacting easily" (Twetten, 2006, p. 22.8). Students describe this classroom as their favorite and feel a close con-nection with their instructor.

Adjustable-Height Furnishings, University of Connecticut School of Business–Hartford

The classrooms at the University of Connecticut School of Business demonstrate another creative way to rethink the concept of a "tiered classroom." Instead of pro-

FIGURE 14.3   Iowa State University, LeBaron Hall. Seats swivel so that students may face each other to work in groups. (Courtesy of Iowa State University.)

posing the construction of a tiered floor, the designers at Schoenhardt Architecture + Interior Design worked with Steelcase Furniture Systems to apply a tiered furniture model to the classrooms (Figure 14.4). The floor remains level while the chairs and tables incrementally increase in height toward the back of the classroom. The chairs and tables are on wheels, are fully adjustable, and are wired for power and data access. This tiered furniture model offers a low-cost design solution to maximize clear sight-lines in the classroom without compromising the accessibility and flexibility of the space to its users. Students who use wheelchairs can access any space within the classroom and choose a table height that is most appropriate for them. The adjustability of the tables and chairs also allows students of any size to find a work area that fits them best (Steelcase Furniture Systems, n.d.).

FURNISHINGS, EQUIPMENT, LIGHTING, AND SOUND

To accommodate the wide range of sizes of people, designers should lay out spaces and choose equipment and furnishings to accommodate the "tallest and the smallest" persons on the anthropometric scale of human measurement (i.e., dimensions that fall within the 5th percentile for women and the 95th percentile for men). It is recommended that seat widths and aisle and row depth are designed to accommodate the largest male, and vertical reach height for equipment and controls are within reach for the smallest female (Allen et al., 1996).

FIGURE 14.4   University of Connecticut, adjustable-height furnishings. The floor remains flat while the height of each row of tables and chairs rises incrementally toward the back of the room. (Copyright Steelcase Inc. 2007.)

Because it is difficult to find one type of classroom seat that will be comfortable for everyone, it is ideal to select a seat that can adjust to the user in a variety of ways (e.g., adjustable seat height, arm height, arm length). If it is not possible to provide adjustable seating within the context of the classroom design, providing chairs in a range of sizes may be a feasible solution.

Using tables for work surfaces in classrooms is recommended over tablet arms attached to chairs because the configuration of tablet arms can limit seating choices for left-handed students versus right-handed students, and tablet arms limit the amount of space available for one to sit comfortably in a seat. Also, tablet arms typically do not have enough surface area to support the materials students need to do their work in class. Each workspace should allow enough room (36 wide × 30 deep) for a student to use a computer or to spread out study materials (Niemeyer, 2003). Table heights should adjust from 28 inches to 34 inches above the finished floor, and it is best to find tables that have T-shaped or L-shaped legs that are positioned at the farthest ends of the table to provide sufficient legroom.

Universal design considerations should also be applied to furnishings used by the instructor. These furnishings should include an adjustable-height podium, a table at least 60 inches wide by 24 inches deep, and adjustable-height seating (Allen et al., 1996).

Lighting and sound quality directly influence how well students and instructors are able to receive and communicate information. Outside noise, uneven sound, and poor lighting can easily interfere with one's ability to concentrate and participate in classroom activities. People with vision and hearing loss can be particularly sensitive to the quality of light and sound in their environment. Classrooms should be located within a building so that they are isolated from areas that will bring unwanted noise into the classroom, such as mechanical systems, elevators, restrooms, and vending areas. It is important that each person in the classroom have the opportunity to hear consistent and clear sound at appropriate decibel levels. Thus, the ceiling should be designed with hard-surfaced materials to reflect sound downward, rather than acoustical tile, which absorbs sound and produces an uneven sound distribution throughout the room (Allen et al., 1996). It is ideal to install a wireless microphone to offer the instructor flexibility to move around the classroom while lecturing without compromising sound projection quality. Assistive listening systems should be available for people with hearing loss (Allen et al., 1996; Niemeyer, 2003).

Flexibility is the key to lighting a classroom space. The more technology is used in classrooms, the more types of lighting options are needed. A zoning system should be implemented so that if, for example, students are viewing a media presentation, lights may be turned off in the projection area while lights remain available for the instructor and students to review or take notes. Lighting should also be flexible enough to spotlight a sign language interpreter for students who are deaf or hard of hearing while the rest of the lights are dimmed. Chalkboards or whiteboards should be uniformly lit across the writing surface. It is also useful to control the lights in sections along the board to allow for a section to be lit while a projection screen is in use (Allen et al., 1996).

Instructors have varying familiarity and comfort with the equipment and technology that is available to them in a classroom, so along with providing a variety of lighting and media options for a classroom, schools should install user-friendly control systems and have standard layouts between all classrooms on campus. Also, the number of control switches should be minimized, clearly labeled, illuminated for use in the dark, and operable from a seated position (Allen et al., 1996).

Technology-Enabled Active Learning Classroom, Massachusetts Institute of Technology, Cambridge

In 2001, the Massachusetts Institute of Technology Physics Department built a three-thousand-square-foot classroom to implement a new teaching model of hands-on active learning for introductory physics courses (Figure 14.5). The technology-enabled active learning (TEAL) classroom is designed so that the instructor and students can easily move between lecture, lab experiment, and discussion sections of the class. By increasing the technology capability of the classroom and the range of instructional activities that this classroom was modeled to support, the TEAL classroom inherently applies barrier-free design principles.

Characteristic of an "in-the-round" design, the instructor's workstation is placed in the center of the room and is surrounded by thirteen round tables that seat nine

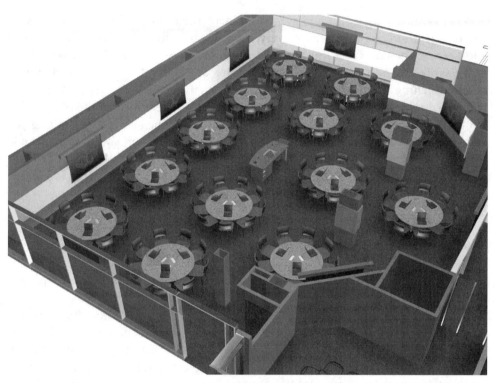

FIGURE 14.5   MIT, TEAL Physics Classroom. Round tables are arranged around a central instruction area with whiteboards and projection screens placed along the perimeter of the room, so that all have equal sightlines of presentation materials. (Courtesy of Mark Bessette of the MIT TEAL/Studio Physics Project.)

students each. There is a networked laptop computer on the table for every three students. Thirteen whiteboards and eight video projectors and screens are arranged around the perimeter of the classroom. The instructor's lecture, class notes, images, and live video can be projected onto each screen, affording everyone a direct sightline to the presentation materials. With presentation and lab materials accessible by a computer at their workstations, students with visual impairments have an opportunity to enlarge the materials on their computer screen for large-print viewing and to utilize audio functions as needed (Keller, 2005). Since students are required to work together to complete lab assignments, chairs are adjustable and mobile to facilitate students working in groups around the computers and using the whiteboard dedicated to their work area.

The classroom affords the instructor flexibility in how she presents a lecture and guides an interactive lab demonstration using the technology the classroom offers. The option of using a wireless microphone allows the instructor to lecture from different parts of the room where mobile lab demonstration stations are set up. The design team placed a storage and preparation room adjacent to the classroom for lab materials and equipment so that instructors could prepare demonstration stations in advance of the lectures without having to transfer them a great distance. Because the technology and equipment allow everyone a direct sightline to class presentations and because the classroom must allow teaching stations and lab demonstrations to move easily around the room, its floor remains at one level. Also, the flexibility of mobile teaching stations and the equitably interactive experience the students have with the presentation and lab materials facilitate greater retention of the physics curriculum. To determine the effectiveness of this classroom model, tests were given before and after the semester to students in the TEAL classroom and to students taking the same course in a traditional classroom. The students who used the TEAL classroom scored significantly higher on these exams, particularly on questions evaluating conceptual understanding of the subject matter (Anthony, 2004).

Learning Studios, Estrella Mountain Community College, Avondale, Arizona

"Radical flexibility" of the classroom environment was the driving design concept for the Learning Studios Project at Estrella Mountain Community College in Arizona. The design team proposed that the more a classroom offers flexibility in space, furnishings, and technology, the greater the potential for students to be engaged and actively learning and retaining information. This vision of radical flexibility was translated by the design team into a classroom that is "changeable on the fly." Each learning studio is nine hundred square feet and accommodates thirty-two students. The studios are equipped with wireless laptops, data projectors, mobile teaching stations, folding tables on wheels, adjustable ergonomic chairs on wheels, adjustable lighting, and combination whiteboards/projection surfaces. None of the furnishings is fixed in place, so all items can be arranged in the configuration that is most appropriate for the instructor to engage students in a particular learning activity (Figure 14.6). The classroom can easily transform from large- to small-group configurations and enables faculty to implement a variety of teaching styles, even within one class period. Tables are easily collapsible so that they can be moved aside when not in use. With approximately thirty square feet allocated per student (instead of the traditional twenty to twenty-five square feet), there is more room for students to spread out their study materials, move their chairs, and comfortably organize a discussion group around a whiteboard or laptop (Figure 14.7).

Being able to arrange seats and position a computer and whiteboard anywhere in the classroom benefits students who are deaf or hard of hearing by allowing the workgroup to sit in a circle or horseshoe configuration for better sightlines within the group. A workgroup also has an opportunity to position itself at a distance from the mix of noise coming from other workgroups, which can also make communication easier for students with hearing loss (Keller, 2005). With movable furnishings and equipment, the instructor is also able to easily maneuver throughout the room and transport a mobile teaching station without having to navigate through narrow aisles or fixed furniture.

Estrella Mountain Community College has found that the "radical flexibility" of the learning studios lowers barriers to student participation and offers students a greater feeling of control, which adds to their sense of comfort and well-being while

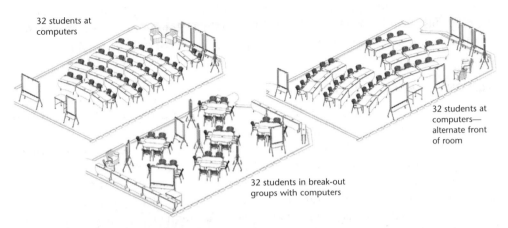

32 students at computers

32 students at computers— alternate front of room

32 students in break-out groups with computers

FIGURES 14.6 & 14.7 Estrella Mountain Community College, Learning Studios. "Radical Flexibility" of the furnishings and equipment allow the room to be configured in a variety of ways to support a range of instructional activities. (Top image courtesy of Herman Miller, Inc. Copyright 2006 Zeeland, MI. Bottom image by Ralph Campbell, copyright 2005 Maricopa Community Colleges.)

building a sense of identity and belonging to the class. Instructors also reported that the learning studios improved peer-to-peer support and permitted more relaxed, less intimidating group collaboration (Lopez & Gee, 2006). Eighty-seven percent (87%) of the faculty surveyed indicated a preference for the learning studios over traditional learning environments, and students viewed the learning studios as more "inviting and comfortable" than traditional classrooms, which were characterized as "oppressive, restrictive, and intimidating" (Herman Miller, Inc., 2006; Lopez & Gee, 2006). Due to this positive feedback, Estrella Mountain Community College has implemented twenty-two learning studios in a new academic building on campus.

LESSONS LEARNED

All the case studies presented in this chapter have in common a collaborative design process that embraces thinking beyond traditional models for building entrances, classrooms, and classroom furnishings, as well as beyond the federal requirements for the built environment mandated by the ADA. Design teams included not only architects and campus administration but also students, faculty, learning and teaching experts, furniture manufacturers, and technology providers. An integrated design process allowed each constituency to contribute a unique perspective to the design program and respond collectively to the needs and concerns of others.

Although it may be impossible to accommodate every person and think of every scenario regarding the use of a space, establishing universal design goals at the beginning stages of a project will positively influence its success in accommodating the widest variety of people. If universal design goals are established on the front end of a project, each design decision can be evaluated in this context, and inform decisions throughout, to create an optimal barrier-free design that is incorporated into and respects the architecture. This approach can avoid accessible design solutions that are "tacked on" as an afterthought and subsequently do not achieve higher levels of functionality, such as equal paths of travel or experience between differently abled people.

The following guidelines provide a good place to start for campus leaders who want to apply universal design to higher education facilities.

Planning and Design
- State universal design goals at the beginning of a design project.
- Let a variety of perspectives inform design decisions: involve students, faculty, staff, and people who are differently abled on the design team.
- Consider possibilities that are beyond traditional models for campus grounds, facilities, and classrooms.

Building Entrances
- Design all main and/or most-traveled entrances of the building to be wheelchair-accessible.
- Design travel paths that do not abruptly change direction or transition unpredictably.
- Keep travel paths clear of protruding objects.

Classrooms
- Locate wheelchair-accessible routes and work areas so that one has a choice of sightlines that is comparable to those provided for people who do not use wheelchairs.

- Provide wide aisles and a generous allocation of space per student.
- Consider how the size and shape of the classroom will affect how furnishings and equipment are configured to facilitate interaction and provide clear sightlines.
- When possible, keep the floor of the classroom at one level.

Furnishings and Equipment

- Provide mobile and adjustable furniture so that it can be located and sized as needed.
- Provide adjustable-height tables (as opposed to tablet arm desks) to give students room to spread out study materials, accommodate legroom as needed, and facilitate use by right-handed and left-handed students alike.
- Consider how students will use computers, view projection screens, and work at whiteboards. Access to computers, for example, can help students customize the information they receive and communicate with their zoom and audio functions.

Sound and Lighting

- Isolate the classrooms from areas that may provide unwanted noise, such as mechanical rooms, elevators, restrooms, and vending areas.
- Allow lighting to be controlled in zones, so that areas can remain lit (e.g., for note taking or to view a sign language interpreter) when other lights are dimmed for projection screen viewing.
- Standardize control system layouts throughout the campus.
- Minimize the number of control switches and make sure they are clearly labeled, illuminated for use in the dark, and operable from a seated position.

CONCLUSION

The built environment directly affects how people feel and behave. Welcoming, comfortable, and barrier-free classrooms, facilities, and overall campus design can positively influence how well students interact and learn, as well as promote a sense of well-being, physically and psychologically, within the campus community. Applying universal design to physical spaces can support an institution's goal of creating a welcoming, inclusive, and usable environment for all students, faculty, staff, and campus visitors.

REFERENCES

Allen, R. L., Bowen, J. T., Clabaugh, S., DeWitt, B. B., Francis, J., Kerstetter, J. P., & Rieck, D. A. (1996). *Classroom design manual* (3rd ed.). College Park: University of Maryland Academic Information Technology Services.

Anthony, R. (2004). TEAL Teaching: Technology enabled active learning (TEAL) is transforming physics education. *Massachusetts Institute of Technology Spectrum,* Winter.

Bain, B. (1989). *The entry experience: Preferences of the mobility impaired, changing paradigms.* Proceedings of the Environmental Design Research Association. Raleigh: North Carolina State University.

Herman Miller, Inc. (2006). *Rethinking the classroom.* Zeeland, MI: Author. Retrieved from http://www.estrellamountain.edu/awareness/download/06/RethinkingTheClassroom.pdf

Keller, E. (2005). *Strategies for teaching students with vision impairments.* Retrieved from http://www.as.wvu.edu/~scidis/vision.html

Kirschbaum, J. B., Axelson, P. W., Longmuir, P. E., Mispagel, K. M., Stein, J. A., & Yamada, D. A. (2001). *Designing sidewalks and trails for access, Part II of II: Best practices design guide.* U.S. Department of Transportation: Federal Highway Administration.

Lopez, H., & Gee, L. (2006). Estrella Mountain Community College: The learning studios project. In D. G. Oblinger (Ed.), *Learning spaces.* Boulder, CO: Educause.

Mace, R. (2007). *About universal design (UD).* Retrieved from http://www.ncsu.edu/ncsu/design/cud/about_ud/udhistory.htm

Niemeyer, D. (2003). *Hard facts on smart classroom design: Ideas, guidelines, and layouts.* Lanham, MD: Scarecrow Press.

Steelcase Furniture Systems. (n.d.). *Case study: University of Connecticut School of Business Graduate Learning Center.* Grand Rapids, MI. Retrieved from http://www.steelcase.com/na/files/96f8baadda344caf9f39a24c63a9178b/Full%20version%20of%20this%20story.pdf

Twetten, J. (2006). Iowa State University: LeBaron Hall Auditorium. In D. G. Oblinger (Ed.), *Learning spaces.* Boulder, CO: Educause.

University of Oregon Planning Office. (n.d.). *Association of University Architects 1998 Case Study Awards Program.* Retrieved from http://planning.uoregon.edu/recognition/AUA98_3.html

PART 4

Universal Design of Technology in Higher Education

In Part 4, Sheryl Burgstahler provides an overview and then other chapter authors share perspectives and strategies for applying universal design principles to technology such as web pages, multimedia, and online learning. The chapters detail how such practices make all technological applications welcoming to, accessible to, and usable by all students, faculty, staff, and visitors.

Universal Design in Higher Education

Instruction	Services	Information Technology	Physical Spaces
Class climate	Planning, policies, & evaluation	Procurement, development policies, & procedures	Planning, policies, & evaluation
Interaction	Physical environments & products	Physical environments & products	Appearance
Physical environments & products	Staff	Physical environments & products	Entrances & routes of travel
Delivery methods	Information resources & technology	Staff	Fixtures & furniture
Information resources & technology	Events	Input, output, navigation, & manipulation	Information resources & technology
Feedback & Assessment		Compatibility with assistive technology	Safety
Accommodation			Accommodation

Source: S. Burgstahler (2015). *Applications of universal design in education.* Seattle: University of Washington. Retrieved from http://www.washington.edu/doit/applications-universal-design-education

229

15

Universal Design of Technology
From Principles to Practice

Sheryl E. Burgstahler

When universal design (UD) is applied, technological environments are accessible and usable for people with a wide range of abilities. The author of this chapter shares highlights of the history of the application of UD to information technology (IT) as well as strategies for applying UD to technological environments in colleges and universities.

Have you ever used a software application and found yourself stuck, unable to accomplish what you set out to do? Of course you have. Do you blame yourself for not knowing enough about the product or about computers in general? Or do you wonder why the product does not give more guidance in how to operate it? Someone who embraces UD would look first to the product itself and ask how it might be made more intuitive, guide users through key steps, and provide useful hints when users make incorrect selections.

This chapter covers issues related to the UD of IT on postsecondary campuses. This topic is of particular importance because of the explosive development of IT (e.g., hand-held computing devices, websites, software applications, multimedia, telecommunications devices, electronic equipment), which has changed the way stakeholders in postsecondary institutions teach, learn, share information, and provide services. Depending on how it is implemented, IT can either level the playing field or further widen the gaps in educational opportunities and attainment between individuals of minority groups (e.g., individuals with disabilities, people from poor communities, older participants) and those of the majority. On a campus where ubiquitous technology places many people on the right side of what has been called the "digital divide" (Waddell, 1999), some faculty, students, or staff may find themselves on the wrong side of the "second digital divide":

> This line separates people who can make full use of today's technological tools, services and resources from those who cannot . . . People with disabilities who are on

the right side of the first digital divide, too often find themselves on the wrong side of the second digital divide. They have technology but do not have full access to all of the benefits it delivers to others. (Burgstahler, 2005, p. 84)

ASSISTIVE TECHNOLOGY, ACCESSIBLE TECHNOLOGY, AND UNIVERSAL TECHNOLOGY DESIGN

Some individuals with disabilities operate standard IT using specialized software and hardware called *assistive technology*, or AT (Closing The Gap, n.d.). Head control, speech input, Morse code input, and dozens of alternative keyboard and mouse options make it possible for individuals with mobility impairments to fully operate computers (see Figure 15.1). Many of these systems provide full access to keyboard functions, but emulating mouse behavior is more difficult or cumbersome and, in some cases, not supported at all. Therefore, to be accessible to these users, websites, online learning courses, and software applications need to be operable with the keyboard alone. In addition, people who are blind can use screen reader technology to access the functions, navigation, and content of software products. Screen reader technology reads aloud the text and structural content on the screen. However, it cannot access the content presented within a graphic image unless this content is alternatively described in a text-based format. Many students who have learning disabilities that affect their ability to read text (e.g., dyslexia) are English language learners, or are auditory learners who also use speech output to read documents.

To create IT products—including software, hardware, websites, videos, electronic documents, content management systems and learning management systems, social media, and databases—that are fully accessible to and usable by everyone, IT developers must consider in their design process the wide range of abilities of potential users and the assistive technologies they may employ. Then they must enhance a product's accessibility and usability for the broadest audience without diminishing its function. In other words, they must practice UD. The definition of UD established by Ron Mace of the Center for Universal Design (CUD) is "the design of products and environments to be usable by all people, to the greatest extent possible, without the need for adaptation or specialized design" (CUD, 2008, p. 1). Sometimes *universal access* and *design for all* are used as synonyms for UD (Stephanidis, 2009). In contrast, *accessible design* is often used to describe design efforts more narrowly focused on individuals with disabilities, often in response to legislation that requires accessibil-

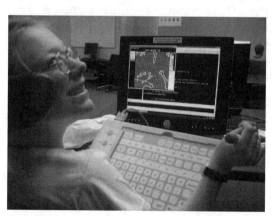

FIGURE 15.1 A student with a disability uses an expanded keyboard and other assistive technology to achieve independent access to a computer.

ity. *Usable design*, as discussed in Chapter 1, is measured by "the extent to which a product can be used by specified users to achieve specified goals with effectiveness, efficiency, and satisfaction in a specified context of use" (International Organization for Standardization, 1998). Usability engineers are concerned with subjective views on how well a design enables performance and contributes to well-being (Iwarsson & Stahl, 2003). Even IT that is technically accessible may not be very usable for individuals with disabilities. Universal designs are both accessible and usable.

Examples of UD features in IT products are video presentations with captions and audio descriptions, transcriptions offered along with audio clips, office equipment with large control buttons that can be reached from a seated position, operating systems that include an option to enlarge characters on the screen, and hand-held computing devices that are compatible with assistive technologies. UD not only minimizes the need for AT, but it is also compatible with commonly used AT.

IT products are often composed of two parts that must both be designed in an accessible format: (1) the technology-based delivery system, such as a learning management system, and (2) the content delivered by that system, such as the course materials in an e-learning course. In many cases, including a UD feature in an IT product is easy to do, results in cost savings to consumers, and benefits other people in addition to those for whom the feature was originally designed. For example, today it is required that television sets include decoder chips that allow the display of captions whenever they are provided by a video presentation. This built-in feature is inexpensive compared to the decoder device that, in the past, had to be purchased separately in order to make captions appear on television screens. Designed for individuals who have hearing impairments, the built-in feature has also benefited people in noisy environments (e.g., a sports bar, an airport, a conference exhibit) or noiseless areas (e.g., a library, a bedroom where a baby is sleeping), and individuals viewing the video in a foreign language. It also promotes the inclusive goal of UD, as it allows individuals with a wide range of characteristics to use the same product (see Figure 15.2).

A decision to adopt accessible or universal IT design practices in higher education is sometimes motivated by legal mandates. For example, almost all institutions of higher education in the U.S. are covered entities under Section 504 of the Rehabilitation Act of 1973, the Americans with Disabilities Act of 1990 (ADA), and the ADA Amendments Act of 2008. These laws prohibit discrimination on the basis of disability. They do not specifically mention IT, but are generally interpreted to require that postsecondary institutions make IT accessible to people with disabilities unless it would pose an undue burden to do so. When an institution develops or selects IT that is not usable by individuals with disabilities, the subsequent expense of providing access is not generally considered an undue burden; in most cases the cost could have been significantly reduced had accessibility been considered at the time of product development or selection (Patrick, 1996; Waddell, 2007). Legislation has also been interpreted to mean that the institution should have a plan in place for ensuring that technology is accessible:

Figure 15.2 Three students with a variety of disabilities cluster around a computer to complete a project.

The courts have held that a public entity violates its obligations under the ADA when it only responds on an ad-hoc basis to individual requests for accommodation. There is an affirmative duty to develop a comprehensive policy in advance of any request for auxiliary aids or services . . . The bottom line, according to OCR [Office for Civil Rights] is that effective communication imposes a duty to solve barriers to information access that the entity's purchasing choices create. Whenever existing technology is "upgraded" by a new technology feature, it is important to ensure that the new technology either improves accessibility or is compatible with existing assistive computer technology. (Waddell, 2007, p. 3)

Similar legislation has been enacted in other countries (Seale, 2006), and the Preamble of the Convention on the Rights of Persons with Disabilities states its purpose to be "to ensure to persons with disabilities access, on an equal basis with others, to the physical environments, to transportation, to information and communications, including information and communications technologies and systems" (Narasimhan, 2012, p. v).

Providing appropriate AT is necessary, but not sufficient, to ensure that IT is welcoming to, accessible to, and usable by all faculty, students, and staff at a postsecondary institution. As an analogy, consider an exterior door to a building. It may be accessible to most individuals approaching the door. However, wheelchair users with limited arm and hand functionality may be unable to open it. Providing an electronic door opener activated by a large button increases the number of individuals who can open the door, but it is an add-on product (e.g., an assistive technology) that still does not make the door fully operable by everyone. Replacing it with a door that opens automatically when it senses someone moving toward it is an example of UD. In the UD option, the function of the door is available to everyone in the same manner. With respect to IT, the ideal is for campuses to provide seamless *access* and *usability* for everyone in an *inclusive* manner. Achieving this goal requires the provision of universally designed IT.

GUIDELINES AND STANDARDS FOR THE ACCESSIBLE AND UNIVERSAL DESIGN OF IT

Coordinated efforts to create IT that is usable by a broad audience began with a focus on accessibility for people with disabilities. In the 1980s, cooperation between key stakeholders, including the IT industry, consumers, researchers, and government, led to the development of guidelines for more accessible design (Vanderheiden & Vanderheiden, 1992). Organized by IT function, these guidelines address issues related to sensory, physical, cognitive, and language abilities, as well as seizure disorders. Each guideline is phrased as an objective followed by examples of how the objective might be achieved (Vanderheiden & Vanderheiden, 1992, Part III, Sections 1–5):

1. *Output/Displays* includes all means of presenting information to the user. [The design should] maximize the number of people who can
    - O-1   hear auditory output clearly enough.
    - O-2   not miss important information if they can't hear.
    - O-3   have line of sight to visual output and reach printed output.
    - O-4   see visual output clearly enough.
    - O-5   not miss important information if they can't see.
    - O-6   understand the output (visual, auditory, other).

2. *Input/Controls* includes keyboards and all other means of communicating to the product. [The design should] maximize the number of people who can
    - I-1   reach the controls.
    - I-2   find the individual controls/keys if they can't see them.
    - I-3   read the labels on the controls/keys.
    - I-4   determine the status or setting of the controls if they can't see them.
    - I-5   physically operate controls and other input mechanisms.
    - I-6   understand how to operate controls and other input mechanisms.
    - I-7   connect special alternative input devices.

3. *Manipulations* includes all actions that must be directly performed by a person in concert with the product or for routine maintenance; e.g., inserting [a] disk, loading [a] tape, changing [an] ink cartridge. [The design should] maximize the number of people who can
    - M-1   physically insert and remove objects as required to operate a device.
    - M-2   physically handle and/or open the product.

    M-3 remove, replace, or reposition often-used detachable parts.

    M-4 understand how to carry out the manipulations necessary to use the product.

4. Documentation primarily [focuses on] operating instructions. [The design should] maximize the number of people who can

    D-1 access the documentation.

    D-2 understand the documentation.

5. Safety includes alarms and other protections from harm. [The design should] maximize the number of people who can

    S-1 perceive hazard warnings.

    S-2 use the product without injury due to unperceived hazards or [the] user's lack of motor control.

More recently, federal agencies in the U.S. were required to take steps to ensure the accessibility of their electronic and information technology (E&IT). Section 508 of the Rehabilitation Act of 1973 mandates that any E&IT federal agencies develop, maintain, procure, or use must be accessible to people with disabilities. According to the Department of Justice, accessible E&IT

> can be operated in a variety of ways and does not rely on a single sense or ability of the user. For example, a system that provides output only in visual format may not be accessible to people with visual impairments and a system that provides output only in audio format may not be accessible to people who are deaf or hard of hearing. (U.S. Department of Justice, 2005, p. 18)

The 1998 amendments of Section 508 directed the United States Access Board to produce minimum accessibility standards for the E&IT of federal agencies. Published in 2001, E&IT products covered by the standards include computers, web pages, software, video and multimedia, telecommunications products, and office equipment (United States General Services Administration, n.d.). The Section 508 standards promote the integration of flexible and inclusive features within mainstream IT products. Although they apply only to E&IT products of federal agencies, these standards have been voluntarily adopted by some states, educational institutions, and other organizations as one way to meet their obligations under the ADA. Although the Access Board is charged with periodically reviewing and amending the standards to reflect changes in technology, as of the writing of this book, a refresh of the standards has not yet been published.

The European Standardization Organizations collaborated in the creation of the European Standard on accessibility requirements for public procurement of information and communications technologies (ICT) products and services, which was published by the European Telecommunications Standards Institutes (ETSI) in 2014. As with Section 508, these standards are comprehensive, covering hardware, software, websites, and other ICT products and services.

UD principles can be applied not only to the technology itself, but also to a computer lab, learning commons, office space, library, or other physical environment in which it is located. For example, computers available in a career services office can be placed on adjustable-height tables to accommodate individuals of different sizes and those who use wheelchairs of various dimensions. Additionally, universally designed computing areas are located in wheelchair-accessible facilities, have wide aisles that are clear of obstructions, employ high-contrast and large-print signage, situate at least part of a service counter at a height accessible from a seated position, make lighting adjustable, and/or have window blinds available to reduce glare on computer screens (Burgstahler, 2012). Discussed in the following paragraphs are specific UD considerations for IT commonly used in higher education.

UD of the Web

The World Wide Web emerged in the 1990s and has grown to be ubiquitous in post-secondary settings. Early on, articles about accessible design (e.g., Laux, McNally, Paciello, & Vanderheiden, 1996; Nielsen, 1996; Rowland & Smith, 1999) and UD (e.g., Burgstahler, Comden, & Fraser, 1997; Waters, 1997) of web pages began to appear.

The World Wide Web Consortium (W3C), which develops and maintains protocols to ensure interoperability of the Web, has always been committed to UD. According to Tim Berners-Lee, the computer scientist who is credited with inventing the Web, "The power of the Web is in its universality. Access by everyone regardless of disability is an essential aspect" (Berners-Lee, n.d.). W3C's vision of the Web is that of an inclusive environment that allows for the expression of cultural nuances and language differences. In 1997, W3C announced that its Web Accessibility Initiative (WAI) would develop guidelines for the accessible design of websites. The WAI promotes universal as well as accessible design, pointing out that

> web accessibility also benefits people without disabilities. For example, a key principle of web accessibility is designing websites and software that are flexible to meet different user needs, preferences, and situations. This flexibility also benefits people without disabilities in certain situations, such as people using a slow Internet connection, people with "temporary disabilities" such as a broken arm, and people with changing abilities due to aging. (WAI, n.d.d)

In 1999, the Web Content Accessibility Guidelines 1.0 (WCAG 1.0) were published as a W3C recommendation. WCAG 1.0 and, later, WCAG 2.0 are widely regarded as international standards for web accessibility. WAI created these standards with input from a large number of volunteers representing a wide variety of stakeholder groups. The U.S. Access Board adopted much of the WAI's early work when it developed the Section 508 accessibility standards for IT of the federal government, and it has incorporated WCAG 2.0 Level AA by direct reference into the latest draft of updated standards and guidelines (U.S. Access Board). Both the WAI guidelines and Section 508 standards demonstrate that accessibility of web pages and applications is possible and that standards, methods, and techniques exist that support the creation of accessible content. Guidelines and standards also make it possible to objectively measure whether web pages are accessible, and several software tools have been developed for checking or validating content for accessibility. Designers and developers can also test web pages by using a variety of monitors, computer platforms, and web browsers; by turning off the sound and graphics capabilities; and by using a keyboard alone (WAI, n.d.a).

WAI's current version of WCAG, WCAG 2.0, includes recommendations for making web content

> accessible to a wider range of people with disabilities, including blindness and low vision, deafness and hearing loss, learning disabilities, cognitive limitations, limited movement, speech difficulties, photosensitivity, and combinations of these. Following these guidelines will also make web content more usable to users in general (WAI, n.d.e).

The guidelines are organized around four principles that lay the foundation necessary for anyone to access and effectively use web content. These principles (WAI, n.d.c) suggest that web content be

- *Perceivable*—Information and user interface components must be presentable to users in ways they can perceive.
- *Operable*—User interface components and navigation must be operable.
- *Understandable*—Information and operation of user interface components must be understandable.
- *Robust*—Content must be robust enough that it can be interpreted reliably by a wide variety of user agents, including assistive technologies.

The guidelines are technology independent in that the success criteria for each can be applied across a wide range of existing and emerging web technologies. According to WAI, it is essential that different components of web development and interaction work together in order for the Web to be accessible to people with disabilities. These components include the following (WAI, 2005):

- content in a web page or web application, including text, images, and sounds, as well as markup that defines structure and presentation;
- user agents such as web browsers and media players;
- assistive technology such as screen readers, alternative keyboards, and switches;
- users' knowledge, experiences, and adaptive strategies for using the Web;
- developers, designers, coders, authors, and others, including those with disabilities;
- authoring tools used to create websites;
- evaluation tools such as web accessibility evaluation tools and HTML validators.

Some quick tips (WAI, n.d.b) for ensuring web accessibility are as follows:

1.1 *Text alternatives.* Provide text alternatives for any nontext content so that it can be changed into other forms people need, such as large print, braille, speech, symbols, or simpler language.

1.2 *Time-based media.* Provide alternatives for time-based media.

1.3 *Adaptable.* Create content that can be presented in different ways (for example, simpler layout) without losing information or structure.

1.4 *Distinguishable.* Make it easier for users to see and hear content, including separating foreground from background.

2.1 *Keyboard accessible.* Make all functionality available from a keyboard.

2.2 *Enough time.* Provide users enough time to read and use content.

2.3 *Seizures.* Do not design content in a way that is known to cause seizures.

2.4 *Navigable.* Provide ways to help users navigate, find content, and determine where they are.

3.1 *Readable.* Make text content readable and understandable.

3.2 *Predictable.* Make web pages appear and operate in predictable ways.

3.3 *Input assistance.* Help users avoid and correct mistakes.

4.1 *Compatible.* Maximize compatibility with current and future user agents, including assistive technologies.

WCAG is part of a series of W3C accessibility guidelines that include the Authoring Tool Accessibility Guidelines (ATAG) and the User Agent Accessibility Guidelines (UAAG). W3C continues to expand the reach of the Web to everyone (e.g., regardless of culture, abilities), to everything (e.g., on devices ranging from power computers with high-definition displays to mobile devices to appliances), from everywhere (from high- to low-bandwidth environments), and through diverse modes of interaction (e.g., touch, mouse, voice, assistive technologies). Other countries have developed standards for web accessibility as well (e.g., the British Standard BS 8878; British Standards Institute, 2010).

UD OF TELECOMMUNICATIONS, SOFTWARE, AND OTHER PRODUCTS

The design of standard telecommunications equipment can potentially erect barriers to individuals attempting to use it. A person who is hard of hearing cannot understand people speaking on a telephone without an amplification feature. A person who is deaf needs a nonaudio alternative to communicate with someone calling on a standard telephone. An individual who cannot use a voice for communication needs alternatives to speech communication. An individual without full hand function may not be able to operate some telephones without AT. A person who is blind cannot access the content of the visual presentation of a videoconference unless audio options are available.

Many laws have promoted the development and use of accessible telecommunications products. Their purposes include protecting the civil rights of individuals with disabilities, establishing procurement requirements for specific agencies, and mandating accessibility standards for the manufacture of products. For example, the Americans with Disabilities Act of 1990 requires that public programs and services provide accessible, "effective communication," regardless of what medium is typically used for that communication (U.S. Department of Justice, 2005). It mandates a nationwide system of telecommunications relay services (in which a human being is involved in translation), which make it possible for standard voice telephone users to talk to people who have difficulty hearing or speaking. Section 255 of the Telecommunications Act of 1996 requires that manufacturers of telecommunications equipment and providers of telecommunications services ensure that such products and services are accessible to people with disabilities, if readily achievable. Section 508 standards for telecommunications products procured, developed, or used by the federal government are similar to the Section 255 design standards for manufacturers.

As with telecommunications, websites, and other IT, the U.S. Access Board developed technical and functional performance criteria necessary for software to comply with Section 508. Guidelines for software accessibility of human-computer interfaces within the ISO Technical Specification 16071 were created by the Organization for Standardization Technical Specification (Gulliksen & Harker, 2004). The Instructional Materials Accessibility Act of 2002 (IMAA) required the U.S. Department of Education to develop accessibility standards for electronic textbooks (Waddell & Hardy, 2004). Additionally, design guidelines for educational software were developed by the National Center on Accessible Media (2006).

STATUS OF THE UD OF TECHNOLOGY

Although UD has the potential to increase product markets and help institutions meet their legal obligations, and accessibility guidelines and standards are available to help developers create accessible IT, companies rarely take the full spectrum of user diversity into account when they develop their products and, as a result, unintentionally erect barriers to product use (National Council on Disability, 2004). Some designers are unaware of accessibility issues; some are aware but place a very low priority on employing accessible practices; others consider the market for accessible IT to be too small to address. A research study, undertaken by the National Council on Disability (2004) to analyze the market for universally designed mainstream IT products, documented consumer needs and UD processes, facilitators, and barriers. It found that rapid changes in technology often cause decreases in accessibility, and that even when accessibility features exist, sales associates for these products are often unaware of them. Additional findings of this study suggest that Section 508 has had an impact on increasing accessibility and UD efforts by industry, that a sizeable market for universally designed products and services exists, and that it is not difficult to incorporate many UD principles into the design practices of manufacturers. However, the study reported, even products designed to be accessible are often not effective because developers do not fully understand the needs of users with disabilities, and people with disabilities are not integrated into design and testing processes. Authors of the final report concluded

> People with disabilities want to use the same products that everyone else uses. Implementation of universal design satisfies this desire of people with disabilities, while also providing more cost-effective products for all users. While it is impossible to satisfy the needs of all users, products and services that come closer to accommodating a variety of physical and cognitive differences will benefit both users and companies. (National Council on Disability, 2004, p. 20)

It can be argued that it is simply good business practice for IT companies to avoid excluding large populations of consumers from effectively using their products. The increasing number of people using computer-based devices includes the aging "baby boomer" generation as well as people with a wide range of language proficiencies, cultures, ages, technology expertise, and abilities.

In spite of efforts to make IT accessible to and usable by everyone, many websites of postsecondary institutions continue to be inaccessible to and/or unusable by many faculty, staff, students, and visitors with disabilities (e.g., Behzad, 2011; Espadinha, Pereira, Da Silva, & Lopes, 2011; Comeaux & Schmetzke, 2013; Hackett & Parmanto, 2005; Kelly, 2002; Seale, 2014a, b; Thompson et al., 2013; Wijayaratne & Singh, 2010). Some evaluators measure website accessibility according to technical guidelines and standards; some test for functional accessibility (to determine if individuals can use the functions of the application). Regardless of the methods employed, studies have consistently found that the websites of postsecondary institutions worldwide present significant accessibility barriers to visitors with disabilities (Thompson, Comden, Ferguson, Burgstahler, & Moore, 2013). One study found that only 60.4% of the images on the top ten web pages at higher education institutions had alt text on images; only 77.9% had headings; only 39.8% had labels on form fields; only 37.3% identified the language of the page; and only 3.3% had ARIA landmark roles—all important characteristics of websites that are universally designed (Thompson et al., 2013). Clearly, much work remains to be done to ensure that web resources provided by institutions of higher education are accessibly designed; even greater efforts are needed to ensure that these resources are universally designed. Contributing to this problem are webmasters' and administrators' lack of awareness of the barriers erected by their websites, of legal obligations to provide accessible content, of guidelines for designing accessible sites, and of the benefits of UD for all web users.

Results from a survey indicate that many postsecondary institutions around the world are working to ensure that their IT is accessible, to deploy assistive technologies (often in multiple labs across campus), to develop and implement IT accessibility policies, to consider accessibility when purchasing enterprise-wide IT (such as learning management systems), and to produce or procure documents in alternative formats for students who require them (Thompson, Draffan, & Patel, 2009). Fewer than 10% of the institutions reviewed had accessibility policies specifically focused on IT. However, the results also make it clear that these institutions still have considerable work to do in each of these areas in order to even come close to the goal of full accessibility of IT for all students, faculty, staff, and visitors.

Employing a UD process goes beyond ensuring accessibility for individuals with disabilities to address usability issues such as ease of use, simplicity of learning, efficiency in performing tasks, memorability, user satisfaction, low levels of user errors for all IT users (Nielsen, 2012). UD is the "one solution to accommodating people with disabilities that also improves the usability of products for the rest of the population" (National Council on Disability, 2004, p. 8).

A prominent example of a worldwide effort that promotes the UD of IT is the Global Public Inclusive Infrastructure (GPII), a project of Raising the Floor (2011).

The purpose of GPII is to eliminate barriers to access and use of the Internet that are related to disability, literacy, digital literacy, aging, or financial resources. As countries build their broadband infrastructures to reach everyone, GPII leaders work to ensure that "everyone" includes people with a broad range of characteristics, including disability. The purpose of the GPII is not to create new assistive technologies or services, but rather to create the infrastructure for making their development and use easier, less expensive, and more effective. GPII leaders provide the following analogy:

> Like building a road system does not provide transportation but greatly enhances the ability of car companies and others to do so—and provides an infrastructure that car companies themselves cannot do. The Internet is the infrastructure for general information and commerce. The GPII enhancements to the Internet would provide the infrastructure to enable the Internet to be truly inclusive for the first time. (Raising the Floor, 2011, p. 1)

STEPS TOWARD THE UD OF IT IN HIGHER EDUCATION

In a Dear Colleague letter (2010), the U.S. Department of Justice and U.S. Department of Education stated, "It is unacceptable for universities to use emerging technology without insisting that this technology be accessible to all students." Making an institution-wide commitment to using accessible IT is an important step, but translating that commitment into action takes significant effort. Companies may not have a legal obligation to manufacture products that are fully accessible, but there are legal obligations for educational entities to use IT products and services that are accessible to individuals with disabilities. Institutions can use their purchasing power to increase industry awareness of the importance of IT accessibility and usability through procurement policies and procedures (e.g., University of Illinois, 2013). Imagine if all library procurement officers, as they communicated with database vendors, routinely stated the libraries' commitment to equitable access for all patrons and then inquired about current product accessibility features and the company's future plans in this regard. Such efforts would put companies on notice that institutions of higher education expect universally designed products to be available.

Postsecondary institutions must consider myriad issues when cultivating a campus culture that promotes UD of IT: vision, leadership, legal issues, technical standards, development and procurement policies, procedures, support and training, accountability, and enforcement (Bohman, 2007). For example, the GOALS (Gaining Online Accessible Learning through Self-Study) project created a set of four institutional indicators of web accessibility; evaluated the social validity of the indicators to determine if stakeholders found them appropriate, understandable, usable, and satisfactory; and created resources as a framework for implementing and promoting institution-wide web accessibility through multiple stakeholders (e.g., administrator, faculty, technology specialist) at a variety of institution types. The four indicator categories are:

1. institutional vision and commitment of leadership,
2. planning and implementation,
3. resources and support, and
4. assessment (Mariger, 2011).

To help schools reach the goal of web accessibility campus-wide, WAI's 2002 *Implementation Plan for Web Accessibility* still resonates over a decade later:

1. *Establish responsibilities.*
   - Establish a coordination team with a communication plan.
   - Identify a high-level champion or spokesperson for accessible IT.

2. *Conduct an initial assessment.*
   - Find out whether the institution is subject to external requirements regarding IT accessibility.
   - Conduct an initial assessment of the accessibility of campus websites and other IT.
   - Assess current awareness of the need for IT accessibility by survey or interviews within the institution.
   - Assess expertise of campus IT developers with regard to accessible design.
   - Assess suitability of current software to support development of accessible websites and other software.
   - Estimate resources required to address the needs identified in the initial assessment.

3. *Develop institutional policy.*
   - Find out whether the institution has an existing policy that mandates IT accessibility.
   - Establish an institutional policy on IT accessibility.

4. *Develop initial and ongoing promotion plans to increase awareness of the institution's IT accessibility policy.*

5. *Provide training.*
   - On a regular basis, offer a range of training options to meet the needs of administrators, technical support staff, and others with relevant roles in the institution.
   - Integrate training within mainstream IT training (e.g., web design classes).

6. *Develop accessible websites/software.*
   - Make UD a priority throughout the development process.
   - Provide development teams with resources and software tools that promote accessibility.

7. *Promote IT accessibility awareness.*
   - Incorporate the organization's IT accessibility policy into key documents where appropriate.
   - Enforce the organization's policy on IT accessibility.

8. *Monitor IT accessibility.*
   - Specify the evaluation process to be used for IT accessibility.
   - Conduct ongoing monitoring of the accessibility of the organization's IT.
   - Invite and respond to user feedback on campus IT.
   - Periodically review all aspects of the implementation plan for effectiveness.

Although training is often recommended for promoting accessible IT, little research supports its efficacy. One study of the impact of accessibility training on nineteen postsecondary webmasters—where the impact was measured by testing the accessibility of web developer websites before and after training and support—provided mixed results (Thompson, Burgstahler, & Moore, 2007).

Policies and guidelines can encourage the accessible design of all types of IT in order to provide a more inclusive institutional environment (University of Washington [UW], n.d.a). Some steps toward IT accessibility have been motivated by civil rights complaints reported to the Department of Justice and the Office of Civil Rights of the U.S. Department of Education (UW, n.d.b). Complaints and resolutions have covered a wide variety of aspects of the procurement, development, and deployment of IT on postsecondary campuses. Among them are policies and procedures; grievance procedures; training and support; procurement practices; library services; IT in classrooms; AT in computer labs; and learning management systems, websites, instructional materials, clickers, and other technology.

Civil rights complaints and resolutions at other schools have motivated some postsecondary institutions to develop policies, guidelines, and procedures regarding the accessibility of IT. After reviewing civil rights history and the legal complaints and resolutions relevant to the accessibility of IT on postsecondary campuses, Paul Grossman, retiree from the Office of Civil Rights, summed up developments in civil rights legislation and enforcement. His observations about changes over time include that

- the measures or characteristics of equity have expanded (e.g., to increase consideration of the independence and integration of the user, ease of use of technology, completeness and timeliness of the delivery of accessible information);
- the goal of equal access to information is achieved by making it available in formats compatible with AT and making AT readily available; and
- the goal of equal access to information is further achieved by making access a required element in acquisition, implementation, and support of IT; providing training; providing effective alternatives to address delays and complications; and assigning responsibility for compliance to specific individuals (Grossman, 2014).

Salome Heyward, a civil rights attorney with more than thirty years of experience in the field of disability discrimination law, recommends that campuses follow the road map created by the resolutions of civil rights complaints to develop policies, procedures, and staff assignments for accessible IT on their campuses. She encourages campuses to consider taking action in the four areas of application listed below, along with several examples under each category (Heyward, 2014, p. 3):

- *Key compliance standards* (e.g., ensure equal access to benefits afforded by IT and equal treatment in its use; do not rely on an accommodations-alone approach; ensure communications with individuals with disabilities is as effective as with others; when alternative access is necessary, provide the same ease of use, ready access and completeness, functionality and timeliness of response; provide access in integrated settings);

- *Institutional approach to compliance* (e.g., adopt accessible IT policies, procedures related to procurement, development, and use of accessible IT; include accessible IT support and compliance in job assignments);
- *Compliance strategies* (e.g., conduct campus-wide audits regarding the accessibility of IT; identify accessibility barriers and develop plans for addressing them; provide support services; develop a system for alternative media creation); and
- *Enforcement advice* (e.g., post guidelines for IT accessibility; require that web pages and instructional materials created, purchased, or made available adhere to accessibility requirements; monitor progress in making IT accessible; provide training and support).

Many campus policies and guidelines that do exist point to relevant laws and existing institutional policies, to procedures for campus units and individuals, and to WCAG 2.0 Level AA as a standard for web accessibility and for guidance on the accessible design of other IT (e.g., videos, PDF files). Resolutions of civil rights complaints in the U.S. articulate an expectation that institutions be proactive in developing, procuring, and using accessible IT and electronic documents. Practices commonly required of targeted institutions include: conduct accessibility audits of web pages and learning management systems; set institutional standards relating to accessible technology and create a method to monitor compliance; set timelines for making specific IT accessible; provide training and resources about accessibility to those responsible for online instruction; consider accessibility in IT procurement processes; and create a procedure for students to report the inaccessibility of IT products (UW, n.d.b, c). Some organizations have created materials with guidelines and examples from other campuses to help institutions develop their policies and procedures regarding accessible IT (e.g., National Center on Disability and Access to Education, n.d.; Jisc TechDis, n.d.; UW, n.d.c).

What would a campus that embraces the UD of IT look like? Here is one scenario:

There would be a focus on proactively developing, purchasing, deploying, and using IT that is accessible to and usable by everyone, including faculty, staff, students, and visitors to the campus websites. This would require a campus-wide commitment. Specifically, there would be responsibilities for the disability services office and the central IT unit and close collaboration between them, with the IT group focused on overall universal design of technology provided on campus and disability services focused on additional accommodations individual students might need. The central IT organization would have accessibility built into all of its procurement and technology design steps and consider accessibility in product upgrades. IT staff would take responsibility for the accessibility of the IT infrastructure, technical support, and training, and would promote universal design within distributed computing organizations. In this environment, the need for individual accommodations would be minimized. For example, disability services could recommend assistive technology for the computer labs on campus, but the managers of those labs would purchase, maintain, and support the software and hardware so that any students can use it. An individual or unit within IT with specialized knowledge and skills related to assistive technology and accessible design of technology can consult with the IT developers, purchasers, and support personnel, as well as provide a liaison with disability services. This group could maintain a showroom and consulting facility that includes a wide variety of assistive technology for testing and use, while commonly used AT would be deployed throughout campus so that students with disabilities can work side-by-side with their peers. Throughout campus, procedures regarding accessible IT would be incorporated into existing workflows, such as those employed with designing online learning, purchasing library databases, training faculty, and designing technology centers.

Such universally designed models of services benefit students with documented disabilities that receive accommodations through the disability services unit, those who have not disclosed their disabilities, and those who do not have disabilities at all. The model retains the domains that these units typically work in—for example, deploying technology for computing services units and ensuring accommodations for the disability services unit.

APPROACHES FOR EXPLORING AND MEASURING THE UD OF TECHNOLOGY

Design methods that support human values and engage users with a wide variety of characteristics hold promise for exploring the efficacy of UD with respect to e-learning, websites, and other IT practices (Emiliani, 2009; Friedman, Kahn, Borning, & Huldtgren, 2013). In the U.K., Jane Seale, a leader in promoting accessible e-learning in higher education, stated:

> We need new methodological approaches to "liberate" disabled students' voices; methods that offer us opportunities for critical self-reflection but also enable a dialogical relationship to be established with disabled students in which they are genuinely heard. (Seale, 2014c, p. 192)

For example, Seale employed a *participatory design* approach to explore the complex interactions between students and technologies in an e-learning setting within a higher education institution. Participatory design engages users in all steps of the design process (e.g., Bjerknes & Bratteteig, 1995), tests in real-life contexts, and uses development and evaluation within iterative cycles until an acceptable solution is reached.

Another approach is *design-based research,* a term commonly used to describe a set of research practices in the learning sciences when the subject of the study is a complex system involving emergent properties that arise from the interaction of variables that come to light during the design process (Brown, 1992; Collins, 1990). It does not try to isolate individual variables because it strives to study the lived experiences of human beings (Collins, Joseph, & Bielaczyc, 2009).

Design approaches that maximize the engagement of users include *value-sensitive design,* which is grounded in the design of technology that accounts for human values within a cultural context in a principled and comprehensive manner (Friedman et al., 2013). Human values addressed in the literature on system design include human welfare, privacy, freedom from bias, trust, autonomy, informed consent, identity, universal usability, and courtesy. Suggestions for applying value-sensitive design include:

(1) identify values, technology, and context of use, (2) identify both direct and indirect stakeholders, (3) for each stakeholder group, identify benefits and harms, (4) map benefits and harms onto corresponding values, (5) conduct a conceptual investigation of key values, (6) identify value conflicts, (7) integrate potential value conflicts, and (8) integrate value considerations into one's organization structure (Friedman et al., 2013).

Usability testing practices hold promise to inform design practices and to ensure the UD of technology, as long as individuals with diverse characteristics perform some of the tests. The term *usability* has at least two distinct meanings when applied to product development. One meaning refers to the iterative testing and feedback process wherein users are observed as they interact with the product features. A second meaning is related to a user's ability to effectively perform tasks using a product and to their satisfaction. Jakob Nielsen, a key proponent of usability processes, identifies five quality components of usability:

1. *Learnability.* How easy is it for users to accomplish basic tasks the first time they encounter the design?
2. *Efficiency.* Once users have learned the design, how quickly can they perform tasks?
3. *Memorability.* When users return to the design after a period of not using it, how easily can they reestablish proficiency?
4. *Errors.* How many errors do users make, how severe are these errors, and how easily can they recover from the errors?
5. *Satisfaction.* How pleasant is it to use the design? (Nielsen, 2012)

The usability process is often employed during multiple phases of product development, in order to make the developing product more efficient and attractive to customers. For example, a collaborative project between a university and technology corporation that explored computer software usability and accessibility with individuals with visual impairments, people with mobility impairments, and older adults—some of whom used AT—found that, in order for IT products to be considered "usable," they should be universally designed to meet a wide range of user needs (Burgstahler, Jirikowic, Kolko, & Eliot, 2004). The researchers recommended that more usability testing practices be employed to ensure that products are usable by members of a diverse population. For usability to contribute to UD, designers must consider a broad range of users, including those with disabilities. Sometimes, this has been referred to as *universal usability* (e.g., Schneiderman, 1999).

Many other design approaches incorporate user involvement in the process, including *user-centered design* and *learner-centered design* (Nesset & Large, 2004). Clearly, many researchers consider involvement of the user critical in designing IT, but they differ in their views regarding how best to involve them.

CONCLUSION

Although legislation, guidelines, standards, promising practices, design approaches, and resources are available, the inaccessible design of IT on postsecondary campuses continues to create barriers to some members of the community. Applying UD practices benefits students with disabilities, as well as those with nontraditional learning styles, students learning in a foreign language or from a different culture, those with a low level of technical skills and comfort, and people with age-related visual impairments. Proactively purchasing, developing, and deploying accessible IT can address the needs of these groups and minimize the need for assistive technology. The efforts of all stakeholders are needed to reach the goal of a fully inclusive campus with respect to technology access. The next chapter shares the history of assistive, accessible, and universally designed technology from the perspectives of leaders in the field who represent a variety of stakeholders. Then, in Chapter 17, Terrill Thompson discusses the process of universally designing video presentations and a media player. In Chapter 18, Roberta Thomson, Catherine Fichten, Alice Havel, Jillian Budd, and Jennison Asuncion discuss how UD, e-learning, and information and communication technologies can blend in online courses, thereby connecting the content in Parts 2 and 4 of this book.

REFERENCES

Americans with Disabilities Act of 1990. 42 U.S.C.A. § 12101 *et seq.*

Americans with Disabilities Act Amendments Act of 2008. 42 U.S.C.A. § 12101 note (2011)

Berners-Lee, T. (n.d.). *W3C Web accessibility initiative.* Retrieved from http://www.w3.org/WAI/

Behzad, H. (September 01, 2011). Analyzing web accessibility in Finnish higher education. *ACM SIGACCESS Accessibility and Computing, 101,* 8–16.

Bjerknes, G., & Bratteteig, T. (1995). User participation and democracy: A discussion of Scandinavian research on system development. *Scandinavian Journal of Information Systems, 7*(1), 73–97.

Bohman, P. (2007). Cultivating and maintaining Web accessibility expertise and institutional support in higher education. *ATHEN Access Technologists Higher Education Network, 2.* Retrieved from http://www.athenpro.org/node/40

British Standards Institute. (2010). *BS 8872:2010 Web accessibility; Code of practice.* Retrieved from http://shop-bsigroup.com/en/ProductDetail/7pid=000000000030180388&rdt=wmt

Brown, A. L. (1992). Design experiments: Theoretical and methodological challenges in creating complex interventions in classroom settings. *Journal of the Learning Sciences, 2*(2), 141–178.

Burgstahler, S. (2005). Web-based distance learning and the second digital divide. In M. Khosrow-Pour (Ed.), *Encyclopedia of information science and information technology* (pp. 3079–3084). Hershey, PA: Idea Group Inc.

Burgstahler, S. (2012). *Equal access: Universal design of computer labs.* Seattle: University of Washington. Retrieved from http://www.washington.edu/doit/equal-access-universal-design-computer-labs

Burgstahler, S., Comden, D., & Fraser, B. (1997). Universal access: Designing and evaluating Web sites for accessibility. *CHOICE: Current Reviews for Academic Libraries, 34 Supplement,* 19–22.

Burgstahler, S., Jirikowic, T., Kolko, B., & Eliot, M. (2004). Software accessibility, usability testing and individuals with disabilities. *Information Technology and Disabilities E-Journal, 10*(2).

The Center for Universal Design (CUD). (2008). *About UD.* Raleigh: North Carolina State University. Retrieved from http://www.ncsu.edu/ncsu/design/cud/about_ud/about_ud.htm

Closing The Gap. (n.d.). *Resource directory.* Henderson, MN: Author. Retrieved from http://www.closingthegap.com/solutions/search/

Collins, A. (1990). *Toward a design science of education.* New York: Center for Technology in Education. Retrieved from http://cct2.edc.org/ccthome/reports/tr1.html

Collins, A., Joseph, D., & Bielaczyc, K. (2009). Design research: Theoretical and methodological issues. *Journal of the Learning Sciences, 13*(1), 15–42.

Comeaux, D., & Schmetzke, A. (2013). Accessibility of academic library web sites in North America: Current status and trends (2002–2012). *Library Hi Tech, 31*(1), 8–33.

Emiliani, P. L. (2009). Perspectives on accessibility: From assistive technologies to universal access and design for all. In C. Stephanidis (Ed.), *Universal access handbook* (pp. 2-1–2-18). Boca Raton, FL: CRC Press.

Espadinha, C., Pereira, L., Da Silva, F., & Lopes, J. (2011). Accessibility of Portuguese public universities' sites. *Disability & Rehabilitation, 33*(6), 475–485.

European Telecommunications Standards Institute. (2014). *European standard: Accessibility requirements suitable for public procurement of ICT products and services in Europe.* Retrieved from http://www.etsi.org/deliver/etsi_en/301500_301599/301549/01.01.01_60/en_301549v010101p.pdf

Friedman, B., Kahn Jr., P. H., Borning, A., & Huldtgren, A. (2013). Value sensitive design and information systems. In N. Doorn, D. Schuurbiers, I. van de Poel, & M. E. Gorman (Eds.), *Early engagement and new technologies: Opening up the laboratory* (pp. 55–95). Dordrecht, The Netherlands: Springer Netherlands.

Grossman, P. (2014). The greatest change in disability law in twenty years: What you need to know. In M. L. Vance, N. E. Lipsitz, & K. Parks (Eds.), *Beyond the Americans with Disabilities Act.* Washington, DC: National Association of Student Personnel Administrators.

Gulliksen, J., & Harker, S. (2004). The software accessibility of human-computer interfaces: ISO Technical Specification 16071. *Universal Access in the Information Society, 3,* 6–16. Retrieved from http://link.springer.com/article/10.1007%2Fs10209-003-0079-1#close

Hackett, S., & Parmanto, B. (2005). A longitudinal evaluation of accessibility: Higher education Web sites. *Internet Research, 15*(3), 281–294.

Heyward, S. (2014). Providing access to technology doesn't have to be mystery. *Disability Compliance for Higher Education, 20*(5), p. 3.

International Organization for Standardization. (1998). *Guidance on usability.* (ISO 9241-11).

Iwarsson, S., & Stahl, A. (2003). Accessibility, usability and universal design—positioning and definition of concepts describing person-environment relationships. *Disability and Rehabilitation, 25*(2), 57–66.

Jisc TechDis (n.d.). *Jisc TechDis is...* Retrieved from http://www.jisctechdis.ac.uk/

Kelly, B. (2002). Web Watch: An accessibility analysis of UK university entry points. *Ariadne, 33.* Retrieved from http://www.ariadne.ac.uk/issue33/web-watch/

Laux, L. F., McNally, P. R., Paciello, M. G., & Vanderheiden, G. C. (1996). Designing the World Wide Web for people with disabilities: A user centered design approach. *Proceedings of the Second Annual ACM Conference on Assistive Technologies, Association for Computing Machinery, Special Interest Group on Accessible Computing,* Vancouver, BC, 94–101.

Mariger, H. A. (2011). The social validation of institutional indicators to promote system-wide web accessibility in postsecondary institutions (Dissertation). Logan, UT: School of Graduate Studies, Utah State University. Retrieved from http://digitalcommons.usu.edu/cgi/viewcontent.cgi?article=1899&context=etd

Narasimhan, N. (Ed.). (2012). Web accessibility policy making: An international perspective. Retrieved from http://g3ict.org/resource_center/publications_and_reports/p/productCategory_whitepapers/subCat_7/id_150

National Center on Accessible Media. (2006). *Accessible digital media guidelines.* Retrieved from http://ncam.wgbh.org/invent_build/web_multimedia/accessible-digital-media-guide

National Center on Disability and Access to Education. (n.d.). *Looking to the work of others as you create your institution's web accessibility policy.* Retrieved from http://ncdae.org/blog/web-accessibility-policy

National Council on Disability. (2004). *Design for inclusion: Creating a new marketplace.* Washington, DC: Author. Retrieved from http://www.ncd.gov/publications/2004/10282004

Nesset, V., & Large, A. (2004). Children in the information technology design process: A review of theories and their applications. *Library and information science research, 26*(2004), 140–161.

Nielsen, J. (1996). Accessible design for users with disabilities. *Alertbox: Current Issues in Web Usability.* Retrieved from http://www.useit.com/alertbox/9610.html

Nielsen, J. (2012). *Usability 101: Introduction to usability.* Fremont, CA: Nielsen Norman Group. Retrieved from http://www.nngroup.com/articles/usability-101-introduction-to-usability/

Patrick, D. L. (Correspondence to Senator Tom Harkin, September 9, 1996). Retrieved from http://www.justice.gov/crt/foia/readingroom/frequent_requests/ada_tal/tal712.txt

Raising the Floor. (2011). *GPII.* Retrieved from http://gpii.net

Rehabilitation Act of 1973. 29 U.S.C. § 79 *et seq.*

Rowland, C., & Smith, T. (1999). Web site accessibility. *The Power of Independence, Summer,* 1–2.

Schneiderman, B. (1999). Universal usability: Pushing human-computer interaction research to empower every citizen. *ISR Technical Report 99–72.* College Park: University of Maryland, Institute for Systems Research.

Seale, J. K. (2006). *E-learning and disability in higher education. Accessibility research and practice.* London: Routledge.

Seale, J. K. (2014a). Evaluating accessibility practice. In *E-learning and disability in higher education* (2nd edition) (pp. 92–120). Abingdon, Oxon, UK: Routledge Taylor & Francis Group.

Seale, J. K. (2014b). Opening up spaces for dialogue, critique and imagination in accessibility research and practice. In *E-learning and disability in higher education* (2nd edition) (pp. 3–20). Abingdon, Oxon, UK: Routledge Taylor & Francis Group.

Seale, J. K. (2014c). Re-imagining accessibility research: Methods to enable a democratic voice to be heard. In *E-learning and disability in higher education* (2nd edition) (pp. 192–214). Abingdon, Oxon, UK: Routledge Taylor & Francis Group.

Section 255 of the Telecommunications Act of 1966. 47 U.S.C. § 255.

Section 504 of the Rehabilitation Act of 1973, as amended. 29 U.S.C. § 794.

Section 508 of the Rehabilitation Act of 1973, as amended. 29 U.S.C. § 794d.

Stephanidis, C. (2009). Universal access and design for all in the evolving information technology. In C. Stephanidis (Ed.), *Universal access handbook* (pp. 1–11). Boca Raton, FL: CRC Press.

Thompson, T., Burgstahler, S., & Moore, E. (2007). Accessibility of higher education websites in the Northwestern U.S.: Current status and response to third party outreach. In *Proceedings of the First International Conference on Technology-based Learning with Disability* (pp. 127–36), July 19–20, 2007. Dayton, OH: Wright State University. Retrieved from http://www.wright.edu/lwd/documents/FinalLWD07.pdf

Thompson, T., Comden, D., Ferguson, S., Burgstahler, S., & Moore, E. (2013). Seeking predictors of web accessibility in U.S. higher education institutions. *Information Technology and Disabilities Journal,* 13(1).

Thompson, T., Draffan, E. A., & Patel, P. (2009). 2008 ATHEN survey on accessible technology in higher education. *ATHEN E-Journal,* 4. Retrieved from http://athenpro.org/node/86

United States Access Board. (2011). Draft updated standards and guidelines. Retrieved from http://www.access-board.gov/guidelines-and-standards/communications-and-it/about-the-ict-refresh/draft-rule-2011

United States Department of Justice. (2005). *A guide to disability rights laws.* Washington, DC: U.S. Department of Justice, Civil Rights Division. Retrieved from www.ada.gov/cguide.pdf

U.S. Department of Justice and U.S. Department of Education. (2010, June 29). Joint "Dear colleague letter": Electronic book readers. Retrieved from http://www2.ed.gov/about/offices/list/ocr/letters/colleague-20100629.html

United States General Services Administration. (n.d.). Summary of Section 508 Standards. Washington, DC: U.S. General Services Administration. Retrieved from http://www.section508.gov/summary-section508-standards

University of Illinois. (2013, November 20). *Minimal functional accessibility requirements for software candidates.* Retrieved from https://itaccessibility.illinois.edu/sites/itaccessibility.illinois.edu/files/Purchasing_Accessibility_Checklist.pdf

University of Washington (UW). (n.d.a). *Example policies in higher education.* Seattle: Author. Retrieved from http://www.washington.edu/accessibility/requirements/example-policies/

UW. (n.d.b). *Legal cases by issue*. Seattle: Author. Retrieved from http://www.uw.edu/accessibility/requirments/legal-cases-by-issue

UW. (n.d.c). *Resolution agreements and lawsuits*. Seattle: Author. Retrieved from http://www.washington.edu/accessibility/requirements/accessibility-cases-and-settlement-agreements/

Vanderheiden, G. C., & Vanderheiden, K. R. (1992). *Guidelines for the design of consumer products to increase their accessibility to people with disabilities or who are aging (Working Draft 1.7)*. Madison, WI: Trace Research and Development Center. Retrieved from http://trace.wisc.edu/docs/consumer_product_guidelines/toc.htm

Waddell, C. D. (1999). The growing digital divide in access for people with disabilities. Overcoming barriers to participation in the digital economy. Paper presented at the *Understanding the Digital Economy Conference*, May.

Waddell, C. D. (2007). Accessible electronic & information technology: Legal obligations of higher education and Section 508. *ATHEN Access Technologists Higher Education Network, 2*. Retrieved from http://www.athenpro.org/node/39

Waddell, C. D., & Hardy, B. (2004). Education student to serve information seekers with disabilities. *Journal of Education for Library and Information Science, 45*(2), 137–148.

Waters, C. (1997). *Universal web design*. Indianapolis, IN: New Riders.

Web Accessibility Initiative (WAI). (2002). *Implementation plan for web accessibility*. Retrieved from http://www.w3.org/WAI/impl/Overview

WAI. (2005). *Essential components of web accessibility*. Retrieved from http://www.w3.org/WAI/intro/components.php

WAI. (n.d.a). *Complete list of web accessibility evaluation tools*. Retrieved from http://www.w3.org/WAI/ER/tools/complete

WAI. (n.d.b). *How to meet WCAG 2.0*. Retrieved from http://www.w3.org/WAI/WCAG20/quickref/

WAI. (n.d.c). *Introduction to understanding WCAG 2.0*. Retrieved from http://www.w3.org/TR/UNDERSTANDING-WCAG20/intro.html#introduction-fourprincs-head

WAI. (n.d.d). *Introduction to web accessibility*. Retrieved from http://www.w3.org/WAI/intro/accessibility.php

WAI. (n.d.e). *Web content accessibility guidelines (WCAG) overview*. Retrieved from http://www.w3.org/WAI/intro/wcag

Wijayaratne, A., & Singh, D. (2010). Is there space in cyberspace for distance learners with special needs in Asia? A review of the level of web accessibility of institutional and library homepages of AAOU members. *The International Information & Library Review, 42*(1), 40–49.

This material is based on work supported by the National Science Foundation under grant numbers CNS-1042260 and HRD-0833504. Any opinions, findings, and conclusions or recommendations expressed in this material are those of the author and do not necessarily reflect the views of the National Science Foundation.

16

A Brief History of Assistive, Accessible, and Universally Designed Technology

Perspectives of Practitioners Who Lived It

Fourteen Leaders in the Field

This book would not be complete without providing some perspective regarding the history of assistive technology, accessibly designed technology, and universally designed technology from leaders in the field. The following text was first published in 2014 as a preface to the twentieth anniversary issue of the Information Technology and Disability (ITD) Journal. The guest editors share their perspectives, after which they summarize the contributions of twelve additional practitioners in the field. A reference with a link to the full content of this issue is included at the end of the excerpt.

Terrill Thompson
Sheryl E. Burgstahler
University of Washington

Twenty years ago, Norm Coombs and colleagues from Project EASI (Equal Access to Software and Information) established a free online e-journal that has informed, inspired, and captured the ever-evolving state of the assistive technology (AT) and information technology (IT) accessibility fields. This special issue of the *Information Technology and Disabilities (ITD) Journal* celebrates its impact over two decades. It features articles from a dozen pioneers in the field, most of whom have published articles in past issues of the *ITD Journal*. Authors share their stories about how assistive technology and accessible IT have evolved over the years and what new challenges and hopes they envision for the future.

In the paragraphs below, the editors each share their journeys in this field and then introduce the authors and the stories they share in this twentieth anniversary issue of the *ITD Journal*.

SHERYL'S JOURNEY

My journey in the field of assistive technology began more than twenty years ago. In 1982, I hired an engineering student at Saint Martin's College—where I taught mathematics, computer programming, and computer applications in education—to modify an Apple II computer with a switch box to lock the shift, control, and repeat keys. It needed to be designed in such a way that a six-year-old boy, Rodney, could operate the switch box, and therefore all of the functions of the computer, with his mouth wand. Passing through a chain of education technology leaders at the time, I found Gregg Vanderheiden and his colleagues at the University of Wisconsin, who mailed me a hand-drawn picture showing how to build an external switch box. Included in this article is a picture of me with Rodney (Figure 16.1), who is operating the computer using his mouth wand, the computer keyboard, and the switch box.

I learned about Rodney several weeks before meeting him from his special education teacher, who was teaching him to type on an electric typewriter. She wondered if I thought he could operate a computer. I invited her, Rodney, and his family to come to the Microcomputer Resource Center we had created at the college. When she shared with me a copy of the first letter Rodney wrote on the typewriter, I knew this young man was someone I wanted to get to know. In part, he said:

FIGURE 16.1   Sheryl with six-year-old Rodney at the computer with a switch box

May 3. 1982,

Dear President Reagan,

I want to tell you my name. My name is Rodney and I Am 6 years old . . . I am handicapped bebecause I can't use my legs or my hands because I have little muscles and dbones.

I go to Skyline Exceptional School . . . I get to learn to type with my special mouth wand. Someday I will get to use a computer because I am smart even tho handicapped.

This is my first letter L typed. I Worked hard typing. TThank you for being nice . . .

Rodney

So, Rodney and I embarked on our own little journey, exploring how technology could enhance his performance in school and his life overall. Back then, we did not imagine that by today there would be thousands of commercially available AT products, let alone the many features that benefit individuals with disabilities that are integrated into IT products. Word about Rodney spread, and St. Martin's became a magnet for those exploring computer access issues for individuals with disabilities. I recruited any experts I could find to teach Saturday workshops on computer use by students with physical disabilities, visual impairments, and learning disabilities. Because of these experiences, when I was hired to lead the new Microcomputer Support Group (MSG) at the University of Washington (UW) in 1984, I immediately added making IT accessible to faculty, students, and staff with disabilities to the MSG mission statement.

I teamed up with the founders of Project EASI when it began in 1989 as a special interest group of the EDUCOM conference and professional organization of postsecondary IT leaders. Daniel Hilton-Chalfen became chair in 1990; we recruited Norm Coombs to be the next chair of EASI, and the rest is history. Meanwhile, Dan Comden joined the UW team as the access technology manager for the UW and as the technology specialist when I founded the Disabilities, Opportunities, Internetworking, and Technology (DO-IT) Center with National Science Foundation funding in 1992. At the time, the Internet was emerging; we used e-mail, telnet, and file transfer protocol. Content was limited and mostly text-based and therefore accessible to students who were blind using early screen-reader technology. A moment comes to mind when Randy, a high school student at the time and one of our first DO-IT Scholars, described his first experience reading a newspaper independently because of its availability on the Internet. Randy is blind. Our UW team also networked with AT leaders at the Closing The Gap conference on technology for people with disabilities and the California State University, Northridge (CSUN) International Technology and Persons with Disabilities Conference. Later, Terrill Thompson, coeditor of this *ITD* issue, joined our UW team.

In the early days, when we talked about accessible web design there were no standards or guidelines to point to, so we made them up as we went. We often called the effort, borrowing from terminology in the field of architecture, simply the *universal design* (UD) of websites. In those early years, I would not have imagined that in twenty years there would be standards and guidelines for the accessible design of websites, that the technology used to present websites would be so complex, that the range of devices used to access the Web would be so diverse, and that UD would be broadly promoted as an approach for the design of a wide range of technologies as well as instruction and student services. I'm excited to be part of what comes next!

TERRILL'S JOURNEY

My journey in the technology accessibility field began in 1994, as coordinator of the Computer Learning Center at Independence, Inc., the independent living center in Lawrence, Kansas. There we provided computer and assistive technology training to individuals with disabilities. Some of these individuals joined us in the challenge of keeping the lab up and running, dealing with conflicts that invariably emerged as assistive devices collided over interrupt requests (IRQs), direct memory access (DMAs), or input/output (I/O) addresses. Together we puzzled over how to install AT software applications in ways that would reduce the possibility of their stumbling over each other. Those were fun times!

The technology itself was grass roots, built by small companies or individuals, many of whom had disabilities themselves. Our screen reader of choice was Provox, created by Chuck Hallenbeck, a blind professor at the University of Kansas and advisor to our center. Provox was built for DOS, and we were honored to be using a beta release that exclaimed "Holy @!#, Batman, here comes Windows!" whenever the user would launch Windows from the DOS prompt. This single exclamation summed up widespread feelings in the accessibility community at the time: computer users with disabilities were faced with a daunting change in technology and keeping up would require extraordinary effort.

This feeling would be repeated in subsequent years, with the rise of the Internet, the explosion of online (and uncaptioned) video, and even today with the Web emerging as a primary channel for hosting highly interactive cloud-based software applications. History repeats itself: innovation happens that breaks existing accessibility models and individuals with disabilities are shut out. The accessibility community works hard to develop new creative strategies for making the new technology accessible. Then, just as accessibility has started to catch up, innovation happens again and the cycle repeats. Fortunately, we now understand this pattern, which I believe is the first step to changing it.

During that troubled transition to Windows, some of our most dedicated patrons at the Computer Learning Center were students from area colleges and universities. Working with these students and helping them to self-advocate for better accessibility led me to an active interest in improving accessibility in higher education. Boulder, Colorado, was a day's drive from Lawrence, and I discovered kindred spirits at Accessing Higher Ground (AHG), the accessible technology conference organized by Howard Kramer at the University of Colorado. Back then AHG was primarily a regional conference attended by people from the Rocky Mountain states, plus at least one person from Kansas. The conference was well attended by people from higher education who were working to implement accessibility solutions on their campuses.

Once I found my way into higher education, first at North Carolina State University and now at the University of Washington, I acquired a new respect for the vast breadth of the accessibility problem. We faced inaccessible websites; inaccessible documents; inaccessible software with very few accessible alternatives available on the market; and inaccessible textbooks and other print resources that required extraordinary effort to convert into accessible formats, with little or no help from publishers. These problems still exist today, but there are many signs that the state of accessibility is improving. This is the result of tireless work on the part of hundreds of people, including individuals with disabilities, accessibility advocates and evangelists, standards organizations, and many others who have elected to devote their time and energy to breaking down barriers and working hard for equal access.

In 2002 at CSUN's Annual International Technology and Persons with Disabilities Conference, I and a few dozen other people met in what would be the first annual meeting of a new association that adopted the name ATHEN, for Access Technology Higher Education Network. ATHEN is a network of higher education professionals committed to improving accessibility for students, faculty, staff, and administrators. Its purpose is to collect and disseminate best practices in access technology in the higher education environment as well as present a collective voice for the professional practice of access technology in higher education. One of the channels through which it has realized this purpose is its online publication, the *ATHEN e-Journal*. Four issues of the journal were published between 2005 and 2009, after which ATHEN and EASI began their collaboration on a combined e-journal, keeping the name from the original EASI publication, *ITD Journal*. The first issue from this collaboration was published in April 2013. The second is the current issue, which commemorates the *ITD Journal's* twentieth anniversary.

THIS TWENTIETH ANNIVERSARY ISSUE

The people who contributed to this twentieth anniversary issue are among those who have worked tirelessly over the years to break down barriers for people with disabilities.

Steve Noble was one of the original contributing editors of the *ITD Journal* since its beginning, and was editor of several issues after Tom McNulty's tenure, including the tenth anniversary issue. Therefore, it is fitting to feature Steve in the opening article of the current issue. In his article, Steve reflects briefly on the past, then gazes into the future and describes four things he expects to see in 2024 if enough accessibility advocates work together toward a few key goals.

Daniel Hilton-Chalfen looks back to the first issue of the *ITD Journal* in 1994, leads us through key milestones over the last twenty years, and predicts the future in the field, particularly as it relates to accessible text.

George Kerscher also focuses on accessible text, and describes developments with EPUB 3 that have the potential to eventually make content accessible "from day one."

John Gardner shares the history, current state, and future of making graphic images accessible to those who cannot see them.

Sharron Rush acknowledges the contributions of our colleague John Slatin until his death from leukemia in 2008, and repeats his words, "Good design is accessible design." She talks about the value of competitive activities like the Accessibility Internet Relay for Austin (AIR-Austin) in stimulating awareness, excitement, and development of accessible websites.

Cyndi Rowland also focuses on web accessibility, sharing developments that have occurred during her fifteen years in the field and organizing her impressions around the issues of awareness; complexity; guidelines, standards, and laws; harmonization; and supports. She then discusses challenges that remain.

Harry Murphy and *Howard Kramer* describe the roles of conferences—the CSUN Conference and Accessing Higher Ground, respectively—as agents of change and facilitators of networking that lead to new connections such as ATHEN.

Sean Keegan talks about the history, importance of, and goal for "transparency" in accessible technology design.

Dan Comden shares his "long, strange trip" through the history of assistive technology, which he describes as "exciting, always changing, often frustrating, and when it's done properly, truly liberating."

Susan Kelmer shares her journey with alternate format production. As she says, "There will never be an alternate format destination. There will only be the continued journey."

Finally, *Darren Gabbert* shares his experiences through milestones in the evolution of speech recognition technology.

Enjoy your journey through the history of IT through the lens of accessibility over the past twenty years. Consider the challenges, frustrations, solutions, and partial solutions of others and compare your views to the predictions for the future through the eyes of leaders in this historical movement.

REFERENCE

Thompson, T. & Burgstahler, S. (Eds.). (2014). ITD twentieth anniversary issue. *Information Technology and Disabilities E-Journal, 14*(1). Equal Access to Software and Information (EASI) and Access Technology Higher Education Network (ATHEN). Retrieved from http://itd.athenpro.org/volume14/number1/index.html

This material is based on work supported by the National Science Foundation under grant numbers CNS-1042260 and HRD-0833504. Any opinions, findings, and conclusions or recommendations expressed in this material are those of the author and do not necessarily reflect the views of the National Science Foundation.

17

Video for All

Accessibility of Video Content and Universal Design of a Media Player

Terrill Thompson

This chapter provides background on the variety of ways that individuals access video, including barriers and benefits to particular populations. It also provides a brief history of web standards as they apply to online video, and culminates in a case study that explores how universal design (UD) was employed in designing and developing Able Player, a fully accessible open source media player.

Video is everywhere. More than one billion unique users visit YouTube each month and watch over six billion hours of video, and one hundred hours of video are uploaded to YouTube every minute (YouTube, 2014). In higher education, videos are used with growing regularity to deliver both academic and administrative content. The proliferation of lecture capture products makes it possible for instructors to easily provide video recordings of each of their lectures and make them available to students immediately following the end of class.

Video engages students. It offers an alternative to lectures, readings, and other activities, and, combined with these other delivery mechanisms, can be part of a compelling curriculum that satisfies the first principle of universal design for learning, "provide multiple means of representation" (Center for Applied Special Technology [CAST], 2012).

However, despite the beneficial contributions video can make to inclusive instruction, it can also exclude groups of users unless it is produced and delivered with universal design in mind. This chapter provides an overview of video accessibility issues, and describes the process that went into creating *Able Player*, an open source cross-browser media player that was specifically created to follow the principles of universal design. As the product was conceived, developers carefully considered a wide variety of users and scenarios for how those users would be engaging with the video content. Although some of the content in this chapter is technical, even nontechnical readers are encouraged to follow the process of UD as applied to the development of this media player in order to better understand how developers can create products that can be used by people with the widest range of potential characteristics.

VIDEO ACCESS ISSUES

Many groups of individuals have difficulty fully accessing the content of video. Several are discussed in the paragraphs below.

People Who Are Unable to Hear or Understand the Spoken Language

Users who are unable to hear the audio are missing an important part of most video productions. A solution is to accompany video with captions. Captions are text that is displayed in sync with the video, typically at the bottom of the video display. They provide a synchronized transcript of all spoken audio as well as descriptions of other important audio content, such as "a knock at the door."

Captions benefit individuals who are deaf or hard of hearing, but, like curb cuts and automatic door openers, they also benefit society as a whole. People with more typical hearing abilities are often in situations where they are unable to hear: for example, in a noisy environment such as a gym, sports bar, or airport; or in a quiet environment such as a library or computer lab where audio output is unavailable or impractical. In settings such as these, individuals are unable to access the audio content unless captions are provided.

Also, people who do not natively speak the language spoken in a video, people with language processing disorders, or anyone else who has difficulty understanding a video's verbal content can all benefit from captions, as they can read along while listening.

People who do not understand the language of the video at all can benefit from having the video's content translated into another language. Translation plays a major role in UD, as language is arguably the greatest barrier that prevents access to information. For example, this book was originally written in English. Unless it's translated into other languages, only 14% of the world's population can access its content (Crystal, 2003). Translations of video content are typically delivered as subtitles, which, like captions, are displayed as timed text, synchronized with the video. Unlike captions, subtitles provide access only to spoken dialogue, since other audio content (e.g., "a knock at the door") requires no translation.

Captions and subtitles can be produced by various parties. Sometimes the producer of a video includes captioning as part of their production workflow; other times, captioning is outsourced to organizations that specialize in that service. In fact, the Described and Captioned Media Program lists hundreds of providers of captioning services (n.d.a). Also, several free web-based tools make it easy for individuals to caption their own videos (e.g., amara.org, dotsub.com, subtitlehorse.com, captiontube.com); some of these tools are frequently used to caption video through *crowdsourcing*, relying on the efforts of a dedicated "crowd" or community of volunteers. Similarly, subtitles are typically produced by professional translation services, but many of the free crowdsourcing platforms can be used to support volunteer subtitling.

In the future, technology could play a more integral role in captioning and translating video content. Already, Google uses automatic translation technology to automatically generate subtitles for any YouTube video that has closed captions. Users can click the CC button on the YouTube player and choose to have the video translated into any of more than seventy-five supported languages. Google also uses automatic speech recognition (ASR) technology in an effort to automatically caption many of the videos that are uploaded to YouTube (Harrenstien, 2009). However, ASR faces many great challenges given the complexities of human speech and language, and results from this experimental effort are not yet reliable for people who depend on captions.

American Sign Language, not English, is the native language of many people who are deaf or hard of hearing in the United States (Mitchell, Young, Bachleda, & Karchmer, 2005). Since English is not their first language, these individuals do not necessarily gain full access to video content through English captions. Instead, a solution is to provide a videotaped sign language interpreter who appears in a supplemental window or overlay, translating spoken content into sign language as the video plays.

Another feature that benefits users who have difficulty understanding the language of a video, whether due to language barriers or cognitive functioning, is the ability to change the rate of playback without changing or distorting pitch. There are differences in the optimum speed at which people process information. For some, slowing down playback can be helpful. For others, such as people who are easily distracted, speeding up playback can help them stay focused. Speeding up playback also helps people who are busy, as they can get through the video content more quickly.

People Who Are Unable to See

People who are unable to see video can often gain some understanding of the content by listening to the audio. However, if content is purely visual or has insufficient audio cues to accurately convey what's happening on the screen, that content is inaccessible to nonvisual users. A common example in higher education is when video includes multiple speakers, and each speaker's name, title, and affiliation appear visually in a graphic on the screen. If this same information is not also provided audibly, nonvisual users have no idea who is speaking.

One strategy for ensuring that individuals who are unable to see the video still have access to its visual content is to integrate the necessary audio content into the production. For example, on-screen text can be read aloud by a narrator. This benefits individuals who are blind or visually impaired, and also benefits others who have difficulty reading text, as well as people who are looking away. Similarly, if a lecturer is conducting a demonstration on-screen, she should describe what she's doing, just as she should in a live lecture, based on the reasonable assumption that some people in the audience are unable to see the demonstration.

For those situations where it is not feasible to integrate audible versions of the visual content into the production, another solution is a technique known as *audio description* (also called *video description, descriptive video, descriptive narration,* or simply *description*). Audio description is a separate audio track that injects brief narration at key points in the video, describing important visual content.

Audio description is both a science and an art form. The words chosen to describe visual content can have an effect on meaning; therefore, description must be carefully scripted in order to minimize that effect. Good description is concise and objective, and accomplishes its purpose without being distracting. Timing is also an important consideration, since the description needs to be injected into the content at moments that avoid collision with dialogue or other critical program audio.

Given the specialized skills required to produce audio description, it has historically been outsourced to audio description professionals. The Described and Captioned Media Program lists twenty-seven providers of audio description services in the U.S. and thirteen international providers (Described and Captioned Media Program, n.d.b). When video is intended for online distribution, the typical deliverable is a new described version of the video, featuring a human narrator whose recorded narration is mixed with the program audio, with volumes adjusted as needed to attain an optimum balance. The described version of the video can be distributed as an alternative to the original.

The specialization and cost associated with producing audio description has resulted in very little video content being described. However, many videos used in higher education, especially those featuring "talking heads," could feasibly be self-described. In 2013, the Video Description Research and Development Center at the Smith-Kettlewell Eye Research Institute unveiled YouDescribe, a free tool that anyone can use to add human-voiced description to YouTube videos (Kendrick, 2013; YouDescribe, n.d.). The output produced by YouDescribe is a set of audio clips that can be played back at appropriate times in sync with the video, using the custom player on the YouDescribe.org website.

Still another method for delivering audio description is to create a timed text file, similar to a closed caption file. With this approach, when someone using a screen reader plays a video, each short segment of description text is exposed at its appropriate time during video playback, at which time it can be read aloud by the person's screen reader or, in the future, self-voiced by media players themselves. Researchers at IBM Tokyo and WGBH found that individuals who are blind in Japan and the United States tend to prefer human-narrated description, but that synthesized description is also acceptable (Kobayashi, O'Connell, Gould, Takagi, & Asakawa, 2000). Text-based audio description is the type that is now supported by HTML5, as explained later in this chapter.

People Who Are Unable to See or Hear, plus Everybody Else

People who are deaf-blind typically access the computer using a braille output device, which includes a row of braille dots that refreshes as the user moves about the web page, document, or application. Users control their own reading pace, so reading live caption text in braille is largely impractical. Instead, braille users can read a transcript. The ideal transcript is one that includes both the audio content (captions) and visual content (audio description), since people who are accessing a video's content through a transcript otherwise have no access to either of these components.

Transcripts are beneficial to other users as well. They benefit users who have slow Internet connections or other technical limitations that prevent online video from playing on their devices. They also benefit anyone who is busy. People might have too little time to sit through an entire video, but they can quickly read, scan, or search a transcript, looking for content that specifically matches their interests or needs.

For this latter group, transcripts are particularly beneficial if they're interactive, with time data associated with the text in the transcript. Interactive transcripts include features such as clickable text that enables users to launch the video starting from any point in the transcript. Being able to search, scan, and selectively play video in this fashion can be extremely beneficial for students who are reviewing videotaped lectures as they prepare for an exam. Here again, captions demonstrate that UD provides great benefit to society as a whole.

WEB STANDARDS AND ONLINE VIDEO

The World Wide Web was invented in 1989 by Tim Berners-Lee, an English computer scientist who was then working as a contractor for CERN. Berners-Lee also drafted the earliest versions of Hypertext Markup Language (HTML), the markup language in which most web pages are coded (Berners-Lee, 1991; Berners-Lee & Connolly, 1993a, b), and founded the World Wide Web Consortium (W3C), an international community where member organizations, a full-time staff, and the public work together to develop web standards. Since its establishment, the W3C has produced multiple revisions of HTML, as well as dozens of other specifications and standards for the Web.

In 1999, the W3C published version 1.0 of the Web Content Accessibility Guidelines (WCAG). WCAG has served as the defining standard for web accessibility ever since. An updated version, WCAG 2.0, was published in 2008. WCAG 2.0 is organized into four broad principles. In order to be accessible, web content must be *perceivable*, *operable*, *understandable*, and *robust*. Each of these principles is defined and clarified with specific guidelines, and each guideline includes precise success criteria that must be met in order to satisfy that guideline. Each success criterion is assigned one of three levels (Level A, AA, and AAA) in descending order of priority, with Level A success criteria being the most critical.

Both WCAG 1.0 and WCAG 2.0 have provided an international standard on which several countries have based their web accessibility laws (Rogers, 2012). Both versions of WCAG have also included checkpoints or success criteria that specifically apply to media accessibility. In WCAG 2.0, the most directly relevant success criteria all fall under the *perceivable* principle, and require captions, transcripts, audio description, and synchronized sign language in order to meet the guidelines at various levels. By providing these alternative formats for video content, video producers or distributors ensure that their video content is perceivable by all users, regardless of whether those users perceive the content using sight, sound, or touch.

The W3C's latest version of HTML, HTML5, was finalized in October 2014 (W3C, 2014a) and provides some of the markup necessary to meet the success criteria required by WCAG 2.0. Specifically, HTML5 introduces two new media elements, <audio> and <video>, which make it possible to add media to web pages using HTML alone. Prior to HTML5, adding media to web pages was dependent on proprietary, platform-specific plug-ins that users had to download and install, most of which didn't work universally across operating systems. Adobe Flash eventually rose to prominence as the leading platform for delivering online media. Flash still required users to download a third-party plug-in, the Adobe Flash player, but it was available for all major operating systems at the time (Apple's iOS would later change that) and it had attained an installed base that was much higher than any of the individual media plug-ins (at its peak, Adobe claimed that 98% of computers had Flash installed).

Flash made it possible for developers to easily create their own media players, and the Web became saturated with a tremendous variety of players, all of which offered a means of playing media on web pages. They differed primarily in their visual appearance. A few of these players included support for closed captions, but most players were not created with UD in mind and failed to support the needs of users with disabilities. For example, buttons and controls were often operable only with a mouse, and could not be operated with a keyboard alone. Further, they were often not assigned proper labels (e.g., Play, Pause, Forward, Rewind, Stop, Volume Up, Volume Down) in order to make them accessible for screen reader users.

With the introduction of HTML5 media elements, we now have a promising method for adding media to web pages that works across browsers and operating systems and does not require any third-party plug-ins. As a standard web component, the challenge of making the controls accessible via a variety of input modalities (e.g., mouse, keyboard, stylus, touch, voice commands) rests on the companies that create browsers (most prominently, Microsoft, Google, Mozilla, Apple, and Opera). This increases the likelihood of web-based media players being accessible, as opposed to the situation when media players were the domain of hundreds of third parties.

The HTML5 specification includes a variety of accessibility features that specifically support UD, including captions, subtitles, text-based audio description, and adjustable playback rate. Each of these features is described below.

Captions and Subtitles in HTML5

In addition to new <audio> and <video> elements, HTML5 introduces a new <track> element. This is used in conjunction with the <video> element to identify caption files or other files that contain timed text tracks to be synchronized with the video. With the new <track> element, HTML5 supports five distinct kinds of text tracks:

- captions
- subtitles
- descriptions
- chapters
- metadata—essentially any other text that is intended to be synchronized with the video (e.g., pop-up comments, supplemental content, advertisements)

Each kind of text track is delivered in a new proposed standard format called Web Video Timed Text ([WebVTT]; W3C, 2014b).

WebVTT is a plain-text file format that includes start and stop times for rendering blocks of text. WebVTT also supports a variety of optional features, such as voice spans to identify speakers and markup that enables authors to control the spatial positioning of text on the video. For example, when two speakers are having a conversation, the caption text for each speaker could be positioned near that speaker to help clarify who's speaking.

All major browsers now support captions, and some additionally support subtitles. If a caption track is available, browsers typically display a CC button on the control bar of their built-in media player so users can toggle captions on and off.

Audio Description in HTML5

As noted in the preceding section, one of the five kinds of timed text tracks supported by the HTML5 <track> element is "descriptions." A WebVTT description file is essentially the same format as a WebVTT caption file, but contains description text rather than captions. Each segment of description text is intended to be exposed to screen readers, or perhaps self-voiced by media players, at the start time indicated within the WebVTT file.

With this approach to delivering audio description, the description text can be written and timestamped using the same free online tools that are used to create captions and subtitles. This greatly simplifies the process of creating descriptions, and therefore increases the likelihood that higher education institutions will add descriptions to their video, as is required by WCAG 2.0.

The HTML5 Media API

One of the most important features of HTML5 media support is its *application programming interface* (API). This is a set of methods, properties, and events that enables developers to build their own media players using JavaScript to control the <audio>, <video>, and related HTML elements. This opens the door to the possibility of creating a media player that fully embraces principles of UD, probably to a much greater extent than any of the browser makers will in designing their built-in players. In fact, several HTML5 media players are now available that include support for accessibility (e.g., AccessibilityOz, n.d.; Brightcove, Inc. n.d.; Colceriu, n.d.; Lembree, 2014; Nomensa, n.d.; Web Experience Toolkit, n.d.). The remainder of this chapter describes one HTML5 media player named *Able Player* that was designed and developed to adhere to the principles of universal design.

BUILDING A MEDIA PLAYER USING UD

The UW-IT Accessible Technology Services (ATS) group (ATS, n.d.) at the University of Washington was among those who decided to build their own custom media player using the HTML5 Media API. ATS is the parent organization of the DO-IT Center, where DO-IT stands for "Disabilities, Opportunities, Internetworking, and Technology." The DO-IT Center has worked since 1992 to promote the success of individuals with disabilities in postsecondary education and careers, using technology as an empowering tool (DO-IT, n.d.a.). Since DO-IT's formation, the Center has produced over fifty videos on a wide range of topics related to individuals with disabilities accessing curriculum, using technology, and pursuing challenging careers. DO-IT has always strived to deliver these videos in a variety of formats to ensure that everyone can access them. At various points in history, the videos were distributed on VHS tapes, DVD, and online. Prior to HTML5, the online videos were available as downloadable files in formats supported by QuickTime, RealPlayer, and Windows Media Player. Since the beginning, the video products have always been captioned and audio-described.

In 2011, the DO-IT Center began delivering their videos online using a custom HTML5 media player that DO-IT staff built from scratch using the HTML5 Media API. The DO-IT Video website (DO-IT, n.d.b.) features the accessible player, and allows people to perform a keyword search on the entire video library and jump to particular starting points within videos from the search results.

In 2014, the DO-IT Center, with funding from the National Science Foundation as part of the AccessComputing project (n.d.), entered a new phase of development for their player and released their player under the name *Able Player* to the open source community, where it is now freely available (Able Player, n.d.). Because Able Player is an open source project, people around the world are now contributing toward improving its feature set. In particular, the Committee on Institutional Cooperation (CIC), a consortium of the Big Ten universities plus the University of Chicago, has contributed significantly toward development of the player (CIC, n.d.).

The remainder of this chapter documents the requirements, features, problems, and solutions relative to the design of Able Player to this point. At each step, leaders of the project carefully considered the needs of all users and strove to develop a player that would serve as a model of UD.

Humble Beginnings: An Accessible Audio Player

Able Player originated as an audio player named Accessible Audio Player (AAP). Audio players have fewer accessibility requirements than video players since audio does not need to have synchronized captions or descriptions. However, careful consideration of how all users will interact with an audio player reveals several important design requirements:

- Player controls must be fully operable without a mouse.
- Player controls must be labeled in such a way that they are fully accessible to screen reader and/or braille users.
- Any changes to playback status (e.g., Playing, Buffering, End of track), which are typically written on the status bar of media players, must be coded in such a way that they are announced to screen reader users.
- Player controls must be reasonably large and have sufficient foreground-background contrast to be easy to see, even by people with low vision.
- Player controls must be visible and easy for users to see in Windows High Contrast Mode (which changes foreground and background colors and strips out background images).
- The labels for player controls (e.g., Play, Pause, Stop, Mute) must be easily discoverable so people using speech input software such as Dragon Naturally Speaking

can locate the commands needed to operate the player with voice commands (e.g., by saying "click Play").

Next Step: Add Support for Accessibility Features of the HTML5 Specification

The HTML5 Media API is used to control both audio and video, so extending the accessible audio player to support accessible video was a logical next step. As described earlier in this chapter, the HTML5 specification includes support for captions, subtitles, text-based audio description, and adjustable playback rate, so, at a minimum, an accessible video player should support each of these features. However, when one considers how best to support these features, the importance of accounting for individual differences becomes apparent. For example, people who use closed captions are not an otherwise homogenous group. Like all users, they have varying needs and preferences related to font size and color contrast. Also, some people might benefit from having text in a transcript highlighted while it's read, while others might find these features distracting.

Therefore, Able Player was designed to offer users flexibility and choice, key concepts in designing an interface that is capable of meeting individual differences. The following sections describe the role of various user preferences in applying UD to Able Player.

Caption preferences

The earliest captions were *open captions* (which are always on). However, these were soon replaced by *closed captions* (which can be toggled on or off) in order to provide user flexibility, as some people benefit from captions while others find them distracting.

Able Player, like most online media players that support captions, includes a CC button on the controller bar that enables users to toggle captions on or off. By default, captions are on, based on the belief that captions benefit many individuals, including those who don't realize they might benefit. If users find the captions distracting or otherwise undesirable, there is a checkbox within the Preferences dialog (accessible via the Preferences button on the player's controller bar) that enables users to uncheck the option "Closed captions on by default." The player uses browser cookies to store and remember users' preferences.

The font size for captions in Able Player is the default font size within users' browser preferences. If users increase or decrease the default font size for web pages, this change is reflected in the size of caption text as well. The color of caption text is white, and it appears on a black background beneath the video player. If individuals are using a high contrast color scheme, the caption text (and all other player prompts and controls) honors the user's color scheme.

At the time of this writing, Able Player designers are considering the incorporation of preferences to the Preferences dialog that would give users more targeted control over the appearance of caption text. Since captions appear in a context and serve a function that is distinctly different from other readable text on a web page, users might conceivably need or prefer seeing that text presented differently. Therefore, future versions of Able Player are likely to have a color palette within the Preferences dialog to allow users to select both the foreground and background colors.

Audio description preferences

As described earlier in this chapter, there are multiple ways of delivering audio description. One method is to provide a separate video that includes voiceover narration mixed into the program audio. This method results in *open description* (like *open captions*, *open description* is always on). Another method, the HTML5 method, is to provide text-based audio description that can be read by a screen reader. Since text-based audio description is contained in a distinct file separate from the video, this method results in *closed description*, which, like *closed captions*, can be toggled on or off.

Able Player's creators opted to support both methods. If description is provided in a WebVTT file and added to the video using the HTML5 <track> element, the player supports this feature in the same fashion that it supports closed captions. When the video is playing and reaches the start time of the next block of description text, the player exposes that text to screen reader users in a way that instructs screen readers to read the text immediately. By default, the description text is hidden from sighted users, although this too can be changed within the Preferences dialog.

One problem with delivering audio description as screen-readable text is that users operate their screen readers at varying reading speeds. A timestamp in a WebVTT description file can tell a screen reader when to start reading a description, but there is no way to know when the description will stop. Therefore, when writing the description text the author should find a gap in the program audio that is sufficiently long to allow the description content to be read even at a slow speed. But how long is long enough? This requires guesswork. A duration that is sufficiently long for some users might not be sufficiently long for others.

To address this problem, Able Player's designers added support for "extended audio description," a feature through which the video is automatically paused when audio description starts. The user must then press Play (a user-configurable hotkey) in order to resume playback. This method ensures that audio description and program audio don't collide, but it also prevents described video from playing through without user intervention, which could be a problem if users are watching video in the background while engaged in another activity away from their computer. Therefore, this option can be turned on or off within the Preferences dialog, and is off by default.

Providing a description in a separate described version of the video is also supported by Able Player, using another new feature in HTML5, custom data attributes. In HTML5, elements can be extended with custom attributes using the *data-* prefix. Able Player is utilizing this feature with built-in support for a *data-desc-src* attribute for the <source> element, the value of which is a path to the video file for the described version. Following is an example:

```
<source type="video/mp4" src="myvideo.mp4" data-desc-src="myvideo_described.mp4">
```

FIGURE 17.1   The Role of User Preferences in Delivery of Audio Description in Able Player

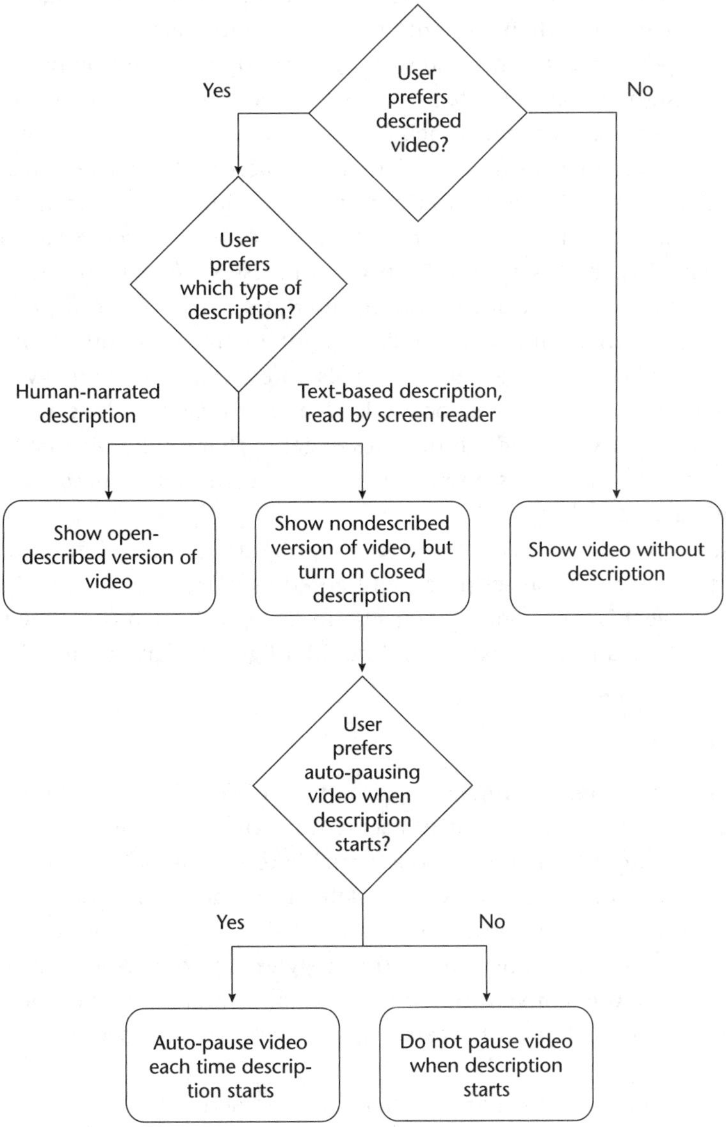

If a separate described version is available, and the user has indicated a preference for a described version in the Preferences dialog, Able Player will play the described version rather than the nondescribed version. Regardless of whether description is delivered as a separate video or as text that's readable by a screen reader, descriptions can be toggled on and off with a button on the player, just like closed captions. See Figure 17.1 for a flowchart showing the critical role that user preferences play in delivering audio description in Able Player.

Transcript preferences

If a caption file and/or description file is available, Able Player automatically parses the available files and uses their content to produce an interactive transcript. Description text is wrapped in a container and styled differently than caption text in order to clearly distinguish between the two. Since screen reader users are unable to see these visual style differences, each new block of description text is prefaced with a label, *Description:*, that is hidden from sighted users but accessible to screen reader users. Users can click anywhere in the transcript to play the video starting from that point.

Since some individuals are unable to use a mouse, the transcript can optionally be keyboard-enabled. If this feature is turned on, users can tab through the transcript, landing on each block of caption or description text, and can press Enter to play the video from that point. This makes the interactive functionality of the transcript accessible to keyboard users, but it can also present a problem if keyboard users are trying to get to a link or other focusable element outside of the transcript. They may have to tab dozens or hundreds of times to get to that link! Therefore "keyboard-enable interactive transcript" is offered as a choice in the Preferences dialog, and is turned off by default.

Another user preference pertains to text highlighting within the transcript. By default, the text within a transcript is highlighted as it's spoken in the video. Some users will find that this functionality helps them to cognitively process the video, but other users will be distracted by it. Therefore, highlighting can be turned off within the Preferences dialog.

Language preferences

Able Player supports foreign language subtitles in a WebVTT file using the HTML5 <track> element. Captions and subtitles serve different functions. Captions provide access to audio content for people who are unable to hear it. Subtitles provide a version of the spoken audio that has been translated into another language. Despite this fundamental difference in purpose, media players that support subtitles typically do so via the CC button, the same button that toggles captions. Able Player's designers opted to follow this convention. If subtitles are available in one or more languages, selecting the CC button triggers a menu that provides users with a choice of languages.

The subtitle tracks are also parsed when the interactive transcript is built, so if subtitles in a specific language are available, a transcript in the same language is also available. Users can select the language of the transcript independently of the caption or subtitle language. These features were designed to be controlled independently because having both written languages operating in parallel (e.g., captions in English, adjacent transcript in Spanish with text highlighted in real time) might be helpful to non-native language speakers or for students who are learning a foreign language.

Able Player was also developed with localization in mind. All default text, including English labels, prompts, and help text, is contained within a single English language file, which can easily be translated into other languages. The player automatically detects the language of the website and if a translation table is available in that language, it deploys the player in that language. If it is unable to detect the language of the web page, it attempts to determine the user's language set within the web browser, and again, if it's a supported language, it deploys the player in that language.

Hotkey preferences

Able Player is operable with the following keyboard shortcuts from anywhere on the web page:

> p or spacebar = Play/Pause toggle
> s = Stop
> r = Rewind
> f = Forward
> m = Toggle Mute
> c = Toggle Captions
> n = Toggle Descriptions
> h = Help

For some users these keys might conflict with keys that are used by other tools, including browser plug-ins or assistive technologies. Therefore, users are given the ability within the Preferences dialog to assign any combination of modifier keys (Alt, Control, or Shift) to the supported keystrokes. Also, if the web page includes more than one instance of Able Player, the behavior of the keyboard shortcuts is necessarily changed so that a player must have keyboard focus before the keys will trigger their usual effect.

Finally, if user focus is on a page element in which users would logically be typing keystrokes (e.g., a form field) the player stops listening for keyboard commands. Otherwise, if users attempted to type (for example) the letter *p* in a form field the media would begin playing or would pause, either of which would probably be surprising and undesirable.

Fallback Content: No HTML5? No problem!

All major browsers have supported HTML5 media elements for years now, spanning several browser versions. However, there are still people using older browsers. Although browsers are available for free, successive versions tend to require newer and more powerful computers and people with low income or low interest or aptitude in technology may be slow to upgrade. WebAIM's Screen Reader User Survey #5 (WebAIM, 2014) found that 19.8% of screen reader users who responded to the survey were still using Internet Explorer (IE) versions 8 or earlier, and IE began supporting HTML5 media elements in version 9.

In the spirit of UD, all users should have access to the content, even those who are using older technologies. However, "users should have access to the content" is not the same as "users must be able to play the video online." At a certain point it seems reasonable to expect users to meet specific minimum technical requirements. However, it is important to avoid simply dismissing people who don't meet these requirements. Instead, consideration should be given to alternative means for delivering comparable content. Strategies for providing access to the video content if the user can't play the video include:

- Provide links to the original media files so users can download the media and play it on their computers using software.
- Provide a transcript. Be sure to include both audio and visual content (e.g., captions and descriptions).

The creators of Able Player opted to build an alternative fallback player using JW Player, a commercial media player that is free for noncommercial use but is licensed separately and is not distributed with *Able Player*. Historically, JW Player has used Adobe Flash, but it now supports HTML5. Since it is being used in this case as a fallback player for people whose browsers don't support HTML5, the Flash version is used. JW Player, like HTML5, has a robust API that allows developers to control the player using their own custom HTML elements. This made it possible to build a fallback player that is nearly identical to the HTML5 player in both appearance and functionality. Therefore, users with older browsers, including Internet Explorer 6, 7, and 8, can have the same experience with *Able Player* as users with newer browsers.

CONCLUSION AND FUTURE CONSIDERATIONS

The W3C has drafted a set of Media Accessibility User Requirements (W3C, 2014c) that provide a comprehensive inventory of media-related user needs for people with blindness, low vision, atypical color perception, deafness, hearing impairments, physical impairments, cognitive and neurological disabilities, and deaf-blindness. As Able Player's designers and developers continue to employ UD in improving and advancing their media player, they will actively consult this resource to gain better understanding of user needs that perhaps have not been fully considered. The developers will also conduct usability tests with a wide variety of users in order to learn how people interact with the player. Working with users, including those with disabilities, is an indispensable practice for understanding user expectations and applying lessons learned to improving the design of products. The best products are those that are easy for everyone to understand and use.

REFERENCES

Able Player. (n.d.). *Able Player.* Retrieved from http://ableplayer.github.io/ableplayer

AccessComputing. (n.d.). *AccessComputing.* Seattle: University of Washington. Retrieved from http://www.washington.edu/accesscomputing/

AccessibilityOz. (n.d.). *OzPlayer.* Retrieved from http://www.accessibilityoz.com/ozplayer/

Accessible Technology Services. (n.d.). *Accessible Technology Services.* Seattle: University of Washington. Retrieved from http://www.washington.edu/doit/accessible-technology-services-0

Berners-Lee, T. (1991). *HTML tags.* Retrieved from http://info.cern.ch/hypertext/WWW/MarkUp/Tags.html

Berners-Lee, T., & Connolly, D. (1993a). *Hypertext Markup Language (HTML) 1.1.* Retrieved from http://tools.ietf.org/html/draft-ietf-iiir-html-00

Berners-Lee, T., & Connolly, D. (1993b). *Hypertext Markup Language (HTML) 1.2.* Retrieved from http://www.w3.org/MarkUp/draft-ietf-iiir-html-01.txt

Brightcove, Inc. (n.d.) *Video.js.* Retrieved from http://wet-boew.github.io/v4.0-ci/demos/multimedia/multimedia-en.html

Center for Applied Special Technology (CAST). (2012). *The three principles of UDL*. Retrieved from http://www.udlcenter.org/aboutudl/whatisudl/3principles

Colceriu, I. (n.d.). *Acorn Media Player*. Retrieved from https://ghinda.net/acornmediaplayer/

Committee on Institutional Cooperation. (n.d.). *Committee on Institutional Cooperation (CIC)*. Retrieved from http://www.cic.net/

Crystal, D. (2003). *English as a global language*, 2nd edition. Cambridge: Cambridge University Press.

Described and Captioned Media Program. (n.d.a). *Captioning service providers*. Retrieved from http://www.dcmp.org/ai/10/

Described and Captioned Media Program. (n.d.b). *Description service providers*. Retrieved from http://www.dcmp.org/ai/179/

Disabilities, Opportunities, Internetworking and Technology (DO-IT). (n.d.a.) *Disabilities, Opportunities, Internetworking and Technology*. Seattle: University of Washington. Retrieved from http://www.washington.edu/doit

DO-IT. (n.d.b) *DO-IT videos*. Seattle: University of Washington. Retrieved from http://www.washington.edu/doit/video

Harrenstien, K. (2009). *Automatic captions in YouTube*. Retrieved from http://googleblog.blogspot.com/2009/11/automatic-captions-in-youtube.html

Kendrick, D. (2013). Series: The work of the Smith-Kettlewell Institute: Part II: The Video Description Research and Development Center. *AFB AccessWorld Magazine*. Retrieved from http://www.afb.org/afbpress/Pub.asp?DocID=aw140607

Kobayashi, M., O'Connell, T., Gould, B., Takagi, H., & Asakawa, C. (2000). Are synthesized video descriptions acceptable? In *Assets '00: Proceedings of the fourth international ACM Conference on Assistive technologies* (pp. 172–179). New York: ACM.

Lembree, D. (2014). *Introducing an accessible HTML5 media player*. Retrieved from https://www.paypal-engineering.com/2014/09/05/introducing-an-accessible-html5-video-player/

Mitchell, R., Young, T., Bachleda, B., & Karchmer, M. (2005). *How many people use ASL in the United States? Why estimates need updating*. Retrieved from http://research.gallaudet.edu/Publications/ASL_Users.pdf

Nomensa. (n.d.). *Nomensa Accessible Media Player*. Retrieved from https://github.com/nomensa/Accessible-Media-Player

Rogers, M. (2012). *Government accessibility standards and WCAG 2.0*. Retrieved from http://blog.powermapper.com/blog/post/Government-Accessibility-Standards.aspx

WebAIM. (2014). *Screen reader user survey #5 results*. Retrieved from http://webaim.org/projects/screenreadersurvey5

Web Experience Toolkit (n.d.). *Multimedia player – video*. Retrieved from http://wet-boew.github.io/v4.0-ci/demos/multimedia/multimedia-en.html

World Wide Web Consortium. (2014a). *HTML*. Retrieved from http://w3.org/TR/html5

World Wide Web Consortium. (2014b). *WebVTT: The Web video text tracks format*. Retrieved from http://dev.w3.org/html5/webvtt/

World Wide Web Consortium. (2014c). *Media accessibility user requirements: W3C editor's draft 28 May 2014*. Retrieved from http://www.w3.org/WAI/PF/media-a11y-reqs/

YouDescribe. (n.d.). *YouDescribe.org*. Retrieved from http://youdescribe.org/

YouTube. (2014). *Statistics*. Retrieved from https://www.youtube.com/yt/press/statistics.html

This chapter is based on work supported by the National Science Foundation (grant number CNS-1042260). Any opinions, findings, and conclusions or recommendations are those of the author and do not necessarily reflect the policy or views of the federal government, and you should not assume its endorsement.

18

Blending Universal Design, E-Learning, and Information and Communication Technologies

Roberta Thomson
Catherine S. Fichten
Alice Havel
Jillian Budd
Jennison Asuncion

The authors of this chapter examine how to blend universal design (UD) with e-learning tools used by postsecondary faculty and with information and communication technologies (ICTs) used by students in traditional classroom, hybrid, and online courses. The focus is on how instructors can design and deliver their courses in an accessible way using e-learning.

E-learning is in a state of constant flux and is partly dependent on developments in different disciplines. Here we define *e-learning* as instruction that involves technology, online course delivery systems, digital communication, and educational paradigms used by higher education faculty (Sangrà, Vlachopoulos, & Cabrera, 2012). This includes information and communication technologies and the learning management systems (LMSs) that are used to support instruction in traditional, hybrid, and completely online courses, including massive open online courses (MOOCs). In this chapter, we examine how ICTs are used by students in these courses to facilitate their learning.

E-learning and ICTs hold the potential for greater access to higher education than ever before. However, just because a course is digital does not ensure that it is usable by everyone or that it is accessible to all (Berkowitz, 2008). It is our premise that the application of UD principles can promote increased access by focusing on how students learn and how instructors teach using e-learning tools and ICTs. At the core of

FIGURE 18.1   Learner variability, course components, and accessible e-learning tools result in blending UD, e-learning, and ICTs. This results in accessible learning environments.

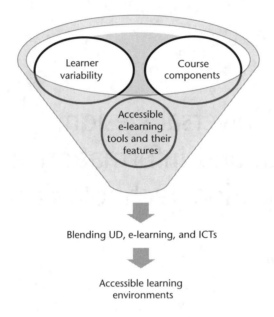

Blending UD, e-learning, and ICTs

Accessible learning environments

this notion is the combination of three key components described below and illustrated in Figure 18.1:

- The diversity of students in a course—for example, their learning preferences, abilities, processing speeds, cultural backgrounds, and prior knowledge.
- The course components—for example, delivery, content, communication, and evaluation.
- E-learning tools, ICTs, and their features—for example, LMSs, mobile devices, software, and applications used by both instructors and students.

UNIVERSAL DESIGN PRINCIPLES AND FRAMEWORKS

UD, which originated in architecture, offers a method to design structures that work for everyone because the physical, sensory, and other needs of all potential users are taken into account during the planning stages. One benefit of the UD approach is that it avoids costly retrofits by responding to the diversity of users from the outset (e.g., making curb cuts as the sidewalk is being built rather than after it is completed). Seven principles governing the UD of products and environments were initially proposed by the Center for Universal Design (CUD) (Story, Mueller, & Mace, 1998). These were later adapted to other fields, including education. As discussed in Chapter 2 of this book, several frameworks for the application of UD to instruction have emerged. They include universal design of instruction, universal design for teaching, and universal design for learning. These have a common goal, which is to render learning environments welcoming, accessible, and usable by all students (Burgstahler, 2008).

TABLE 18.1   Universal Design for Learning (UDL) Principles

Principles	Descriptions
Multiple means of representation	Course content is offered in a multitude of formats (e.g., PowerPoint, video, podcast, images).
Multiple means of engagement	Instructors offer multiple pathways to engage students in the course material (e.g., wikis, group chats, online mind mapping).
Multiple means of action and expression	Instructors offer multiple methods of expression/evaluation of students' knowledge of course content (e.g., participation in discussion forum, online multiple-choice quiz, virtual group project).

Adapting the UD approach to higher education is intended to create inclusive learning environments that respond to the diversity of the student population, thus ensuring the accessibility of learning activities, environments, and products. For example, the universal design for learning (UDL) framework extends UD by promoting flexibility in curriculum design through the application of three principles: (1) multiple means of representation, (2) multiple means of engagement, and (3) multiple means of action and expression (Rose & Meyer, 2002). Addressing the diversity and variability of potential students enrolled in a course, UDL provides students with multiple pathways to perceive, engage with, act upon, and express course content (Center for Applied Special Technology [CAST], 2011). Table 18.1 includes the three principles of UDL, along with descriptions of the principles, and examples of their applications in online learning.

The proactive application of UD has the potential to reduce the need for disability-related accommodations and expand access to learning for all students (Fovet & Mole, 2013). However, taking one step in applying a principle of UD does not always lead to full accessibility to all learners. For example, offering students a video as an alternative to text provides multiple means of representation, but will not provide full access for a student who is deaf unless the video is captioned.

ACCESSIBILITY, E-LEARNING, AND ICTS

There are many opportunities for instructors to blend e-learning and ICTs with UD to respond to learner variability. However, in the rush to integrate technology into teaching, instructors and those responsible for designing, supporting, and implementing e-learning often fail to think about the specific accessibility requirements of students with different needs (Bissonnette, 2006). For example, those in charge of supporting and deploying e-learning generally do not confirm ahead of time whether academic software being considered for purchase is compatible with assistive technology (AT) used by students with disabilities. AT includes screen reader technology used by students who are blind or who have learning disabilities that impact their ability to read printed text, and technology used by individuals with limited hand function that fully emulates the keyboard, but not the mouse. To be accessible and usable to these students, all LMS functions need to be accessible via screen reader and through the use of the keyboard alone. Although U.S. laws and court challenges have increased the accessibility of software and hardware sold by vendors of e-learning products (Rowland, 2012), there are still accessibility issues regarding specific types of ICTs used in higher education institutions (U.S. Department of Justice and U.S. Department of Education, 2010; U.S. Department of Education, 2011).

In addition to accessibility problems, there are also barriers due to the high cost of ICTs and to inadequate opportunities to experiment with them before purchasing. Some organizations have addressed this issue. For example, the Adaptech Research Network (n.d.) maintains a database of free or inexpensive hardware and software for both Windows and Macintosh platforms, as well as applications for Apple and Android mobile devices. These tools may support not only students with disabilities, but also the many individuals looking for tools that match their needs and budget.

At least five postsecondary groupings have a stake in promoting UD of e-learning in colleges and universities: the students themselves, professionals who provide disability-related services to the campus community, instructors who use and implement e-learning in their courses, e-learning professionals on campus who provide leadership and select e-learning products for campus-wide use, and the vendors who develop and sell e-learning products to colleges and universities. Because of their different perspectives, these groups are likely to have different views about UD and e-learning accessibility (Fichten et al., 2009).

When choosing e-learning tools and digital course components, instructors need to keep in mind that students use a variety of ICTs to access learning materials. Thus, in reviewing the various elements of e-learning it is important that instructors ensure the following: that the LMS works on multiple platforms (e.g., desktops, laptops, mobile technologies); that lecture presentations are inclusive of students with a variety of skills, preferences, and abilities; that course materials are accessible and usable by the largest number of students possible; that a variety of communication modalities, content representations, engagement methods, and evaluation techniques are made available; and that accessibility to learners with diverse disabilities has been taken into account.

USING UD, E-LEARNING, AND ICTS TO FACILITATE ACCESSIBILITY

Described in this section are accessibility challenges related to e-learning tools and methods, as well as examples of solutions that apply the UDL principles of multiple means of representation, multiple means of engagement, and multiple means of action and expression to on-site, hybrid, and fully online courses including MOOCs.

Web Platforms and Learning Management Systems

Web platforms and LMSs (for example, Blackboard, Moodle, Desire2Learn, VClass, SAKAI) used by higher education institutions offer an assortment of features, which allow instructors to customize their courses. As these platforms have evolved, some of the features offered have enhanced accessibility while others have created barriers (Rangin, 2013). Some accessibility features have even been lost once a provider moves from one version of the product to the next.

There is much that the instructor can do to apply UD principles to a course design within the structure the LMS provides. For example, instead of presenting material in an idiosyncratic manner, which can lead to confusion for students, an instructor can organize the content in clearly identified modules or chunks of learning material that are obviously tied to the course learning objectives. In addition, specific learning objectives should be reflected in the course calendar feature provided in the LMS. Both in-person and virtual office hours can also be noted on the LMS course calendar. Instructors can verify that their material is presented in an organized way by using the "student view" feature available in most LMSs. By doing so, instructors are placing themselves in the students' position and verifying that what they have posted is, indeed, presented in an organized manner from the students' perspective and that a diverse group of students will be able to access the material.

Specific Course Methods and Materials

Some of the many online resources available for directions on implementing specific suggestions made below can be found in the Training and Support section at the end of this chapter.

Syllabus. A student's customary first contact with a course is the syllabus/course outline. A universally designed course syllabus would include a photo or captioned video introducing the instructor, a course tour presented in printed and captioned video formats, a link to instructions on how to use the LMS, a description of the multiple pathways to reach the course objectives, and information on how to arrange for disability-related accommodations. The syllabus should be presented in an accessible format. Guidance for the UD of a syllabus can be found in several of the online resources listed in the Training and Support section at the end of this chapter.

Lectures. When using presentation software, such as PowerPoint, instructors can ensure that their presentations are accessible and usable by all students by considering the amount of content per slide, font size, colors, contrast, and animations. A basic listing from WebAIM (n.d.) includes the following:

- Ensure that font size is sufficient.
- Provide sufficient contrast.
- Do not use color as the only way to convey content.
- Avoid automatic slide transitions and use simple slide transitions when possible. Complex transitions can be distracting.
- Use simple language.
- Check the reading order of text boxes that are not part of the native slide layout. A screen reader usually reads these last.
- If you have embedded video, ensure that the video is captioned, and that the player controls are accessible.
- If you have embedded audio, ensure that a transcript is included.

Instructors often post their PowerPoint presentations or lecture notes online. For instructors concerned about copyright, this can be assigned through a free license provided by Creative Commons (n.d.). When notes are posted online, they should be presented in an accessible, text-based format—not, for example, as scanned PDF documents, as described in the Documents section below. If notes are supplied before an in-class presentation, they should be posted early enough to allow sufficient time before the class session so that students can modify the format to be compatible with their note-taking preferences.

Some universities and colleges provide lecture recordings, including video and audio capture, especially in large classes (Leadbeater, Shuttleworth, Couperthwaite, & Nightingale, 2013). These recordings are typically stored on the university or course website, allowing students to review the lecture at their own preferred time and pace. Providing captions benefits not only students with hearing impairments or auditory processing difficulties, but also English language learners and all students as they learn to spell terminology used in the video.

Textbooks. To access course content, students are often required to read textbooks, book chapters, journal articles, and other academic material. If these are provided only in printed format, the disability services office on campus may be required to convert them into accessible digital text for a student who uses screen reader technology to read aloud digital text. Digital textbooks have become increasingly popular and are being used in addition to traditional textbooks because they provide advantages that include portability among devices, such as laptops, tablets, e-readers, and smartphones (Lepi, 2012). While digital textbooks seem to promote accessibility overall, many academic book publishers use proprietary formats that may, in fact, restrict accessibility (for example, they may not allow the option to select text for reformatting or have the capability to be used with screen readers, or they may use complicated navigation schemes). Before selecting a digital textbook, instructors should ask the vendor to provide specific information about accessibility and usability features.

Documents. All documents that students are expected to read before class should be made available in advance and in accessible formats. To make images on digital documents accessible to students with visual impairments, alternative text, also known as "alt text," can be provided. Alt text is a brief, meaningful description connected with an image. It allows individuals who cannot see the image to obtain the necessary information with screen reading software that can read the alt text. In the same vein, instructors should select videos with captioning or subtitles—or add captions themselves or through a campus unit—and verify that they are, indeed, accurate. If the video is captioned or subtitled in-house or by the professor, there will need to be an internal review of this work for accuracy. In addition, the provision of audio description (which inserts commentary into the video that describes body language, expressions, and movements) ensures full accessibility to students who are blind.

Students are frequently required to read course materials, such as course handouts and journal articles, that have been posted online as a PDF file. Although many journal articles now found online are accessible, many are not, particularly to screen readers used by students who have a visual or print impairment. When a paper document is simply scanned and saved as a PDF file, the text is saved as an image and cannot be selected, copied, or read by screen reading software. The scanned PDF must be rendered accessible through the use of optical character recognition (OCR) software. This process extracts the text from the image and creates an editable, selectable, and accessible document that can also be read by a screen reader. Students can use accessible PDF files in many ways, including highlighting, taking notes, listening to text, searching terms, and looking up definitions. Some instructors have posted PDF files from old photocopies of book chapters and journal articles that have been annotated or highlighted. These files are very difficult to render accessible and should be avoided whenever possible. Some of these documents can be found online and can be downloaded to use instead of the older, illegible documents.

Communication. Students can engage with course content by communicating with their professors and their peers, both with individuals as well as with the whole class, through online synchronous or asynchronous communication built into the LMS (Giesbers, Rienties, Tempelaar, & Gijselaers, 2014). Online communication options are used in e-learning courses, but they are also useful to students who are unable to attend class or be on campus due to mobility issues, illness, or inclement weather. There are also students who are better able to communicate with others through technology than in person. These individuals may include students with speech and hearing impairments, with anxiety disorders, who are on the autism spectrum, or who are second language learners.

Asynchronous communication, such as e-mail and Internet forums, can be used in courses to facilitate online discussions where individuals can post content and then reply to one another. Providing asynchronous communication methods ensures that all students have the opportunity to communicate with one another at a convenient time and at their own pace, allowing for self-review of content and grammar. If a discussion board provided within an LMS is not accessible to a specific student, perhaps because they are blind and using screen reader software, an accessible alternative such as e-mail should be used.

Synchronous communication, which occurs in real time (for example, chat rooms and instant messaging), presents more accessibility and usability challenges than asynchronous options. There are potential barriers for second language learners, beginner typists, students using specific types of AT that do not allow input at a high speed, and students with spelling difficulties who may be uncomfortable with rapidly written communication. Providing multiple means of engagement is key. Since Skype and other videoconference programs may not be accessible to and usable by all students, instructors should provide multiple communication options that include e-mail. Another application of tools such as Skype or Adobe Connect is to host guest lecturers; in those cases, accessibility solutions include the creation of a captioned recording of the presentation, using features included in the LMS or external tools. Audience response tools (clickers), surveys, and other synchronous tools are not all universally designed. For example, certain brands of clickers have small screens that are not accessible to students with low vision or to some individuals with mobility impairments. UD requires that engagement alternatives be provided to ensure that everyone can participate.

Evaluation

To ensure that students can optimally demonstrate their learning, multiple evaluation activities should be employed and students should be given options to demonstrate their knowledge. Instructors can conduct evaluations by reviewing written papers, virtual group projects, online tests, blogs, portfolios, mind/concept mapping, discussion forums, hands-on demonstrations, student presentations, and online oral examinations through Skype or similar tools. Course participation can also be measured in multiple ways, including in-class and online discussions.

Providing the option of completing testing online outside of or within the LMS (such as online quizzes) may be beneficial for students who are disadvantaged by a paper format. In the same vein, when completing in-class essay writing, students may benefit from working on a mobile device that can e-mail the essay to the instructor at the end of class. To ensure that exams are accessible to the majority of students, lengthy online exams and speed testing need to be avoided when possible and if academically appropriate. In keeping with UD principles, it is best to design a test so that adequate time is given for all students to complete it. However, because some students may be eligible for extended time on tests, it is important to ensure that extended time can be specified on the LMS on which the exam is delivered or that other options can be employed to ensure that reasonable accommodations are provided. It is also important that all testing options are accessible to those using screen readers and other assistive technology. Providing students with an option to submit their test via e-mail is a possible solution when testing features in the LMS are not accessible.

DESIGNING A NEW COURSE

Based on our experiences as instructors in traditional and online environments, disability service providers, students, and educational technologists, we suggest seven key questions to ask when developing a course where blending UD and e-learning is expected to contribute to increased access and reduction of barriers.

1. Has careful thought been given to the diversity of learners in the course? Are there barriers in any area of the course for learners with different abilities (e.g., artistic, numerical), circumstances (e.g., second language learners), concerns (e.g., finances), and disabilities (e.g., visual impairment)?
2. Has the accessibility of the LMS, including its various components, been considered for all persons, including those with different disabilities (for example, are the calendar, announcements, discussion board, chat, and quizzes accessible; can students easily distinguish new discussion threads; does the announcements tool indicate the number of new announcements posted)?
3. Has consideration been given to the variety of platforms and mobile devices students could be using to interact with the e-learning course and the course material?
4. Are there alternative digital representations of course content that are accessible and usable?

5. Are there options offered for student engagement with the course content and the course objectives through accessible e-learning tools (such as online mind mapping and discussion forums)?

6. Are there alternatives offered to students to demonstrate what they have learned through accessible ICTs or e-learning tools (such as audio, visual, written, and demonstrations)?

7. Has the institution's access technologist been consulted as the e-learning and digital learning modules and activities are designed (to ensure that all aspects of the course structure and components are accessible and usable—for example, how readily and easily can the website be navigated)?

TRAINING AND SUPPORT

It is important to note that many instructors need training on how to use their LMSs, on how students with different access needs use ICTs, and on how to employ UDL in designing course materials and methods. Support can include direct instruction as well as providing links and contact information to personnel who can provide assistance with making IT accessible. The following resources are particularly relevant to the application of UD to e-learning courses.

- AccessDL: http://www.washington.edu/doit/programs/accessdl
- Adaptech Research Network Database of Free and Inexpensive Computer Technologies: http://www.adaptech.org/en/research/fandi
- CAST: http://www.udlcenter.org/aboutudl/udlguidelines
- Center for Universal Design in Education: http://www.washington.edu/doit/programs/center-universal-design-education
- JISC TechDis Inclusion Technology Advice: http://blog.jisctechdis.ac.uk
- Province of Ontario: Making Your Website Accessible: http://www.mcss.gov.on.ca/en/mcss/programs/accessibility/info_sheets/info_comm/website.aspx
- UDL-Universe: UDL Course Changes: http://www.udluniverse.com
- UDL On Campus: Selecting Media and Technology: http://udloncampus.cast.org/page/media_landing#.VK8Rg1Z3E3g
- WebAIM: http://webaim.org/techniques/powerpoint/
- Web Content Accessibility Guidelines: http://www.w3.org/WAI/intro/wcag

CONCLUSION

Considering UD when selecting and using e-learning materials in traditional, hybrid, and online courses can ensure an accessible learning experience for the diversity of students in today's colleges and universities. Collaboration between the wide array of stakeholders is needed to design, implement, and support accessibility and usability. This includes the students, instructors, ICT vendors, institutional IT procurement specialists, and campus disability service providers.

REFERENCES

Adaptech Research Network. (n.d.). *Database of free and inexpensive computer technologies.* Retrieved from http://www.adaptech.org/en/research/fandi

Berkowitz, D. (2008). *Just because it's digital doesn't mean it's accessible.* Retrieved from http://net. educause.edu/ir/library/pdf/NCP08082.pdf

Bissonnette, L. A. (2006). *Teaching and learning at Concordia University: Meeting the evolving education needs of faculty in providing access for university students with disabilities* (Doctoral dissertation). Retrieved from ProQuest Dissertations & Theses. (UMI No. NR16269).

Burgstahler, S. E. (2008). Universal design of instruction: From principles to practice. In S. E. Burgstahler, & R. C. Cory (Eds.), *Universal design in higher education: From principles to practice* (pp. 23–43). Cambridge, MA: Harvard Education Press.

Center for Applied Special Technology (CAST). (2011, February 1). *Universal design for learning guidelines full-text representation version 2.0.* Retrieved from http://www.udlcenter.org/aboutudl/udlguidelines

CAST. (n.d.). *UDL OnCampus: UDL syllabus.* Retrieved from http://udloncampus.cast.org/page/planning_syllabus

Creative Commons. (n.d.). *Creative commons.* Retrieved from http://creativecommons.org/

Fichten, C. S., Ferraro, V., Asuncion, J. V., Chwojka, C., Barile, M., Nguyen, M. N., Wolforth, J. (2009). Disabilities and e-learning problems and solutions: An exploratory study. *Educational Technology and Society, 12*(4), 241–256.

Fovet, F., & Mole, H. (2013). UDL—From disabilities office to mainstream class: How the tools of a minority address the aspirations of the student body at large. *Collected Essays on Learning and Teaching, 6,* 121–126.

Giesbers, B., Rienties, B., Tempelaar, D., & Gijselaers, W. (2014). A dynamic analysis of the interplay between asynchronous and synchronous communication in online learning: The impact of motivation. *Journal of Computer Assisted Learning, 30,* 30–50. doi:10.1111/jcal.12020

Leadbeater, W., Shuttleworth, T., Couperthwaite, J., & Nightingale, K. P. (2013). Evaluating the use and impact of lecture recording in undergraduates: Evidence for distinct approaches by different groups of students. *Computers & Education, 61,* 185–192. doi:10.1016/j.compedu.2012.09.011

Lepi, K. (2012). *11 real ways technology is affecting education right now.* Retrieved from http://www.edudemic.com/new-study-finds-11-real-ways-technology-is-affecting-education-right-now/

Rangin, H. (2013, March). *A comparison of learning management system accessibility.* Paper presented at the 28th Annual International Technology and Persons with Disabilities Conference, San Diego, CA.

Rose, D. H., & Meyer, A. (2002). *Teaching every student in the digital Age: Universal design for learning.* Alexandria, VA: Association for Supervision and Curriculum Development.

Rowland, C. (2012, November 19). Review of recent legal issues in higher education and web accessibility [Blog post]. Retrieved from http://ncdae.org/blog/recent-legal-issues/

Sangrà, A., Vlachopoulos, D., & Cabrera, N. (2012). Building an inclusive definition of e-learning: An approach to the conceptual framework. *The International Review of Research in Open and Distance Learning, 13*(2). Retrieved from http://www.irrodl.org/index.php/irrodl/index

Story, M. F., Mueller, J. L., & Mace, R. L. (1998). *The universal design file: Designing for people of all ages and abilities.* Raleigh: North Carolina State University, The Center for Universal Design.

UDL Universe. (n.d.). *Ensuring access through collaboration and technology (EnACT).* Retrieved from http://www.udluniverse.com

U.S. Department of Education. (2011). Electronic book reader Dear Colleague letter: Questions and answers about the law, the technology, and the population affected. Office for Civil Rights. Retrieved from http://www2.ed.gov/about/offices/list/ocr/docs/504-qa-20100629.html

U.S. Department of Justice and U.S. Department of Education. (2010, June 29). Joint "Dear Colleague": Electronic book readers. Retrieved from http://www2.ed.gov/about/offices/list/ocr/letters/colleague-20100629.html

WebAIM. (n.d.). *Center for persons with disabilities.* Retrieved from http://webaim.org/techniques/powerpoint/

PART 5

Promotion and Institutionalization of Universal Design

In Part 5, Sheryl Burgstahler provides an overview and then other chapter authors share strategies for institutionalizing universal design in all campus policies and procedures. The result is an institution with instruction, services, physical spaces, and technology that is welcoming to, accessible to, and usable by everyone.

Universal Design in Higher Education

Instruction	Services	Information Technology	Physical Spaces
Class climate	Planning, policies, & evaluation	Procurement, development policies, & procedures	Planning, policies, & evaluation
Interaction	Physical environments & products	Physical environments & products	Appearance
Physical environments & products	Staff	Staff	Entrances & routes of travel
Delivery methods	Information resources & technology	Input, output, navigation, & manipulation	Fixtures & furniture
Information resources & technology	Events	Compatibility with assistive technology	Information resources & technology
Feedback & Assessment			Safety
Accommodation			Accommodation

Source: S. Burgstahler (2015). *Applications of universal design in education*. Seattle: University of Washington. Retrieved from http://www.washington.edu/doit/applications-universal-design-education

19

Promoters and Inhibitors of Universal Design in Higher Education

Sheryl E. Burgstahler

Earlier chapters in this book have provided strategies for the implementation of universal design in higher education (UDHE). This chapter touches on factors that can promote and inhibit the widespread practice of UDHE. Roles that government, industry, educational entities, professional organizations, researchers, and consumers might play in the promotion of UDHE are suggested.

What would it take to make universal design in higher education as commonplace on campuses as recycling is in Seattle? Most people would know what UDHE is, accept it as the right thing to do, and make an effort to achieve it. Because of a shared belief, people would encourage one another toward the goal and, together, many small efforts would make a difference. The authors of this book make a compelling case that a more inclusive campus can result when UDHE is routinely applied to instruction, information technology, physical spaces, and student services. Despite the promise of universal design (UD), however, this paradigm has not yet been widely embraced by colleges and universities.

PROMOTERS AND INHIBITORS

It is relatively easy to sell the general idea of UD; the bigger challenge is to put UD principles into practice. The following paragraphs touch on a few of the many factors that can serve to promote or inhibit the widespread application of UDHE: vision, change, championship, legislation and litigation, awareness, attitudes, diversity efforts, equity, time and cost, research, and market forces.

Vision

Lack of a shared vision, or the presence of a shared vision that promotes a medical model of disability with a resulting accommodations-only approach to access, can interfere with the implementation of UDHE. A shared vision that embraces the social model of disability and values diversity, equity, and inclusion can promote it. With this shared vision, all stakeholders would celebrate all types of diversity and take steps to ensure that all campus products and environments are "usable by all people, to the greatest extent possible, without the need for adaptation or specialized design" (CUD, 2008). Thus, individuals with diverse characteristics would experience the campus fully through the same venues, with the need for accommodations at a minimum.

A team of disability service professionals and faculty from more than twenty states nationwide explored the characteristics of campuses that might achieve this ideal state. These leaders were part of a UDHE initiative of the Disabilities, Opportunities, Internetworking, and Technology (DO-IT) Center at the University of Washington that was funded by three grants from the Office of Postsecondary Education of the U.S. Department of Education. Team members engaged in an iterative process to develop a list of Campus Accessibility Indicators that describe the characteristics of an institution that fully includes individuals with disabilities (DO-IT, 2015). These indicators can help administrators identify key issues to address as they develop a more inclusive campus and provide a starting point for campus-wide conversations. Although these indicators focus on individuals with disabilities, they can be modified slightly to ensure, in the spirit of UD, that individuals with a wide variety of characteristics are fully included (DO-IT, 2015, p. 2). The Campus Accessibility Indicators include:

- University conversations
  - The university-level mission statement is inclusive of people with disabilities.
  - Disability is included in discussions of diversity and special populations on campus.
- Administrative empowerment
  - Policies, procedures, and practices are regularly reviewed for barrier removal and inclusivity.
  - Administrators, staff, faculty, and student leaders are trained, encouraged, and empowered to take action around disability and universal design issues.
  - People with disabilities are visible (even if their disabilities are not) on campus, including in positions of power and authority.
- Infusion of universal design in all campus offerings
  - Budgeting reflects the reality of the cost of universal design and of accommodating current and prospective employees, students, and visitors with disabilities.
  - Measures of student success are the same for all student populations; institutional research includes this data.
  - Campus marketing, publications, and public relations are accessible and include disability representation.
  - Campus websites, including online courses, meet established accessibility and usability standards.

- Relevant disability issues are addressed in curricula.
- All campus facilities are physically accessible and universally designed.

Change

Infusing UD throughout a campus may require a paradigm shift from the accommodation model to a more inclusive one. An inhibitor to the acceptance of UD is adherence to "the way we have always done things" (e.g., reactively provide accommodations for students with disabilities rather than employ proactive measures).

Levy and Merry (1986) suggested that aspects of a proposed change include (1) the reason(s) for change, (2) the content of change, and (3) the process of change. For a reason to embrace UD, a campus can look both externally (e.g., legislative mandates) and internally (e.g., to meet the needs of an increasingly diverse student body). As far as the content of change, campus leaders can present UD as an approach for addressing the needs of students with diverse characteristics and a complement to the accommodations already provided for individual students with disabilities. The process of change toward the UD paradigm can be incorporated into campus-wide strategic plans and the workflows of campus units and individuals. For example, routine consideration of teaching performance with respect to a diverse student body in faculty evaluations can promote UD.

Adopting the ADKAR (Haitt, 2006) model for promoting and sustaining change can help campus leaders avoid some roadblocks.

- *Awareness of the need to change.* Help stakeholders understand why changes are needed.
- *Desire to participate and support change.* Motivate stakeholders through knowledge, engagement, encouragement, examples, and results.
- *Knowledge of how to change.* Share strategies for implementing UD in specific areas (e.g., to instruction, recreational facilities).
- *Ability to implement the change on a day-to-day basis.* Provide engagement, resources, and professional development to support stakeholders as they create change in their respective areas.
- *Reinforcement to keep the change in place.* Engage with stakeholders to sustain efforts to change.

Through all of these steps it is important to tailor change strategies according to the culture of the institution.

Championship

Championship has been identified as an important predictor of change (Creamer & Creamer, 1986). Champions for UD can come from the disability services unit, but also from all other areas of a campus—such as the faculty, IT services, student services, facilities, and student groups. For example, a teaching and learning center can champion UD as an approach to help faculty address the increasing diversity of their students. UD champions can maximize their impact by banding together as task forces, standing committees, and informal gatherings. These groups can explore ways to increase campus-wide awareness of accessibility issues and implementation of UD.

Legislation and Litigation

When he signed the Americans with Disabilities Act (ADA, The U.S. Equal Employment Opportunity Commission, 2002), President George H. W. Bush said:

> With today's signing of the landmark Americans with Disabilities Act, every man, woman, and child with a disability can now pass through once-closed doors into a bright new era of equality, independence, and freedom.

Campus responses to legislation can promote or inhibit the widespread adoption of UDHE. The practice of UD is inhibited when institutions focus only on meeting minimum mandates for nondiscrimination, such as those that result in "ADA-compliant" physical spaces. UDHE is promoted when institutions look beyond minimal legal mandates and focus instead on the spirit of civil rights legislation as well as broad institutional values and goals related to equity, diversity, and inclusion.

The results of legal challenges can promote change as well. For example, the National Federation of the Blind and students with visual impairments have registered multiple complaints with the U.S. Department of Education's Office of Civil Rights and the Civil Rights Division of the Department of Justice regarding the inaccessibility of technology on campuses. These complaints have resulted in resolutions for compliance that are being used to guide other campuses as they seek to comply with Section 504 of the Rehabilitation Act and the ADA and its 2008 Amendments with respect to the accessibility of websites, applications software, documents, and other information technology (Luna, 2014; University of Washington, n.d.).

Awareness

Many faculty members do not have extensive knowledge about how students learn or about effective teaching practices (Rebora, 2014) or UDHE, and many do not perceive that they need such knowledge. They do not yet understand how accommodations alone cannot ensure a fully inclusive class (Smith & Buchannan, 2012) or program. With increased knowledge, resources, and/or engagement with disability services personnel, these practitioners could become promoters of UDHE. Awareness of practices at other institutions can also promote the application of UD at an institution interested in keeping pace with the practices of its peers. One promising practice to increase awareness of UD among students is for faculty members to look for ways to include accessibility- and disability-related content in their courses. For example, an engineering professor could require that students employ UD in their design projects, ensuring that products created are accessible to and usable by a diverse audience (Bigelow, 2012; Chang, Tremblay, & Dunbar, 2000; Erlanson, Enderle, & Winters, 2007).

Attitudes

Discriminatory attitudes can create barriers to higher education. For example, Hehir (2002) describes *ableism* as a devaluation of disability that

> results in societal attitudes that uncritically assert that it is better for a child to walk than roll, speak than sign, read print than read braille, spell independently than use a spell-check, and hang out with nondisabled kids, as opposed to other disabled kids. (Hehir, 2002, p. 3)

Such attitudes perpetuate inequality and inhibit the acceptance of UDHE as a way to support social integration. The attitude of some faculty and staff that students with disabilities are an extra burden also inhibits the adoption of UD, as does a "survival of the fittest" attitude about students in general. Attitudes are often reflected in the language people use. Inhibitors to the adoption of UDHE can be the use of terms that marginalize groups of people (e.g., labeling people as "inspiring" or "special" just because they have disabilities) or that label some aspect of the disability experience as negative (e.g., saying someone "suffers" from a disability or is "confined" to a wheelchair—which is an odd expression since people actually gain mobility because of this empowering technology). Wording that promotes the UD paradigm focuses on function, and even then only if it is relevant to the conversation. Hopefully, as more students with diverse characteristics succeed in academic programs and careers, negative attitudes about specific groups of students will change for the better. (See Figure 19.1.)

FIGURE 19.1 Working with a student with a disability can make faculty more comfortable working with other students with disabilities.

Diversity Efforts

Although significant efforts have been made toward better serving a diverse student body at many institutions, too often disability is not included in how a campus defines *diversity*. Diversity efforts of many postsecondary institutions focus only on gender, race, and ethnic issues. Institutions with such a narrow vision of diversity are unlikely to embrace UDHE. On the other hand, institutions that have expanded their definition of diversity to encompass such characteristics as sexual orientation, religion, age, socioeconomic status, nationality, and disability are

FIGURE 19.2 When students with diverse characteristics work together they learn to advocate for one another.

fertile ground for the promotion of the UD paradigm. Working toward the full participation of members of all of these groups in the campus environment can be achieved in part through the adoption of UD practices. For example, including students with a wide range of disabilities in focus groups and on design committees related to new construction, renovation, and program development is one strategy for promoting the adoption of UD (Burgstahler & Moore, 2009; Staeger-Wilson & Sampson, 2012).

Positioning UD as an approach that upholds the principles of nondiscrimination and equal opportunity may promote its application. Helping stakeholders develop "cultural competence"—which refers to an ability to interact effectively with people of different cultural, socioeconomic, and other backgrounds—can lead to discussions of disability and the application of UD. (See Figure 19.2.)

Equity

A promoter of UDHE is stakeholder recognition that the experience of a person receiving an accommodation is not always equivalent to that of other individuals. For example, students who require course materials in electronic formats so that they can use screen reader software to read the text aloud may have access to the course content at a later time than other students, unless the faculty member takes steps proactively to universally design course materials. Not recognizing this inequity may hinder the adoption of UD practices in favor of an accommodation-only approach.

Time and Cost

Time and cost are often reported as deterrents to the widespread application of UDHE. Designing products and environments that are not fully accessible may be easier and less expensive initially, but result in greater expense and effort for the institution further down the road. For example, designing the institution's online registration system to be fully accessible to individuals using assistive technologies may ultimately cost less and minimize legal challenges than providing accommodations to every student for whom the online system is inaccessible.

Until UD is routinely applied, extra time and resources may have to be expended to redesign inaccessible products and environments and to train and support staff in the practice of UD. However, setting incremental goals can address these barriers to change. For example, administrators of a distance learning program may employ UD practices each time a new course is developed or an existing course is updated. A sensible practice of addressing potential design barriers incrementally rather than all at one time serves to spread out costs over time.

Research

Much has been said in this book about the lack of research supporting the effectiveness of UD strategies and the need for interdisciplinary efforts in this regard. An inhibitor to the adoption of UD is research that does not address the needs and experiences of individuals with diverse characteristics. A potential promoter of UD is traditional educational research that analyzes specific outcomes for students with disabilities and other subgroups. Design-based research methods should also be explored; in this approach experimentation is done in real-life settings, the design is refined through an iterative process, and the experiences of students with a wide variety of characteristics, including disabilities, can be analyzed (Collins, Joseph, & Bielaczyc, 2004). There is a need for research to "clarify the benefit of tools and strategies that serve as scaffolds (temporarily needed and discarded) [versus] tools that augment performance (always needed for acceptable performance)" (Edyburn, 2010, p. 39). Researchers should ensure that the voices of multiple stakeholder groups are represented in studies. For example, in researching the effectiveness of an online learning course, researchers should be sure to gain perspectives from students who dropped out of the course in addition to those who completed it. Care should be taken to ensure that the opinion of one student with a disability is not assumed to reflect the opinion of the entire group of students with this type of disability. It is also important in UD research to make sure that UD is defined broadly; it is not unusual to find individuals promoting a UD practice that benefits students with learning disabilities, but does not address making the practice accessible to students who are blind, deaf, or have other disabilities.

Market Forces

The large and aging baby boomer population and the veterans of recent conflicts are increasing the demand for and availability of products and environments with built-in accessibility features. Campus administrators with purchasing authority are in a good position to promote UD by making it clear to vendors that accessibility is a consideration as they choose information technology and other products. Conversely, purchasers who do not consider accessible and usable design when making institutional purchases inhibit widespread application of UD.

STAKEHOLDER ROLES FOR PROMOTING UNIVERSAL DESIGN IN HIGHER EDUCATION

Institutionalization of UD practices is a group effort. Industry, institutions of higher education, professional organizations, researchers, consumers, and government can play important roles in promoting the widespread application of UDHE.

Industry

Industry can promote UD in a variety of ways. It can hire a diverse workforce, engage consumers with a wide range of abilities and perspectives in product design and usability testing, make accessibility features readily apparent and promote them in advertising, and train sales representatives and other employees on accessibility and usability issues and universally designed product features as they are developed.

Institutions of Higher Education

To implement UDHE as a paradigm shift requires that people and processes throughout the institution be involved. Institutions can use print, video, and online materials to increase awareness of UD practices. Such efforts can include disseminating UD guidelines customized to specific audiences (e.g., webmasters, administrators, faculty), publishing articles on UD in campus periodicals, and delivering presentations on UDHE. All stakeholders should have access to training that is tailored to their specific application areas. Administrators can promote the adoption of UD practices by redefining the role of the disability services office to include proactively assisting faculty and staff in applying UD in their respective areas of responsibility and providing incentives for stakeholders to participate in UD training. Faculty can also be encouraged to collaborate with staff in the disability services office to design their courses to be more accessible and to voice accessibility concerns to textbook publishers, use accessible technologies, apply UD to their instruction, and teach UD content in their courses (see Figure 19.3). Campus units that offer professional development to faculty and staff can be encouraged to incorporate UD in their regular training options. Administrators can also adopt procurement policies that promote the purchase of universally designed products.

FIGURE 19.3 Faculty can learn to work with students who have a variety of disabilities through professional development in UD.

Professional Organizations

Professional organizations can further UDHE by publishing UD articles in their journals, making their meetings and websites accessible to all potential participants, offering presentations and exhibits on UD topics at conferences, and encouraging members to adopt UD practices. Professional organizations can also promote consideration of the needs of students and staff with diverse characteristics in the evaluation of educational entities, such as in assessments of university quality.

Researchers

Efforts to get UD on the research agendas of disciplines such as technical communications, information sciences, education, and usability can promote its adoption in higher education. Researchers can examine the impact, efficacy, and cost of UDHE. There is also a need to further develop and validate guidelines and checklists to measure levels of application of UDHE to specific products and environments and to share best practices. Dissemination of research results can be tailored to specific audiences to encourage effective applications of UD. Industry and consumers can participate in the research agenda with the goal of creating more economically viable products and environments that employ UD.

Consumers

Consumers of higher education offerings can affect the adoption of UDHE through advocacy groups and individual input to various campus units. People with disabilities tend to advocate only for specific accommodations when they need them. A student UD advocate could take the next step of providing suggestions to the institution that would eliminate the need for an accommodation in the future. For example, a student who cannot access the content of a video on a website because it is not captioned might need to use a sign language interpreter to meet an immediate access need, but she could also advocate for captions on videos campus-wide. Individuals with disabilities can further the adoption of UDHE by learning about access issues and solutions for their peers with different types of disabilities, such has been done in the DO-IT Scholars program since 1993 (DO-IT, n.d.b). This would help increase awareness and promote advocacy that goes beyond the specific needs of individuals with disabilities similar to their own. Similar efforts can make a more welcoming and usable campus for racial and ethnic minorities and other underrepresented groups.

Government

To promote UDHE, government agencies can fund research and research-to-practice projects to apply UD to specific applications, disseminate information about UD, develop and enforce legislation and standards, and use accessible products and processes in their own agencies. Government could provide tax breaks to encourage companies to develop universally designed products and make accessible products more affordable. One federal effort to promote UDHE provided funding through the Office of Postsecondary Education of the U.S. Department of Education to support successful postsecondary outcomes for students with disabilities, primarily through the professional development of faculty and administrators. One project in DO-IT's UDHE initiative supported the creation of the Center for Universal Design in Education (DO-IT, n.d.a), which shares resources regarding the applications of UD to instruction, services, technology, and physical spaces.

CONCLUSION

There is no magic formula for applying UDHE across campus. Clearly, much work needs to be done before the application of UD is as widespread in higher education as recycling is in the Northwest. However, the UDHE practices discussed in this book present models that others can adopt. For many, the only motivation needed for making UDHE efforts is the ultimate goal: to create an institution that is welcoming to, accessible to, and usable by all faculty, staff, students, and visitors.

The authors of the remaining chapters in this part of the book share specific strategies for infusing UD throughout postsecondary campuses. In Chapter 20, Kimberly Bigelow explains how UD principles can be incorporated into an engineering course. In Chapter 21, Susan Yager discusses how faculty development can be used to promote UD. Sally Scott and Joan McGuire in Chapter 22 describe how a case study approach can promote UD. In Chapter 23, Donald Finn, Elizabeth Evans Getzel, Susan Asselin, and Virginia Reilly discuss how collaborations across campus can promote UD. Finally, in Chapter 24, Tara Buchannan and Rachel Smith share a case study in partnerships that promoted UDHE.

REFERENCES

Americans with Disabilities Act of 1990. 42 U.S.C.A. § 12101 *et seq.*

Americans with Disabilities Act Amendments Act of 2008. 42 U.S.C.A. § 12101 note (2011)

Bigelow, K. E. (2012). Designing for success: Developing engineers who consider universal design principles. *Journal of Postsecondary Education and Disability, 25*(3), 212–231.

Burgstahler, S., & Moore, E. (2009). Making student services welcoming and accessible through accommodations and universal design. *Journal of Postsecondary Education and Disabilities, 21*(3), 155–174.

Center for Universal Design (CUD). (2008). *About universal design (UD)*. Raleigh: North Carolina State University. Retrieved from http://www.ncsu.edu/ncsu/design/cud/about_ud/about_ud.htm

Chang, B. V., Tremblay, K. R., & Dunbar, B. H. (2000). An experiential approach to teaching universal design. *Education, 121*(1), 153–158.

Collins, A., Joseph, D., & Bielaczyc, K. (2004). Design research: Theoretical and methodological issues. *Journal of the Learning Sciences, 13*(1), 15–42.

Creamer, D. G., & Creamer, E. G. (1986). Applying a model of planned change to program innovation in student affairs. *Journal of College Student Personnel, 27*, 19–26.

Disabilities, Opportunities, Internetworking, and Technology (DO-IT). (2015). *Self-examination: How accessible is your campus?* Seattle: University of Washington. Retrieved from http://www.washington.edu/doit/self-examination-how-accessible-your-campus

DO-IT. (n.d.a). *The Center for Universal Design in Education (CUDE)*. Seattle: University of Washington. Retrieved from http://www.washington.edu/doit/programs/center-universal-design-education/overview

DO-IT. (n.d.b). *DO-IT Scholars Program*. Retrieved from http://www.washington.edu/doit/programs/do-it-scholars/overview

Edyburn, D. L. (2010). Would you recognize universal design for learning if you saw it? Ten propositions for new directions for the second decade of UDL. *Learning Disability Quarterly, 33*(1), 33–41.

Erlandson, R. E., Enderle, J. D., & Winters, J. M. (2007). Educating engineers in universal and accessible design. In J. M. Winters & M. F. Story (Eds.), *Accessible medical instrumentation: Accessibility and usability considerations* (pp. 101–116). Boca Raton, FL: CRC Press, Taylor & Francis Group.

Haitt, J. (2006). *ADKAR: A model for change in business, government and our community*. Loveland, CO: Prosci.

Hehir, T. (2002). Eliminating ableism in education. *Harvard Educational Review, 72*(1), 1–32.

Levy, A., & Merry, U. (1986). *Organizational transformation: Approaches, strategies, theories*. New York: Praeger.

Luna, R. (2014). Accessible technology in student affairs. In M. L. Vance, K. Parks, & N. Lipsitz (Eds.), *Beyond the Americans with Disabilities Act: Inclusive policy and practice for higher education* (pp. 51–67). Washington, DC: NASPA.

Rebora, A. (2014). Learning by universal design. *Education Week*. Retrieved from http://www.edweek.org/tm/articles/2014/06/18/gp_rose_interview.html

Section 504 of the Rehabilitation Act of 1973. 29 U.S.C. § 794.

Smith, R. E., & Buchannan, T. (2012). Community collaboration, use of universal design in the classroom. *Journal of Postsecondary Education and Disability, 25*(3), 271–279.

Staeger-Wilson, K., & Sampson, D. H. (2012). Infusing just design in campus recreation. *Journal of Postsecondary Education and Disability, 25*(3), 247–252. Retrieved from http://files.eric.ed.gov/fulltext/EJ994289.pdf

The U.S. Equal Employment Opportunity Commission. (2002). *Remarks of President George Bush at the signing of the Americans with Disabilities Act*. Retrieved from http://www.eeoc.gov/eeoc/history/35th/videos/ada_signing_text.html

University of Washington. (n.d.). Resolution agreements and lawsuits. Retrieved from http://www.washington.edu/accessibility/requirements/accessibility-cases-and-settlement-agreements/

This chapter is based on work supported by the U.S. Department of Education Office of Postsecondary Education (grant number P333A050064) and the National Science Foundation (grant numbers CNS-1042260, EEC-1444961, and HRD-0833504). Any opinions, findings, and conclusions or recommendations are those of the author and do not necessarily reflect the policy or views of the federal government, and you should not assume its endorsement.

20

Raising Awareness of Universal Design in the Engineering Curriculum
Strategies and Reflections

Kimberly E. Bigelow

In this chapter the author reflects on the importance of integrating universal design (UD) considerations into the engineering design curriculum. She considers strategies that engineering educators can use to help engineering students develop an awareness of UD that can be applied to design decisions and ultimate products, processes, and services.

As an engineering educator I teach students each day who are eager to learn how to design. These students will go on to work on the designs of everything from components of airplane engines to automotive seats to surgical instruments. In some cases the human-centered nature of engineering will be apparent—for example, when designing an assistive device for an individual with a disability. However, in many cases, a focus on human-centered design is absent or limited to the consideration of only a small percentage of potential users. An opportunity therefore exists to better educate our students, who will go on to design all sorts of products, processes, and services, about the need to practice design with a fundamental consideration for all of those individuals who may use, maintain, repair, or otherwise interact with what has been developed. Thus, universal design has an important place in the engineering curriculum. Yet, to date, the inclusion of UD in engineering design curricula has been predominantly absent. In this chapter I seek to describe this need and opportunity in more detail, describe ways that UD has been implemented in engineering design courses at the University of Dayton, and reflect on how we can continue to raise awareness nationwide moving forward. A full paper describing some of this work has been published in the *Journal of Postsecondary Education and Disability* (Bigelow, 2012).

A PLACE FOR UD IN ENGINEERING DESIGN

It is important to clarify that *engineering design* refers to the process by which engineers design, not just the ultimate output that is generated ("the design" itself). This process serves as the foundation of all engineering design activity, one of the predominant tasks of the engineering profession. Though the specific steps of the process sometimes take on different names and there may be some subtle differences in convention, the overall engineering design process is consistently applied by engineers and taught similarly in engineering courses across the nation. At most academic institutions, students get their richest experience in engineering design in a project-based senior design capstone course, spending a semester or more working with a team to solve a real-world problem. Similar courses, termed "cornerstone" design classes, have also begun to appear at the first-year level so that the engineering design process is learned and practiced from day one.

The engineering design process is initiated when a problem is presented that must be solved. In the real world, this problem is generally ill-defined and open-ended. In recent years, academic institutions have begun to adopt strategies to try to mimic this open-ended nature in their courses so that students can develop the important and critical skill of learning how to define, and subsequently refine, the problem. These problems are generally presented to the design team by the "client," an individual or small group of key stakeholders who are invested in seeing their problem solved. For example, an executive from a shoe company might approach a design team because there are too many customer complaints related to a certain shoe type and the company wants to design a solution. Prior to trying to solve the problem, during the *problem definition phase*, the design team must understand all aspects related to the problem: Who are the customers? What don't they like? How are they using the product? Are all the users dissatisfied, or only a select group of them? What characteristics about that subgroup—the dissatisfied—prevent the design from meeting their needs in the way that it does for others? Have some users come up with their own one-off solutions to make the product work ad hoc for them? Is there something on the market that works better? Should the solution be a low-cost add-on to the product or a total replacement? The list goes on and on, and it is up to the design team to do due diligence and walk through this entire process. A team who does this best will seek to understand multiple facets of the problem: they will conduct interviews and focus groups, do field observations, try to experience the problem firsthand, look through product catalogs, and read customer feedback reviews. They will try to sort through the angles and opportunities, seeking to identify which opportunity will result in creating the most valuable and useful solution. They will also consider possible new markets and groups of people who weren't immediately targeted for the design but might benefit if features were changed in some way. This entire introductory process provides an ideal opportunity to move students toward a broader awareness and appreciation of the human-centered nature of engineering.

The problem definition phase of the engineering design process is also perhaps the single most important step to ensure a successful and useful end product. This is largely because the problem definition efforts culminate in the establishment of functional requirements and constraints that will guide the design. These criteria, which are developed from the design team's efforts to better understand the problem, as well as their own values, become the standard by which all design ideas are evaluated.

This phase of the engineering design process presents a significant opportunity to ensure that the design of products and processes is more universal through the application of universal design. UD is defined by the Center on Universal Design (2008) as "the design of products and environments to be usable by all people, to the greatest extent possible, without the need for adaptation or specialized design." Covering UD topics in engineering courses may result in increasing the numbers of future engineers with the habit of considering UD during the problem definition phase of projects in the field. A heightened awareness of UD may lead designers to ensure that perspectives and opinions of a diverse user group are obtained and to consider alternative users and possible markets beyond the traditional scope. Most significantly, though, if engineers truly view UD as important, that should be conveyed through their inclusion of guiding UD principles in their design criteria. These principles—which include equitable use, flexibility in use, simple and intuitive use, perceptible information, tolerance for error, low physical effort, and size and space for approach and use—are arguably considerations that would make any design better (Story, Mueller, & Mace, 1998; The Center for Universal Design at North Carolina State University, 1997; Zeff, 2007). And, after all, it is the role of the engineer to strive to develop the best and most useful solutions.

Despite the opportunity and potential benefits of better incorporating UD topics into the engineering design curriculum, the topic remains largely absent in engineering courses. One reason may be that many engineering practitioners have not been educated in the topics of UD in the way that many architects, industrial designers, and student learning providers have. In fact, much of the UD content I have brought into my engineering courses came from my own multidisciplinary academic preparation, which included coursework outside of engineering, specifically in geriatrics and gerontology classes.

Some building blocks are already in place to begin to promote the development of a UD mind-set in our engineering students. One of these key pieces is the overarching sense of responsibility and ethics in design that is cultivated in engineers throughout their education and career. This ethical responsibility to the welfare of those for whom we are designing products is articulated in everything from our national accreditation criteria to our professional societies' codes of ethics. To date, this has largely come to mean a focus on disaster avoidance and safety, and, in recent years, on sustainability and appropriate technology. Ideally, we envision that engineering programs extend this sense of ethical responsibility to ensure that designs are created in a way that promotes equitable use by all. Another key piece is the education related to understanding and meeting the legal requirements for ensuring accessibility (e.g., the Americans with Disability Act of 1990 [ADA] along with its 2008 Amendments), which some engineering students, especially those who will be involved with the design of public buildings and structures, are well versed in. Though it is important to recognize that meeting accessibility requirements is different from the ideal goal of designing for all through the application of UD principles, it is a start in getting future engineers to think more inclusively in their design process.

There is, therefore, an opportunity to integrate UD into the engineering design curriculum so that it will more often be applied to the design of products, services, and processes that we all use every day. The remainder of this chapter explores some of the ways that we have strived to do this at the University of Dayton, examines the outcomes, and discusses the implications and strategies others can try. It also suggests the role that UD practitioners from any discipline can play in helping in this process.

FOCUSING ON THE PROBLEM PRESENTED: A CASE STUDY

I decided to begin my efforts to increase emphasis on UD by focusing on my first-year engineering design course. This course is a semester-long, project-based learning class focused on applying the engineering design and innovation process to real-world problems. It is the instructor's job to identify an appropriate problem for the class to work on, as well as engage community partners who have a stake in the problem. In teams, students move through the steps of the engineering design process to define the problem, set design criteria, generate multiple design solutions, perform a decision analysis to evaluate their design alternatives against their established criteria, solicit feedback on their proposed design, refine it, prototype it, test it, and document their work and future recommendations.

During my first few semesters teaching the course, I chose problems focused on designing products for individuals with disabilities. In framing these problems, I tried to emphasize opportunities for creating designs that would work well not only for the individuals with disabilities for whom we were designing, but also for their peers without disability who would be interacting with them. For example, the Playground Project tasked students with designing playground equipment that would encourage interaction between children with disabilities and their peers. In reflecting on the choice of problems I was presenting to the class, I came to realize that though the problems were ripe for encouraging the incorporation and integration of UD principles, I was not effectively capitalizing on this. I also realized that though I thought the nature of the problem would lead students to develop this background on their own as they went through the problem definition stage of the process and developed their guiding objectives and constraints, it did not.

As a first step toward resolving these issues, I decided to be more strategic in the problem I chose and the way in which I presented it to the class. In spring 2011, I chose a course project with an explicit emphasis on UD. The university's director for Student Learning Services, a practitioner of UD, served as the project "client." The problem definition that I posed tasked students with addressing aspects of our laboratory-classroom space that were difficult to use and maintain efficiently and effectively, with the goal of making the space more usable and accessible to all potential users by specifically applying UD principles. This specific room space was chosen in part because increasing numbers of students with disabilities were utilizing the room, and the student project served as an opportunity to evaluate and find solutions for any barriers that could prevent these students from fully participating in the engineering design process. As a class, we referred to the project as the "UD Project" to help further emphasize the goal.

Approximately three class periods were devoted to problem definition, none of which included a formalized lecture or lesson on the principles of UD. Rather, through instructor-facilitated class discussion, students were led through the same approach traditionally used for the problem definition process. Asking questions such as "Who uses the room?", "What do we know about these users?", "What do we assume about the abilities required for an effective user-environment interaction?", and "What about the room does not work for you?" helped lead most students toward an initial understanding of issues addressed through UD. After the students had a chance to begin to process and reflect on the various issues of the room, I provided suggestions of specific aspects of the project on which they might want to focus. These suggestions included the ability to meet all users' needs in entering, exiting, and moving about the classroom space; the ability to locate, identify, reach, and use equipment, tools, and building supplies; and the ability for all users to sit and work comfortably and efficiently in the classroom space.

During the next class period, a guest panel came in to help define the problem in additional detail. This panel included the director of Student Learning Services, who gave a brief introduction to UD and shared challenges that can be faced by students with a variety of disabilities. Also on the panel were individuals who spoke about personal experiences working in the room while on crutches, teaching in the room while in a wheelchair, and assisting a custodian who has cerebral palsy. In retrospect, I would have preferred to increase the diversity of this panel to avoid the appearance of focusing on individuals with physical disabilities; however, the panel was helpful in providing guiding information to the class.

In addition to this in-class learning, students were required to find at least three resources of their choosing that helped them better understand the problem. These resources could include websites, news articles, academic journals, personal interviews, field observations, and so on. Emphasis was placed on finding online resources that helped increase knowledge related to UD, for example, by doing web searches using keywords like "universal design." Students were then expected to synthesize this knowledge and use it to develop a refined design focus and subsequent requirements, criteria, and constraints associated with the design, which would guide the project/product evolution.

The UD Project provided an explicit context in which students could learn and apply the guiding principles of UD. To determine its effectiveness at doing so, the outcomes of the project were compared with those of the Playground Project. To compare how these two projects contributed to raising awareness and highlighting the importance of considering principles of UD within the engineering design process, the students' design decision analyses were examined. Decision analysis is the process in which the design team evaluates the best ideas they have generated against the criteria previously established at the conclusion of the problem definition phase. This is done to ensure that the design ultimately chosen for prototyping best meets the requirements and constraints of the project. Each criterion is assigned a weighted importance value—generally a score of 0 through 10, with 10 being most important. In this way the decision analysis conveys what criteria the student teams, based on their understanding of the problem, view as most important, as well as the criteria's perceived respective importance.

To analyze the data, the design decision analysis criteria and their relative weights were compiled separately for each project. The criteria were then reviewed to reveal the common themes that emerged. These themes, chosen based on the goals of getting students to consider UD principles, included: (a) criteria that clearly conveyed a correct understanding and recognition of the importance of UD principles, such as "universal design" and "equality"; (b) criteria that conveyed UD by focusing on accessibility, such as "accessible to many people" and "wheelchair accessible"; (c) criteria that indirectly conveyed UD knowledge through consideration of functions and requirements, such as "movable" and "comfort"; and (d) criteria tangentially related to UD by focusing on safety. The average weight of the criteria within each grouping was calculated so that thematic groupings could be compared.

For the UD Project, the six design teams used a total of fifty-one criteria in their decision analyses. Five of the six student design teams included at least one criterion that clearly and directly conveyed a correct understanding of UD principles. There were nine criteria fitting this category: "universal design," "avoids setting people up for failure," "easy for all to use," "feeling of equality," "versatility," "obvious use," "versatile height," "easy to move by all," and "doesn't inhibit ability to reach storage." Whereas most teams had only one criterion fitting this category, one team seemed to develop a deeper understanding and appreciation of UD principles and included four of these "directly related" criteria into their decision analyses. The average weighted importance of the nine criteria in this category was calculated to be 7.7 ± 1.1 (standard deviation [SD]), with some students using a highest importance score of 9, and others 10.

An additional seven criteria were categorized as considering UD by focusing specifically on accessibility. These criteria were largely, though not exclusively, meant to describe features relating to physical accessibility. The seven criteria had a mean score of 8.3 ± 1.4 (SD), indicating the design teams felt accessibility was generally more important than the more global aspects of UD. The third category included criteria that indirectly reflected an understanding of UD through the selection of certain design features and requirements. Criteria in this category included requirements like "moves up and down," "easy to clean," and "weight." The average importance of these criteria was 6.0 ± 1.8 (SD). The criterion in the last thematic category that tangentially touched on UD was "safety." All six teams included "safety" in their decision analyses, with the average importance weighting of 9.29 ± 0.45 (SD), indicating that safety was perceived as the most important criterion for all designs.

In comparison, not one decision analysis included any criteria directly emphasizing UD principles of designing for all. Accessibility, though, was considered as important by five of the six teams, who included some aspect of it in their decision analyses. Additional criteria focusing specifically on applying knowledge related to disability into their decision analyses also emerged. For example, several teams included "texture" as an important criterion in their playground design, because they had learned through their reading that children with developmental disabilities often benefit from tactile feedback. As with the UD Project, "safety" was ranked as the most important criterion by every team.

The results of the UD Project suggest that the students working on that project were able to learn and appropriately apply fundamental knowledge of UD into their design decisions. This is in contrast to the results of the Playground Project, which suggests that students don't inherently consider UD principles without some prompt. Though the results of the UD Project are promising, several points remain unclear: (1) whether this increased awareness of UD principles will transfer to future projects with a less explicit UD focus, (2) whether increased education on topics of UD would have led to stronger or more sustained connections as viewed by the criteria, and (3) whether a similar outcome could be achieved by emphasizing UD without making it the explicit central topic of the project.

ADDITIONAL STRATEGIES FOR INCREASING UD EDUCATION

Following the completion of the UD Project, I began to address the three issues identified above. Most notably, knowing that an explicit problem focus on UD helped raise awareness, I began to seek more subtle opportunities to work UD into the curriculum in the semesters that followed. This was especially necessary as I initiated a partnership with our regional health-care network, which agreed to sponsor multiple projects that were focused predominantly on designing assistive devices for individuals with neurologic diseases and conditions. I wanted to be sure, even though the choice of the project focus would not be as explicitly related to UD as the UD Project, that I did what I could to avoid having the students consider only disability-related criteria, as they had done with the Playground Project.

I did this by adding in clauses to the problem description that suggested that the design solution be achieved through the use of UD principles. I also included a brief overview of UD and a specific suggestion that students include UD as one of the topics to learn more about for their problem definition research. For the most part this was enough to get students to begin thinking in this direction, though I still felt there was a need for further educational opportunities.

More recently, I developed a specific assignment that sought to better promote the integration of UD principles into the design process through student-led learning. I gave this assignment to one of the classes that was trying to design solutions for individuals with neurological impairment. The assignment first asked students to locate and explore resources related to UD. After establishing this base knowledge, the students were presented with the list of the seven guiding principles of UD and guidelines on applying them as prepared by the Center for Universal Design at North Carolina State University (1997). Upon reviewing the list, the students were tasked with generating three to five specific criteria that would guide their projects in becoming more universally designed, with the hope that some of these would then transfer to serve as criteria for the decision analysis. Students were finally asked to look for examples of good, commercially available, universally designed products and explain how each product exhibited the guiding principles of UD.

A review of the decision analyses of the resulting projects showed that this emphasis led most students to include criteria relating to UD into their decision analysis—however, not to the same degree as was achieved with the earlier UD-specific problem. For example, for the UD Project, many student teams included multiple criteria aligning with the various guiding principles of UD, but for this project many students simply listed "universal design" as an all-encompassing criterion. There was at least one team, though, that did an excellent job researching UD and achieved a much deeper understanding of it, which was well reflected in their decision analysis. This particular team included criteria such as "beneficial for any level of ability," "simplicity," "ease of operational use," "easy to grasp (in shape and comfort)," and "ambidextrous." This result suggests that easy-to-implement UD-focused activities may be influential in developing the UD mind-set we want to ultimately foster in future engineers.

As I increased my efforts to incorporate UD into the curriculum, I was surprised by how easily I found opportunities to educate and encourage the students in this topic. For example, whenever we spoke about objectives and constraints, I found myself providing the class examples that resonated with the goals of UD, such as mentioning "high visual contrast" and "usable with either hand" as constraints. In my current courses, we also talk a lot about the importance of diversity in engineering, especially in the ideation and brainstorming process. I try to highlight this by talking to the class about how this diversity not only provides unique input but also ultimately helps ensure that products are more universally usable. When we talk about diversity, I lead the class in a brainstorming session about what kinds of diverse perspectives might be important to include, regardless of the topic of focus. I make sure to draw on examples that students might not always consider, such as individuals who are pregnant, individuals who are in the 5th and 95th percentiles for height, nonnative English speakers, and individuals with a hearing or visual impairment. This seems to help students begin to appreciate the different perspectives that each of these individuals might bring to design discussion—and ultimately how their needs and desires might differ, and sometimes even conflict. I then encourage each design team to invite these diverse potential users to participate, in person or virtually, in their ideation and brainstorming sessions. This simple opportunity takes what we are already doing in class and expands it and hopefully helps with my goal of instilling a UD mind-set. Anecdotally, I have noticed increased student awareness and comfort in talking about UD this semester; however, we are still too early in the semester to determine whether this will impact their project decision analyses.

Though more work is necessary to determine best practices to maximize learning, for now I would encourage engineering educators to consider opportunities to integrate these types of small but seemingly influential changes into their problem definitions and course assignments. In addition to the types of activities mentioned above, one step that all engineering educators can quickly and easily implement is to word design problem definitions to include a clause such as "by applying UD principles." As design teams are already expected to immerse themselves in resources to better understand the problem, even without additional prompting or education this would cause more students to minimally research "universal design." This may be enough to familiarize students with the guiding principles and incorporate aspects of them into their design criteria. It is also worth noting that, based on my experience, educators assigning projects related to the needs of individuals with disabilities should be careful to promote the distinction between designing for individuals with disabilities exclusively and designing to include individuals with disabilities by maximizing flexibility of use for all. This approach may help students begin to grasp UD as an ultimate goal for all designs.

Many of these approaches are most appropriate for engineering design courses; however, it is also important to consider how to extend these efforts to include a focus on UD throughout the curriculum. As detailed above, there are often simple and subtle opportunities to work UD principles into classroom conversation. To date, this has been done very effectively in the engineering curriculum as related to focusing on the importance of safety. This is largely attributable to the well-known, powerful examples of the need for safety that engineering educators seem to universally draw on, such as the Tacoma Narrows Bridge collapse when teaching statics and the *Challenger* explosion when teaching thermodynamics. Though such powerful examples may not be as obvious or immediately come to mind when focusing on UD, educators can start simply by using the example of curb cuts and asking the class who benefits from them (everyone from travelers in busy cities to individuals pushing strollers, not just wheelchair users). Given time and growth in the area of a UD focus within the engineering curriculum, hopefully there will be many more examples that will come immediately to mind.

CONCLUSION

Although work is needed to continue to grow and expand UD integration into engineering and design classes, it is hoped that the information presented here provides support and motivation to develop engineers who possess a guiding mind-set that values UD, as well as offering some strategies for doing so. Hopefully, as awareness is raised, engineering educators will begin to explore and evaluate best practices to most effectively instill UD principles into engineering curricula and ensure that a UD mind-set stays with their students throughout their future, just as the criteria of safety does now. One way that this can happen is through encouragement, engagement, and interaction of UD practitioners with engineering faculty at the institutional level. The majority of campuses nationwide conduct much of their design work out of a central location (e.g., at the University of Dayton, our Innovation Center, housed in the School of Engineering, oversees all senior design capstone courses). Professionals knowledgeable in UD across a wide range of disciplines are encouraged to reach out and foster relationships with engineering faculty so that change and empowerment can begin.

REFERENCES

Bigelow K. E. (2012). Designing for success: Developing engineers who consider universal design principles. *Journal of Postsecondary Education and Disability, 25*(3), 211–224.

Center for Universal Design (CUD). (1997). *Principles of universal design.* Retrieved from http://www.ncsu.edu/ncsu/design/cud/about_ud/udprinciples.htm

CUD. (2008). *About UD.* Retrieved from http://www.ncsu.edu/ncsu/design/cud/about_ud/about_ud.htm

Story, M. F., Mueller, J. L., & Mace, R. L. (1998). *The universal design file: Designing for people of all ages and abilities.* Raleigh: Center for Universal Design, North Carolina State University.

Zeff, R. (2007). Universal design across the curriculum. *New Directions for Higher Education, 137,* 27–44.

21

Small Victories
Faculty Development and Universal Design

Susan Yager

Many college and university faculty receive "accommodations" in the placement of their classrooms, setting of teaching and office hours, and so on, but they may not think pro-actively about accessible course design and accommodations for students with disabilities. Time constraints and institutional pressures may be factors preventing faculty from imple-menting universal design principles in their teaching. Faculty development centers, as well as teaching and learning centers, can play a significant role in educating faculty on this issue by building faculty awareness, celebrating incremental change, consistently applying principles of both good teaching and universal design, and modeling inclusive practices.

Many faculty members receive accommodations without realizing what they are. For example, I was pregnant with my second child when I requested to move my class from an old building with poor elevator service to a first-floor room in a more mod-ern building. The move was made without question, and in the past twenty years I have never again been assigned a room in that older hall. It was only years later, how-ever, that I learned how closely this courtesy of a new classroom assignment resem-bled the reasonable accommodation process for persons with disabilities. It was easy for me, and it should be an easy process at both the logistical and curricular levels for anyone on campus who has a disability.

At many colleges and universities, permanent faculty are among those most likely to find accommodations easily available, whether that entails a preferred teaching schedule, carefully scheduled committee meetings, hardware or software as part of a startup package, or a classroom accessible by elevator. These preferences can be built into the faculty's daily lives—arranged, that is, by design. In contrast, I am aware anecdotally that students, who often must take specific required courses, have far greater restrictions on their time and mobility. Students with physical or social dis-abilities may need coordination of services and support from staff and faculty who are aware of the necessity for accommodations. However, their need for accommodations can be minimized, and student success optimized, when faculty apply universal design principles in teaching and professional work (Getzel, 2008). One of the functions of faculty development centers is to build faculty awareness of students' diverse needs and to provide ongoing support to instructors to enhance teaching and learning. One major element of this support is to encourage instructors to understand and implement universal design principles to maximize the learning of all students.

Universal design, true to its name, involves the application of broad-based principles of inclusiveness and accessibility at every stage of a process, whether that process is designing a building, creating a transit system, or teaching a course. One impressive example of universal design in architecture is an entrance to the main library at the University of Arizona, Tucson, a campus that prides itself on accessibility. Stairs flank a central ramp, which puts access by foot or by wheel at the heart of the library entrance. That no one is inconvenienced by this design underscores the fact that everyone is welcome in the building. Attractive and accessible buildings include such elements as wide doorways, automated water faucets and towel dispensers in bathrooms, and automatic doors. These elements of universal design are necessary to some, but efficient for all. In the same way, universal design in the classroom emphasizes inclusiveness of learning styles and preferences, as well as awareness of physical and social differences. (By contrast, my pregnancy-related relocation to a different classroom was an accommodation for a specific circumstance.) Universal design contributes to the learning of all students, not just those with a documented need for accommodation. To the extent that universal design is successfully applied, requests for individual accommodations should become less frequent.

CONSTRAINTS ON FACULTY AWARENESS

Three constraints may impede the use of universal design: time, exposure to information about universal design and its principles, and institutional and professional situations. To some extent, knowledge and awareness of students with disabilities may also act as a constraint (Izzo, Murray, & Novak, 2008).

Time, of course, is the universal constraint. Even when faculty acknowledge the need for accommodations, they do not always take steps to meet this need (Lombardi, Murray, & Gerdes, 2011). In an era of increasing demands and diminishing resources, time to reflect is increasingly precious, and schedules are unrelentingly full. Textbooks and supplies are sometimes obtained just before term begins; films and videos may be ordered without being previewed; or older media and technology that are already on campus may be pressed into service. Such haste can result in classroom materials or plans that are incompatible with universal design. Such materials could include, for example, videos without captioning, student-response technology (like classroom "clickers") without large buttons or braille accommodation, or assignments that do not consider the needs of students with physical or social differences. Universal design may seem to be a simple matter of thinking globally, considering diversity in learning materials and experiences, and merely looking ahead, and indeed these are all components of thoughtful course design. However, for harried faculty who are ordering next term's books under this term's pressures, nothing is really simple.

Level of exposure to information is a second element that may prevent faculty from thinking in terms of universal design. It can also be, I believe, a major impediment to instructors' implementing active, student-centered learning. Almost by definition, successful academics thrived, as students, under traditional teaching methods. Thus, insofar as human beings tend not to think beyond the dimensions of their own experiences, faculty will likely use teaching methods that worked well for them, although these methods may not work as well for a variety of students. Without systematic reflection on how their own learning preferences may differ from others', faculty have little impetus to redesign, or consciously universally design, their teaching. As a result, when students do require accommodation, particularly if faculty have little advance notice, a temporary solution must be constructed. Such a quick fix solves the immediate problem but leaves thoughtful redesign of the course for another, perhaps ever-deferred, day.

A greater concern than the constraints of time and experience may be the limitations imposed by the structure of academe, especially the structure of large research universities. At these institutions, a set amount of faculty time is devoted to classroom work and office hours, with much of the remainder devoted to disciplinary research. Students' lives outside the classroom may therefore remain mysterious to busy faculty members. For workers in such large institutions, the divide between the provost's office and that of the dean of students is a sharp one, so faculty often know little about student affairs or other offices that support students. Again, the cause is relative lack of experience: Who would seek out the office of disability resources if it were not necessary? Where research is the primary concern of faculty, teaching sometimes receives less attention, and the university as it exists beyond the provost's purview may receive less still. Certainly, many faculty do interact with student affairs offices, but many others occupy a narrow academic channel, never coming in contact with supporting offices until a classroom accommodation requires it.

THE ROLE OF FACULTY DEVELOPERS

Given these challenges, faculty development centers or centers of teaching and learning can play a significant role in promoting universal design among faculty. These centers can help to build a culture in which universal design is a part of teaching and professional practice rather than accommodations as an emergency add-on or afterthought. Faculty development offices can provide a number of functions and services to help promote universal design and shape institutions that pay attention to the issue. For example, the professionals might

- build partnerships between academic and student support units;
- build faculty awareness at both the grassroots and institutional levels;
- celebrate small successes, applauding progress in thinking about and acting on universal design principles;

- at the same time work for larger, more systemic changes;
- promote the realization that the principles of good teaching and the principles of universal design are congruent; and/or
- practice critical self-awareness so as to model and promote principles of universal design themselves.

Building partnerships is perhaps the simplest of these tasks, although it takes commitment and persistence. At Iowa State University, a research-extensive institution, strong partnerships have been forged between the Office of the Dean of Students, which includes the disability resources office, and the Center for Excellence in Learning and Teaching (CELT), which is part of the Office of the Provost. The staff of these offices work together to publicize disability awareness weeks on campus and to support expert speakers on campus who offer workshops on universal design, and have participated in one another's programming in order to cement and publicize the tie between universal design and good teaching. For example, when students or staff watch a student affairs video on finding campus accommodations, they will see and hear CELT's message, and when CELT organizes its annual orientation for new faculty, information from the Office of the Dean of Students is included. Clear and ongoing communication—via orientation as well as CELT's website, weekly e-mails, and newsletter—is vital to this partnership effort because the population of instructors, teaching assistants, and students continually changes. Because the university has legal obligations to community members who have disabilities, CELT's communication efforts also function as a reminder of the legal, ethical, and professional responsibilities faculty and staff have in common. Perhaps the most important component of building these partnerships—and this may be felt more strongly at a large research university than elsewhere—is to maintain mutual understanding and respect between faculty and professional staff, including Office of the Dean of Students personnel and advisors. CELT's mission statement makes explicit the notion that professional staff and faculty are partners in the teaching effort.

Because CELT exists to forge connections among campus educators, its staff members strive to overcome the isolating effect of self-contained and independent departments and offices. This goal requires working for awareness and for change at both the grassroots and institutional levels. At the grassroots level, for example, CELT staff have worked to make instructors aware of creative and innovative assistive technologies available for students on campus through in-campus networking and via its campus newsletter. Most effective, and an important follow-up, was talking with individual faculty about how the assistive technologies can help meet their students' needs. A film professor whose classes were very long, for example, needed a writing board for a student who uses a wheelchair. It needed to be large enough to cover the arms of the chair and comfortable enough for the student to use for the entire class. Fulfilling this request was a simple matter for assistive technology professionals, but the key element was making the connection, promoting faculty awareness. Faculty development personnel can publicize and promote campus resources but must be ready to forge these connections and to spread the word about both accommodation and universal design. Even simple changes in classrooms—for example, posting the day's goals on a PowerPoint slide—can make a real difference for many students with disabilities (Ouellett, 2004). Faculty developers must let instructors know that help is available and that they are not to blame for needing such assistance or for not having foreseen every pedagogical circumstance.

EFFECTIVE INSTITUTIONAL SUPPORT

Faculty awareness also needs to be built in a top-down or institutional manner, again through some of the communication channels mentioned above. For example, Iowa State has instituted a campus-wide practice regarding course syllabus statements about students with documented disabilities. Each term, a set of sample statements published by the Disability Resources Office is promoted by the Office of the Dean of Students, the Office of the Provost, and CELT, particularly through the orientation for new faculty. Several slightly different statements are offered, varying in formality and tone, from which instructors may choose. The first such statement is probably the most widely used; it reads simply:

> If you have a documented disability and anticipate needing accommodations in this course, please make arrangements to meet with me soon. Please request that a Disability Resources staffer send a SAAR [Student Academic Accommodation Request] form verifying your disability and specifying the accommodation you will need.

Although the development of the syllabus statements had strong institutional support, it was more a matter of institutional ethos than of explicit policy or directive that brought about this change. Reminders, widespread and ongoing communication, and instructor autonomy as to the wording and style of the statement helped to create a new expectation for course syllabi.

Although it may seem like a small matter, this change in culture regarding the course syllabus deserves to be celebrated. Because of this now institution-wide practice, every instructor thinks at least once per course preparation about the needs of students with disabilities. Since each sample statement describes both the student's and the instructor's role in providing necessary accommodations, instructors are reminded of the possibility that a quiet room, an untimed test, a captioned video, or a comfortable lap desk may be necessary for students in the upcoming class. As instructors consider the likelihood that some students will have unusual needs, universal design principles enter into the instructors' conscious course planning, even if it may be years before a student with a particular need enrolls in one of their classes.

In addition to celebrating culture changes such as this, CELT celebrates successes by bringing faculty to conferences to recognize their efforts in promoting universal design and good teaching, and to call the institution's attention to that work. There are both indirect and direct ways to recognize good faculty work in implementing universal design. For example, CELT's annual Teaching Tips workshop features excellent faculty and can provide recognition and praise for teachers who have made strides in this area. Sharing stories on a one-to-one or small-group basis (i.e., "Professor X tried this technique, and it worked well") can both get the word out and provide public approbation for faculty, thereby rewarding efforts toward implementing universal design. More discreetly but still quite effectively, faculty developers who are appointed to teaching award committees or similar bodies can affect how the institution recognizes and rewards such efforts.

WORKING TOWARD SYSTEMIC CHANGE

At the same time, however, faculty developers must continue to work toward larger, systemic improvements. For example, Iowa State spent a year examining various personal-response units, or clickers, used to elicit instant feedback in lectures. As various kinds and features of personal-response systems proliferated, the university considered whether to support a single brand. Faculty developers, with a natural interest in the pedagogical value of these systems, played a significant role in reminding faculty and support staff that not all students would find these easy to use: larger keypads, raised numbers, or audible feedback may sometimes be necessary. In my limited experience, sales demonstrators had not thought about universal design as an issue in creating these systems. This particular technology is becoming obsolescent with the advent of mobile devices and apps, but the principle will remain the same no matter the delivery device: consistent, persistent reminders communicated to technology developers and campus decision makers can keep universal design in everyone's consciousness.

Classroom design is another area in which faculty developers may influence institutional change. When I was new to faculty development, I had an opportunity to participate with faculty, students, and staff on a committee charged with imagining the optimal, if not the ideal, classroom. The imagined room would be wider than it was deep, full of light and air, and attractive. It would have excellent acoustics, good sightlines from every angle, and room enough to let students gather in groups. Equipped with both high- and low-tech equipment, such a classroom would be flexible, accessible, and learner-friendly. We waxed eloquent about the need for aisles by which students could easily reach the seats and faculty could easily reach the students, even in a large lecture hall. Such a committee and its recommendations report may seem like an exercise in futility, but in this case the ideal was at least partially realized. A short time after the committee wrapped up its work, the university set out to replace an aging lecture hall, one with steep steps and a narrow focus on the speaker's lectern, with a new, more student-friendly classroom (Twetten, 2006). Part of the role of the faculty development office was to help bridge the ideal and the possible. Working with such diverse groups as faculty users, planning and maintenance personnel, and the project's architects, CELT staff helped to create a large hall that, while only twelve rows deep, seats more students than the original facility. It contains tiered rows of alternately fixed and turnable chairs, allowing for unprecedented comfort and ease of student interaction in large-format classes. The room is accessible by elevator at three levels, giving mobility-limited students a number of seating options. Generous space between seats and rows as well as two broad aisles allow all students ease of access within the classroom and encourage the instructor to move around. The room's instructional technology is also designed for diverse student needs. For example, the hall is equipped for distance captioning, which allows students with difficulty hearing to read the instructor's spoken words on a computer with only a second's delay.

The faculty development office was not the sole, or even leading, actor in building this redesigned lecture hall. Many units, from academic departments to the instructional technology experts to classroom equipment and furnishings managers, played a role in its construction, and the success of the remodel has led to the building or remodeling of several large-lecture classrooms since then. The faculty development role was one of mindfulness, continually keeping the principles of universal design in the forefront and bearing witness, as it were, to the benefit to all students of a well-designed—a universally designed—teaching space.

If I learned anything about universal design as a faculty developer, it is that universal design *is* good teaching: it helps instructors to think of students as individuals and promotes planning for learners with differing strengths and abilities. Universal design is also a boon to students with strong tendencies or preferences that might impede learning but do not rise to the level of a documented disability. Universal design offers what one might call a diverse approach to diversity, a habit of thought that creates options rather than limitations.

And yet, like the cobbler whose children went shoeless, faculty developers need to look to their own areas of responsibility as well. Do faculty developers themselves adhere to universal design principles? Are workshops and other sessions offered at the same times of day, the same days each week? Are workshops often presented in the same way, or are large-group, small-group, ongoing, online, and one-time events offered? In conversations about teaching and learning, do faculty developers include diverse voices, including untenured faculty, teaching assistants, and students? Faculty developers must practice critical self-awareness in order to model and encourage the use of universal design principles.

CONCLUSION

Faculty developers who persist in efforts to communicate about, encourage, and practice the implementation of universal design can play a significant and central role in making universal design a part of campus cultures nationwide. As colleges and universities seek ways to diversify their campuses for reasons of fairness and justice, as well as for such pragmatic reasons as student recruitment and retention, faculty developers can serve their institutions and their colleagues by maintaining a focus on this campus issue.

REFERENCES

Getzel, E. (2008). Addressing the persistence and retention of students with disabilities in higher education: Incorporating key strategies and supports on campus. *Exceptionality: A Special Education Journal 16*(4), 207–219. doi:10.1080/09362835.2013.865530

Izzo, M. V., Murray, A., & Novak, J. (2008). The faculty perspective on universal design for learning. *Journal of Postsecondary Education and Disability, 21*(2), 60–72.

Lombardi, A. R., Murray, C., & Gerdes, H. (2011). College faculty and inclusive instruction: Self-reported attitudes and actions pertaining to universal design. *Journal of Diversity in Higher Education, 4*(4), 250–261.

Ouellett, M. (2004). Faculty development and universal instructional design. *Equity & Excellence in Education, 37*(2), 135–144.

Twetten, J. (2006). LeBaron Hall auditorium. In D. G. Oblinger (Ed.) *Learning spaces* (Chapter 22). Boulder, CO: Educause. Retrieved from http://www.educause.edu/research-and-publications/books/learning-spaces

22

A Case Study Approach to Promote Practical Application of Universal Design for Instruction

Sally S. Scott
Joan M. McGuire

The confluence of classroom diversity, a changing professoriate, and expectations for collaborative learning environments has provided an environment in higher education that is ripe for examining innovative approaches to working with faculty as they rethink their teaching strategies and methods. This chapter provides an overview of the use of case studies as a strategy to support faculty reflection and application of universal design for instruction. Table 22.1, "The Nine Principles of Universal Design for Instruction," provides faculty with a framework for considering a range of inclusive practices. Case study methodology assists faculty in moving from general principles to guided practice in implementing inclusive teaching strategies.

The first two decades of the twenty-first century are notable for postsecondary education for several reasons. First, the trend toward an increasingly diverse student population continues to grow. In 1995, 72% of undergraduate students were Caucasian, 11% were African American, and 8% were Hispanic. In 2012, 55% were Caucasian, 13% were African American, and 13.6% were Hispanic (Chronicle of Higher Education, 2014). The 2011 undergraduate demographic profile included 42% of enrolled students who were of nontraditional age (i.e., twenty-five years of age and over) and 38% who were attending college part-time (U.S. Department of Education, 2013). The most recent figures show that in 2007–2008, 11% of students indicated they had a disability (in 1978, this figure was 2.3%) (Henderson, 1999; U.S. Department of Education, 2013). Diversity in college classrooms brings an array of experiential backgrounds, learning styles, and learning needs.

Other noteworthy trends include projections about the changing model of college and a shift in philosophy about college teaching. Escalating costs, student demands for more options for taking courses (including online courses), and changing student demographics will challenge colleges to be flexible (Van Der Werf & Sabatier, 2009). Faculty will also need to be more flexible by becoming "less an oracle and more an organizer and guide, someone who adds perspective and context, finds the best articles and research, and sweeps away misconceptions and bad information" (Van Der Werf & Sabatier, p. 5). With this change will come a new cadre of instructors, who will incorporate more information technologies into their instruction at a time when the paradigm of college teaching is changing from providing instruction (the teaching paradigm) to producing learning (the learning paradigm) (Fink, 2013).

Finally, the development of the construct of universal design (UD) and the articulation of its guiding principles underlie the possibility of creating environments and products that are usable by the greatest number of people, without a need to retrofit accommodations to ensure equitable use (Center for Universal Design, 2007). The UD paradigm, from the field of architecture, is now being proposed as a model for implementation in creating accessible and inclusive learning environments. One such adaptation, universal design for instruction (UDI), is specifically targeted for college faculty, with the assumption that faculty are content experts who can refine their pedagogical skills to enhance instructional accessibility (McGuire & Scott, 2006). In keeping with theory development and application, the nine principles of UDI in Table 22.1 (Scott, McGuire, & Shaw, 2001) serve as guidelines for practice in intentionally developing and refining instruction using the UDI paradigm.

With the confluence of classroom diversity, a changing professoriate, and expectations for collaborative learning environments comes the opportunity to examine innovative ways to work with faculty as they rethink their approaches to teaching. Whether through institutional structures, such as centers focused on teaching and learning, or through a more decentralized departmental or individual model, the time is prime for using UDI as a tool of reflection to support faculty endeavors.

The purpose of this chapter is to provide an overview of the use of case studies as a strategy that can be instrumental in supporting faculty reflection on and application of UDI.

CASE STUDIES AND PROFESSIONAL DEVELOPMENT

Case studies are an approach to training and professional development that have a long tradition in the fields of law, business, and medicine. The approach is characterized by the presentation of a compelling story that poses a dilemma that is realistic to participants. Participants identify issues embedded in the case and generate possible solutions or courses of action (Hughes, Herston, & Stein, 2010; Wasserman, 1994). The case study method guides participants through a reflective process that draws on professional knowledge and experience to solve realistic professional problems and complexities (Lynn, 1999). A component of the case study methodology can include teaching notes that "address issues that might be raised, alternative methods for discussion (such as the use of leaderless small groups), ideas about background

TABLE 22.1   The Nine Principles of Universal Design for Instruction

Principle	Definition	Example(s)
Principle 1: Equitable use	Instruction is designed to be useful to and accessible by people with diverse abilities. Provide the same means of use for all students, identical whenever possible, equivalent when not.	Provision of class notes online. Comprehensive notes can be accessed in the same manner by all students, regardless of hearing ability, English proficiency, learning or attention disorders, or note-taking skill level. In an electronic format, students can utilize whatever individual assistive technology is needed to read, hear, or study the class notes.
Principle 2: Flexibility in use	Instruction is designed to accommodate a wide range of individual abilities. Provide choice in methods of use.	Use of varied instructional methods (lecture with a visual outline, group activities, use of stories, or web board–based discussions) to provide different ways of learning and expressing knowledge.
Principle 3: Simple and intuitive	Instruction is designed in a straightforward and predictable manner, regardless of the student's experience, knowledge, language skills, or current concentration level. Eliminate unnecessary complexity.	Provision of a grading rubric that clearly lays out expectations for exam performance, papers, or projects; a syllabus with comprehensive and accurate information; a handbook guiding students through difficult homework assignments.
Principle 4: Perceptible information	Instruction is designed so that necessary information is communicated effectively to the student, regardless of ambient conditions or the student's sensory abilities.	Selection of textbooks, reading material, and other instructional supports in digital format or online so students with diverse needs (e.g., vision, learning, attention, English as a second language) can access materials through traditional hard copy or with the use of various technological supports (e.g., screen reader, text enlarger, online dictionary).
Principle 5: Tolerance for error	Instruction anticipates variation in individual student learning pace and prerequisite skills.	Structuring a long-term course project so that students have the option of turning in individual project components separately for constructive feedback and for integration into the final product; provision of online "practice" exercises that supplement classroom instruction.
Principle 6: Low physical effort	Instruction is designed to minimize nonessential physical effort in order to allow maximum attention to learning. *Note:* This principle does not apply when physical effort is integral to essential requirements of a course.	Allowing students to use a word processor for writing and editing papers or essay exams. This facilitates editing of the document without the additional physical exertion of rewriting portions of text (helpful for students with fine motor or handwriting difficulties or extreme organization weaknesses while providing options for those who are more adept and comfortable composing on the computer).
Principle 7: Size and space for approach and use	Instruction is designed with consideration for appropriate size and space for approach, reach, manipulations, and use regardless of a student's body size, posture, mobility, and communication needs.	In small class settings, use of a circular seating arrangement to allow students to see and face speakers during discussion (important for students with attention deficit disorders or who are deaf or hard of hearing).

(continued on next page)

TABLE 22.1 (continued) The Nine Principles of Universal Design for Instruction

Principle	Definition	Example(s)
Principle 8: A community of learners	The instructional environment promotes interaction and communication among students and between students and faculty.	Fostering communication among students in and out of class by structuring study groups, discussion groups, e-mail lists, or chat rooms; making a personal connection with students and incorporating motivational strategies to encourage student performance through learning students' names or individually acknowledging excellent performance.
Principle 9: Instructional climate	Instruction is designed to be welcoming and inclusive. High expectations are espoused for all students.	A statement in the class syllabus affirming the need for class members to respect diversity in order to establish the expectation of tolerance and encourage students to discuss any special learning needs with the instructor; highlighting diverse thinkers who have made significant contributions to the field; sharing innovative approaches developed by students in the class.

Source: S. Scott, J. McGuire, & S. Shaw. (2001). *Principles of universal design for instruction.* Storrs: University of Connecticut, Center on Postsecondary Education and Disability. Copyright 2001 by S. Scott, J. McGuire, & S. Shaw. Reprinted with permission.

and follow-up readings to enrich analysis, and ways to link the case with other teaching-improvement activities" (Hutchings, 1993, p. 13). The use of case study methods has been widely recommended in the professional development of teachers, including college faculty (Souza, Carey, McMartin, Ambrosino, & Grimes, 2011). Shulman (1992) observed that the case study approach is particularly well suited to training instructors in the "day-to-day ambiguities of the classroom" (p. xiii). In structure, cases may be of varied length, format, and level of detail, ranging from a brief paragraph to multipage descriptions. Wasserman (1994) observed that good cases, regardless of length, are "based on problems or 'big ideas' that warrant in-depth discussion" (p. 13). Cases in teaching may focus, for example, on such topics as the relationships of instructional strategies to student outcomes, examination of teacher assumptions in the classroom, or cultural factors affecting student learning. Darling-Hammond and Baratz-Snowden (2007) described case study methods as a means of assisting instructors in building a schema for their decision making and continued professional growth. Through a process of analyzing teaching situations, applying strategies, and considering alternatives, instructors are provided with a model to "seek out and add knowledge of specific techniques throughout their careers" (Darling-Hammond & Baratz-Snowden, 2007, p. 115). This schema allows instructors to progress from "novice" decision makers in the classroom to "expert" instructors, with a broader and more flexible repertoire of responses in the classroom.

USING THE INSTRUCTIONAL CYCLE TO PROMOTE REFLECTION

The process of designing and teaching a college course is multifaceted, time-consuming, complicated, and iterative. Decisions about what to teach, how to teach it, and how to determine student learning are integral to course development and revision. Factors such as theories of learning (cognitive, constructivist, multiple intelligences, social-cognitive) can be instrumental in guiding the teaching process (Bransford, Brown, & Cocking, 2000; Bruning, Schraw, & Norby, 2011; Morrison, Ross, & Kemp, 2004). Practices derived from research on ways that learners acquire, process, integrate, retrieve, and apply new knowledge are instrumental in creating learner-centered approaches to course design and implementation (Davis, 2009). Recently, resources for developing and implementing effective instruction and assessing learning outcomes promote the principles of universal design (Bacigalupo, 2010; Davis, 2009; McGuire & Scott, 2006; Pliner & Johnson, 2004). A practical approach to course design, the instructional cycle, adapted from the literature on effective instructional practices (Algozzine, Ysseldyke, & Elliott, 1997–1998; Brophy & Good, 1986; Kame'enui & Carnine, 1998), offers a tool for facilitating reflection. Three components include examining (a) what is taught (planning and delineating learning goals and outcomes); (b) how it is taught (delivering or orchestrating instruction and monitoring the extent to which the content is understood or acted on by students), and (c) how learning is assessed (designing activities to determine the extent to which students have met the instructional goals). While this instructional cycle is logically sequenced for the purpose of application, in reality its components are not solely discreet and autonomous since one element should inform the other two (i.e., assessment should guide planning; implementation activities should relate to learning objectives, etc.). In our approach to using case studies with faculty, we have found that using the instructional cycle framework adds a dimension that faculty can readily identify with and apply in their reflection on their own teaching. A minicase, questions for reflection, and teaching notes are presented for each of the three elements of the instructional cycle.

SAMPLE MINICASES, QUESTIONS FOR REFLECTION, AND TEACHING NOTES

Case 1: Planning Instruction

Peter Miller is a faculty member in the psychology department in a four-year state university. He teaches a required undergraduate course that meets for two hours every week. In this blended course, which includes lectures and use of the Canvas learning management system, he posts the class syllabus, assignments, and links to readings and articles. He finds the Canvas discussion board convenient because he can reach all the students in his class and respond to student queries at any time. He typically has forty to fifty students per semester in his class. The student population is varied and includes traditional- and nontraditional-age students. This semester he has been contacted by one of the students in his class who disclosed that she has a language-based learning disability. The letter from the disability services office states that the student is entitled to reasonable accommodations under the Americans with Disabilities Act. According to the student's disability documentation, she is eligible for extended time on tests and use of a note taker.

Questions for Reflection and Teaching Notes

What are the issues for Dr. Miller as he prepares to teach this course?
The class is diverse, comprising traditional- and nontraditional-age students who may vary in their skills with the use of a web-based teaching platform. There is also a student with a language-based learning disability who may be reluctant to post questions and responses online because of weaknesses in her writing skills. Dr. Miller incorporates lectures into his teaching, with implications for note taking, an area for which one student uses accommodations.

Which of the principles of UDI are most important for him to consider?
Given the diverse students in this class, principles 1 (equitable use), 2 (flexibility in use), and 6 (low physical effort) are particularly relevant.

Using the principles of UDI as a guide, what strategies do you suggest for Dr. Miller in planning an inclusive course?
Dr. Miller could plan to send a "Welcome" e-mail message before the first class begins that includes a link to the class website, a description of sections and their purpose on the class home page, and a link to the university's technical support for using Canvas (principle 1). Topics and dates for which discussion board postings are required could be identified in advance on the course syllabus, so that the student with the learning disability could develop a draft and seek editing assistance before posting (principle 2). PowerPoint notes for class lectures could be posted in advance so that *all* students have the opportunity to come to class with a working outline (principle 6). While Dr. Miller does not currently use an online test format for the course, it is possible to permit extended test time online, should he modify the course in the future (principle 1).

Case 2: Delivering Instruction

Mr. Stegman teaches a satellite summer course offered by ABC Community College to students in the nursing program. The course spans four weekends and is held in a public school classroom. Each session is a full day of lessons and activities. The room is small and has no air conditioning. Although the class has only seventeen students, he finds that many of them are distracted by the physical challenge of being in a small room in the summer heat. He has talked to the administrative personnel about the physical size and space of the classroom, but he has not received much sympathy. The budget is tight at the college, and the registrar is not always able to get air-conditioned rooms for summer classes. Mr. Stegman has talked to a faculty colleague about the impact of the classroom conditions on student learning. She told him to ignore the problem; if students are less engaged because of physical elements beyond his control, there is nothing he can do about it.

Questions for Reflection and Teaching Notes

What are the issues for Mr. Stegman as he considers how he is delivering instruction?
The physical environment of the classroom and the length of the daily schedule for delivery of the course content are major concerns.

Which of the principles of UDI are important for him to consider?
Principles 4 (perceptible information), 7 (size and space), and 8 (community of learners) are relevant in this case.

Using the principles of UDI as a guide, what strategies do you suggest for Mr. Stegman in revising his course delivery?
Given the challenges of the learning space and schedule, creating a sense of community among students is particularly important. Before the first class, Mr. Stegman could contact students to acknowledge the rigor of the class schedule and encourage them to share ideas about the instructional environment (e.g., building in enough time for lunch, varying the structure of a class day; principle 8). With advance planning, Mr. Stegman could vary the environment for delivering instruction by scheduling several class meetings in alternative, more user-friendly settings. For example, they could use the college's library, which is air-conditioned and has space allocated for instruction, including seminar rooms for small-group work (principle 7). On specific dates, class time could be structured so that small groups work on tasks (e.g., content-specific research questions, problem-based activities) outside of the allocated classroom, then come together to debrief and brainstorm about the topic (principles 4 and 7).

Case 3: Assessing Learning Outcomes

Professor Mancini is planning assignments for her History 206 class. She usually assigns the class a set of readings, two quizzes, a midterm exam, and a final exam. It is a fairly large class, so all tests are in multiple-choice format. She feels this works well, since students have to be able to recall a large amount of declarative knowledge. However, she realizes that not all students are equally comfortable with multiple-choice questions. Though she is aware that some students perform better on other test formats, such as oral presentations, she is uncomfortable changing the test format due to the size and nature of the class.

Questions for Reflection and Teaching Notes

What are the issues for Dr. Mancini as she considers her assessment of learning outcomes?
While Dr. Mancini would like to be sensitive to students' test-taking abilities and preferences for test format, she also knows that factual learning is critical to the course objectives and that efficiency in the amount of time required for grading is essential.

Which of the principles of UDI are most related to these issues?
Principles 1 (equitable use), 2 (flexibility in use), and 5 (tolerance for error) are germane to the issues.

Using the principles of UDI as a guide, what strategies do you recommend for Dr. Mancini to make her assessment of student learning more inclusive of diverse students?
Dr. Mancini might consider an alternative to the two quizzes that she has previously structured as multiple-choice. Students could use class notes as well as chapter summaries they have developed while taking the quiz in class. This would reinforce students' class attendance and completion of reading assignments and accommodate

diverse abilities in recalling facts (principle 2). Dr. Mancini could also design a multiple-choice test option for which students could explain their selection of the answer, affording a flexible alternative based on the rationale for item choice (principle 5). She could also set a threshold for dropping an item based on the percentage of the class answering incorrectly (e.g., 75% or more missing an item; principle 1).

DISCUSSION

The case study method is well suited to the challenges of supporting college faculty in enhancing their knowledge and practice of inclusive instruction. While the principles of UDI provide faculty with a framework for considering a range of inclusive practices, case studies are a complementary approach to assisting faculty in building a schema for implementing UDI. Guiding faculty through the process of applying the principles in the classroom and providing a forum for faculty dialogue and exchange with colleagues around realistic dilemmas promote faculty movement along a continuum, from novice to more expert instructional decision makers. As Shulman (1986) concurred, the development of instructional decision making should entail the "careful confrontation of principles with cases, of general rules with concrete documented events—a dialectic of the general with the particular" (p. 13).

Moving from general principles to guided practice in instructional problem solving allows faculty to consider unique classrooms and specific context considerations affecting instruction, such as campus missions or academic disciplines. The engaging format and flexible structure of cases make this approach adaptable to a number of different professional development strategies and settings. While it is important to be in tune with campus opportunities for training as they arise, we have found pre-semester professional development days, new faculty orientation, and teaching assistant orientation sessions to be prime settings for case study training and discussions. Often, departmental-level training in the form of brown-bag lunches that focus on teaching and online discussion boards provide engaging platforms for case study dialogue. Collaborating with campus resources such as centers for teaching excellence and instructional design professionals offers another approach to extending the dialogue on inclusive instruction.

The use of a case study approach to promoting the application of UDI should be tempered by the awareness that finding ways to engage faculty in a process of examining their views and approaches to teaching comprises a major challenge (Saroyan, Amundsen, McAlpine, Weston, Winer, & Gandell, 2004). It is not unusual for faculty to view themselves as content experts and scholars rather than teachers. To effectively engage in a collaborative process of exploring the use of UD principles in instruction requires acknowledgment that a professor's "area of expertise is a matter of professional self-identity" (Saroyan et al., 2004, p. 16). It is also important to understand the broader context of the institution and its culture. Promoting a philosophy of proactively designing and using inclusive instructional strategies to benefit a wide range of learners, including students with disabilities, will be successful only if a systemic process is developed, with the clear support of top-level administrators (Saroyan et al., 2004; Seldin, 1995).

In the 2006 report of the Secretary of Education's Commission on the Future of Higher Education (U.S. Department of Education, 2006), the quality of student learning in our colleges and universities is described as inadequate and, in some cases, declining. The Commission has called for "a robust culture of accountability and transparency," including the measurement of student learning outcomes (pp. 20, 23). Although the literature on the effects of implementing UD-based instructional practices on student learning is sparse and only two studies could be located (Scott & Edwards, 2012; Street et al., 2012), results of other studies indicate favorable outcomes such as the effectiveness of UD-based faculty training to increase inclusive teaching practices and positive student attitudes about such practices (Davies, Schelly, & Spooner, 2013; Izzo, Murray, & Novak, 2008; Lombardi, Murray, & Dallas, 2013; Moon, Utschig, Todd, & Bozzorg, 2011). Precision in clearly articulating the theory and its principles, as well as rigor in investigating the work of faculty in creating accessible instruction, hold great promise as higher education seeks to address the learning needs of a diverse student population. As noted, the use of case studies that incorporate principles and focus on practice has received a great deal of attention as an approach for training instructors. We believe that this methodology is well suited for advancing the dialogue about UD and its application to instruction. With a diverse audience of participants (e.g., faculty, disability services professionals, administrators, graduate students) and systematic data collection that includes qualitative comments based on reflection about the case study process, another tool for promoting inclusive teaching may contribute to efforts to refine teaching in more engaging ways.

REFERENCES

Algozzine, B., Ysseldyke, J., & Elliott, J. (1997–1998). *Strategies and tactics for effective instruction.* Longmont, CO: Sopris West.

Bacigalupo, M. (2010). An inclusive model for articulating curriculum in higher education. In L. Fox & L. Ijiri (Eds.), *Changing lives through metacognitive relationships: LD/ADHD and college success* (pp. 101–129). Milton, MA: Curry College.

Bransford, J. D., Brown, A. L., & Cocking, R. R. (2000). *How people learn: Brain, mind, experience, and school.* Washington, DC: National Academy Press.

Brophy, J., & Good, T. L. (1986). Teacher behavior and student achievement. In M. Wittrock (Ed.), *Third handbook of research on teaching* (pp. 328–375). Chicago: Rand McNally.

Bruning, R. H., Schraw, G. J., & Norby, M. N. (2011). *Cognitive psychology and instruction* (5th ed.). New York: Pearson.

Center for Universal Design (CUD). (2007). *About universal design: Universal design history.* Center for Universal Design. Retrieved from http://www.ncsu.edu/ncsu/design/cud/about_ud/udhistory.htm

Chronicle of Higher Education. (2014). *Almanac of Higher Education 2014.* Retrieved from http://chronicle.com/article/RacialEthnic/147373/

Darling-Hammond, L., & Baratz-Snowden, J. (2007). A good teacher in every classroom: Preparing the highly qualified teachers our children deserve. *Educational Horizons, 85*(2), 111–132.

Davies, P. L., Schelly, C. L., & Spooner, C. L. (2013). Measuring the effectiveness of universal design for learning intervention in postsecondary education. *Journal of Postsecondary Education and Disability, 26*(3), 195–220.

Davis, B. G. (2009). *Tools for teaching* (2nd ed.). San Francisco: John Wiley & Sons.

Fink, L. D. (2013). *Creating significant learning experiences.* San Francisco: Jossey-Bass.

Henderson, C. (1999). *College freshmen with disabilities: Statistical year 1998.* Washington, DC: American Council on Education.

Hughes, B., Herston, T., & Stein, J. (2010). Using case studies to help faculty navigate difficult classroom moments. *College Teaching, 59*(1), 7–12.

Hutchings, P. (1993). *Using cases to improve college teaching: A guide to more reflective practice.* Washington, DC: American Association for Higher Education.

Izzo, M. V., Murray, A., & Novak, J. (2008). The faculty perspective on universal design for learning. *Journal of Postsecondary Education and Disability, 21*(2), 60–72.

Kame'enui, E. J., & Carnine, D. W. (1998). *Effective teaching strategies that accommodate diverse learners.* Upper Saddle River, NJ: Merrill.

Lombardi, A., Murray, C., & Dallas, B. (2013). University faculty attitudes toward disability and inclusive instruction: Comparing two institutions. *Journal of Postsecondary Education and Disability, 26*(3), 221–232.

Lynn, L. (1999). *Teaching and learning with cases: A guidebook.* Chappaqua, NY: Seven Bridges Press.

McGuire, J. M., & Scott, S. S. (2006). Universal design for instruction: Extending the universal design paradigm to college instruction. *Journal of Postsecondary Education and Disability, 19*(2), 124–134.

Moon, N. W., Utschig, T. T., Todd, R. L., & Bozzorg, A. (2011). Evaluation of programmatic interventions to improve postsecondary STEM education for student with disabilities: Findings from Sci-Train university. *Journal of Postsecondary Education and Disability, 24*(4), 331–349.

Morrison, G. R., Ross, S. M., & Kemp, J. E. (2004). *Designing effective instruction* (4th ed.). San Francisco: John Wiley & Sons.

Pliner, S. M., & Johnson, J. R. (2004). Historical, theoretical, and foundational principles of universal instructional design in higher education. *Equity and Excellence in Education, 37*(2), 105–113.

Saroyan, A., Amundsen, C., McAlpine, L., Weston, C., Winer, L., & Gandell, T. (2004). Assumptions underlying workshop activities. In A. Saroyan & C. Amundsen (Eds.), *Rethinking teaching in higher education: From a course design workshop to a faculty development framework* (pp. 15–29). Sterling, VA: Stylus.

Scott, S. S., & Edwards, W. (2012). Project LINC: Supporting lecturers and adjunct instructors in foreign language classrooms. *Journal of Postsecondary Education and Disability, 25*(3), 253–258.

Scott, S. S., McGuire, J. M., & Shaw, S. F. (2001). *Principles of universal design for instruction.* Storrs: University of Connecticut, Center on Postsecondary Education and Disability.

Seldin, P. (1995). Improving college teaching. In P. Seldin et al., *Improving college teaching* (pp. 1–12). Bolton, MA: Anker.

Shulman, J. (Ed.). (1992). *Case methods in teacher education.* New York: Teachers College Press.

Shulman, L. (1986). Those who understand: Knowledge growth in teaching. *Educational Researcher, 15*(2), 4–14.

Street, C., Koff, R., Fields, H., Kuehne, L., Handlin, L., Getty, M., & Parker, D. (2012). Expanding access to STEM for at-risk learners: A new application of Universal Design for Instruction. *Journal of Postsecondary Education and Disability, 25*(4), 363–375.

Souza, T., Carey, T., McMartin, F., Ambrosino, R., & Grimes, J. (2011). Using multimedia case stories of exemplary teaching for faculty development. *To Improve the Academy, 29*, 60–73.

U.S. Department of Education. (2006, September). *A test of leadership: Charting the future of U.S. higher education.* Washington, DC: Author.

U.S. Department of Education. (2013). *Digest of education statistics, 2012* (National Center for Education Statistics 2014–015), Table 269.

Van Der Werf, M., & Sabatier, G. (2009). *The college of 2020: Students.* Washington, DC: Chronicle Research Services, The Chronicle of Higher Education. Retrieved from http://www.gvsu.edu/cms3/assets/61697910-910A-8DF3-C277AFB5E6D3E506/spcdocs/the_college_of_2020_students.pdf

Wasserman, S. (1994). *Introduction to case method teaching: A guide to the galaxy.* New York: Teachers College Press, Columbia University.

23

Implementing Universal Design
Collaborations Across Campus

Donald E. Finn
Elizabeth Evans Getzel
Susan B. Asselin
Virginia Reilly

Beginning in the late 1990s, the Rehabilitation Research and Training Center at Virginia Commonwealth University (VCU) conducted structured faculty and student interviews to help identify areas of need for instructing students with disabilities. The findings led to the implementation of disability awareness workshops for faculty and subsequent identification of the need for understanding how to best design and deliver instruction. Developing partnerships with established on-campus entities helped to extend the reach of the information to faculty. Outreach strategies included workshops and the distribution of print- and web-based materials. The success of the VCU efforts led to a replication project at Virginia Polytechnic Institute and State University (Virginia Tech), a land grant university in the southwestern section of the state. The authors of this chapter outline the approaches to disability awareness and instructional techniques of the VCU and Virginia Tech projects, including the projects' development, unique characteristics, and outcomes.

As greater numbers of students enter college with diverse learning and support needs, and as new technologies and teaching strategies emerge, faculty must continue building and expanding professional development activities. Helping to create instructionally accessible environments is a growing theme of professional development activities on college campuses across the country (Brinckerhoff, McGuire, & Shaw, 2002; Getzel & Finn, 2005; Scott & Gregg, 2000; Wilson & Getzel, 2001). Collaborative relationships between instructional faculty, staff, college administrators, and students with disabilities create an atmosphere where everyone's input is valued. This collaborative atmosphere can help determine the most effective instructional and support

326 UNIVERSAL DESIGN IN HIGHER EDUCATION

strategies and resolve issues that may arise when educating students with disabilities in higher education (Alfano, 1994; Brinckerhoff, McGuire, & Shaw, 2002; Getzel & Finn, 2005; Scott & Gregg, 2000). A concerted effort is needed to respond effectively and efficiently to emerging trends in educating a diverse college population. Scott and McGuire (2005) emphasize that the impact of diversity on educational strategies in higher education cannot be overstated. They contend that as universities respond to changes in higher education, including more new faculty members and the use of emerging technologies on campus, instructional strategies will broaden to include more inclusive methods and techniques to reach all students.

Since the late 1990s, Virginia Commonwealth University has worked on a campus-wide approach to determine the professional development needs of faculty, staff, and administrators. Using an extensive evaluation process, VCU obtained input from these groups and from students with disabilities. Structured interviews were conducted to determine the professional development needs on the university's academic and medical campuses. The first evaluation focused on how students with disabilities at VCU are currently educated. Most of the instructional faculty and staff who were interviewed taught courses in which one or more students with disabilities were enrolled. Both faculty and administrators reported limited knowledge of disability-specific legislation and other related issues and were generally uninformed about resources, accommodations, and assistive and educational technology (Wilson & Getzel, 2001). As a result of this study, VCU implemented a training initiative designed to provide the university at large with the knowledge, awareness, and sensitivity necessary to interact with and serve VCU students with disabilities more effectively.

At the end of the three-year implementation, a second university-wide evaluation was conducted to determine the outcomes of the training and technical assistance provided. Again, the evaluation process included instructional faculty and staff, administrators, and students with disabilities. Faculty and staff members wanted more training and information, especially on the integration of disability-related information, materials, and resources. In particular, universal design strategies emerged as a campus-wide interest. Faculty members contributed professional development ideas, including guides on teaching students with disabilities and collaborating with other professionals on campus, more workshops or seminars through the VCU Center for Teaching Excellence (CTE), and ongoing communications via e-mail (e.g., sharing helpful websites). The two evaluations provided an invaluable tool for determining how to meet the expressed needs of instructional faculty and staff across the university.

The initial evaluation helped VCU to focus on specific information related to the educational learning needs of students with disabilities, the process for requesting accommodations at VCU, and campus resources. During the first series of professional development activities, universal design was introduced as a framework for instructing and assessing student learning in a more inclusive manner. In response to the evaluations, a team of faculty members from the VCU Rehabilitation Research and Training Center (RRTC) who specialize in the educational needs of college students with disabilities worked with CTE staff members to develop a two-day workshop that focused on effectively instructing large classes. This workshop included a two-hour segment that introduced participants to universal design philosophy, and the entire workshop demonstrated universal design techniques that faculty members could incorporate into their classes.

The team at VCU-RRTC formed a partnership with the CTE to disseminate disability-related information and resources through the CTE. The materials focus on universal design techniques, with the goal of ensuring that disability-related information is fully integrated into university-sponsored professional development activities. According to Getzel, Briel, and McManus (2003), several universities have found that incorporating universal design concepts into information that faculty and staff received through their center for teaching excellence (or similar entity) was an effective outreach method. Providing information on universal design enables teaching professionals to learn how adjustments in their instruction, curricula, and use of technology can benefit all students. The VCU-RRTC team determined that establishing this partnership and evaluating its effectiveness could assist other universities and colleges across the country.

THE PARTNERSHIP WITH THE CENTER FOR TEACHING EXCELLENCE

At VCU, the CTE is the primary source of instructional support and information about the teaching and learning process for faculty. It incorporates a variety of approaches, including holding group workshops, authoring and distributing self-study materials, providing individual consultations, and offering PowerPoint presentations and other materials through its website. The VCU-RRTC team worked closely with the CTE director and associate director to identify outreach approaches to reach VCU's faculty members. The two primary approaches identified were face-to-face faculty workshops and the publication of a print newsletter. The team agreed that the best approach for introducing universal design instructional practices to faculty was to discuss the diversity of college learners. Using this approach establishes a context for discussing learner differences along a continuum of diversity that includes individuals with disabilities. This context gives faculty a new framework and sensitivity toward students with disabilities. It also helps to cultivate a receptive atmosphere to universal design concepts and practices as applied to classes (both face-to-face and online) and materials (print- and web-based) (Getzel & Finn, 2005).

Collaborative Sponsorship of Workshops and Training

The initial outreach method resulting from the CTE-RRTC partnership was the presentation of universal design concepts at the annual winter and summer CTE institutes. These institutes are designed for instructional faculty and last for two to four days. Each institute operates under a theme, such as Effective Instructional Strategies for Large Classes, Integrating Technology into Instruction, and Teaching with Blackboard. The institutes attract faculty from across VCU who want to learn more about effective and innovative instructional methods. The VCU-RRTC team has offered presentations and brief workshops at a number of these institutes.

Print Material Developed Through Collaboration

Another effective faculty outreach method is the collaborative effort of developing a newsletter for faculty, *VCU Teaching*. In its original form, *VCU Teaching* was a web-based newsletter produced by the CTE with a limited readership. The new version is designed for online viewing and for print distribution via campus mail semiannually to all faculty, including adjuncts. Currently, *VCU Teaching* reaches thousands of faculty members on both campuses. CTE staff write the bulk of the publication, but a column on universal design principles and effective practices for working with students with disabilities is written by VCU-RRTC faculty. This endeavor has provided excellent exposure of disability-specific information as well as an effective means for presenting topics of student diversity and universal design techniques on a regular basis.

The collaboration resulted in more original outreach publications about universal design and effective work with diverse groups of learners. Publications have included postcards, fact sheets, and newsletters offering concise universal design information and links to additional materials about VCU-RRTC services and upcoming workshops and events.

Online Resources

Because of time constraints and scheduling issues, the project team worked to develop a self-paced, Internet-based module introducing universal design to faculty. The module content and sequence were based on participant feedback and evaluation data from the face-to-face workshops delivered at VCU and other venues. The module begins with an overview of learner diversity, including subtopics of learning styles or preferences, international students, and disabilities. Next, the rationale for universal design is presented, along with examples of universally designed materials in the college setting. Tools for locating and creating universal design–friendly materials are introduced, along with an overview of assistive technology and software packages available for use by students and faculty. Consistent with universal design principles, the module design incorporates universally designed elements, including alt tags for all pictures and diagrams, easy-to-read Arial font, and minimal use of italic, bold, and underlined text. For further study, Internet-based resources are included with the URLs written out to ensure recognition by screen readers. In the pilot stage, professors who completed the module confirmed that it was an effective method for introducing universal design and showing examples of universally designed materials. Additionally, they reported that the module prompted them to reexamine their classroom materials and instructional practices to help address the needs of diverse learners (Finn, 2005). Because of this module's success, future self-paced modules are being considered.

Direct Outreach Methods

In addition to the partnership with the CTE, VCU-RRTC team members conducted universal design outreach efforts across the VCU campuses. They tailored workshops and information sessions about universal design and methods for working effectively with diverse students for groups requesting subject-specific presentations and workshops. Those requesting presentations or workshops included faculty and administrators from the schools of education and social work, and supervisors of graduate teaching assistants from schools across the academic campus. Universal design workshops were also developed for student groups, including medical residents who supervise first-year medical students, art education and special education majors, master's of social work students, and undergraduate honors-level students from various disciplines.

As the benefits of the partnership with the CTE emerged through evaluation results and other feedback, the VCU-RRTC team sought to determine the effectiveness of this type of partnership in another setting. The team decided to seek another university to collaborate with, offering resources and support to facilitate their replication effort. Because of previous collaborative projects and other associations with the director of Americans with Disabilities Act (ADA) services at Virginia Tech, team members approached the ADA director and her associates about establishing a replication site. Virginia Tech was chosen because its geographic and student population differences would help to determine the effectiveness of the VCU model in a different setting. The two universities are comparable in size, each serving more than twenty-six thousand students, five to six hundred of whom have disclosed their disabilities to the university. These are primarily individuals with learning disabilities, attention deficit hyperactivity disorder (ADHD), psychiatric disabilities, medical disabilities, and combinations thereof. However, VCU is an urban university in the heart of the city of Richmond, covering two campuses, whereas Virginia Tech is located in the rural southwestern part of the state and has a more homogeneous student population than VCU. After initial discussions, the ADA director formed a team to discuss the VCU model and determine the professional development needs at Virginia Tech.

PROJECT REPLICATION EFFORTS AT VIRGINIA TECH

University-wide Collaboration

The staff in the offices that provide services to students with disabilities and support faculty at Virginia Tech have a long-standing relationship with each other. Universal design philosophy was commonly discussed and embraced by University ADA Services and the ADA Executive Advisory Committee; however, these groups have struggled to find ways to introduce this philosophy to the academic side of campus. The VCU initiative offered a systematic approach to facilitate campus-wide understanding and acceptance of universal design principles. The director of University ADA Services at Virginia Tech and the VCU-RRTC faculty began talking about how the work at VCU could be continued at Virginia Tech (Finn, Reilly, & Asselin, 2005). These talks led to the formation of the Universal Design Faculty Initiative at Virginia Tech to assist faculty in teaching all learners more effectively, especially those with disabilities.

Universal Design Planning Committee

The first and most important step was forming a committee of key leaders who would support and communicate the project's goals to the teaching faculty. The Universal Design Planning Committee consists of the director of University ADA Services, the director of the Center for Excellence in Undergraduate Teaching (CEUT), the assistant provost and director of the Center for Academic Enrichment and Excellence, the director of Services for Students with Disabilities (SSD), and a teaching faculty member from the School of Education. Each of these members brings special expertise and the ability to publicize, grow, and manage a sustained effort.

The Universal Design Planning Committee informally polled a sample of teaching faculty to determine the most effective method for receiving information about teaching techniques; the overwhelming preference was for face-to-face professional development opportunities. This venue offers opportunities for interaction with a presenter and with peers to share experiences and to secure practical solutions to take back to the classroom. The planning committee worked with the VCU-RRTC team to plan a strategy based on the survey results that would capture the interest of a diverse faculty population. A model that included elements of the approach used at VCU was developed for Virginia Tech; it included a plan for multiple mailings and events to reach faculty several times throughout the next year. The plan was to begin with "awareness" information about the basics of universal design in the fall, followed by more in-depth information in the spring to equip faculty with tools and ideas to adapt their own curricula.

Workshops

The first strategy was to invite faculty, particularly new members, to a universal design workshop facilitated by a VCU-RRTC faculty member. Recruitment began at the fall Graduate Teaching Assistant Training and New Faculty Orientation, with members of the planning committee promoting the upcoming two-hour, introductory universal design workshop. The next step was campus-wide outreach using an article about universal design written for the CEUT newsletter. Faculty members rely on this newspaper-style publication for announcements about workshops, study group opportunities, and pedagogical articles. The introductory workshop was marketed as providing approaches and information that would assist diverse learners, not only those with disabilities. Shortly after the CEUT newsletter was distributed, an adaptation of a postcard designed and used by the VCU project the previous fall was mailed to faculty members at Virginia Tech. The caption on the front of the postcard asked, "Are They Getting It?" and showed scenes of students in various learning settings. On the back, some practical universal design techniques were offered, along with an announcement about the upcoming workshop. In addition to these announcements, the workshop was also featured on the university website.

The multiple outreach methods were successful, as evidenced by the diversity of departments and schools represented at the two-hour workshop presented in late September. Don Finn, a faculty member and replication project liaison from the VCU-RRTC, facilitated the workshop, called An Introduction to Universal Design: Strategies for Reaching ALL Students. Participants included representatives from veterinary medicine, education, engineering, and other administrative and academic departments. In addition to an overview of universal design, this presentation introduced various types of assistive technologies and software. Inspiration software was demonstrated as a tool for designing materials for effective instruction, including presentations and handouts. Several copies of Inspiration were given as prizes to encourage faculty to explore ways to integrate universal design–friendly materials and techniques into their instruction. Workshop attendees received practical information, and many were anxious to learn more.

Following the fall workshop, the Planning Committee designed a newspaper-style publication about the Universal Design Faculty Initiative. The CEUT director contributed the lead article about the philosophy, tenets, and benefits of universal design. Additional articles described the missions of and services offered by the partnering offices involved in the Virginia Tech Universal Design Faculty Initiative. A faculty perspective on universal design revealed teaching practices that exemplify universal design strategies, such as including accommodation statements for students with disabilities in syllabi, offering alternative assignments, and using a variety of methods and materials to supplement lectures.

The second workshop built on the materials and concepts introduced in the first workshop. It was taught by Dr. Sally Scott, codirector of the Universal Design for Instruction Project at the University of Connecticut, and provided hands-on group activities that allowed attendees to apply techniques for designing instructional materials and syllabi for their curricula.

Faculty Study Group

At the end of the workshop, the planning committee announced the formation of a universal design faculty study group. Members of the group would meet at the CEUT, could apply for study group stipends, and would support each other in learning more about universal design in reevaluating and redesigning their instructional materials. The invitation resulted in a diverse group that included faculty from the colleges of Human Sciences and Education, Science, and Architecture and Urban Studies, and representatives from the SSD. The study group was instrumental in helping the planning committee identify faculty needs for a final workshop.

Faculty-Designed Workshop

The faculty group explored student assessments and determined that a major challenge faculty faced was that the design and delivery of tests often inadvertently create barriers for students, particularly those with disabilities. The group reviewed examples of poorly designed tests from a collection on file at SSD. Faculty had sent these tests to SSD for administration to students served by the office. An examination of the tests provided a starting point for the inquiry. Could faculty apply universal design concepts to create more accessible instruments? The result was a collaborative effort between the study group and the Universal Design Planning Committee to develop a two-part workshop called All Tests Are Not Created Equal. Workshop recruitment was done through a modified version of a newsletter from the VCU project, *The Professor's Assistant*, which was mailed to faculty members in the early spring. Its lead article outlined research-based guiding principles of universal design (McGuire, Scott, & Shaw, 2003; Scott, McGuire, & Foley, 2003) and an overview of the benefits of integrating universal design concepts into the college curriculum (Finn & Thoma, 2006).

The All Tests Are Not Created Equal workshop was delivered by a VCU-RRTC faculty member, with the assistance of the study group members. The second part of the workshop included a breakout activity in which study group members worked with small teams of participants to examine test formats and recommend changes through implementing universal design principles covered in the presentation. Changes made to the tests included using consistent font size and style (e.g., Times or Arial were suggested), limiting the use of special text formatting (e.g., bold, italics, or underlining to highlight important words or concepts), revising wordy or vague questions, grouping questions by type (e.g., true/false, multiple-choice, short-answer), ensuring consistency of layout (e.g., alignment of choices for multiple-choice questions, consistent placement of blanks or locations for inserting answers), and determining which illustrations or diagrams would be useful and which could be eliminated.

Several faculty participants agreed to revise their tests by applying universal design principles with assistance from the study group. Following the workshop, study group members conducted research to determine the impact of revised assessments; this research was supported by a grant from the university Office of Multicultural Affairs (Asselin & Reilly, 2006). Initial data on test format changes were collected from students with and without disabilities. The data revealed that the changes were recognized by students, made the items clearer and easier to read, and enhanced student performance. The faculty participants reported that the changes were relatively easy to implement and they were pleased to offer more accessible assessment instruments.

OUTCOMES OF THE REPLICATION PROJECT AT VIRGINIA TECH

Faculty Awareness

Over the course of the replication project, nearly two hundred faculty, administrators, and teaching assistants participated in the series of universal design workshops offered at Virginia Tech. Of the faculty members attending the initial workshop, nineteen completed an informal follow-up survey regarding specific teaching practices that they employed (Finn, Reilly, & Asselin, 2005). The respondents were tenure-track faculty with eleven or more years of teaching experience, primarily with undergraduates. The group reported that of their overall enrollment, 5% or less were students with disabilities, with one-third reporting having less than 1%. Certain trends in teaching practices could be drawn from the responses. In general, these faculty participants provided a positive learning environment by inviting students to spend time with them to discuss accommodations and verify course expectations. They willingly offered lecture notes or outlines in advance of classes, and more than half reported checking their classrooms or labs for accessibility in size, space, and physical effort. Half the participants implemented other aspects of universal design by supplementing their lectures with multiple learning experiences and helping students make the connection to real-life situations.

Faculty Initiatives

An outcome that was particularly pleasing to the Universal Design Planning Committee was the level of faculty ownership and contributions to the initiative. The members of the initial CEUT-sponsored study group met to enhance their own awareness of universal design and to integrate universal design principles into their instruction.

The study group then served alongside the Universal Design Planning Committee to contribute to the design and delivery of faculty workshops. A core group of these faculty members remained together for two years, making strides to implement, evaluate, and disseminate the results of their efforts. One of the group's first activities included a visit to the Assistive Technology Lab at Virginia Tech to see a demonstration of available software and hardware to increase accessibility of instruction. Several study group members submitted internal and external grant proposals to further their universal design research interests, with some presenting their findings at national, regional, and university-sponsored conferences. Some faculty members are analyzing data to compare student performance on tests, before and after universal design revisions are applied, to determine if the changes have an impact on student learning.

Next Steps

Like the VCU-RRTC project, the Universal Design Planning Committee is exploring more ways to reach the faculty at Virginia Tech, including offering print and electronic documents, arranging for additional face-to-face trainings, and creating online informational modules. Additionally, the group is seeking ways to build on current faculty training offered through the Faculty Development Institute on various aspects of instruction, such as web accessibility, student assessment, and new software programs. Possible topics for this training include using assistive technologies and applying universal design principles to instruction.

Lessons Learned Through the Replication Effort

Faculty who participated in workshops, individual projects, and interviews expressed the realization that universal design strategies are "good teaching practices" and appreciated the opportunity to enhance their own skills. We found that, given the information, faculty were more than willing to try out universal design strategies and were pleasantly surprised by the impact on student achievement.

The Universal Design Planning Committee recognized the importance of collaboration with various departments across the university that support students and faculty and enhance the emphasis on diversity in the mission of the university. The synergy created by the individuals in the committee extended their impact to faculty as well as students. Most important was the fact that faculty members who became involved in the Universal Design Faculty Training Initiative were able to provide input into the process and guide implementation of various professional development opportunities.

RECOMMENDATIONS FOR SUCCESSFUL FACULTY OUTREACH PROGRAMS

Project staff make the following recommendations to other postsecondary institutions who wish to conduct similar activities on their campuses.

Use Evaluation Strategies to Understand the Learning Environment

At both sites, evaluation studies, or study groups, were used to obtain input from key individuals to assess the learning environment and the professional development needs of faculty and staff. Because universal design is based on the inclusive nature of learning, we recommend including students with disabilities in evaluation activities to obtain their perceptions of the learning environment.

Create Collaborative Partnerships

At both universities, partnering with individuals and administrative offices proved to be critical to the success of the projects, particularly because of the visibility and good reputations of these entities among the faculty. Networking efforts within the universities provided access to faculty members who otherwise may not have considered the benefits of applying universal design principles to their instruction.

Determine a Strategy for Implementation

It is important to develop a plan for implementation. Having evaluation or needs assessment results will offer a direction for planning professional development activities. Consideration of how the activities will be disseminated is equally important.

Develop Training Using Several Formats

Programs at seventeen colleges and universities that have developed professional development activities found that face-to-face, online, and print methods were effective strategies for infusing information and resources with universal design techniques (Getzel, Briel, & McManus, 2003). Offering different formats not only models the use of universal design techniques but also helps to address the challenge of faculty and staff finding time to participate in professional development activities.

Create Incentives for Faculty Participation

A primary lesson learned from the activities at both sites was that some faculty members need incentives and some type of recognition or reward for their commitment to improving instruction. Several incentive options were explored. At VCU and Virginia Tech, faculty members who attended workshops were eligible to receive Inspiration software. Both sites were also able to offer minigrants to purchase equipment and software, as well as stipends for faculty to develop and incorporate universal design strategies into their coursework.

CONCLUSION

Providing university-wide professional development activities infused with universal design strategies to create learning environments for all students, especially students with disabilities, has shown promising results at VCU, Virginia Tech, and other universities and colleges across the country (Getzel, Briel, & McManus, 2003). However, achieving positive results requires an ongoing commitment between highly visible university departments and academic faculty. Additionally, faculty should receive outcomes research that demonstrates the impact of universal design on student learning. Further study is needed on the long-term impact of these collaborative relationships and on outcomes for students with disabilities who take courses designed using universal design principles. Innovative practices should be shared among institutions of higher education in order to add to the growing body of knowledge in the field of disability and higher education.

REFERENCES

Alfano, K. (1994). *Recent strategies for faculty development.* (ERIC Document Reproduction Service no. ED371807). Los Angeles: ERIC Clearinghouse for Community Colleges.

Asselin, S., & Reilly, V. (2006). *Improving the learning climate for students with disabilities.* Blacksburg: Virginia Tech, Office of Multicultural Affairs.

Brinckerhoff, L. C., McGuire, J. M., & Shaw, S. F. (2002). *Postsecondary education and transition for students with learning disabilities* (2nd ed.). Austin, TX: Pro-Ed.

Finn, D. E. (2005). *Measuring the effectiveness of online faculty development: Exploring factors related to the integration of universal design concepts by community college professors.* Unpublished doctoral dissertation, Virginia Commonwealth University.

Finn, D. E., Reilly, V., & Asselin, S. (2005, August). *A collaborative model: Helping college faculty implement principles of universal design.* Paper presented at the annual international conference of the Association on Higher Education and Disability, Milwaukee, WI.

Finn, D. E., & Thoma, C. A. (2006, January). What is a universal design approach to learning? *The Professor's Assistant: An Informational Publication for University Instructors at Virginia Tech.*

Getzel, E. E., Briel, L. W., & McManus, S. (2003). Strategies for implementing professional development activities on college campuses: Findings from the OPE funded project sites (1999–2002). *Journal of Postsecondary Education and Disability, 17*, 59–76.

Getzel, E. E., & Finn, D. E. (2005). Training university faculty and staff. In E. E. Getzel & P. Wehman (Eds.), *Going to college: Expanding opportunities for people with disabilities* (pp. 199–214). Baltimore: Paul H. Brookes.

McGuire, J. M., Scott, S. S., & Shaw, S. F. (2003). Universal design for instruction: The paradigm, its principles, and products for enhancing instructional access. *Journal of Postsecondary Education and Disability, 17*, 11–21.

Scott, S. S., & Gregg, G. (2000). Meeting the evolving educational needs of faculty in providing access for college students with LD. *Journal of Learning Disabilities, 33*, 158–167.

Scott, S. S., & McGuire, J. M. (2005). Implementing universal design for instruction to promote inclusive college teaching. In E. E. Getzel & P. Wehman (Eds.), *Going to college: Expanding opportunities for people with disabilities* (pp. 119–138). Baltimore: Paul H. Brookes.

Scott, S. S., McGuire, J. M., & Foley, T. E. (2003). Universal design for instruction: A framework for anticipating and responding to disability and other diverse learning needs in the college classroom. *Equity and Excellence in Education, 36*, 40–49.

Wilson, K. E., & Getzel, E. E. (2001). Creating a supportive campus: The VCU professional development academy. *Journal for Vocational Special Needs Education, 23*, 12–18.

Professional development activities at VCU and Virginia Tech were developed under a grant from the U.S. Department of Education Office of Postsecondary Education (grant number P33A020046). However, the content of this chapter does not necessarily represent the policy of the Department of Education, and you should not assume endorsement by the federal government.

24

Collaboration for Usable Design

A Case Study in Partnerships to Promote Universal Design in Higher Education

Tara Buchannan
Rachel E. Smith

This chapter details how the original collaboration between a faculty member and disability service professional led to the development of a program designed to embed universal design (UD) strategies in various environments at their university. The authors discuss how they have engaged the campus community to create partnerships and share the responsibility for a usable and accessible environment. As a result of this program, the implementation of UD is growing exponentially at Western Illinois University (WIU).

Historically, higher education in America has been tailored to meet the needs of English-speaking, able-bodied, white male students. However, on today's college campus, diversity is the norm. The number of students from underrepresented groups is growing, and disability is no exception. In 2013, the National Center for Education Statistics reported that 10.9% of all college students have a disability. While colleges and universities have made many attempts to keep up with expanding diversity, when it comes to disability, requesting retrofit accommodations through disability service departments is the primary modality through which students with disabilities gain access to programs and services in higher education (Cory, White, & Stuckey, 2010). Requesting accommodations typically requires a student to self-identify to a disability services office, submit disability documentation, and await approval of requested modifications by a disability service professional. However, it has been estimated that only 40% of youth who received special education services while in secondary school choose to engage the accommodation process in the postsecondary setting (Wagner, Newman, Cameto, Garza, & Levine, 2005). If this is the case, are institutions of higher education really meeting their diversity goals of equal access and inclusion? Furthermore, is it equal to place additional responsibilities for access on a certain population? While the accommodation process will likely always have a place in higher education, additional strategies for achieving the equal access and inclusion intended in the spirit of disability legislation should be considered.

One such strategy is universal design, an approach that considers the diversity of users in all phases of the creation of products and environments. However, broad implementation of UD within a complex organization requires education, collaboration, leadership, and advocacy from many voices across the boundaries of discipline, division, and position. While the disability service staff should play a key leadership role in such an initiative, they cannot do it alone. Disability service providers must reach beyond the borders of their department and connect with faculty and staff allies across the university community. A program developed on the campus of Western Illinois University attempts to foster such partnerships to increase the usability of a midwestern university community. The program, Faculty and Staff Partnerships for Accessible Solutions (FASPAS), is designed to embed UD strategies into every facet of the university community for the purpose of creating usable, sustainable, and inclusive environments that reduce the need for retrofit accommodations.

ORIGINAL COLLABORATION

FASPAS was conceived through a partnership between the authors, one a disability service professional and the other a faculty member. The two have a long-standing relationship involving advocacy and education related to accessibility issues on campus. Through earlier collaborations, they gained an understanding of each other's views on disability and began to learn about universal design. The initial partnership involved modifications to the faculty member's courses. The authors identified the most commonly requested accommodations and assessed course design to explore how those frequently requested accommodations could be woven into the fabric of courses. The results were positive and included increased student satisfaction, decreased need for accommodation, and overall student success. The full results can be viewed in the practice brief "Community Collaboration, Use of Universal Design in the Classroom" (Smith & Buchannan, 2012).

Likewise, the operating procedures of the Disability Resource Center (DRC) were reviewed and modified with UD in mind. DRC made changes to office literature, its website, and faculty training that encouraged the implementation of UD. DRC changed procedures for students connecting with the department and for scheduling exams. The authors of this chapter consulted with each other as changes were made. The relationship was one of collaboration where each party brought a relevant, yet unique, perspective.

Due to the success of this collaboration, the authors wanted to share their experiences with others and encourage the implementation of UD not only in the classroom but also in other areas on campus. Using their partnership as a model, the authors initially developed a campus training program entitled Faculty Partnerships for Accessible Solutions (FPAS). The program was later expanded to include university staff and administrators and thus its name was changed to Faculty and Staff Partnerships for Accessible Solutions (FASPAS).

THE PROGRAM

FASPAS is rooted in social model thinking, where disability is situated within a spectrum of human variation. Rather than viewing disability as a physical, sensory, psychological, or medical condition causing limitations within an individual, FASPAS participants are encouraged to view disability as a problem that arises from design that does not anticipate diversity on campus. Through the UD process, diversity is anticipated and reflected in the design of our educational programs and environments. The program aims to assist faculty and staff in implementing UD, to grow campus allies and UD advocates, and to develop examples of practical applications for a variety of contexts and disciplines. The overarching goals are to change the way our campus views disability and to start a grassroots movement toward the implementation of UD in the learning, physical, and procedural environments at the university.

Content

FASPAS consists of a series of workshops presented by a team of facilitators with various experiences with respect to UD. Sessions include an introduction to UD, Universal Design for Learning (UDL), and Universal Design of Instruction (UDI); examples of how UD principles have been applied; and possible applications in various courses. We also discuss what UD *isn't*. Other topics discussed include disability history, disability legislation, and a comparison of legal minimums versus UD practices. As technology is often central to the campus experience, the training includes demonstrations on how to design accessible online content and how to use the learning management system to create a usable online experience for students. Each session builds upon the previous one, and the series concludes with a discussion of practical applications and commitments for UD implementation. The program emphasizes small changes that make a significant difference to the student experience. Ongoing training and support is offered in various formats at the conclusion of the workshops.

By the third iteration, the scope of the program was expanded to include university processes and environments other than the classroom. Presentations were redesigned to be inclusive of nonfaculty personnel. With the addition of staff as participants, we offered two breakout sessions—one on using the learning management system to make courses more usable and the other covering UD of policy, procedure, and physical space.

Methodology

UD is modeled throughout the workshops. The program uses a multimodality approach involving presentation, group discussion, group work, individual reflection, and hands-on learning. The sessions are held in a computer lab to ensure faculty access to their course materials and to allow for work time supported by facilitators. The program begins with an overview of the series and discussion of expectations of both the facilitators and the participants. A safe space is created for the group to grapple with new ideas by recognizing that none of us are experts and that we are there to learn from each other. We also discuss the locations of restrooms and exits and welcome participants to take breaks as needed. Relevant reading materials, offered in print and electronic format, are distributed prior to each workshop to allow participants to prepare for workshop discussions. Presentation slides are also available to participants in electronic or print format. All visual images are audio described and all videos are captioned. At the beginning of each workshop we offer an overview of the day and a review of the previous session. Each workshop ends with a preview of what is to come in the next session and an opportunity for participants to complete a quick feedback form on the current session. Throughout the program and beyond, participants are encouraged to collaborate with one another through a course electronic discussion board and at the program reunion. Originally, an e-mail-based distribution list was used for communication, but this proved ineffective and was phased out by the second cohort. Facilitators provide ongoing support to participants via the learning management system and scheduled work labs.

Program Leadership Team

The initial group of facilitators was established based on areas of expertise. The team included a disability service professional, a faculty member familiar with UD experience, an instructional technology professional familiar with accessibility and web design, an instructional technology professional familiar with the learning management system, the university's ADA compliance officer, and the president of Students for Disability Awareness. Information on UD was presented to all facilitators prior to the initial session, and all facilitators committed to attending all sessions to ensure cohesion of the message. The facilitation team has been expanded to include past participants who have implemented UD techniques in their classrooms.

Participants

Participants are recruited in one of two ways. First, personal invitations are sent to potential participants referred by program leaders, past participants, or department heads. The remaining positions are filled through a general campus invitation. Thus far, twenty-nine faculty and staff from a variety of departments have enrolled in the program. Detailed demographics on participants are available in Table 24.1. Departments represented include Health Sciences and Social Work; Agriculture; Kinesiology; Curriculum and Instruction; Dietetics, Fashion Merchandising, and Hospitality; Law Enforcement and Justice Administration; Educational and Interdisciplinary Studies; History; English and Journalism; and Geography. Participants also include staff from Facilities Management, the Provost's Office, and Health Sciences and Social Work. Those participating in the program are asked to commit to attending all FASPAS workshops, to implement at least one UD strategy, and to share what they learned with others.

Evaluation

The training includes ongoing assessment. Participants are given quick-response evaluations after each session to allow for feedback and guide possible modifications in future years. Facilitators also discuss, post-session, any needed modifications to content or layout of the program. At the end of the spring semester, faculty participants are sent two voluntary surveys. One survey is for the faculty member to complete a self-assessment on implementation of UD in a course of their choosing. The faculty participant then administers a second survey of students in one of their courses in which they have implemented UD techniques.

TABLE 24.1   Demographics of FASPAS Participants

Cohort	Departments Represented	Number of Staff	Number of Faculty
Spring 2012	Agriculture Curriculum and Instruction Dietetics, Fashion Merchandising, and Hospitality Health Sciences Kinesiology	0	6
Fall 2012	Agriculture Educational and Interdisciplinary Studies Geography History Law Enforcement and Justice Administration	0	5
Fall 2013	Educational and Interdisciplinary Studies English and Journalism Facilities Management Health Sciences Provost Office School of Social Work	4	5
Fall 2014	Beu Health Center Campus Recreation Centennial Honors College Communications Disability Resource Center Geology Kinesiology Recreation, Park, and Tourism Administration Student Assistance and Parent Service Center	3	6

OUTCOMES

Many professionals attend trainings and leave with good intentions, but not enough time or other resources to implement what they have learned. The success of FASPAS is in its participants enthusiastically implementing UD in their work environments and immediately using the knowledge they have gained. As participants model UD for their students and colleagues, they become advocates and allies. As a result, UD is spreading exponentially on our campus. Of the twenty-nine participants in four cohorts, a documented 60% have promoted UD to colleagues and/or students. This number may in fact be low, as some participants may be casually using UD techniques and not reporting. Instead of one faculty member changing one course, there are dozens of faculty including UD techniques in three or more courses and several staff members changing department procedures and practices across campus. The following sections provide specific examples in the words of those faculty and staff who are actively implementing UD across various disciplines.

Department of Geography: Julie's Story

Julie uses technology, redundancy, and tolerance for error to foster a UD learning environment. She reports:

> I provide my syllabus in three formats: hard copy, accessible Word document, interactive online. The lectures are interactive discussions supplemented with PowerPoint that include video-imbedded images (if available) and alternate text maps and photos. Lectures open with announcements, summary of previous content; end with reminder announcements, preview of content for next class. While in-class participation is important, online discussion forums allow for students to participate outside of the classroom. Maps are used in color, pattern, and black and white format to avoid color/vision biases. Alternate format maps are available at request; this includes electronic maps with alternative text. Interactive maps are used to allow students to manipulate images to their best use (blank, outline, color, pattern) for outside study. Materials are provided via the course management system with opportunities to study, communicate, and review. The chosen textbook is furnished in hard copy and/or electronic version at the student's choice.

Julie has also incorporated UD into assessment with the use of choice assignments and grading rubrics.

Department of English and Journalism: Alisha's Story

Alisha uses similar techniques to Julie in redundancy and access of material via a course management system. The classroom techniques vary due to discipline, but she too offers choice.

> Whenever possible I use visual note taking to provide examples and illustrations for complex or abstract concepts. For the classrooms with chalkboards only, I use my telephone to photograph the notes so that I can post them to the course page. Prewriting activities for each paper are meant to scaffold the development of the paper. I offer choices in prewriting activities (students can create an outline, jot list, or mind map to plan papers). Examples from two assignments are Review Essay and Visual Analysis Essay. The Review Essay offers choice in which media they review. Students can choose a book, movie, video game, or music album. Prewriting activities include discussing sample reviews. The Visual Analysis Essay teaches methods for analyzing images, and while there are specific sections that must be included in the paper, students choose which image they want to analyze and which aspects of the image to discuss. In addition, to scaffold development of visual analysis methods, we do several examples together. With an image projected in front of the class, I do a "think aloud" of how I would analyze the image, talking through what I notice when looking at the image and modeling the language used to discuss images. We do a couple examples as a whole class and then students analyze art on postcards in small groups. We also visit the University Gallery so they have practice with images with guidance from the gallery curator. To accommodate students with vision impairments, I offer the option of choosing black and white images and 3-dimensional art (sculptures or textiles).

Department of Agriculture: Andy's Story

Collaborative note taking reduces the need for a note taker accommodation. Groups take notes and share publicly. This method ensures notes are being taken and that everyone has access to the material.

> I used the note taking technique shared in the FASPAS training. Each day I would walk into class and list three random names on the board. These were my three note takers for the day. They had 48 hours to type notes into a Word document and send them to me. I would post these notes on the course management system under the dates of the lecture.

Department of History: Jen's Story

Jen uses multiple means of expression and engagement, allowing students various ways to express what they know using a method that interests them.

> In my senior-level courses (400-level), I allow students to meet course writing requirements in multiple ways. I allow them to either (a) select a series of guided essays on course reading materials responding to prompts I have devised OR (b) conduct individual research and write an original historical essay. The total length requirement for each track is the same, roughly 12–15 pages. I find that some students feel much more comfortable in following the path I have set while others thrive on the opportunity to research an area of their own interest.

Jen also uses technology to assist all her students.

> Many of my upper-division courses are discussion-driven, but I know that not all students are comfortable yet in the classroom with their peers to speak out to express their ideas. I create discussion threads on the course management system that parallel the discussions we have in class and encourage students who are reticent about speaking in class to post their responses to questions and their colleagues' comments there. The same strategy is also helpful for students who miss class, whether due to illness, university events, family or personal emergencies, etc. Posting something allows me to ascertain where they might be missing vital information or misinterpreting information discussed in class or in their readings.

Educational and Interdisciplinary Studies: Sarah's Story

Sarah outlines five distinct areas in which she is using UD.

> First, I use a learning contract. I invite students to select percentages for some of their assignments. Second, I start class with what I call a "check-in." This is a time for students to share how they are doing . . . if they are having a bad day, they can express it, for example. This allows all of us to understand a bit what is going on with the student. I participate in this as well. It is facilitated by asking for a volunteer, and going around the circle. Students can pass if they would prefer. Third, I have worked hard to make sure that the books I use are also in the library; I notice if they are available in an audio version, as well as an electronic version, and I let my students know about it. Fourth, I use Facebook [FB] as a forum for classroom announcements and discussion. This supplements the time in class. One of the best parts of FB is that it doesn't

go away, and is free for all students. I share classroom handouts, articles, video clips, etc., through FB, so that the students have them. Fifth, I establish group classroom norms with my students at the beginning of the semester, which allows students a chance to contribute to the kind of learning environment they want to establish. Items such as helping to set up and put back the classroom are usually on the list, but so is allowing everyone a chance to contribute (being mindful of the amount one participates). There is also an assignment tied to the group norms for each semester learning environment.

Facilities Management: Michael's Story

Michael has taken up advocating for UD within the Facilities Management division of campus. He started by hanging posters explaining UD and followed by providing two separate UD training workshops for the Facilities Management staff.

Michael reports that "UD is now a part of Facilities Management design guidelines that all architectural and engineering firms working on WIU projects must follow."

As a result of such advocacy, academic departments are being encouraged to purchase classroom furniture that can be used by all to the greatest extent possible. Projects are being viewed through a UD perspective. This small change will have a long-standing impact on campus.

BENEFITS

FASPAS has not only affected attitudes about disability, but it has also become a pipeline for collaboration on disability programming on campus. Participants have become advocates by leading training sessions, speaking at conferences, speaking in colleagues' courses, facilitating at disability cultural events, sharing at faculty meetings, and actively engaging in many other formalized learning environments. Two former participants became FASPAS facilitators. One former participant developed and provided training for additional faculty on campus through the Center for Innovation in Teaching and Research.

An unanticipated benefit of the program is that, through discussion, administrators and staff garner a better understanding of the challenges they each face and the culture of respective positions and departments. This connection fosters a support network to serve as not only a UD resource, but also a more supportive environment. Faculty support and encourage one another in pedagogical choices that embrace UD across disciplines. Administrators are better able to advocate for supports and resources for a more broadly inclusive campus community. Disability service professionals have been able to better understand their role as a resource not only to students, but also to the campus overall. Accordingly, the disability service staff makes themselves available to faculty and staff as consultants on the design of courses and other university environments and processes. As a direct result of FASPAS, DRC has been invited to consult on both course design and classroom design. Participants and facilitators have provided valuable feedback to the campus Master Planning Implementation Team and included disability culture events in curricula to encourage education on UD to all students.

FASPAS participants were given a fast-feedback paper survey after each session. Participants rated the sessions on a five-point Likert scale from 1 (poor) to 5 (excellent). Categories included knowledge gained, quality of presentation, practical application, and space/seating/location. Session feedback ranks at a 4 or higher for every category. The data reflects participant satisfaction and knowledge gained. Their actions on campus following the training reflect a true, long-standing change at a grassroots level, propelling both the structural and intellectual environments toward a social model of UD.

FUTURE CONSIDERATIONS

As we look to further develop the program, we review participants' feedback, facilitator observations, reported barriers to participation, challenges, goals, and open source materials available on the topic. There are scheduling difficulties for faculty and facilitators. There is an ongoing time commitment for disability service professionals in identifying participants and conducting trainings. The first program was offered every semester, but due to a limited number of facilitators, the program is now being offered once per academic year.

Participants are asked to commit to the entire program due to each session building upon the previous one. Often we are asked to shorten the program, offer an online format, or excuse participants from missed sessions. While FASPAS participants do not receive a grade, it is assumed that completion means the participant has the knowledge of the program. Not attending all sessions makes this problematic. Alternative trainings using technology are being considered. However, face-to-face delivery has allowed for collaborations among colleagues and a sharing of ideas that may not be as seamless in a virtual environment. A weekend-condensed session may serve as an alternative to either synchronous or asynchronous online training.

Another limitation of the program relates to lack of facilitators' time. Additional facilitators and staff are needed to measure outcomes of UD on retention, accommodation requests, and campus attitudes, as well as to conduct the training, follow-up, and ongoing support requests in relation to the UD techniques taught. With some participants joining the team, a rotational teaching method is being explored.

Finally, the response to surveys administered once the program concludes is low. Training is conducted during the fall semester, and two follow-up surveys are sent to participants toward the end of the spring semester, presumably after they've had the opportunity to redesign with UD in mind. One survey gathers information on faculty or staff perception of the effectiveness of UD. The other survey is administered to students and gathers information on their perception of the usability of courses. Currently, surveys are sent through campus mail, and the participant completes the faculty/staff survey and administers the student survey, then returns their survey also via campus mail. Facilitators send reminder e-mails to complete the survey. One possible solution for improving the response rate is for facilitators to take a more active role in the administration of follow-up surveys by administering surveys in person. Another possible solution would be to develop an online survey. However, both experience and research show that online surveys result in lower response rates. The facilitators are exploring incentives to increase the survey response rate without influencing the data.

CONCLUSION

Using an accommodation process as the primary method by which to address accessibility is deeply rooted in the culture of higher education. However, the accommodation process promotes the marginalization of students with disabilities by means of segregated access (Burgstahler & Cory, 2008). Furthermore, overreliance on a system that imposes additional responsibilities on a certain population and serves only a portion of that population fails to meet equal access and opportunity goals espoused by institutions of higher education (Loewen & Pollard, 2010). Changing that culture is a long-term effort requiring collaboration and cooperation across the campus community. While it will take many years for UD to become firmly rooted in our campus culture, the FASPAS program has shown promise in creating change and making strides toward broader utilization of UD as a method by which we address access and inclusion. FASPAS encourages participants to anticipate diversity and emphasizes the shared responsibility in creating a welcoming environment for all. Through training and opportunity for mastery, faculty are using universal design to make courses more usable for all students, and staff are beginning to evaluate practices and procedures in light of UD. Overall, the partnerships cultivated through FASPAS are proving effective in producing usable design that is practical for diverse populations.

REFERENCES

Burgstahler, S. E., & Cory, R. C. (2008). Indicators of institutional change. In S. E. Burgstahler and R. C. Cory (Eds.), *Universal design in higher education: From principles to practice* (pp. 247–253). Cambridge, MA: Harvard Education Press.

Cory, R. C., White, J. M., & Stuckey, Z. (2010). Using disability studies theory to change disability services: A case study in student activism. *Journal of Postsecondary Education and Disability, 23*(1), 29–38.

Loewen, G., & Pollard, W. (2010). The social justice perspective. *Journal of Postsecondary Education and Disability, 23*(1), 5–18.

Smith, R. E., & Buchannan, T. (2012). Community collaboration: Use of universal design in the classroom. *Journal of Postsecondary Education and Disability, 25*(3), 271–279.

U.S. Department of Education, National Center for Education Statistics. (2013). *Digest of Education Statistics, 2012* (2014–2015), Chapter 3. Retrieved from http://nces.ed.gov/fastfacts/display.asp?id=60

Wagner, M., Newman, L., Cameto, R., Garza, N., & Levine, P. (2005). *After high school: A first look at the postschool experiences of youth with disabilities.* A report from the National Longitudinal Transition Study2 (NLTS2). Menlo Park, CA: SRI International.

The authors would like to thank the following WIU FASPAS participants for sharing their stories:
Dr. Andrew Baker, Chairperson, Department of Agriculture
Dr. Julie Lawless, Assistant Professor, Department of Geography
Dr. Alisha White, Assistant Professor, Department of English and Journalism
Dr. Jennifer McNabb, Professor, Department of History
Dr. Sarah Schoper, Assistant Professor, Educational and Interdisciplinary Studies
Mr. Michael Hott, Architectural Superintendent, Facilities Management

The Last Word

This book has revealed how universal design (UD), although not the only design consideration, can contribute to the development of a high-quality product or environment. UD cannot rescue a poorly designed application, but it can make a good one better: UD makes a good course better, a well-conceived building better, a useful service better, an informative website better, and so on.

UD is a simple idea. The Center for Universal Design defines it as "the design of products and environments to be usable by all people, to the greatest extent possible, without the need for adaptation or specialized design." Although the concept is simple, newcomers to the UD paradigm soon learn that UD requires no less than a different way of thinking . . . about almost everything! With full inclusion as the ultimate goal, UD provides a framework for approaching the ideal and thereby making the world more welcoming, accessible, and usable. UD accepts that when it comes to human beings, variability is not the exception; it's the rule. UD is not "one size fits all"; it's about built-in flexibility that makes a single product or environment usable by nearly everyone.

Opinions vary and can change over time regarding what is "possible" and what is "reasonable" with respect to a specific application of UD. Like human abilities, UD practices could be placed on a continuum. Maybe we need UD benchmarks—perhaps from "really, really, really universally designed" to "not so much"—based on the diversity of an audience for which it is welcoming, accessible, and usable. Regardless, we can all advocate for designs that are toward the more inclusive end of the continuum. My advice is to play nice, but never lose your capacity for outrage. Point out barriers to decision makers, along with providing suggestions for more inclusive design and, possibly, offering to assist in making improvements. As the great philosopher Aristotle pointed out, "Anyone can get angry, but to do this to the right person, to the right extent, at the right time, with the right motive, and in the right way, that is not for everyone, nor is it easy."

Many questions remain regarding universal design for higher education (UDHE). Here are a few of mine.

- How can UD practices be fully informed by the voices of all stakeholder groups?
- What have we learned from providing academic accommodations to students with specific types of disabilities that can be more generally applied as a UD strategy to benefit all students?
- What specific outcomes of UDHE practices with respect to learning, access to technology, and inclusion in campus services and activities do we need to measure?

- From what disciplines—including disability studies, special and regular education, rehabilitation, computer science, engineering, policy studies, social sciences—can we find the best research methods for analyzing the impact of UD practices?
- Are some learning theories, philosophies, and practices more conducive to the incorporation of UD? If so, which ones, and how can UD principles work within various models to maximize learning?
- What policy, training, and support strategies impact the adoption of the UDHE paradigm?
- For specific applications, where should we draw the line between what accessibility features should be part of a UD strategy (e.g., creating accessible PDF files) and what access barriers should be dealt with through accommodations (e.g., providing a sign language interpreter)?
- When UDHE is embraced campus-wide, is there a reduction in requests for accommodations by students with disabilities and/or a change in the types of accommodations they request?

To answer key questions about UDHE we can look to traditional educational research methods, but we should also consider methods developed for usability studies and design research. It is not enough to see how well the class performs as a whole when a UD practice is employed; we need to know how effective it is for individuals with diverse characteristics. Without a strong research base, we are left with many UD "promising" practices rather than "research-based" practices.

My passion for inclusion—grounded in my personal, academic, and professional experiences—runs deep. I see UD opportunities everywhere. So how can you get started as a UD advocate? In the words of Mother Teresa, "Help one person at a time and always start with the person nearest you." Take her advice and start right where you are and universally design something at your worksite, in your home, or in your community, or share the idea with someone who will!

One last word: UD is a journey, not an endpoint. And, according to the Chinese philosopher Lao Tzu, "The journey of a thousand miles begins with one step." Go ahead, take that step.

Sheryl E. Burgstahler, PhD
Founder and Director, DO-IT and Access Technology Centers
University of Washington, Seattle

About the Authors

ALICE ANDERSON, emerita, Division of Information Technology, was the technology accessibility program coordinator at the University of Wisconsin–Madison. She played a significant role in strategic planning, policy, and resource development in the area of technology accessibility and coordinated campus advisory committees that addressed access issues with respect to people with disabilities. She was a leader in the Universal Design in Higher Education initiative of the Disabilities, Opportunities, Internetworking, and Technology (DO-IT) Center at the University of Washington.

SUSAN B. ASSELIN, PhD and professor emerita of special education at Virginia Tech, prepares aspiring and currently employed career and technical, general academic, and special educators for their future roles. Dr. Asselin received several grants from the Office of Special Education and Rehabilitative Services to prepare resource/transition educators, established the Commonwealth's first regional transition services technical assistance center, and provided the groundwork for a statewide system of technical assistance with education and rehabilitation. She has published numerous articles and book chapters related to career development and transition and universal design for learning.

JENNISON ASUNCION, with a BA in political science and an MA in educational technology from Concordia University, codirects the Adaptech Research Network at Dawson College. His research interests include the use and accessibility of information and communication technology by postsecondary students with disabilities and how that usage impacts their academic and career success.

KIMBERLY E. BIGELOW, who holds a doctorate from Ohio State University, is an assistant professor in the Department of Mechanical and Aerospace Engineering at the University of Dayton. Dr. Bigelow directs the Engineering Wellness and Safety Laboratory, which focuses on improving the balance, gait, and mobility of individuals with disabilities. Her research interests include clinical biomechanics, assistive device design, and engineering design education.

TARA BUCHANNAN is the director of the Disability Resource Center at Western Illinois University. She has over twelve years of experience advocating for students with disabilities in higher education and is particularly interested in the application of the social model of disability and universal design in higher education. She holds a master's degree in rehabilitation administration and services from Southern Illinois University at Carbondale.

JILLIAN BUDD, with an MA from McGill University, is a doctoral student at McGill University studying school/applied child psychology with interests that include learning disabilities, attention deficit hyperactivity disorder, and assistive technology. She has been a research assistant at the Adaptech Research Network at Dawson College since 2007. The numerous projects in which she has been engaged include testing and maintaining a database of free and inexpensive information and communication technologies.

SHERYL E. BURGSTAHLER, PhD and affiliate professor in education, founded the Disabilities, Opportunities, Internetworking, and Technology (DO-IT) and Access Technology Centers at the University of Washington, as well as the Center on Universal Design in Education. Dr. Burgstahler has delivered over two hundred presentations worldwide; is author or coauthor of nine books and more than one hundred articles and book chapters; is editor of five peer-reviewed books and journal issues; and serves on the editorial review panel for the *Journal of Postsecondary Education and Disability*. Dr. Burgstahler and her projects have received numerous awards, including those from the Association of Higher Education and Disability, the Trace Center, the California State University, Northridge Technology and Persons with Disabilities Conference, the National Information and Infrastructure Association, and the president of the United States.

CHRISTOPHER J. BUTTIMER is a doctoral student in culture, communities, and education at the Harvard Graduate School of Education. Mr. Buttimer previously taught middle school English language arts and currently provides professional development in adolescent literacy to teachers. His research focuses on youth participatory action research in schools.

DEB CASEY, PhD, is vice president of student affairs at Green River Community College in Auburn, Washington. Dr. Casey has been actively engaged in executive leadership and has led traditional and entrepreneurial functional areas within student affairs. She is committed to access, equity, and success, particularly among members of traditionally underrepresented populations. She has published articles on diversity issues, universal design, student affairs administration, and students with psychological disabilities. Dr. Casey has received the College Student Educators International's Outstanding Senior Level Administrator Award and the American College Personnel Association (ACPA) Disability Service Award.

REBECCA C. CORY, PhD, is associate dean of instruction at Bellevue College. She has dedicated her professional career to the inclusion of students on the margins in higher education. She served as disability services director at three institutions and has coedited two books on accessible pedagogy, *Building Pedagogical Curb Cuts: Incorporating Disability in the University Classroom and Curriculum* (Syracuse University Press) and *Universal Design in Higher Education: From Principles to Practice*, first edition (Harvard Education Press). Currently, she directs graduate programs in adult learning and higher education leadership.

PATRICIA L. DAVIES earned a BS in occupational therapy from Colorado State University (CSU) and a PhD in neuroscience from University of Wyoming; she is now a professor at CSU. Dr. Davies is the research specialist on two federally funded projects: ACCESS (emphasizing universal design for learning) and the Opportunities for Postsecondary Success (focusing on strategies to improve persistence and retention in college for students with disabilities). She has experiences in assistive technology evaluation and intervention and conducts research on brain development and brain-computer interfaces using electroencephalography.

IMKE DURRE, PhD, is a climatologist for the National Oceanic and Atmospheric Administration. She holds a bachelor's degree in applied mathematics from Yale University and a doctoral degree from the University of Washington. Dr. Durre's work focuses on compiling international data from weather balloons and surface instruments into research-quality datasets as well as extracting information about our climate from these data. She is a member of two national committees fostering diversity in science and mathematics and serves as a lead mentor for blind and visually impaired students who are DO-IT participants.

LAURA A. EDWARDS is a doctoral student in human development and education at the Harvard Graduate School of Education. She researches the neural mechanisms underlying learning behaviors in children with autism spectrum disorders, with the aim of informing the design of developmentally appropriate curricula and interventions for this population. She is also passionate about arts education and its role in universally designed education. She has previously served on the editorial board of the *Harvard Educational Review*, where she cochaired a special issue, *Expanding Our Vision for the Arts in Education*.

SCOTT FERGUSON has a master's degree in policy studies from the University of Washington, Bothell.

CATHERINE S. FICHTEN received her MA from Concordia University and her BSc and PhD in psychology from McGill University. She is a professor in the Department of Psychology at Dawson College and an associate professor in the Department of Psychiatry of McGill University. She has codirected the Adaptech Research Network and worked as a clinical psychologist at the Behavioural Psychotherapy and Research Unit of the Jewish General Hospital in Montreal. Dr. Fichten's research interests include factors affecting the success of postsecondary students with disabilities.

DONALD E. FINN, PhD, is an associate professor of Adult Education at Regent University in Virginia Beach, Virginia. He has developed and conducted workshops on effective inclusive instructional practices for teachers and college/university professors. Dr. Finn has authored and coauthored chapters and articles for journals, newsletters, and other publications and has served as a journal article reviewer. He chairs the University Curriculum Committee, the MEd in Curriculum & Instruction, and the PhD and EdD programs in the School of Education. Dr. Finn has served on state and national adult education committees and boards. He was named the Regent School of Education Faculty Member of the Year in 2010 and was recognized as Virginia's Adult Education Leader of the Year in 2013. Dr. Finn's research interests include the integration of various technologies into online and face-to-face instruction, effective curriculum design and delivery techniques for diverse students, and the impact of family and professional demands on adult students in higher education.

ELIZABETH EVANS GETZEL is the director of the Center on Transition Innovations at Virginia Commonwealth University's Rehabilitation Research and Training Center. Ms. Getzel directs projects on collaborative career planning, STEM as a viable career option for veterans with disabilities, employer-based internship programs for youth with disabilities, and the use of a supported education model for college students with disabilities. She has authored or coauthored journal articles and book chapters on transition, career development, postsecondary education, and employment and is coeditor of the book *Going to College: Expanding Opportunities for People with Disabilities* (Brookes Publishing).

ELISABETH GOLDSTEIN, an architect, has worked with postsecondary institutions on their master plans as well as new construction and renovation projects for student housing, academic buildings, and student service spaces. Her experiences as an accessibility designer and management consultant have made Ms. Goldstein keenly aware of the importance of understanding each client's unique needs and requirements to achieve the best design solutions.

JENNA W. GRAVEL, EdM, is a doctoral student in education policy, leadership, and instructional practice at the Harvard Graduate School of Education. Her research interests focus upon inclusive education and expanding learning opportunities for all students through universal design for learning (UDL). Specifically, Ms. Gravel's research explores the application of UDL in ways that encourage rich, disciplinary thinking in English language arts among diverse learners. Prior to coming to HGSE, Jenna worked as a middle school special educator and as a research assistant/project manager at the Center for Applied Special Technology (CAST).

PAM GRIFFIN, MA, has retired from her position as the coordinator of General Disability Services at the University of Minnesota–Duluth. She was responsible for providing academic accommodations to students with physical, psychological, systemic, and visual disabilities as well as resources and information to faculty and staff on accessibility and instructional strategies that meet the needs of students with disabilities. She also taught introduction to college learning classes, in which she applied universal design principles.

ALICE HAVEL, with a PhD in counseling psychology from McGill University, is a member of the Adaptech Research Network. She was the coordinator of Dawson College's AccessAbility Center for students with disabilities for over twenty years.

JEANNE L. HIGBEE earned her BS in sociology from Iowa State University and her MS in counseling and PhD in higher education administration from the University of Wisconsin–Madison. Now retired, she worked in student affairs in Wisconsin and Maryland and then as a faculty member at the University of Georgia and in the Department of Postsecondary Teaching and Learning at the University of Minnesota (UM), Twin Cities. Her many awards include UM's Access Achievement Award and Horace T. Morse Award, as well as awards from American College Personnel Association (ACPA)—College Student Educators International, the College Reading and Learning Association, and the National Association for Developmental Education. Dr. Higbee has published more than one hundred fifty book chapters and journal articles, is the editor or coeditor of five books and sixteen monographs, and is the editor of the *Journal of College Teaching and Learning*.

CHRISTOPHER J. JOHNSTONE, PhD, is a research associate at the National Center on Educational Outcomes and Director of International Initiatives and Relations for the College of Education and Human Development at the University of Minnesota. He has published several articles and book chapters on the universal design of large-scale assessment and contributed to an article on this topic in the *Journal of Postsecondary Education and Disability*. Dr. Johnstone's most recent research investigates disability issues in international settings.

LEANNE R. KETTERLIN-GELLER, PhD, is an associate professor at Southern Methodist University. She engages in research focused on instructional leadership principles and practices in supporting all students in mathematics education. She has served as principal investigator for federal, state, and locally funded research grants focused on the development of formative assessment systems and instructional interventions to support the success of all students in mathematics; she has also presented research and published articles and book chapters on the universal design of assessment.

JOAN M. MCGUIRE, PhD, is a professor emerita of special education in the Educational Psychology Department and senior research scholar in the Center on Postsecondary Education and Disability at the University of Connecticut. Dr. McGuire's research interests include universal design for instruction; postsecondary disability program development, administration, and evaluation; and adults with learning disabilities. She served as the coeditor of the *Journal of Postsecondary Education* and has published widely.

KAREN A. MYERS, PhD, is an associate professor and director of the Higher Education Administration Graduate Program at Saint Louis University and cofounder and director of the international disability education project *Allies for Inclusion: The Ability Exhibit*, the Ability Ally Initiative, and the Saint Louis University Ability Institute. She has been a college teacher and administrator at many institutions; is a disability consultant and trainer and author of numerous journal articles, book chapters, and books; teaches the graduate course Disability in Higher Education and Society; has received multiple awards from ACPA; is cofounder of the ACPA Standing Committee on Disability and past ACPA Foundation Trustee; and is coauthor of *Allies for Inclusion: Disability and Equity in Higher Education* (Jossey-Bass).

HYE-JIN PARK, EdD, is an associate professor at the University of Hawaii Center on Disability Studies. Her research areas include program evaluation as well as curriculum and instruction to address the needs of diverse learners including students with disabilities, gifted students, and culturally and linguistically diverse students.

ERIC PATTERSON, who is blind, graduated from Portland State University in 2007. He also attended Portland Community College, where he earned a career pathways certificate in Windows server administration and is seeking a job in information technology (IT) support. He began participating as a DO-IT Scholar in 1993 and now mentors younger Scholars.

LACEY REED is a student at Shoreline Community College and participates in therapeutic horseback riding in Washington. Having multiple disabilities, she is one of the many beneficiaries of universal design. She has quadriplegia (both arms and legs) and cerebral palsy. Her disabilities affect her fine and gross motor movement and speech. Ms. Reed employs adapted computer equipment and operates a power wheelchair. Along with her physical disabilities, she also has specific learning and processing disabilities that require accommodations. Ms. Reed began participating as a DO-IT Scholar in high school and now mentors younger Scholars.

VIRGINIA REILLY, PhD, is the director of University Americans with Disabilities Act (ADA) Services at Virginia Tech and has served as president of the Association on Higher Education and Disability. Dr. Reilly has conducted research on standards of accessibility for higher education, is coauthor of the book *The ADA Coordinator's Guide to Campus Compliance* (LRP Publications), and wrote a chapter in the book *Going to College* (Brookes Publishing). Dr. Reilly has served as the project coordinator for the Southwest Virginia Assistive Technology System site.

MICHAEL RICHARDSON is the director of the Northwest ADA Center and is responsible for coordinating the activities of the Technical Assistance Unit. He provides technical assistance, continuing education, and technical consultation services related to the Americans with Disabilities Act and other related federal and state requirements for professionals, businesses, state and local government agencies, and consumers. Prior to this position, Mr. Richardson was an assistant director of the Disability Resources for Students office at the University of Washington and program manager at the DO-IT Center.

PATRICIA J. RICHTER, MA, is director of Disability Services at Kutztown University of Pennsylvania. Prior positions include assistant director of the ACT 101 Program at Kutztown University (a state program for access to higher education) and learning specialist in the Program for Learning Disabled College Students at Adelphi University in New York. Ms. Richter holds a bachelor's degree from New York University and a master's degree in special education from New York University.

KELLY D. ROBERTS, PhD, is a professor at the Center on Disability Studies at the University of Hawaii, the director of the Pacific Basin University Centers on Excellence in Developmental Disabilities, and chair of the Association of University Centers on Disabilities Council on Research and Evaluation. Her research currently includes two large-scale randomized control trials and research on promoting access and retention of individuals with disabilities in postsecondary education, both of which incorporate universal design principles.

DAVID H. ROSE, with an EdD from Harvard University, is cofounder of the nonprofit research and development organization, CAST, and a lecturer in developmental neuropsychology and universal design for learning at the Harvard Graduate School of Education. Dr. Rose is the recipient of many awards, including the Computerworld/Smithsonian Award for Innovation in Education, and is the author or editor of numerous articles, books, and educational software programs.

MAYA SATLYKGYLYJOVA is a doctoral candidate in cultural foundations of education at Kent State University. Her background includes working at the University of Hawaii Center on Disability Studies as a teaching assistant. Her research focuses on the concept of hybridity and identity formation of female immigrant students in the U.S. education system.

CATHERINE L. SCHELLY is an assistant professor; the director of the Center for Community Partnerships, a service and outreach arm of the Department of Occupational Therapy, at Colorado State University; the director of the New Start for Student Veterans program; and the principal investigator on the Opportunities for Postsecondary Success project. Her research interests include the impact of universal design for learning implementation and student self-advocacy on persistence and retention of students with disabilities.

SALLY S. SCOTT, PhD, is a postsecondary disability specialist and educational consultant based in Richmond, Virginia. She specializes in the development and evaluation of services for college students with disabilities. She has published widely and is a frequent presenter on topics including young adults with cognitive disabilities, faculty development, and universal design for instruction. She currently serves as senior research associate for the Association on Higher Education and Disability.

JESSIE AMELIA SHULMAN is an operations program manager at Amazon Web Services. She graduated from the University of Washington with a bachelor's degree in informatics and a minor in dance. Ms. Shulman coauthored the article "A Web Accessibility Report Card for Top International University Web Sites." She began her involvement with DO-IT in 1998 as a DO-IT Scholar and has continued to serve as a mentor.

CARSON SMITH is a graduate of the University of Washington, where he participated in the DO-IT program and worked as a consultant in his university's adaptive technology lab helping to transform math textbooks into braille. Mr. Smith now works in digital media, with an emphasis on using data to help improve decision making and usability for all.

RACHEL E. SMITH received both her BS in psychology and MS in recreation, park, and tourism administration from Western Illinois University. She is a certified therapeutic recreation specialist. Her experience includes nineteen years as an advocate and educator in the many facets of disability. She is currently an assistant professor, fieldwork coordinator, and internship coordinator in the Department of Recreation, Park, and Tourism Administration at Western Illinois University.

AL SOUMA, MA, is a rehabilitation counselor who has been coordinating disability support services at Seattle Central College since 1991. He offers presentations and workshops on accommodating students with psychiatric disabilities in the classroom in venues sponsored by organizations such as the American College Personnel Association, the National Association of Student Personnel Administrators, and the Association of Higher Education and Disability, which presented him with the 2002 Professional Recognition Award. He also presented at the Sixth International Conference on Higher Education and Disability in Innsbruck, Austria.

CRAIG L. SPOONER earned his BA in anthropology from University of California, Los Angeles, and his MA in education from the University of New Mexico. His academic credentials include both classroom instruction and departmental leadership at the University of New Mexico, Gallup, as well as many years of training faculty and providing instructional design at Colorado State University (CSU), where he is currently employed. His interests in accessibility, technology, and universal design for learning have led to collaboration with CSU's Institute for Learning and Teaching and the creation of widely used online UDL resources.

SARAH STEELE is a graduate of Seattle Pacific University. She is active in her church as a member of the weekly bible study and chancel choir. She uses an electric wheelchair to get around. She has fibrodysplasia ossificans progressiva, a rare disease that causes muscle to turn to bone. She was a participant in the DO-IT Scholars program.

TERRILL THOMPSON, who has twenty years' experience in the IT accessibility field, is technology accessibility specialist with Accessible Technology Services at the University of Washington, which includes the Access Technology and DO-IT Centers. He promotes information technology accessibility by working collaboratively with a wide variety of stakeholders on campus and around the world. Mr. Thompson has presented at numerous conferences and consulted widely with government, private industry, and K–12 and postsecondary entities on IT accessibility issues.

ROBERTA THOMSON received her BSc in computer science from Acadia University and her MA in educational technology from Concordia University. She is currently the project coordinator on the collaborative higher education UDL Faculty/Toolkit project for four Montreal-area colleges and McGill University, as lead institution. She is also a course instructor for the Faculty of Education at McGill University in the inclusive education, diverse learners, and assistive technology areas, and at LaSalle College for disability related courses. Her background includes work in the technology field as well as with individuals with disabilities in a multitude of settings.

MARTHA L. THURLOW, PhD, is the director of the National Center on Educational Outcomes and senior research associate at the University of Minnesota. During the past decade, Dr. Thurlow's work has emphasized the need to obtain valid, reliable, and comparable assessment measures while ensuring that the assessments are truly measuring the knowledge and skills of students with special needs, rather than their disabilities or limited language when these are not the focus of the assessment. Her research studies have covered a range of topics that include participation decision making, accommodations, universal design, computer-based testing, graduation exams, and alternate assessments.

SUSAN YAGER, PhD, is a professor of English at Iowa State University and former associate director of Iowa State's Center for Excellence in Learning and Teaching. Her primary research interests are in medieval British literature and the scholarship of teaching, especially as it pertains to literary studies.